LLOYD
AXWORTHY

NAVIGATING
A *New* WORLD

CANADA'S
GLOBAL FUTURE

Vintage Canada

For Denise, who has made all the difference.

VINTAGE CANADA EDITION, 2004

Copyright © 2003 Lloyd Axworthy International, Inc.

Published in 2004 in Canada by Vintage Canada, a division of Random House of Canada
Limited, Toronto. Originally published in hardcover in Canada by Alfred A. Knopf
Canada, a division of Random House of Canada Limited, Toronto, in 2003.
Distributed by Random House of Canada Limited, Toronto.

Grateful acknowledgment is made to the Crossroad Publishing Company
for permission to reprint from *The Analogical Imagination* by David Tracy;
and Aris & Phillips for permission to reprint from
Lands of Castile and Other Poems by Antonio Machado.

Vintage Canada and colophon ar registered trademarks of
Random House of Canada Limited.

NATIONAL LIBRARY OF CANADA CATALOGUING IN PUBLICATION

Axworthy, Lloyd, 1939–
Navigating a new world : Canada's global future / Lloyd Axworthy.

Includes bibliographical references and index.
ISBN 0-676-97464-3

1. Security, International. 2. Human rights. 3. International cooperation.
4. Humanitarian assistance, Canadian. 5. Canada—Foreign relations.
6. International relations. 7. War—Protection of civilians. I. Title.

JZ1320.A94 2004   327.1'7   C2004-902495-7

www.randomhouse.ca

Book design by CS Richardson
Printed and bound in the United States of America

2   4   6   8   9   7   5   3   1

Contents

Acknowledgments

THIS BOOK COULD NOT HAVE BEEN WRITTEN WITHOUT THE HELP OF many who have contributed in direct and indirect ways. I owe them all for this chance to share in print thoughts and ideas garnered after twenty-seven years in public life.

I begin with the voters of Winnipeg, who through seven elections gave me the privilege of being a member of the provincial legislature and then the Canadian Parliament. It is a rare honour to be chosen by your peers to represent them. The enunciation about the value of democracy that infuses these pages I owe very much to the lessons learned from the people I served.

I also benefited in innumerable ways from association with a remarkable number of Canadians who served in public life as members of Parliament or ministers or who were involved in the workings of party politics. One of the inspired choices I made early in life was to become a partisan of the Liberal Party of Canada, one of the great political institutions in the family of democracies. It has always been headed by good leaders and supported by dedicated members with liberal notions about Canada. I pray it continues in this mode.

Working with public servants of the unelected variety has also been a good part of my experience over the past three decades. Many I have mentioned in this book, but to all those I've worked with I express my admiration for the work you do on behalf of your fellow citizens. The quality of our public service is a Canadian asset.

A special word of appreciation must go to a particular group of public servants, the staff that served me as a member and a minister. They come from all parts of the country, with some predominance from Manitoba, and they are a first-rate, loyal, prodigious, hard-working group of men and women who came to the Hill, regional or constituency office with idealism and a singular dedication to making the political process work.

Before sitting down to write I gathered with a group of former assistants for dinner at the Château Laurier hotel in Ottawa to share recollections of the days on the tenth floor of the Pearson Building, home to Foreign Affairs. Their enthusiasm for the exercise and willingness to help gave me the launch I needed. Several, in particular Joe Stern and Heidi Hulan, read over drafts of certain sections and their comments were extremely helpful.

I also benefited from the excellent research assistance of Hannah Simone and Serena Sharma, graduates of UBC who looked for the detail that I congenitally miss, and of Duart Farquharson, who helped in editing early chapters. My appreciation also goes to several of the staff and faculty at the Liu Institute for Global Issues for helping with the development of ideas, especially Robert Adamson and Andras Vamas Goldman, and for allowing me the time to peck away at the keyboard.

I was also helped by the editors of the op-ed pages at the *Winnipeg Free Press*, *Globe and Mail* and *Toronto Star* who, by inviting me to write from time to time, gave me a chance to test drive some ideas and work on my syntax. And my friend Paul Fraser was as always the source of good counsel and sage advice.

I can't say enough about John Pearce, vice-president and executive editor-at-large, and Louise Dennys, executive publisher of Alfred A. Knopf Canada. First, they convinced me that I could make the transition from the world of the thirty-second clip to actually writing sentences and paragraphs. They gently cajoled me away from writing a potboiler memoir and pushed constantly for a road map—"More prescription," they would say—that has turned into a guide for navigating a new world. They then applied their exceptional editorial skills, along with the other professionals at Knopf, to make this a readable product. Thank you.

Finally, to family. My mother as always gave her support, promising to buy the first copy, regardless of what critics say. To my son Stephen, whose continual questioning of all things established and conventional kept me thinking beyond the current time frame, having to accept through his eyes what a future might hold, an attitude that only deepened with the arrival of Emma, daughter to Louise and Derek, and through testing against the iconoclasm of John.

And to Denise, who read and corrected copy, listened to countless renditions of my latest brainwave and had the diplomacy to know when to dissuade me from further ramblings, and who put up with too many Sunday nights listening to a two-finger typing chorus from the study next door. Merci, ma chérie.

Preface to the Paperback Edition

Heading to Toronto for the official launch of the hardcover edition of this book, I picked up the latest Martha Grimes mystery novel, aptly entitled *Foul Matter,* to while away the hours of a transcontinental flight.

The plot revolves around two hit men hired by a well-known publishing house to "snuff" one of its authors—a somewhat disconcerting introduction to the dangers encountered once your book hits the shelves. One of the biggest challenges, I soon discovered, is "navigating" the literary minefield known as the "publicity tour," a succession of hotline shows, bookstore signings, university talks and early morning interviews where you are given three minutes to explain the impact of globalization, spliced between the weather reports and the hockey scores.

But my tour offered a rare opportunity to take stock of the mood, feelings and opinions of a wide variety of people who clearly feel their lives are being played out against a backdrop of war, terrorism and unremitting violence. Wherever I found myself, the questioning was the same: the turmoil in Iraq and the Middle East; the merciless slaughter of innocents in Liberia, the Congo and Uganda; the search for security against unseen, deadly threats that can strike our towns and cities at any time; the worry over young men and women in our forces being killed by land mines. What do you make of a world where even the neutrality of humanitarian organizations like the Red Cross or the United Nations provides no immunity, and where young children are dragooned into armies to fight adult-inspired battles? In the words of Pierre Teilhard de Chardin, "A great many internal and external portents (political and social upheaval, moral and religious unease) have caused us all to feel, more or less confusedly, that something tremendous is at present taking place in the world. But what is it?"

As I moved from small-town radio stations to bookstores to campuses, I discovered a broadly shared unease that our political system is not addressing that question with care or consideration. Our understandable short-term preoccupation with security has obscured our long-term vision of a world free from conflict—a vision that has motivated Canadians and driven Canadian foreign policy over the last half century. The word "peace" is slipping from the political vocabulary. Instead, we are being exhorted to spend more on weapons such as the still-unproven missile defense system, not because it will be of much use as protection, but as a demonstration of our goodwill towards the American administration.

It is ironic that much of the rhetoric we hear today is about how we must exercise military might to promote the development of democracy in various trouble spots around the globe, while at the same time we are ignoring the signs that our own democracy is beginning to fray around the edges. Increasingly, decisions are being made behind closed doors or by secret arrangements dictated by security priorities. My fear is that the terrible discovery that a Canadian citizen, Maher Arar, was seized in the United States and sent to a prison in Syria without due process of the law was not an anomaly but the tip of the iceberg: it revealed just how far we may have gone down the path of eroding our Charter rights because our decision makers have bought into the teleology that counterterrorism is an end in itself, rather than a means to an end.

In all parts of Canada, I was particularly disturbed by the cynicism and resignation of young people. One young woman at Wilfrid Laurier University seemed to sum it up when she asked why she should be politically active or interested when it was clear that politicians weren't interested in her concerns or issues. She isn't alone in those thoughts—witness the turnoff from voting. And many I spoke to felt there was an increasing distance between what really counts—coming to grips with those "portents that something tremendous is taking place"—and our preoccupation over struggles for political power without much purpose at stake.

Paul Martin became prime minister in 2003 with the promise of addressing such concerns; of governing in a new, more open way, and plotting out a more effective global role for Canada. But his government was side-swiped in its first month by allegations of patronage and financial mismanagement of the sponsorship program. And it fostered further public skepticism by being caught in the contradictions of trying to be more friendly toward the Bush administration while holding to its commitment to be both more responsive to parliamentary and public involvement on crucial issues and more assertive on major international events. In March 2004, when the government called a House of Commons vote on Canada joining the missile defense program, the defection of a significant number of Liberal MPs was an omen of future political reaction if such decisions are made without sufficient public and parliamentary debate.

The efforts to deal with the democratic deficit through parliamentary reform are laudable. But they are not enough to meet the longing I heard from so many Canadians—a longing for democratic accountability and responsiveness. A longing to repair our disintegrated democratic process.

Yet, as I mull over this yearning that I heard on the book trail, what is most impressive to me is that it reflects not passive feelings but the signs of a stirring towards activism. A politics of a different kind is beginning to emerge. Networks of individuals and groups right across North America are beginning to explore, search and even formulate answers; to organize around agendas that are very different from those spoken about in the corridors of power or in the media.

This questing—a search for a different course to follow, and a willingness to explore beyond the conventional wisdoms or elite prescriptions—became most vivid for me when I met with a group of women in Victoria. They told me that it is time Canada has a minister for peace with the resources to help prevent conflict, to aid in reconciliation, to rebuild conflict-ridden societies and to educate young people on the practices of peace and the means of resolving conflict. And in meeting after meeting, I realized that this is more than an idea; it is becoming an agenda for action.

Circles of women are mobilizing, men and women who sing for peace in churches, mosques and synagogues are organizing within their communities, campaigns in schools are being developed. The same spirit was alive in a conference of the Mennonite Economic Development Association that I attended in Winnipeg, where business people had come together to raise capital and supply skills for supporting micro-business overseas as a way of promoting peace. Across the country—most notably in British Columbia, New Brunswick and Quebec—major efforts are underway in various forms of people's assemblies to rethink our democratic institutions.

One of the most important areas in which we can respond to these desires for reform is that of Canadian foreign policy. It is a prospect that may be possible as the government begins a period of review. And the place to start is to move away from the 9/11 mindset that has dominated policy and engage in a real public debate about the meaning of security today.

When I wrote this book in 2003, I decried the rush to war in Iraq. After its publication, and after listening to so many Canadians, it strikes me that it is important to draw further lessons from the unfolding post-Iraq war saga. The pre-war assertions of the threat posed by Saddam Hussein's possession of weapons of mass destruction, and the bold predictions about building democracy in the Middle East, have now been largely discredited. The failure to find those weapons, and the breakdown of society in Iraq, have given pause even to those who until recently proclaimed the virtues of the military campaign.

John Upton, writing in January 2004 in *The London Review of Books,* said: "We are told that we face a complex, overwhelming threat, yet we are given the crudest means of deciphering our predicament: caricatures of Saddam, of bin Laden, of suicide bombers and evil imams. These are the cartoon ogres in whose shadows we are encouraged to unite." On the basis of analysis that we now know was at best faulty and possibly untrue, Western countries have responded by introducing emergency powers, expending vast amounts of money on border security and expanding military action.

Such an evolution of events presents a strong argument for us to reorient our efforts away from this mistaken approach on world issues and towards areas of action that have been powerful sources of Canadian competence and international activism. It is indeed a good time to apply the principles of "human security" I outline in this book. It is instructive that the coalition powers, which before the war were prepared to ignore the UN, have now called on that previously scorned institution to help extricate them from the situation they created and the terrible violence of civil war. They have offered a chance for the UN to reassert its primary role as a centre of peace and security, as proposed under the "responsibility to protect" agenda. (It was encouraging to see that Paul Martin referred to this made-in-Canada international idea in his speech at the World Economic Forum in Davos in early 2004. We have yet to see whether it will serve as a template for his government's proposed foreign policy review.)

Canada can help in this reassessment of the UN—first, by ensuring the UN's role is an autonomous one, not one subordinate to the provisional authority of coalition powers. And second, we can help provide the security that the UN and other international personnel need in situations of conflict by providing our blue-helmeted constabulary to assist in the tricky task of preparing for transfers of authority and the creation of homegrown institutions of governance.

The same diligence to human security should be applied to the 2004 re-engagement in Haiti. We have been there before with troops, police and development assistance. But like most donor countries we lost interest after 9/11. We forgot that this poor country with its long history of difficulties needs constant support to consolidate its fragile democratic system and to counter the military thugs and wealthy elite who never gave up the dark dream of restoring the privileges they enjoyed under the Duvalier dictatorship. A duly-elected president was deposed and our troops sent back to patrol the streets. To what end? To simply provide time for the old gang to consolidate their rule? Or will we lead an effort to plan and mobilize a true multilateral effort to the long-term task of nation building? A real test of Canadian leadership—along with other wealthy countries—will be to assert the same level of assistance to a hemispheric neighbour as we have been compelled to commit to Iraq in the aftermath of the war.

There are other places where international cooperation, and the application of international standards, are reasserting their value in the post-Iraq war era. The new prosecutor for the International Criminal Court, Luis Moreno-Ocampo, has announced that the first cases to be tried will be in northern Uganda, the site of so much killing and abuse (as the story of Emma, which begins this book, shows). The battle to pressure the large pharmaceutical companies to agree to the provision of generic drugs is slowly being won. And the collapse of the trade talks at Cancun is a sign that Third World countries are standing up to market fundamentalisms and demanding a fair, equitable participation in their economic decision making. Even in the field of disarmament a debate is beginning on how to update the Non-Proliferation of Nuclear Weapons Treaty—though we must still contend with the ongoing efforts of the Americans to assert a pre-emptive strategy that contemplates the use of a second generation of nuclear weapons. And with sorrow we learned of the Bush administration's reneging on President Clinton's previous commitment to join in the Anti-Personnel Landmine Treaty.

Yet, like Manitoba crocuses which sprout here and there through the snow as a harbinger of spring, the emergence of a renewed UN, the start-up of the ICC process and the discrediting of the pretensions of superpower omnipotence all signal the resilience of an international system based on an understanding of human security in the world at large.

Herein lies a counterpoint to the "business as usual" political mavens who dominate the mainstream. There are sure "portents that something tremendous" is happening. We can hear all around us the murmuring demands for change. We are on the edge of a political renewal with the ambition to create a kinder, more just and peaceable world. It would be unforgivable to not heed those murmurings, or to fail to clarify and seize the chance for renewal.

Sir Winston Churchill caught the same mood more than half a century ago when he said, "We live in an age of great events and little men, and if we are not to become the slaves of our own systems or sink oppressed among the mechanism we ourselves created, it will only be by the bold efforts of originality, by repeated experiment, and by the dispassionate consideration of the results of sustained and unflinching thought."[1]

Lloyd Axworthy
April 2004

Conflict is our actuality. Conversation is our hope.

—David Tracy, *The Analogical Imagination*

PROLOGUE: CANADA AND THE WORLD

CANADIANS ARE ON THE ROAD TO GLOBAL CITIZENSHIP. INCREASINGLY in work, travel, education and in personal and political engagement the world is our precinct, with international trade, finance, technology and business driving much of our global interests. But there is also a political, cultural and even moral dimension to our emerging role in global society.

Canadians take pride in what we do in the world. Our sense of identity is often tied up in such achievements as peacekeeping, placing in the top rung of the United Nations Human Development Index of best places to live, and winning a gold medal in Olympic hockey or a Man Booker Prize in literature. The values we express internationally help define who we are when other distinctions are being erased. Equally, our welfare is closely tied to international rules and practices. Daily while at Foreign Affairs I saw how little separates what we do inside our border from what happens outside and vice versa. We occupy the global village that Marshall McLuhan prophesied we would half a century ago. What this means is that we win in a stable, equitable, cooperative world. We lose when it is turbulent, divisive and unfair. It only makes sense, therefore, to examine carefully what we can do to tip the global system in a constructive way. That is what I would like this book to achieve.

I don't feel we yet fully understand the responsibilities and obligations that come with being a global citizen or make the full connection between the need for well-resourced international initiatives and our domestic interests. Too often we try to do things on the cheap, and avoid the tough commitments. In the federal election of 2000, I watched with some dismay how the entire campaign unfolded with nary a word about foreign policy. There was great discussion of domestic economic priorities, but nothing on how to strengthen our capacity for effective international action—and this despite growing disenchantment with a variety of global developments, expressed most notably in protests and demonstrations.

My own years at Foreign Affairs were very much occupied with the effort to define a distinctive international place for Canada. When I arrived there in 1996, a decided shift was taking place in the perceptions and calculations arising out of the end of the Cold War and the surge of globalization in economics, technology and information. In the early nineties there had been fond hopes of a new era of prosperity based on the liberalization of markets, deregulation and the global movement of capital. Poverty in the Third World would be whittled away by the powerful forces of the marketplace. By the middle of the decade, though, that tide of optimism was on the wane. Inequities were growing, not receding. The value of global trade and investment agreements was under challenge by Southern countries, and there was growing skepticism from civil-society groups. The spectre of ecological disaster was creeping into prominence.

Similarly, President George Bush Sr.'s bold claims for an emerging system of security based on international cooperation—the "New World Order"—had already run aground in Somalia and Bosnia. The United States was increasingly shy of exerting direct leadership in the security requirements of an era of messy internal ethnic conflicts. The United Nations was discredited by its inaction in Rwanda and impoverished by the nonpayment of dues by the world's superpower and other financial shirkers. There was a definite vacuum in defining security needs and responses.

This was especially so in scoping out answers to the dark side of globalization—the increasing threats from international terrorists, pedophiles, drug dealers, small arms traders, illegal-diamond merchants and people smugglers. The same networks of information that allowed capital to move around the world in seconds, or brought scenes of suffering into living rooms around the globe, gave these predators the capacity to exploit the vulnerable and establish international connections that could overwhelm the capability of individual nations to protect their citizens. Drug trafficking, for example, had become a multi-billion-dollar business and confronted police forces with the most sophisticated tools of communication, transportation and organization. Ugly signs of dangerous terrorist networks were being detected. Already in 1996 I was calling for a starvation policy to deny criminal perpetrators access to money and arms.

There was an obvious demand for more effective international teamwork to meet all these challenges. Halting steps were being organized at the UN, the G-8, the OECD. But there was an opposite pull. The strong hold of beliefs in national sovereignty, and anti-internationalist feelings, meant that many governments resisted multilateral cooperative ventures. The philosophy of go-it-alone was alive and well even in the face of a shared risk. Traditional notions of national interest were stoutly defended even while they simply didn't match the tempo of interdependence that was under way.

Complicating the efforts to govern this global interdependence was the pre-eminent position of the U.S. The collapse of the Soviet Union had confirmed the dominance of American power and influence as the reality of the global system. With this came increasing U.S. claims that its dominant position carried special responsibilities and therefore prerogatives to act unilaterally. The Clinton administration generally set its actions inside the framework of international institutions and laws. But not so the government of George W. Bush. The terrorist attacks of September 11, 2001, launched an aggressive U.S. effort to assert U.S. interests, repudiate multilateral, collaborative governance, and follow a radical security doctrine that prescribes the use of U.S. military supremacy to establish the U.S.'s unchallenged right to determine the character and shape of the world—what might be called imperial ambitions.

From a Canadian point of view, the U.S.'s reluctance to submit to international treaties and agreements, and its new doctrine of pre-emption, are cause for great concern. While over the past decade most agreements in arms control and environmental or human rights have not been ratified by Congress, now the Bush administration is not just a reluctant signatory but also a ferocious opponent of any agreement that does not directly serve specific ambitions of the U.S.—hardly a promising atmosphere in which to construct a new global architecture.

The U.S. stance poses real difficulties for Canadians as we become ever more integrated into a North American economy and security arrangements. The September 11 attacks, the subsequent anti-terrorist campaign and the controversy over the invasion of Iraq have brought pressures for further alignment with U.S. goals and closer military ties. But how far do we go in the integration of our systems before we lose the capacity to pursue independently our own preferences for multilateral, international collective action and collaboration? As we shall see, the paradox is that global interdependence can enhance the scope for distinctive Canadian actions.

By the time I became foreign affairs minister, a realistic and imaginative look was needed to make sense of these conflicting and confusing trends. The old paradigm of nation-state supremacy couldn't deal with evolving interdependence. The alliance system of the Cold War didn't provide a relevant basis for global cooperation. Even the multilateral system centred on the UN was rooted in post–Second World War thinking and didn't encompass forms of governance to meet economic and technological changes and new security threats.

During my time at Foreign Affairs a number of international challenges, from Zaire to Haiti and from Cuba to Kosovo, suggested the need for a new approach that would emphasize the human and humanitarian dimension and also promote Canada as an innovative player. The concept of human security emerged as the lens through which to view the international scene. The security risk to individuals was our focal point, and around that we developed a strategy for working towards new standards of international behaviour, using the soft-power tools of communication and persuasion. While simple in concept, in some ways it was revolutionary, since it set the notion of human rights against deeply held precepts of national rights.

We proposed a way of seeing the world and tackling global issues that derived from serving individual human needs, not just those of the nation-state or powerful private economic interests. This is not through some form of all-powerful, centralized world government. Rather, it is a form of global governance that operates under global rules, works through global institutions and will require a form of global democratic politics to make decisions. It seeks a way to transcend particular interests for a common good.

This new outlook has to date mostly been applied to achieving security from violence. But it can equally be applied to other issues, particularly environmental security. Increasingly, people are asking how we move towards a more effective, enforceable management of environmental problems that might emulate the ways we deal with violence and conflict. For the truth is that there is as much dislocation and suffering through environmental degradation and climate change as there is through conflict situations. The number of refugees caused by environmental damage equals or exceeds that of war. People in one jurisdiction suffer from actions taken in another (as we have seen in North America with smog, or in Southeast Asia with the Indonesian forest fires) and this highlights the need to find solutions that transcend traditional cross-border agreements.

As we shall see, the same lens of human security can be brought to bear on other global concerns such as public health, migration, the management of resources such as water, and even the monumental task of alleviating poverty. As we increasingly struggle with growing gaps in equality and with the exploitation of the world's poor, and as we witness partial and often self-defeating development programs, we have to ask if we are not coming up with answers still rooted in conventional thinking. It's time to look with new eyes.

The idea of human security seems a particularly good fit for Canadians. We are in a position to promote a blueprint for ordering global affairs that improves upon the present, frequently ineffective model. We have inherent strengths as a people of wealth and talent who have forged a community of interests, express a humane set of values, know the struggle to assert and maintain a sense of independence and understand the benefits of working in collegial fashion. In a survey of forty-four countries, with thirty-eight thousand respondents, Canadians showed the highest level of satisfaction with their lives and the general direction of their country.[1] There was not the degree of angst over crime, corruption and the state of public services as in other countries, nor by a long chalk the level of animus against immigration found virtually everywhere else. These characteristics, particularly the latter, translate into real strengths for Canada in pursuing a role in the world.

The accepted wisdom has been that we are an honest broker, a mediator, a peacekeeper, a country that uses our proximity to the U.S. to act as an interlocutor between them and other nations or international organizations. Today such a middle-power role is not enough; indeed, such a role is losing much of its validity. Canadians instead can draw on the strengths I have just listed to take a special kind of leadership in helping manage a world dominated by the power and influence of our continental neighbour. I was once asked in Minneapolis if I agreed with the definition of the U.S. as the "indispensable nation." I demurred answering directly, out of politeness to my American audience. But I did say that I believed Canada was the "value-added nation" in the international system—Canadians can help carve out a global system of security based on protecting individual social, political and economic rights. Such a course would reflect the opening lines of the UN Charter, which begins, "We the Peoples"—not "We the Leaders" or "We the Diplomats." Canadians are in a unique position to help write the new navigation manuals in these stormy times.

It is an approach that stands in stark contrast to those who see a world dominated by military force and naked self-interest. The instinct of the Bush administration to dismiss treaties, disdain common efforts to cope with global issues and argue for "full-spectrum dominance" and pre-emptive, unilateral action needs a constructive response.

So do the fanatical extremists who murder and maim indiscriminately. They need to be brought to justice. We need a strengthened commitment to open democracy and the enhancement of rights to counter the growing power of narrow fundamentalism among all faiths and its translation into acts of intolerance and political violence. Justice and caring are also due the dispossessed of the world who feel cut off and ignored by the rich developed world as they languish in camps of refuge and displacement or are left to die of AIDS or malaria untended and alone. They need inclusion and the better distribution of wealth.

This book, then, is dedicated to the proposition that we in Canada—each and every one of us—can make a difference to the building of a humane global community relevant to our times. It describes a world seen through my eyes from different vantage points over a number of years. It asks that we begin to rethink the international dimension from the perspective of individuals—their security, their needs, their potential, their hopes and dreams. I have attempted to offer and set out choices for Canadians to consider. If Canadians can get this global role right, if we can maintain and strengthen our capacity and will for creative independent action, we will fulfill our duty as global citizens and define our own place in the contemporary firmament.

PART I

Emma *and* Us

CHAPTER I

THE ROAD TO GULU

THE TRUE NARRATIVE OF POLITICS IS NOT THE SOLILOQUY OF THE STATE but the human story. That is why I've chosen to begin this book with a brief encounter I had with a thirteen-year-old Ugandan girl whom I shall call Emma. Discourse on foreign affairs is all too often pitched at a perplexing level of abstraction devoid of emotion or values, where diplomatic jargon and code words like "national interest" mask the human element. For me, Emma provided a corrective.

She had recently been a child soldier, and came all the way to Winnipeg to an international conference on war-affected children to tell her tale of abduction, abuse and violation. It wasn't the only case of extreme suffering I had come across. God knows there are hundreds of acts of inhumanity being committed every day against people like Emma: mine victims who lose their limbs; schoolchildren murdered in a classroom or exploded in a shopping centre; starving thousands in refugee camps; babies infected with the AIDS virus while still in the womb. But Emma's story tells us so much about the kind of world we live in and our opportunity to make changes to help people like her. It is an appalling story that helps us see the complexity of the global situation. To tell it, I need to introduce you to the Gulu region of Uganda.

FEBRUARY 5, 2002
ON THE ROAD FROM PABO, ACHOLILAND

The white Nissan Patrol four-wheel drive, with small Canadian decals on the side mirrors, sped down the middle of the dusty red dirt road back towards Gulu, the main city in northern Uganda. Along each side was a steady stream of travellers, most on foot, many on bicycles, often carrying a passenger or two on the back fender, usually with a brightly coloured jerry can of water in their arms or on their head, perhaps a sheaf of housing thatch or fire-wood. Our driver, Gisaw Shibru, an Ethiopian with long experience in delivering humanitarian assistance in Africa, and Ugandan director of Canadian Physicians for Aid and Relief, or CPAR, explained that this road had been a favourite ambush target of the rebel group the Lord's Resistance Army (LRA), often booby trapped with land mines. But the presence of so many locals using the sides of the road was a sign that the risk had decreased and it was safe to drive.

The air conditioning was turned on high against the mid-afternoon heat, but I didn't find it cooling. I was too angry. A slow anger was rising from the very deep pit of my stomach, an anger fuelled by feelings of indignation, shame, futility, helplessness at what I had just seen. It was the special bile born when one is confronted by gross, ugly injustice.

We were on our way back from a camp for internally displaced persons, at a place called Pabo, about eighty miles from the Sudanese border. Forty-seven thousand men, women and children crowded into a few square kilometres of space, living in unimaginable squalor amidst small, dark thatched huts cramped together with only a foot or two between them, many in disrepair or partially burnt down, with open sewers and rudimentary latrines. Each step had to be carefully placed to avoid the human droppings.

The camp elders showing around three CPAR workers, Dr. Patricia Spittal, who was heading up our project in the region, and me were trying to explain in the most fervent terms that these were man-made disasters and people wanted to leave. Every so often as we walked about, listening to the story of how all these people had been moved from their villages and communities by the army, ostensibly for protection against raids by the LRA, one of the chiefs would stop and point over the tops of the huts to a not too far off range of hills and say that was home.

It was the kids who made the most vivid impact. As soon as we left the cars, hundreds appeared, drawn by the visitors, looking for a handout, or just to shake a hand or have a photo taken. Every time we stopped they crowded about to answer questions or just stare. That gave us a chance for a close look, and it was disturbing—sores on eyes and ears, stomachs swollen by hunger or worms. Chris, one of the CPAR workers, said they had tried months ago to administer treatment, but as soon as the children returned to Pabo, the problem would recur. What we couldn't see directly, but were told about, was the high rate of sexual and physical assault rampant in the camp, leading to a growing incidence of sexually transmitted diseases and HIV. Security or policing was non-existent. Everywhere we looked there was a sense of idleness, listlessness. There was nothing to do, especially noticeable among the young men who lay under the eaves of the thatched huts staring nowhere or playing endless rounds of an ancient board game. It was the women who were occupied, the young ones tending their babies, the older ones foraging for food, water and wood.

These were the victims of a war that has been raging in this remote, forgotten area of northern Uganda since 1986. They weren't combatants, didn't wear uniforms; most were innocent of any act of aggression. But there were four hundred thousand of them in camps like this one, dying of starvation and disease, separated from their communities and any semblance of ordinary life. They faced the special loss of having their children abducted to be child soldiers, or to be maimed or killed by land mines any time they took a misstep on a road or a field as they looked for food and water.

In the "bush," just on the other side of the Sudanese border, Joseph Kony, leader of the LRA, himself an Acholi, was hunkered down in hidden camps, surrounded by young abducted children now acting as hostages against an expected assault by the Ugandan Defence Force. The politics were changing for the LRA. Once they had been supported by the Sudanese and used to fight against the rebels in southern Sudan, but since September 11 and the declared war on terrorism, their Sudanese benefactors, now courting favour in Washington, considered them expendable and were abandoning them.

They are a strange group, deriving from a semi-spiritualist movement led by Kony's cousin against the forces of President Museveni, whose members smeared butter on their bodies to ward off bullets. After their defeat, Kony took up the cudgels and waged a vicious war in northern Uganda targeting his own people. His manifesto, as far as anyone could figure out, was to get better housing and jobs. But over sixteen years of raids, kidnappings and land-mine traps, thousands have died, the area has been devastated; thousands of children have disappeared or been subject to the worst kind of abuse and violation. His actions have immobilized what was once a fertile area, leaving it impoverished and in ruin.

It was clear that everyone wanted to see him go and the war end. The irony was that for parents in Acholiland any military action would result in the killing of their children. Most of the LRA had themselves been abducted as children, and the large number of hostages still held would be caught up in a military attack. They desperately wanted a negotiated settlement, based on amnesty legislation passed by the Ugandan Parliament, but it didn't appear that anyone was listening. After September 11, military action was the preferred way of stopping terrorists. Negotiation and reconciliation were no longer in vogue, and international involvement was thought to be too complicated. Force of arms seemed to be the answer, bringing with it further suffering to the children and families of the region.

As I travelled about, the signs of decrepitude were everywhere. So too was the people's sense of being forgotten, by their government, by the rest of the world. While Uganda had enjoyed an average of 7 to 8 per cent growth in the past few years and had become the poster boy of correct economic principles for international financial institutions, the north was poorer than ever. Not for them the glare of media attention focusing on their sorrow or misery, nor mobilization of vast resources or outside intervention. A few aid agencies from the UN and the NGO community were working in the area, but, as they were the first to admit, they could barely make a dent in the mass of human misery. The Acholi people faced a double jeopardy, further bloodshed and continued insecurity and deprivation. It was that reality that started my slow burn.

It had started earlier in the day in the office of the resident district commissioner, Max Omeda. At first our small delegation was greeted with some suspicion. Max wanted to know what CPAR was and what we were up to. He warmed up a little when he found out that I had been in politics for close to three decades; I was not one of those—in his view—"meddlesome NGOs". Max himself was a former rebel commander, having fought Museveni in the western province of Soroti. But he had been accepted into the government and was now assigned to the northern region to put an end to the LRA. As he stated, there could be no development for the people until security was restored. We agreed, but the question was, By what means?

In the midst of our meeting, in walked two very tough-looking characters, right out of central casting as rebel leaders, which is exactly what they were. They had crossed the border the previous day and were now being given the royal treatment by the district commissioner. Something was up, part of a scheme to isolate Kony, before the push.

Later in the morning I met a group of young women who had already paid the price of ongoing conflict. Spread under a huge mango tree was a gathering of land-mine victims. Most of them were in their early twenties, several nursing their babies as they sat on mats on the ground, their artificial limbs positioned awkwardly out from their bodies. Beside us was a marketplace where they had set up a small business selling food bought from local farmers—part of a self-help project established by CPAR with a grant from the Canadian International Development Agency (CIDA). They had nothing else. After their injuries they were abandoned by husbands, shunned by family and friends and left with no pension or means of support from the government. They were all alone.

The discussion became animated when Patrick, the CPAR worker, tried to explain to the women that they would have to pay back a portion of the start-up capital given them so that other groups could be financed. There was already a list of 380 other land-mine victims who wanted to start projects. The women said they couldn't afford to pay a sum of about $200 in Ugandan shillings. I decided to become a partner with the group and repaid their loan in return for a small share of any profits they someday may earn. As the meeting broke up, Gisaw Shibru started a conversation with a middle-aged man who had sat silently on the edge of the group during our exchange. His name was Vincent. His story was stark. His son had been mutilated and killed by the rebels. His wife, who witnessed the atrocity, had become mentally deranged. A few days after this incident he lost a leg to a land mine. He said he didn't have much to live for and so he didn't see much point to the women's small enterprise. He just had given up.

Leaving this gathering, with the women still bargaining with Patrick, I couldn't help but be reminded of an article I had read just before leaving Canada, reporting how our military in Afghanistan were frustrated at not being allowed to use land mines as they partnered with U.S. troops who were not similarly restrained. They thought it was a mistake for Canada to have promoted the land-mine treaty, thereby limiting their choice of weapons. Too bad they would never spend a morning under a mango tree seeing what a cruel killer and destroyer of innocent people their weapon of choice can be. I calculated that if a small portion of the half-billion dollars being spent to supply Canadian troops for a mop-up operation in the hills of Afghanistan were redirected to resettle displaced persons or help in the rehabilitation of land-mine victims, it would make a huge difference in Afghanistan, just as it would in northern Uganda.

FEBRUARY 6, 2002: LACOR HOSPITAL, ON THE OUTSKIRTS OF GULU

Lacor Hospital was more than just a treatment centre; it was a living repository of basic data on the impacts of war and conflict on people. In the AIDS ward they showed us graphs that directly related the rise of HIV to the intensity of conflict. The surgeons said the incidence of injuries from land mines received during war years was running at five hundred a year and that the horrific statistics on child malnutrition correlated with the incidence of conflict and war. We saw a young boy whose jaw had been shot away at the end of December in crossfire. The courtyard was full of mothers with babies they had brought in to relieve their starvation. A resident took me into the children's ward to show me a case of a rare form of child cancer, whose cause seems to be related to malnutrition. It is treatable by drugs, but the prices set by the international pharmaceutical companies are far beyond the budget of the Lacor Hospital. Even the simple treatment of malnutrition had become problematic. UNICEF had run out of budget in Uganda and hadn't been able to provide a special milk-sugar compound to the hospital for the last three months. Too bad that President Bush didn't divert from his $48-billion increase in defence spending a few dollars for milk supplies.

One hopeful sign was a building under construction to house pediatrics and patients with child-related diseases. Five years earlier, U.S. Secretary of State Madeleine Albright had visited the hospital and pledged U.S.$5 million for this construction.

The most telling experience during my visit to the hospital occurred when I was taken around back to a tree-shaded oasis where two memorials sat amongst large mounds of red dirt. One is for Lucille Corti, a Canadian woman who, with her husband, Piero, founded the hospital in 1959. In 1983 she contracted HIV before it even had a name, and succumbed to AIDS in 1998. During her long stay in Gulu, she and her husband, along with a loyal staff of local doctors and nurses, supported by aid money from international donors, built this small establishment into one of the best hospitals in Uganda. It became a refuge of caring for those wounded and affected by the war. In 1999 a ceremony unveiling a special stamp in her honour was held in Ottawa. Her real tribute, however, is the hospital she founded that still ministers to the health problems of a population desperately in need.

Next to the flowered gravesite of Dr. Corti stands a black marble plaque that recognizes the heroism of medical staff who lost their lives in a valiant—and successful—fight to contain the deadly Ebola virus that affected the region in October 2000. Thought to be carried by soldiers coming out of the bush, the virus spread at a rapid rate, killing hundreds in just a few days. If this virulent strain were to spread into the camps of internally displaced persons it would wreak havoc of gigantic proportions, and would in all likelihood have leap-frogged beyond northern Uganda to become a worldwide threat. The only way to stop the disease was through isolation. Dr. Matthew Lukwiya, a physician from the Gulu area who could have been working at a comfortable practice anywhere in the world, took on the task of containing the disease. The price was his own life. He was called in to deal with a patient who had gone berserk and threatened to break out of confinement. Knowing that any direct contact with the infection is a sure death sentence, he nonetheless wrestled the man back into bed and cleaned his open sores. Five days later, Dr. Lukwiya was dead, followed by twelve other staff of the hospital who became infected.

The heroism of this small group of medical people in a distant part of the world made me think about where, in this global age, responsibility lies for the welfare of others. A group of African doctors and nurses were surely acting as global citizens when they took the decision to arrest a disease that might easily have had widespread repercussions for people living in Europe or North America. They were not hunkering down behind walls trying to protect just themselves or their immediate families or kinfolk. They showed their mettle as their brother's and sister's keeper on a global scale.

There are many African heroes and heroines in the cause of global human security. They generally don't receive knighthoods or appear on the cover of *Time*. Their work and effort give lie to the oft-perceived notion of Africa as a place with no hope. It is amazing how many people I met during my brief stay who showed remarkable resource, courage and leadership: A burly former army officer named Fabius who gave up his commission to go back to law school and now works as a human rights advocate, at some danger to himself. Geoffrey Oyat, a community organizer who plies his trade with a variety of international NGOs to advance the cause of children. The workers at the child rehabilitation centre run by CPAR, the Christian relief and development agency World Vision and a local group called Gulu Support the Children Organisation (GUSCO), who brave retaliation from rebels for their work saving children. The tall, outspoken environmental officer for the local district commission who is trying to arrest the razing of woodlands to prevent desertification, working with no resources, not even a bicycle.

Perhaps September 11 could become the occasion for honouring all those who make a sacrifice on behalf of their global neighbours, making it a day of remembrance for all victims of violence and those who try to protect them.

FEBRUARY 7, 2002: KAMPALA

The outdoor terrace of the Kampala Sheraton Hotel was alive with noisy, animated conversations over bitter lemon and cheeseburgers. This was the other side of the Uganda experience, as well-dressed businesspeople, diplomats, World Bank officials and First World academics mixed with their Ugandan counterparts, also very well dressed, to talk about the latest privatization proposal, trade program or workshop on deregulation. Uganda has been Africa's economic showcase, with high growth rates and full allegiance to economic liberalization. Not too many of those discussing deals on the hotel terrace were fussed about the kids up in Gulu.

One exception was my lunch companion, a savvy, experienced and knowledgeable player in the Ugandan government, himself an Acholi from the north, but one who had made a successful career serving various governments since the days of Idi Amin. He was carefully monitoring events in the north, as they had a bearing on his negotiations with the government of Sudan.

My friend confirmed that there had been talks between the governments of Sudan and Uganda on how to fix the situation of the LRA, which had received the Washington brand of being a terrorist group. The Sudanese were ready to jettison their ally as part of a courting campaign with the Americans, and planning for military action was well under way. But this is a border that sits on the African fault line between Muslim and Christian creeds, and the reaction in the south of the Sudan, he said, could be unpredictable and volatile. The Ugandan government was also trying to do a little international image-making by getting rid of the embarrassing IDP camps. But there was no clear plan for resettlement back to the villages. More likely was a plan of decentralizing people into smaller satellite settlements where the army could still keep an eye on things. There was no suggestion that the camp people themselves would be involved in the decision on whether to attack the LRA, thereby putting thousands of children at risk, or on going back directly to their villages.

I asked if outside intervention could alter the plans. The U.S. could get involved, if it was so inclined, but that was unlikely: their interest was simply taking on the terrorists. So could the British, but it was unclear where they would come down. After all, the LRA were labelled terrorists, and no one wanted to be seen as defending them, even if they were mostly made up of former abducted children; too much of a nuance to try to explain. So the fate of the people of Acholiland was unfolding without a lot of concern for their welfare or interests, leaving their fate to the dynamics of international politics.

What about the Commonwealth and the UN and the East African community? I asked. The response was that the Commonwealth would never act because of the reaction by African leaders to what they might see as an incursion into sovereign affairs. The UN couldn't even get its act together in the neighbouring Congo, even though millions had died. And the East African community was primarily interested in free trade. Not an encouraging assessment, but one that I didn't entirely agree with, either. I thought that if Canada put Africa at the centre of the G-8 agenda, there might just be some leverage to be exercised.

When I got home I tried. Bill Graham contacted his Foreign Affairs counterpart in Uganda to raise concerns. Our UN ambassador drew attention to the problem with UN officials in New York, but was told things were in hand. Prime Minister Chrétien referred the matter to CIDA, and there were several discussions about what might be done. But the wheels ground slowly, and at the G-8 meeting the focus was on NEPAD, the African plan for development. No one wanted to get involved in a nasty situation in a small corner of a country presided over by an influential African leader.[1]

SEPTEMBER 10, 2000: WINNIPEG

I was in northern Uganda on a promise. A year and a half earlier, in my home city of Winnipeg, I had hosted an international meeting on war-affected children. It had been a week-long event, beginning with a discussion among young people from around the world, including conflict areas, who were there to draft their own plan of action to protect children in time of war. This was followed by a session of experts, NGOs and representatives of international organizations who were to add their own recommendations to a document presented to ministers on the final weekend. We had laid on a Canadian Air Force Airbus in New York to fly in a large delegation of foreign ministers attending the UN General Assembly, along with ambassadors and other officials. The goal was to agree on a blueprint that could be taken to a special UN session on children's rights.

Running as a subtext was the opportunity to bring together the foreign ministers from Sudan and Uganda to negotiate the release of several thousand child soldiers still held captive in Sudan. A lot of negotiation, discussion, speech making and persuading had to be packed into a limited time.

During the Friday-night reception for the arriving ministers, Mary Ellen Kenny, one of my staff members, passed on a request to meet directly with some children from the northern war zone in Uganda. I was less than enthusiastic. There was so much going on to get an agreement on a ministerial statement and conclude some deal on the release of the children that I didn't see how I could slot them in. Mary Ellen was persistent, so I agreed to find some time the next morning. That's how I met Emma, and that's how my involvement with Uganda began.

My room at the Fort Garry Hotel had deep, oversized chairs, the kind one sees in the sitting room of a downtown men's club, big enough to almost swallow the slight frames of the two adolescent Ugandan girls who had shyly come into the room, accompanied by

Geoffrey Oyat of CPAR and the Parents' Committee for Abducted Children. It was Emma whom I first invited to speak. Coming from someone so young and looking so innocent, her story packed a powerful punch. She had been kidnapped at the age of nine by the LRA, taken across the border to a camp in Sudan and forced to become the sexual slave of one of the soldiers. At the age of eleven she gave birth to a child and after that, as part of winning status as a warrior, was sent back into northern Uganda to participate in killing raids against her own people. Finally, at age thirteen, she escaped and was now residing in an IDP camp. But as she explained, echoed by the others in the room, that wasn't exactly salvation, as she had to face continued threats of assault, risk disease and live with the fear that if captured again she would certainly be put to death.

It was a sobering, shocking tale. Hard to believe that this young woman in front of me, barely out of childhood, had been through the kind of experience that even the most hardened adult would find unbearable. It wasn't a unique story, by any stretch. As I later found in my trip to Acholiland, similar sagas were experienced by thousands of young people who had their lives twisted by the experience of war and abduction. As I sat listening, and as the minutes wore on way past the allotted time, it put all the rest of the conference into simple perspective—there must be a way to protect these children and give them a chance to restore some normalcy to their lives. When I asked Emma what she most wanted she said, "To go back to school." As she and her companions left the room, I promised to come to Uganda someday to see what could be done.

The chance came after I left government and took up a post as director of the Liu Institute for Global Issues, a policy think-tank at the University of British Columbia. Soon after arriving, I was handed a copy of a report commissioned by CIDA on northern Uganda and written by Stephen Owen. Among the many recommendations Owen made was the idea of establishing in northern Uganda a centre for peace and reconciliation, a place where local community groups could gather, receive training in the skills of peacemaking, apply traditional techniques to justice issues, help mobilize a voice for people in the camps, provide advocacy for children's issues and develop a land-mine program. It seemed an initiative suitable for a university centre with a mandate for action in the field.

Soon after, a group of friends suggested that I come back to Ottawa for a roast, the politician's way of receiving a send-off. I agreed on the condition that it would be a fundraiser for Emma. With the help of the Canadian Landmine Foundation, more than $40,000 was raised from a selection of the Ottawa political crowd; we now had the resources to follow through on the Owen report, and by early 2002 we were launched.

Sitting with Geoffrey Oyat on an outside patio of the Acholi Inn in Gulu (half of the structure had been gutted by fire and had yet to be repaired), I caught up on news of Emma. On her return she had been accepted into a camp for war children run by World Vision, and was now attending school in a town in the neighbour-ing province of Lino, by all accounts doing well. I asked him what it had meant to the two girls to be in Winnipeg. He said that before the meeting they had been very nervous, not knowing exactly what to expect. But he had coached them just to tell their story and be open and candid. Afterwards they felt that this had been their first chance to talk to someone "senior," to be taken seriously, to partici-pate with other young people in looking for solutions. They had been given the basic tools in the rehabilitation camp and were now on their way to achieving what Emma said she so deeply wanted— an education.

With us at breakfast was a world-renowned psychiatrist who deals with children's war trauma, Dr. Elizabeth Jareg, from Norway. She comes to the area once a month to help the agencies working with children to treat the scars left by their captivity. I asked her if it was possible for someone like Emma to put her experiences behind her and go on to a normal life. She said children like Emma can never erase the pain inside, and in later life it will continue to haunt them, but that with the right care they can be given a new start. What she emphasized, however, was the importance of being accepted back into the community, and then being given some-thing useful to do. Nothing is more destructive both for the children and for the community than to have large numbers of young people trained in war and the use of guns feeling alienated from their own people and with no occupation. That is a prescription for lawlessness and a return to violence. Signs of that were already appearing in and around Gulu.

To make matters worse, two months after my visit, the Ugandan army launched Operation Iron Fist, chasing after the LRA into their Sudanese sanctuary. The rebels have fought back, and once again northern Uganda has become engulfed in a war that kills more people, swells the ranks of the IDP camps and shatters any hope for peace. Emma's future is again at great risk.

Dr. Jareg also spoke passionately of the need to put in place some form of justice to deal with the perpetrators of the vicious crimes committed during this war. She believed that without some way of addressing the grievances of families and tribal members related to victims of war crimes, or the remaining victims themselves, there could be no true peace. The sense of injustice would fester and be the cause of further disruption. She touched on what had become a central debate in Acholiland—the need to secure peace with the rebels by offering amnesty and forgiveness. Should Joseph Kony and his troops be brought back to the community without penalty in order to avoid further bloodshed? Or should they be tried for their crimes?

The demand for peace was overwhelming, but there were those who recognized that some form of justice must prevail. Traditional tribal means were being suggested, a concept called Mato Oput, or forgiveness. It was being promoted by the Ugandan Amnesty Commission, which had no money, but did have authority to grant penalty-free re-entry into Uganda for LRA fighters. But, as one aid worker argued, what happens when you come up against the person who mutilated your son walking free on the streets of Gulu? How do you forgive?

This question of trading off holding accountable those who commit serious crimes in return for securing peace is a crucial issue facing all wartorn areas, especially with the International Criminal Court coming into being. Our discussion under a very bright morning sky in central Africa was more than abstract. It went to the very core of how best to secure peace, and how it can be done with justice.

FREEDOM FROM FEAR

The callousness towards the plight of others and the overweening preoccupation with muscle-flexing that has become so prevalent in Western countries since September 11 stands in stark contrast to the problems and concerns I found in this small region of Uganda. And what I saw there is a prime reflection of the global condition. Daily threats and insecurities, violence and conflict that render any form of stable life impossible—these are the sad facts of life for millions around the globe. Finding a way to protect the child in a displaced persons camp from being abducted, raped or mutilated is just as important as protecting the right of the commuter getting on an airplane to be free of a terrorist hijacking. The lament and grief that followed the attack against innocent people on September 11 was echoed by an elderly Acholi woman who broke into a meeting with tribal elders held in a satellite camp just outside the main site at Pabo. She wanted us to understand what the war meant to her and her family: the constant scrambling for bare necessities, the loss of any joy or pleasure for a family faced with starvation, the constant fear of injury or death from attacks or land mines. She simply said, "Stop the war, I want to go home."

Driving on that dusty road to Gulu brought home to me as no other experience has the idea that human security must be a choice for the future—that all people, regardless of who they are or where they live, have a right to feel secure against war, violence, disease, disaster and terror. The anger I felt that day could be assuaged only by working to secure those rights.

Five days in a distant part of the world is not much time to become conversant with the complexity of life and difficulty of issues there. But it is enough to remind one of just how close together we are in the world and how our fates are so closely inter- twined. The reality of our living in a global society far outpaces our ability to understand it; we are still living in a time warp of outdated perceptions. In our search for the right road map, one starting place is to understand the human-security dimension of life in Acholiland and how it mixes with ours, to understand what we can do to help protect and nurture the Emmas of the world.

As I came to realize, the true narrative of politics is the human story of Emma and other children like her who have suffered a violation of body and spirit. It is the story of land-mine victims in Chechnya, Angola and Acholiland whose only crime is wanting freedom to farm or play. It is the story of busboys and stockbrokers in the World Trade Center who became targets for fanatics. It is also the story of innocent villagers in rural Afghanistan bombed from thirty thousand feet, and parched, starving dwellers in Basra, and it is the story of all those denied a minimum of peace from arrest, harassment, unlawful imprisonment, of the 300,000 a year who lose their lives through war and conflict and the other 500,000 who lose their lives indirectly from the same causes. Instead of Emma telling her tale, it could just as easily have been some child from Sierra Leone whose arms had been amputated by rebels, or a young boy from Colombia recruited into the rebel force called the FARC, or a young girl I met in Lebanon who had lost a limb to a land mine.

The morning I met Emma and the other children in the comfort of the Fort Garry Hotel, they were speaking of a human condition experienced by countless others around the world, and their plea took on an urgency I had not felt before in quite the same way. This exchange posed the mysterious question of how far does our range of responsibility extend, of why the fate of one group should concern that of another. That is increasingly one of the dilemmas of living in a global society. Where is the line we draw in setting out the boundaries for being responsible for others? Is it simply family and close friends? Is it tribal or ethnic based? Do we stop at the frontiers of our own country? How far can we reach to be each other's keeper? Does our conscience, our sense of right or wrong, take us as far as the crowded camps of northern Uganda, surrounded by land mines, attacked repeatedly by an army made up largely of child soldiers, crazy on drugs, armed with automatic weapons made by the well-developed industries of the North?

As we know, there are many answers to those questions. Our newspapers are full of the hatreds of class, region, religion and the ultra-nationalisms. But there is also the ultimate sin, that of indifference, which allows human tragedy to occur without a trace of interest as one flicks the channels away from news to sports. Or as Cynthia Ozick puts it, "Hoping to confer no hurt, indifference finally grows lethal."[2]

In the stark plains of Gulu I believe an answer was revealed: there is a duty to become involved. We can't afford to stay aloof or be indifferent. What happens there affects us, what we do to help contributes to the common weal.

Naysayers to this notion of global duty will argue that it constitutes meddling in the affairs of others, that it doesn't serve any specific national interest, or that it will require unacceptably high costs of intervention. Even more disturbing is the growing tendency to automatically exclude large numbers of people from being subjects of our concern and our laws. They are outside the pale. In *Homo Sacer: Sovereign Power and Bare Life*, Giorgio Agamben has reconstituted the ancient legal concept of homo sacer to describe this indifference and exclusion that seems to characterize the attitudes of so many decision makers.[3] Under the Roman law of homo sacer, someone could be killed with impunity. Their death would have no sacrificial or spiritual value. Navid Kermani, in the *Times Literary Supplement*, attributes this to the emergence of a double standard: one set of values and norms for those in the West and their allies, and the "logic" of homo sacer for many others—the refugees, the victims of ethnic war, the Taliban prisoners denied legal status, any number whose plight is dismissed as not being important. Even recipients of humanitarian aid have no particular rights or standing.[4]

On the other hand, can we live in an increasingly economically and socially interdependent world without taking on political responsibility for those who are being excluded from the protection of universal laws and rights? Indeed, there is a larger reality that we in the well-developed, reasonably secure part of the world cannot ignore. Our own security interests are also at stake, not so much by the old calculations of national interest but as measured by the risk to individuals.

The world has become less safe for civilians. Yet the tools that we use to govern ourselves are less relevant to the intermingling of our common fate in today's global conditions. The international system centred on traditional domestic and sovereign concerns is poorly governed when it comes to protection of individuals and is no longer perceived as offering hope for the majority of global citizens who seek escape from the fear of want and the fear for life. This is a breakdown that bodes ill for us all.

Nothing illustrates with more clarity why it is important to shift our sightlines to the protection of people than the slaughter of innocent men and women on September 11 in New York and Washington. No country, not even the most powerful, is immune; no individual safe until we grasp the need to rethink the nature of security risk, and rewire our circuits to promote global cooperation against such threats. Evil triumphs only if we let it.

There is a natural and understandable urge to circle the wagons, to divide the world into friend or foe. That might be the right response if we were living in a divided world, but we're not. The reality is that there can be no wall high enough around any country or continent to keep the barbarians at bay. A fragmented, adversarial approach simply won't work. The serial application of military action, with its attendant destruction, ruin and suffering, is hardly an answer. The answer has to be a form of global political community that can restore a sense of security and provide institutions that can promote mutual well-being.

Fortunately, as we shall see, certain political leaders and certain countries, working with key civil leaders and partnering with non-governmental groups, are trying—slowly but surely—to build an order where the interests of those who are at risk are protected and promoted. Canada has been at the forefront in that cause. It is my fervent hope that we will stay there.

PART II

The Tenth Floor

CHAPTER 2

VOCATIONAL TRAINING

THE NORTHEAST CORNER OFFICE ON THE TENTH FLOOR OF THE Lester B. Pearson Building has a panoramic view of the Gatineau Hills, across the Ottawa River in Quebec. Looking directly down, one can see the elegant residence of the British high commissioner. Farther to the right is 24 Sussex Drive. Off to the left are the imposing spires of the Parliament Buildings.

This is where I found myself shortly after noon on January 25, 1996. It is the office of the foreign affairs minister of Canada, and I was to spend a good part of the next four and a half years within its confines, working at a job to which I had long aspired—for me a dream come true.

In my early teens I had discovered an interest in world affairs, in part the result of my involvement in the local United church my family attended in the north end of Winnipeg. In those days the United Church, especially in the Prairies, was influenced by the theology of the social gospel movement, which put a strong emphasis on responsibility to the community in the broadest meaning of the word. Our ministers were Roy and Lois (later senator) Wilson, and at a weekly Sunday-night young people's group, they exposed us to a variety of world issues, such as poverty, racism, colonialism and nuclear war.

Through them I became involved with the Manitoba Youth Parliament. Every Christmas break for seven years, I took a seat in the chamber of the Manitoba Legislature to debate in parliamentary fashion recognition of Red China, nuclear disarmament or Canada–U.S. relations. This in turn led to my participation in the Model UN Assembly sponsored by the local Rotary Club. One year I represented Yemen, the next year Israel, learning at an early age the intractability of the Middle East. It was also the beginning of a lifelong fascination with the UN and a belief in its core value as a place of peace.

Winnipeg had good public schools with demanding teachers. I attended Sisler High, which sat near the city's northwest boundary. From its second-storey window I could discern the outline of Stony Mountain Penitentiary. One of my English teachers who tired of my sundry forms of disruption predicted that someday I would end up in a federal institution, either Parliament or the imposing building that could be seen in the distance.

One of my most memorable moments was when my history teacher, Mr. R. J. Phillips, assigned me to attend a political speech in the old civic auditorium in downtown Winnipeg. It was not a matter of choice: you had to attend or you lost substantial term marks.

On stage was the new leader of Canada's Liberal Party, Lester B. (Mike) Pearson. At first sight, with his bow tie and slight lisp, he was not very prepossessing, especially to a slightly unruly group of teenagers. But when he began to outline the role Canada had played in helping to resolve the Suez crisis by introducing the idea of a UN peacekeeping force, he struck a chord. I was impressed by the way he related our role in international peacekeeping to Canada's nascent talents as a mediator. His concept of Canada as a bridge-builder, based on our history of working through compromise to establish and preserve our nationhood, was compelling. That night was the dawning of my understanding of what it is to be a Canadian, how our integrity as a people is tied up inextricably with exercising an active, independent and constructive role in the world. But it also made me understand that we can play such a role only by fostering liberal-minded, socially responsible, unity-oriented policies and attitudes at home. It is our values that define us, and our politics that can give those values tangible expression.

This encounter fuelled my interest in public service. Mike Pearson was *the* role model. I became an admirer and a Liberal. It wasn't an unalloyed commitment. I once wrote a letter to my role model condemning his government's decision to accept U.S. Bomarc missiles on Canadian soil, and resigned from the Liberal Party. It was, however, a short-lived absence. Pearson represented to me the quintessential qualities of a Canadian. I rejoined the party after a three-month apostasy.

I went on to study political science and history at United College (now the University of Winnipeg). In 1961, I was accepted for graduate studies at Princeton University, where I landed in the midst of the tumultuous sixties revolution on American campuses. It was the time of civil rights, the anti–Vietnam War movement, student power and the too-brief Kennedy era.

All this contributed to a heady atmosphere of challenge to the existing order, confrontation with authority and the sometimes overweening confidence of our generation that we could create a better world. At times the protest movements were truly anarchic, but they also began to rewrite the ground rules of democracy, since they stood for the ideal that democracy could be enhanced through the sharing of power. Participatory democracy was more than a slogan; it was a model of how ordinary citizens could be directly involved in decisions that affect them. What we witness today in the efforts of non-governmental organizations (NGOs) to influence decisions at the global level, or the protests at global convocations, is a natural extension into the international arena of sixties people power.

Princeton substantially deepened my education about the complexities of international affairs. The professors I had were not only fine scholars and teachers; they were engaged in the real world of policy-making and advocacy. Too often Canadian academics tend to be detached and at times disdainful of involvement in the political process. These Princeton academics brought to their intellectual exercise experience in the State Department, the UN and commissions on international law or stints in elected office.

I wrestled with them over the concept of the "middle power," was introduced to the intricacies of "acceptable losses" in a nuclear exchange and tried to discern what exactly made for democracy. Leon Gordenker taught me the value of working through multilateral organizations, and Richard Falk expounded the creative uses of international law, focusing on how to establish individual accountability for war crimes.

Education of a broader kind also took place at Princeton. I was witness to the enormous weight of responsibility borne by Americans because of their pre-eminent place in the world. I watched spellbound as classmates anguished over American involvement in Vietnam. I admired the young black leaders of the early civil rights groups and became directly involved—including joining the march on Birmingham—as Americans confronted the huge issue of race in their society. And I viewed with horror the virulent strands of xenophobia and jingoism that ran through the American body politic—most particularly at a Madison Square Garden rally of the Young Americans for Freedom, a forerunner to many of the extreme conservative organizations that unfortunately have become part of the political mainstream in today's United States. I was amazed at the rhetoric of hate and intolerance that spewed forth.

My first glimpse of President John F. Kennedy was on the steps of the statehouse in Trenton, New Jersey, on a chilly fall evening, surrounded by the Democratic bosses of the state in their homburgs and long overcoats. He was hatless, coatless and so different in presence from those around him. Kennedy's speech was a call to arms to our generation to think new thoughts and challenge the conventional. It was a new message for me and my classmates who were looking for a political personality who spoke to the fresh spirit of the sixties.

But it wasn't just the style that attracted. Kennedy stood for a different approach to the Cold War. He suggested that there could be coexistence with the Russians, and his initiative on a test-ban treaty gave hope. Most significant of all was his decision to avoid a direct confrontation with the Soviets in the face of extreme provocation during the 1962 Cuban missile crisis, despite the urgings of the generals and the old-guard gurus of diplomacy. He exercised political leadership—he didn't just go along. It was an important lesson.

I came away from the U.S. with respect for both its power and its capacity to use that power positively in the international arena. I remain an admirer of the incredible creativity and enormous resources of American universities, think-tanks, research centres and foundations for innovation and public problem solving. And I became fascinated with the open and dynamic quality of American politics.

And yet. It was while living and studying in the U.S. that I came to appreciate that although we share a continent, are closely tied economically, watch U.S. television and movies and rely on Washington's goodwill to manage our border, we are not Americans. We have our own destiny to fulfill.

Our parliamentary politics are different, and so is the kind of federalism we have developed. Canadian multiculturalism gives us a distinctive answer to the integration of diverse groups. Historically we have a greater respect for the provision of public goods. We don't have a powerful military establishment to contend with. Abroad, we have learned to rely on multilateral, cooperative internationalism. These qualities endow us with a different outlook: they give us the ability to march to the beat of our own international drummer.

A POLITICIAN'S APPRENTICESHIP

I arrived for my first sojourn in Ottawa in the late summer of 1967, asked by John Turner to join his staff as policy assistant and speech writer. Turner was at that time registrar-general, a somewhat archaic title that would soon be transformed into minister of consumer and corporate affairs.

This is not a political autobiography, so I won't get into all the crazy and chaotic happenings of that Centennial year. I do, however, want to touch on one lesson Turner imparted to me. He was preparing to present legislation on compulsory licensing for patent drugs, an eminently good idea for creating competition and thereby bringing prices down for the consumer. As a minister should, he worked primarily with the departmental public servants in drafting the bill. But my instruction, as a political staffer, was to ensure that he receive alternative views from outside experts, soundings from MPs, public reaction and party opinion. This put him in a better position to choose the best policy. The senior officials were not very happy. On occasion they openly expressed displeasure at being challenged by a young ministerial "pup." But it was good practice, bringing to bear views that reflected a broader constituency than that inside Ottawa. It helped Turner achieve a successful legislative coup, against severe opposition from the drug companies. It was a demonstration of the need to open up the policy-making process, a lesson I took to heart when I returned to Manitoba.

In the 1973 provincial election, I won the downtown Winnipeg riding of Fort Rouge. That was done by dint of literally knocking on every door, at least twice, tackling immediate urban issues that had long been ignored in the rural-dominated legislature and benefiting from the exuberant campaign waged by Izzy Asper, then the provincial Liberal leader. In 1979, I decided to run federally and, despite the defeat of the Trudeau government, gained by a very small margin the riding of Winnipeg–Fort Garry. What counted, I believe, was the trust people had in my promise to be an effective day-by-day advocate for Western and Manitoba interests, and my own liberal convictions. I believe that even those who didn't always agree with my positions respected my willingness to speak out on an agenda rooted in well-defined beliefs. I was able to keep that relationship of mutual trust with the electors of Winnipeg–Fort Garry (subsequently Winnipeg South-Centre) until my political retirement in the fall of 2000.

For me, working at the grassroots was the essence of politics. Every time I knocked on a door, and was invited into someone's home, I learned another human story. Those hours in the riding office sorting out pension cases and immigration problems taught me a lot about people's needs and how insensitive bureaucracy can sometimes be. It is the job of the elected public servant to maintain a faith in the system of government by giving people a chance to be heard and have their problems solved. Those countless encounters with people at the street corner, the shopping market or the Legion beer parlour gave me a better feel for the public mood than any pollster could. When I came back to Ottawa after a weekend in the riding and was faced with a policy paper or a briefing note from my civil servants, there was an automatic screen that filtered the proposal through what I had heard out on the street. This applied to foreign affairs as much as to any domestic matter. I have always believed it important to bring an on-the-ground, local perspective to bear as a balance to the advice received from department officials whose interests were often dominated by the view from the overseas region, or issue, for which they were responsible.

I recall having a private dinner with Madeleine Albright in an Upper East Side restaurant in New York City after a UN meeting, a practice we got into so that we could engage in wide-ranging discussion without precooked agendas, briefing papers or advisors in tow. She admitted that being captive inside the Washington Beltway, always meeting other diplomats, never gave her the chance to know if what she was doing had resonance with the American public. It was a telling point. And it leads me to one of the real advantages of the Canadian parliamentary system: it helps to have a foreign minister regularly go back home to press the flesh; it helps make our development of foreign policy more consultative and its execution more firmly based on public acceptance.

Another tangible benefit is the opportunity to develop ideas and notions in a public crucible. In our parliamentary system you are on the firing line every day, having to defend positions and respond to criticism both in the verbal workout known as Question Period and in the media scrum. Your views have to bear open, often unremitting scrutiny. Often when hosting a lunch for a visiting foreign dignitary, I would have to excuse myself just before two p.m. to go to Question Period. Many of my guests were horrified and at the same time fascinated that there would be this daily rendering of accountability by a minister, and by the prime minister, secretly wondering what strange form of masochism the Canadian parliamentary system induced. The great advantage of Canadian democracy is that you can't hide your beliefs or views for long. It is a test of transparency.

The same need to have command of your brief was a hallmark of being in Pierre Trudeau's cabinet, where I served first as

Employment and Immigration minister and then in Transport. Trudeau's rational, deliberative style of governing is well known. In cabinet he expected ministers to know their files and be able to marshal a good defence of their positions. At times this would result in meetings of cabinet that could go on for hours, sometimes days. But he was always prepared to let the debate take place as long as it was based on cogent and effective argument. This is what happened in the case of the cruise missile decision.

The issue arose in 1983 when it was discovered that an agreement between the Department of National Defence and the U.S. Department of Defense on shared testing and evaluation included a clause that granted the U.S. reciprocal rights for the testing of weapons systems on Canadian soil. U.S. officials interpreted this as permitting the testing of the new technology of cruise missiles. There was substantial opposition in the Canadian public, shared by several in cabinet, myself included, who felt this would again destabilize relations between the U.S. and the Soviet Union and lead to an escalation in the arms race. What was telling was that Trudeau encouraged and promoted a far-ranging debate inside cabinet that literally went on for months. At one point George Bush Sr., then vice-president in the Reagan administration, came to Ottawa to push for agreement. In a cabinet-level meeting, when Bush asked what was holding things up, Trudeau looked down the table at me and replied, "Ask him."

Eventually the issue was decided on the grounds that we had signed the agreement and therefore were honour-bound to comply—though I believe that Trudeau himself thought the opposition had the best of the debate.

This experience taught me the importance of having wide-ranging discussions in cabinet on topics of foreign affairs. It gave ministers such as myself, who didn't at the time have direct responsibility in external matters but held strong views, a chance to be heard, and reinforced the importance of constantly injecting the international dimension into policy-making.

For Prime Minister Trudeau, having a world view for Canada was a priority, especially when it came to North-South relations and to "suffocating" the arms race. One of his early important decisions was de-nuclearizing the Canadian military. Trudeau's most imaginative and creative initiative, however, was his launching of a peace mission in 1984 to encourage world leaders to restart a dialogue on nuclear disarmament. Forgotten now is how dismal those times were, with a total breakdown of discussions between the Soviet and American administrations.

It was one of that government's finest hours. The Trudeau mission was strongly opposed by senior officials in External Affairs and Defence who felt it would anger the Reagan White House. That was also the prevailing view of the academic foreign policy establishment, who made their views very vocal. On the other side, we heard from people like peace activist Helen Caldicott, who said that someone, especially someone with the credibility of the Canadian prime minister, had to break the log-jam of silence that characterized the disarmament issue. Cabinet debated these options, and strongly endorsed the Trudeau mission.

It was, I believe, encouraging, maybe even uplifting, for Canadians to see their prime minister travelling the world on an issue of vital security. As for concrete results, the mission got world leaders thinking again. Only two years later, at Reykjavik, Ronald Reagan and Mikhail Gorbachev were negotiating arms control and disarmament.

The Canadian officials were right in one respect, though: at the time, President Reagan and his advisors were sorely displeased. They saw the nuclear issue as the property of a closed club—theirs—and didn't like others butting in. But Canada was speaking for all non-nuclear states in insisting that we have a stake in the game too, as our lives are also on the line.

Here is where Trudeau added a further element to the foreign affairs legacy established by Pearson. This wasn't just Canada as a renowned honest broker and font of fresh ideas—the classic middle-power stance. It was Canada as an independent voice—a voice that doesn't simply echo the interests of the powerful and the privileged but speaks for those without international clout who are in need of representation. This was defining a leading role for Canada in establishing norms of global behaviour and rules of law, and advocating inclusive decision making on issues that affect all humankind. It was a position that suited the growing maturity of Canada, and a lesson that needs to be built upon from generation to generation.

Before leaving the Trudeau period, I should mention the re-organization that brought about the new Department of Foreign Affairs and International Trade, or DFAIT. This was basically the handiwork of Michael Pitfield, the clerk of the Privy Council, the idea being to amalgamate the overseas personnel of Immigration and Trade with the foreign officer corps to create an integrated service, and to move the trade development and promotion functions of Industry into External Affairs. The arguments put forward were ones of efficiency and coherence, but it was well known that Pitfield wanted a stronger economic thrust to our foreign policy.

This was a laudable objective, but the structural arrangement created a hydra-headed department with two ministers of equal standing, thus bifurcating responsibility and resources. Strangely, the Canadian International Development Agency (CIDA), the delivery agency for overseas aid, was left out and continued as an autonomous entity, even though in terms of program dollars and in symmetry of interests it was a major instrument of Canadian international policy. If the idea was to achieve coherence, the structural changes didn't meet the goal.

Combining trade and foreign policy proved a mixed blessing. It has created a condition where economic and political interests coincide, and when there is a good working relationship between the two senior ministers there could be a real synergy. I recall, for example, the cooperative efforts of Art Eggleton, then Minister of International Trade, and myself in protecting Canadian business interests in Cuba after the U.S. Helms-Burton Law sought to penalize any foreign company investing there. The Martin government has now split the department again, which adds to the fragmentation not the coherence. It is ironic, given Trudeau's strong global outlook and his relative indifference towards economic matters, that the structural changes he approved have perpetuated the fragmentation between aid and foreign policy, and built into the foreign ministry a bias towards trade.

The Liberal defeat in 1984 began for me a nine-year spell in opposition—in the slang of Parliament, going on sabbatical. It was neither a welcome nor an easy political time, but it gave me the opportunity to explore a wide range of issues. For example, I travelled in Central America, observing how private organizations and citizens were offering an alternative to the military approach of the Americans. Watching private Canadians taking risks, working in deprived conditions, showing their commitment to values of justice in that period of the wars in Central America was a great lesson in the crucial role played by individual Canadians abroad.

By the time the party started planning for the 1993 election, Jean Chrétien had asked me to become the critic for foreign affairs, and we began a round of consultations in an effort to define a role for Canada in the world after the fall of the Berlin Wall. A major Liberal Party conference in Vancouver on the future of the UN was a good example of how a political party can take on the role of promoting serious policy discussion, inviting NGOs, experts, MPs and international organizations, and feeding the results into the electoral platform of a government-in-waiting. It is a role that is regrettably falling into disuse.

On the personal front, this period saw a wonderfully positive change with my marriage to Denise Ommanney, who brought into my life her two children, John and Louise. We married during the election campaign, and this was followed the next year by the arrival of our son Stephen. I mention this simply because having a good home life is of enormous importance to a politician. Whatever I was able to achieve from that point on was greatly enhanced by the love and support I gained from my wife, and the unique insight that only children can bring. It's fair to say that both my antennae and my commitment on issues like child soldiers were substantially sharpened by the simple experience of being a parent.

After the autumn 1993 election, I was appointed minister of human resources. A political friend of mine called HRD "the mother of all ministries." It was a monster portfolio, drawing together the main social functions of the federal government. With the largest budget of any department—more than $60 billion—it was also the prime target for the budget-cutting exercise that became the hallmark of our government's first term. I was charged with meeting the fiscal requirements without overturning the social system, something of an acrobatic exercise considering the depth of cuts expected.

I won't go into the raucous, rollicking days of the budget exercise and social review we launched. But I did learn how crucial our social structure is to our well-being and distinctiveness. We have neither the laissez-faire approach so often exhibited by our southern neighbours, who have of late treated the idea of public goods as anathema, nor the more centrally directed, *dirigiste* system of the Europeans with its built-in rigidities. Coming up the middle, we can offer a degree of security while retaining an equal degree of incentive for individual action. It is in fact a domestic version of human security. Canadians know this, almost instinctively, even though there has been a concerted effort by neo-conservatives to push us towards the American model.

Our ability to manage the pressures of globalization will depend on how we continually update and modernize our own society, since reforming our social system, rooting out anachronisms and rebuilding supports to respond to changes in family structure, the labour market and the aging of the population has given us an advantage in the international marketplace. Canadians take pride when the UN Human Development Index gives us top ranking as the best place to live. The trick is to keep on the path to continued improvements by setting such priorities as refinancing medicare, reducing the numbers of poor children and, most of all, addressing the deprived state of our aboriginal community.

One turning point for me in extending this notion of human security into the wider international arena was the UN Summit on Social Development, held in Copenhagen in 1995. It brought together more than 117 heads of state and a large gathering of NGOs, and its themes were the eradication of poverty, the need for full employment and the need to build secure, stable societies. At its core was a sense of disquiet about the social dislocation caused by global economic forces and the increasing inequality created by the uneven distribution of the benefits of the emerging global economy.

I was struck by how much the underlying issues were the same internationally as they were domestically. I was beginning to realize the global interconnectedness of employment and security. Global security had evolved to include the security of people, their right to live in a clean and safe environment and the opportunity to build a sustainable livelihood for themselves, their families and their communities. These issues are generally seen as domestic and subject primarily to national decision making, but I was becoming increasingly aware that globalization had brought with it new insecurities to the individual and that solutions are going to depend more and more on international cooperation; answers couldn't be found solely within national authorities.

So when, in late January 1996, the prime minister asked me to move to Foreign Affairs, I was ready and willing.

EARLY DAYS

The cabinet swearing-in ceremony on January 25 transported me into the universe of international diplomacy and global politics. I knew I was in a different world when I asked if some lunch could be sent in as I pored over the transition briefing books. At Human Resources, lunch at one's desk in Hull had usually meant tuna on a bagel delivered in a wax paper bag from the basement cafeteria. You can imagine my surprise when a waiter in white gloves arrived in my Pearson Building suite to lay out an endive salad, cold chicken and a chilled white wine. (I found out later that on virtually any day there is a multiplicity of luncheons and dinners catered in the building as part of the diplomatic routine. I was probably inheriting a part of someone else's lunch.)

It didn't take long, however, for reality to set in. My initial briefings with officials began soon after the chicken was consumed. The first order of business was not some matter of grand strategic global design but the mundane and sticky business of how DFAIT was to meet its financial obligations under the government's program-review and fiscal-restraint requirements. Putting it more bluntly, I was told that "the boys downtown"—at Treasury Board and Finance—were not happy at the lack of a plan for cutting our budget by some 15 per cent. If we didn't come up with something fast, "they would do it for us." This was not going to be easy, as the expenditures of our department were not large, as government departments go, something just over $1 billion. Compared with the $60 billion budget at HRD, this was just a footnote. As a result, the 15 per cent represented proportionally a big slice of resources. In a department where 80 per cent of expenditures were on personnel and operations, not on programs, there was little in the way of discretionary funds. In HRD, for example, my research budget alone was about $100 million. In DFAIT, the money for policy research was a mere $2 million.

And so we had to decide between cutting representation overseas and stripping down the support activities at the Pearson Building, or reducing grants and cutting funds for international culture and education and for international organizations to a bare minimum.

Embedded in those calculations was a choice critical to the style and character of Canada's role abroad. Many other countries faced with similar decisions had opted for a regional network, focusing efforts and resources on those areas of the world of immediate and proximate importance. Australia was a prime example. It had chosen to emphasize its contacts and links in Asia, give up its networks in Africa and become virtually non-existent in the Americas. This option was favoured by the bean-counters in Ottawa, "the boys downtown." It would have meant Canada's withdrawing from a number of long-standing connections in the Commonwealth, in Africa and in the newly democratizing countries of Eastern Europe.

Prime Minister Chrétien had made it clear that he didn't want to see embassies closed. With his crucial support, we decided to preserve our "thin red line" of representation in the major geographic regions and to maintain our membership in the primary international organizations. Our method of budget restraint was to pare and shave rather than to slice and hack. We did close a few offices, mainly consulates, and downsized embassy staff, mainly in London, Paris and Washington. We also reduced direct-grant support.

One telling effect was in changing the character of our representation abroad. Locally hired staff increasingly performed work in our missions, with fewer positions for Canadians, the ratio being about eighty to twenty. Fewer and fewer opportunities for foreign postings understandably affected the morale of our foreign service officers. And it affected the capacity of our missions to fully cover, from a Canadian perspective, the myriad political, social and economic events in their areas. Local staff could be loyal and effective, and many had good local contacts. But they could not see the world through Canadian eyes.

We had to pick and choose carefully where to deploy people and resources. This resulted in gaps in our knowledge and distortions in geographic coverage. For example, in the U.S., our largest trading partner and most important ally, we had, in addition to our embassy in Washington (itself reduced in numbers), only ten consulates, primarily trade oriented. Mexico, meanwhile, had opened more than thirty consular offices and beefed up their Washington complement. No need to ask who was in a better position to advance their case.

In the newly independent states of Central Asia and the Caucasus, freed from the Soviet bloc, rich in resources and with a number of crucial political issues burning, we had one embassy and a few satellite offices run from our mission in Moscow. This hole in our representation became most noticeable when the war in Afghanistan brought the region into major prominence. We simply weren't there officially in any significant way. (We are just now opening a diplomatic post in Kabul to accompany a large military contingent.) When Team Canada missions were mounted to Asian or Latin American countries, personnel were stripped from all the surrounding embassies for months, breaking their own work patterns. Our representation in Europe also far exceeded that in Africa or the Americas.

The programs that took the biggest hit were the so-called third-pillar activities, in culture and education. The foreign policy review undertaken in 1995 had put great emphasis on developing international programs that expressed Canada's cultural strengths and on promoting educational, scientific and research exchanges. This focus reflected a shift towards influencing the behaviour of others through a broad range of public contacts, not just the traditional diplomatic channels. It was the "soft power" approach. It was also an important way of engaging Canadians in international issues and exposing them to new experiences abroad.

Unfortunately, these wise words could be translated only into meagre action. Our allocations for third-pillar activities were minuscule compared with the budgets other countries were dedicating. I recall being more than a little embarrassed during a visit from Klaus Kinkel, the foreign minister of Germany, who was setting up chairs of German studies at several Canadian universities. It was a generous and welcome sign of interest in Canada. But we had no funds to reciprocate.

To deal with this budget crunch, necessity became the mother of invention. As our interests in the Balkans expanded with the eruption of hostilities, sending Canadian peacekeepers to the region, we resorted to a hub-and-spoke system of representation. In Croatia, we established an officer with the title of ambassador but without the embassy, cars and staff of a normal operation. He worked out of a hotel, with a fax machine and one secretary, and drove his own vehicle, a Toyota. All his support services came from our mission in Vienna.

This became a model for what was called the virtual embassy, where contemporary communications could be used to establish mobile, lightly equipped offices, eschewing the usual trappings—a method we later followed in other locations such as Kosovo and spots in Africa. We also experimented with sharing offices with the delegations of other countries, relied on roving ambassadors in trouble spots and greatly expanded our use of honorary consulates.

This lean period drove home the tough lesson that foreign policy needs adequate resources if it is to be effective, an important factor that has never figured in any serious cost-benefit analysis by the Canadian government. Yet it was not a debilitating period. Opportunities beckoned in the shifting conditions of the post–Cold War era. The rigidities of the alliance system were loosened. The new administration in Washington seemed open to new multilateral thinking. All countries were searching for new markers to steer by.

Coming into the Pearson Building, I recognized that even with all the financial restraints there was much inherent strength in our foreign policy infrastructure. Most breathtaking was the realization that as a foreign minister I was at the hub of an amazing information network. Twenty-four hours a day, voluminous intelligence flowed in from around the world through the closed-circuit communications system called SIGNET, all analyzed by skilled officers. The file came home with me every night—my homework, as my son called it. Depending on the urgency, next morning responses could be sent, outlining actions to be initiated or further information required. It was a privilege to have that kind of first-class electronic reach, coupled with expert filtering and assessment, and it led to serious discussion about how the new information technology could and should be used as a tool of foreign policy. SIGNET was for internal use. The next stage was how to exploit the Internet as a way of developing a strategy of "public" diplomacy, connecting us to other international players, including the NGO community, and extending our capacity to transmit our message through multimedia.

We consulted with several of the high-tech wizards who were then transforming Ottawa into a dot-com centre. But the main challenge was to get our own government interested, and in that respect we struck out. While there was a growing commitment to wire up Canada by connecting schools, universities and libraries, we just couldn't convince the cabinet that connecting Canada to the world would also have great value. In fact, one of the ironies of the time was that we had to find funding to keep alive Radio Canada International, the overseas short-wave service operated by the CBC. The campaign to rescue it was such that we had to cough up scarce funds to save an enterprise some would say is based on an obsolescent technology. In the meantime, we were forced to scrape meagre resources together to maintain some semblance of an international multi-media communication strategy based on interactive technology. The information revolution is a vital way of enhancing the soft-power capacity of Canada.

Equally vital are our intellectual resources. Ideas, analysis, research, policy development and education are all critical elements in endowing a creative foreign policy, especially for a country that lacks dominant economic or military clout. I was a great fan of the New York Knicks team of the early seventies, the team of Bradley, Reed, Frazier and DeBusschere. They were smaller and slower than many of their prime competitors, but they won because they were smarter. That's what Canada has to be internationally.

I was aided by the efforts of others. At the initiative of deputy minister, Gordon Smith, my predecessor, André Ouellet, had created in DFAIT the Global and Human Issues Bureau, an innovative body designed to recast the department's thinking on emerging issues such as the environment, crime and terrorism. It acted as a counterpoint to the traditional geographic, desk-officer structure, which tended to interpret and react to issues from the perspective of the region in question.

The bureau helped us give better advice to other government agencies about specialized global problems. For example, before the bureau's establishment, DFAIT had assigned only half a person-year to manage the climate change file and one-tenth of a person-year to oversee international crime issues. With the bureau in place, there were now people who could focus on issues that cut across departments. Within a short time of my arrival, Paul Heinbecker, our ambassador to Germany, took over the bureau and for the next four years was instrumental in shaping a distinctive Canadian response to global security issues.

I also benefited from the inclusion within DFAIT of the Canadian Centre for Foreign Policy Development, brought to fruition by Michael Pearson. This small, autonomous research unit was directly responsive to ministerial priorities and also acted as a connection to outside experts and NGOs. Not particularly popular with the senior levels of the bureaucracy, the centre was important for tapping into the growing and highly influential movement of civil society, both within and outside Canada, through consultation and brainstorming. It was also crucial to have broad public interchange with Canadians, especially young men and women, to get them interested in the international role of Canada. Under its director, Steve Lee, the centre proved essential for our public diplomacy.

The major asset I inherited, however, was the foreign service. The professionalism of External Affairs, as the department used to be called, has long been legendary. In my university days it was the most sought-after calling, with rigorous and demanding entry tests. I used to joke with the first-year class of foreign service officers that I was a little intimidated meeting them because I hadn't made it past the first cut in my application to join, and so had had to get into the foreign service by the political route.

Those strict standards of quality were constantly in evidence. A team of very smart, dedicated people prepared to work long hours and expend enormous physical and intellectual energy was there to serve the minister. I detected some suspicion and wariness when I arrived—I did carry a reputation for being tough on public servants, after all. There was also a group who thought I was too activist, not caring enough about the niceties of always travelling in the good company of our traditional alliances, or not solicitous enough of our trade interests. On the whole, however, I was well served, and I think I can say that many within the department enjoyed the ride.

This was a difficult time for the foreign service. Ill-advised changes under a previous regime had severely reduced the ranking categories down to two levels, thereby creating a bottleneck of salary and opportunity for officers in mid-career. There was an increasing disparity between salaries in the private sector and in the department. Women in the system still faced inequity in promotion to higher levels. Spouses of officers found it difficult to secure work in foreign countries and were given no compensation for the many duties they performed on behalf of the embassy. On these issues it was difficult to overcome the studied indifference of "the boys downtown."

As I mentioned, the cutbacks meant less time for service abroad. And overseas postings were themselves becoming more of a risk in terms of personal and family security and living conditions. In many well-known foreign capitals whose names conjure up exotic and mysterious images, the air is toxic, the traffic in gridlock and the pressures of everyday life overwhelming. The media or opposition critics often expose the supposedly extravagant living style of our diplomats abroad, and no doubt there are some cases of living over the top. Yet, from my observation, there is often hardship and aggravation, especially when young children are involved. Nevertheless, the "thin red line" meet the tough demands of international postings and give Canada very effective representation.

My major criticism would be that the nature of the foreign service leads it to overcaution, a tendency too often to look for a settled solution. It is the stuff of British sitcoms to extol the virtues of "Yes, Minister" (meaning No, Minister), and there is no doubt that an important function of the civil servant is to control the exuberances of the political heads that temporarily lead the department. In the foreign service, diplomats also have a vested interest in always trying to improve relations with whatever country, region or organization they hold in their purview, especially in regional desk operations where there tends to be a little of the Stockholm syndrome.

One result of this diffidence, and at times deference to the interests of others, is a loss of credibility both inside Ottawa and often with the public. A case in point was the "turbot war" fought out with Europeans over the raiding of fish stocks in Canadian waters. It was a vital issue for Canada, and the Fisheries Department under Brian Tobin took the lead in confronting the illegal forays. This caused a rupture in our European relations, especially with the Spanish. DFAIT attempted to moderate the split and apply legal formulae. Unfortunately, Foreign Affairs came across publicly as a voice of appeasement, a posture out of step with the prevailing view in cabinet and the country. As a result, the department ended up playing a marginal role when it should have been in the lead.

I saw the fallout when we faced another critical fishing issue, the dispute with the U.S. over West Coast salmon. Fisheries officials and their minister were understandably a little suspicious of working closely with DFAIT, as they expected a repeat of our department's inclination to back away from confrontation. It took a good deal of effort to ensure that we would work in concert, drafting a joint strategy and sharing our respective tasks. That we developed a mutually satisfactory solution and maintained a good working arrangement with the Americans demonstrated to me the importance of a robust stance for Foreign Affairs on cross-border international resource and environmental issues.

Assuming that stance on an even wider front is what I had been preparing for over a long time. The prime minister had entrusted me with giving direction to Canada's international role, and I had charge of formidable, if somewhat circumscribed, resources. It was up to me to put those talents to work.

Politics in Canada is not generally afforded much respect. It commands substantial media attention, but more as a blood sport, where the daily trappings from Parliament or the latest machinations of leadership are put on display. Most polls show that Canadians suspect the worst of their elected representatives when it comes to probity, competence and intelligence. Yet here I was, given the serious responsibility to represent to the rest of the world thirty million fellow citizens of one of the most favoured nations on earth, all because of our politics.

There are not too many countries in which the opportunity to take on important public responsibilities is as open and as egalitarian as it is here in Canada. For all the foibles of our system, it nonetheless gives a kid from the north end of Winnipeg, who has visions of one day being a foreign minister, the chance to first serve a rich and varied apprenticeship and finally to have the vision come true. That, almost more than anything else, is a message we can give to the world.

CHAPTER 3

CHOICES AND CONSEQUENCES

TO UNDERSTAND WHERE WE STAND IN THE WORLD AND WHERE OUR future might lead, we need to look at what choices are before us, who makes those choices and why. Canadians are a relatively small cluster of people who occupy a large piece of resource-rich geography, highly integrated into the economy and culture of our neighbour, the world's superpower. In such a position we constantly face the pressure to become a compliant satellite, if not a complete satrapy. Our history, our politics and our values, however, propel us towards maintaining an independent stance, providing a push against the pull of continental economic forces, making a distinctive contribution to the global common weal. There is nothing axiomatic about either choice. The outcome is very much determined by the people who are given responsibility to govern by the vagaries of the democratic electoral system.

A central figure in that governmental matrix is the minister of foreign affairs. The incumbent can make a difference in shifting the weight or balance between the two contending pressures. It is a unique position, and today the Foreign Affairs office occupies a strategic place in deciding what Canada will be in the global constellation of this new century. In today's uncertain world, it's on the cusp.

BOOKS AND CALENDARS

I suspect most Canadians don't really know what a minister of the Crown actually does. It is a far cry from the impression gained on nightly newscasts from the raucousness of Question Period or the scramble of a media scrum.

A minister of foreign affairs begins preparing for his or her day the night before, by poring over a mound of briefing books like a college student cramming for an exam. Regardless of how late the House of Commons might have sat for a marathon of votes, or whether there was an official dinner at the National Arts Centre for a visiting dignitary, or whether the Air Canada flight from Winnipeg via Toronto was much delayed, or whether there was a son's peewee hockey game in Cornwall, the "books" are always there waiting. Sandwiched between red leather covers are page after page of letters to sign, briefing notes for the next day, reports from embassies, think-pieces from staffers, memos from the deputy minister, draft speeches, cabinet documents to review, proposed schedules for overseas trips, Treasury Board submissions and updates on constituency affairs, to say nothing of the daily review of press commentary, always the highlight of before-bed reading. To skip this nightly ordeal just once can gum up the works; the system grinds down if next morning everyone finds his or her particular document unread, the pet project unapproved. Any act of negligence in ignoring the "books" is viewed as a cause of embarrassment and shame for the miscreant minister.

At the same time, the books constitute an underestimated source of power given to ministers. Without the scrawled signature or cryptic comment on the bottom of each page, nothing proceeds. (Back in the early eighties, when I was in a dispute with one of my deputies over a directive that he refused to carry out, I reciprocated by refusing to okay his departmental submissions. He eventually gave in.) Most often, the nightly cascade of paper provides the minister with an indispensable daily tableau. Each entry is the product of intense hours of labour by a wide assortment of officials and staffers. Without them, it is impossible to navigate the variety of meetings, encounters and, most of all, judgment calls that the next day will bring.

That next day is itself the product of innumerable discussions and agonizing choices, as it is the building block of that other master discipline of ministers known as the calendar: where and what a minister does with the scarcest of resources—time. Although managing time is a problem for every cabinet minister, the foreign affairs portfolio carries with it the added demand of being out of the country for extended periods. One year I clocked twenty-seven trips abroad, covering more than half a million miles. These are not leisurely swings, but usually quick two- or three-day outings, since overseas travel does not excuse a foreign minister from all the other governmental and parliamentary obligations, which were especially onerous after the 1997 election, when we had a very small working majority, and the opposition delighted in demanding votes frequently and on short notice. Thus the calendar, which includes an ever growing number of set international meetings as well as required regional visits and bilateral engagements, unexpected funerals, inaugurations and special missions, imposes an unforgiving discipline.

To give a flavour, let me take a sampling, drawn from the week of September 29 to October 4, 1996, just preceding the opening of the first land-mine meeting held in Ottawa. On Sunday the twenty-ninth, I was in New York for a meeting of the Commonwealth Ministers' Action Group to discuss the situation in Nigeria. The next morning there was a press conference with UNICEF on the issue of child labour, then back to Ottawa for a meeting with the Brazilian foreign minister, followed by Question Period, a meeting with the Indian foreign minister and a dinner in his honour. Tuesday started with briefings in the morning, then the weekly cabinet meeting, more briefings, Question Period, meetings on constituency matters, followed by the Manitoba caucus and then votes in the House. Wednesday started at 7:30 a.m. with a meeting in the parliamentary restaurant with ministers from Western Canada, then the Western caucus, then full national caucus. At noon I opened a land-mine exhibit at the Canadian War Museum, then met with our ambassador to France, went to QP, attended votes and appeared before the House Committee on Foreign Affairs to speak on child labour issues. Thursday, I opened the land-mines meeting, met with a group of German parliamentarians and the president of the African Development Bank, did some interviews on the land-mines issue, consulted with our ambassador to Spain on ways to re-establish relations after the turbot dispute, met with cabinet colleagues to discuss international indigenous rights, and ended the day by going with my family to a concert sponsored by Mines Action Canada. Friday was taken up by the land-mines conference. While this may appear as a somewhat scattergun selection of appointments and events, countless hours of planning and strategizing by officials and staff go into calculating where best to use the time, whom to see, and the expected value to be gained.

The calendar generates the prime currency of the foreign minister. Each engagement is an opportunity to glean information, advance an argument, stake out a position, establish a rapport. For example, after the funeral of Princess Diana, Prime Minister Tony Blair held a luncheon that included Hillary Clinton, and our conversation opened up a chance to talk about land mines. Similarly, in the course of the interminable bilateral sessions held during the UN General Assembly, there arose an opportunity to approach the Vietnamese foreign minister to attempt the release of a Canadian woman held in prison in that country on a drug charge. In the margin of a G-8 meeting, Madeleine Albright and I had the chance to talk about the Pacific Coast salmon dispute.

The jet-plane world has resulted in a proliferation of occasions for personal diplomacy, demanding a constant and excruciating requirement to update and juggle the time slots to gain maximum advantage, all the while balancing the demands of Parliament, cabinet, constituency and family (did I say family?). The foreign minister plays an especially crucial role by using direct contacts and connections to foster the right impressions of Canada, give personal branding to our positions, resolve differences and, in particular, lay the groundwork for new policy ideas. Making the right decisions on the calendar is of no small importance in pursuing an international agenda.

It is also a headache to organize. Making travel plans, seeing who was available, accommodating domestic responsibilities was a constant preoccupation. The outcome usually had me leaving

Ottawa at night on the government jet, the Challenger, stopping to refuel somewhere four or five hours later. It seems I spent a good part of my life in the airport lobby at Keflavik in Iceland at four in the morning, my nose pressed against the windows of the closed duty free shops, waiting for refuelling. We would arrive somewhere in time for a few hours' sleep, then on to the meeting.

So you see how complicated and demanding are the minister's tasks in a routine twenty-four-hour period—on the days when nothing out of the ordinary happens. But that is something of a rarity. So often the best-laid plans go awry: there is a notice from your ambassador at the UN of an immediate vote on a controversial Middle Eastern resolution; a Canadian citizen is kidnapped in some far-off jungle; fighting has broken out in an African state and a peace-making mission is being contemplated; there is advance warning that tomorrow's *Globe* will carry a leaked story from Washington on the breakdown of negotiations on border controls. Whatever the occurrence, the tenth floor goes into overdrive and a response is developed, interrupted only by the need to phone home and say it will be another late supper.

This is not an effort to elicit sympathy for poor overworked ministers. The constant surge of adrenalin and the opportunity to be in command of constantly shifting circumstances and challenges is the heady whiff that draws people to political power. Being a foreign minister is anything but dull, though it does require a high tolerance for ambiguity and the dexterity of a juggler.

But this exposition of how it works raises the question of what kind of room there is in our system to initiate change and reform if one is so inclined. Equally, in what ways does the system need to be improved? As our well-being and security increasingly derive from global trends, it's crucial that we better understand our international role. The decisions we make in our foreign policy will determine our continued definition as an independent political entity.

MANDATE FROM THE PRIME MINISTER

Every minister's tenure begins with a mandate letter from the prime minister, setting out the responsibilities and indicating special areas of activity and attention. In my case, while I had overriding responsibility for the conduct of Foreign Affairs and Trade, the powers and responsibilities were shared with a minister of trade. He mainly looked after trade promotion, policy and development, although I retained jurisdiction on export, import controls, trade quotas and arms transfers. DFAIT had two secretaries of state, one for Asia-Pacific, the other for the Americas and Africa, whom I was supposed to supervise. (The Martin government subsequently abolished these posts.) I also was responsible for the International Development Research Centre and the International Centre for Human Rights and Democratic Development (now called Rights and Democracy). What was not under my jurisdiction was the Canadian International Development Agency. CIDA had its own minister, who was supposed to follow the broad outlines of foreign policy set by DFAIT, but who was actually quite autonomous. This was the cause of continuing frustration and, sometimes, downright friction between the two organizations. Negotiations between the two were often more arduous than the softwood trade dispute with the Americans or getting the Burmese to acknowledge the need for human rights.

What is particularly significant about the mandate letter is that it asserts the prime minister's prerogative to be the major player in the foreign field if so desired, to take on independent initiatives on which the foreign minister may or may not be informed, and to share or take over key departmental decisions such as the choice of ambassadors, placement of embassies and organization of major international meetings in Canada. The exercise of this prime ministerial prerogative is backed up by a separate foreign affairs apparatus in the Privy Council Office, especially by the PM's special advisor on foreign affairs, usually a senior foreign service officer who gives daily briefings, organizes contacts with other foreign leaders and at times undertakes special missions abroad for the prime minister. Although not possessing the same power as, say, the national security advisor to the U.S. president, the special advisor is in an influential position, and can run counter to the opinions and advice of the foreign minister.

A foreign minister must serve one master, the prime minister, and the relationship that is established, whether close or distant, trusting or indifferent, determines to a substantial degree the effectiveness of the minister. This, in turn, makes a difference in the outcome, harmony of purpose and consistency of foreign policy overall. It was well known, for example, that Prime Minister Brian Mulroney and his foreign minister for much of his government, Joe Clark, did not have a good working relationship, and that Mulroney took over management of key files, especially Canada–U.S. relations, without much consultation.

Prime Minister Chrétien's style for the most part was to give his ministers a fair degree of latitude. He certainly gave me a good deal of space. We had, I believe, a relationship of mutual respect, born out of the many years serving together in the House of Commons, and had forged a bond of loyalty during his leadership run, which I supported after recognizing that fulfillment of my own ambitions was not in the cards. One of the prime minister's favourite comments to visiting dignitaries was that between himself, Deputy Prime Minister Herb Gray and myself, we had over a hundred years of experience in the House—a reflection, I believe, of his own regard for those who make a career of elected public service.

There were, of course, certain prime ministerial lines that one didn't cross without a great deal of care and some trepidation, relations with China being a prime example. The prime minister took a special interest in establishing good ties with the Chinese regime, for he saw China as a major opportunity to advance our trade interests. I, on the other hand, wanted to push on human rights issues. Eventually we agreed on a policy of direct bilateral engagement. I was given the go-ahead to travel to China, initiate a human rights dialogue and provide legal assistance and training. It didn't please the human rights organizations, as they wanted open denunciation of Chinese practices in Tibet and condemnation of the jailing of political dissidents. It did, however, provide the template for a policy of engagement on human rights that extended to many countries, including Cuba and Indonesia. In general, the prime minister focused on trade-related matters, especially the Team Canada initiative, and gave me the political space to work more on human rights and democratic development.

Another area that was closely watched by the PMO, especially the principal secretary, Jean Pelletier, was the assertion by Quebec under the separatist government of Lucien Bouchard of an aggressive international role as part of its sovereignty referendum strategy. The narrow margin of victory for federalism in 1995 created an intense and focused effort, directed out of the Privy Council Office, to counter the creation of "winning conditions" as articulated by the separatists as their priority before calling another vote. One of the prongs of Quebec's strategy was to constantly seek international recognition for their claims and to establish a presence as an autonomous international player. This involved establishing offices abroad, including an attempt to gain standing of a sort at the UN, mounting extensive cultural and educational programs, wooing legislators and officials from other countries for some form of endorsement and insisting on parity in delegations, especially to la Francophonie.

Foreign Affairs was kept busy monitoring these multiple efforts, especially the active campaigns by Quebec in the U.S., France and the Americas, and coordinating responses and counter-strategy with the PM's office and Privy Council officials. Of particular concern was the effective use Quebec made of its rich cultural heritage as a tool for promoting the province's interests abroad. It gave rise to a serious examination of how to employ cultural and educational policy as a means of furthering Canadian interests. One direct result was a plan to use our overseas network of embassies and high commissions as showcases for Canadian culture. This goal led to reopening Canada House in London, restoring the Canadian Cultural Centre in Paris, designing a new embassy in Berlin with open public access in mind, and mounting special cultural programs in key cities. We were constantly plagued, however, with a too-tight limit on funds to really give this third-tier approach full play.

The most valuable lesson I learned from applying our foreign policy to the cause of national unity came through the insightful work of a young Quebecker, Daniel Laprès, who joined my personal staff in 1999. Daniel was a strong Quebec nationalist, but he had given up on the separatist cause because he believed it didn't give

Quebec society room to grow in a globalizing world. Nor did he think much of the traditional federal approach of direct confrontation. He presented me with a plan to bring Canadian foreign policy to the young people of Quebec as a prime illustration of how they could fulfill their ambitions for global activism through participating in making and delivering Canadian policy, rather than through efforts to seek sovereignty.

In particular, he believed that the concept of human security would appeal to the well-developed sense of internationalism in Quebec. This approach was sold to Jean Pelletier, and we launched a campaign of direct involvement with young people and NGOs, focusing particularly on the UN. Opening a French-speaking arm of the Pearson Peacekeeping Centre in Montreal clearly demonstrated our commitment to engaging Quebeckers in the discussion of Canada's global role, and this whole effort was very well received, especially by young Quebeckers.

Our efforts also demonstrated how an activist, internationalist policy can help shape an identity and promote unity in the country. International accomplishments reinforce our basic values and enhance our pride as a people. The extent to which Canadians see their country playing a useful, effective role abroad adds to the sense of cohesion, confidence and pride that is an indispensable part of our national makeup. That is why a continual tension exists between the demands to conform to U.S. interests and the desire of many Canadians to pursue a more independent, humanitarian policy. Our national interests go beyond the economic, and foreign policy can be a nation builder.

Peace-building and Turf Maintenance

Another form of outreach designed to enlist civilian involvement and intervention was called the Canadian Peace-building Initiative. It was the result of several months of effort in 1996 to give expression to the human security idea, and involved officials and ministerial staff from both Foreign Affairs and CIDA—an attempt at shared policy-making and coordinated delivery that was unusual, one might say groundbreaking.

While it might seem natural for there to be a synergy of approach, and a high degree of common action between the two government structures that share responsibility for the conduct of our foreign affairs, the reality was that there existed a rivalry that bordered at times on animosity, and remarkably little coordination of policy or integration of effort. In one very effective joint program, called the Canada Fund, there was discretion at the field level of CIDA to invest in local programs of community support, at the behest of the ambassador. I remember visiting one such project in northern Thailand where the fund was being used to support a farm project that trained street kids who were drug addicts or the offspring of addicts to be self-sufficient in producing their own food and flowers for market. For the original $100,000 investment, we were making a real difference in the lives of those children.

But the Canada Fund was the happy exception. Generally there was a divorce between our foreign policy and our development policy, with different structures drawing up the programs and delivering them, and often a separation of purpose and contradiction in result. For example, I recall returning from a tour of the Canadian Forces in Bosnia and meeting officials from my own department, CIDA and Defence. We discussed how we might deliver Canadian aid more directly into our own sector, using our troops, who had expressed interest in working on such things as housing and infrastructure. I felt a more identifiable Canadian presence could also help us lever a greater say in determining policy in Bosnia. To my surprise and annoyance, I was told point-blank that it was not CIDA policy to work in conjunction with the military, as that might compromise the humanitarian nature of the aid; CIDA preferred to make donations directly to multilateral efforts in Bosnia. Whatever the merits of the case, the message was clear: as foreign minister I had no say in CIDA policy.

After an interesting and frank discussion with the CIDA minister, the policy was altered and we began some direct programming. But it was clear that we had to find some way of overcoming this disconnect between Foreign Affairs and CIDA.

The prime minister in his mandate letter had stated that part of my task was to promote the coordination of Canada's international effort. The problem of trying to find common ground between CIDA and Foreign Affairs was in fact endemic throughout the system. There was an increasing level of international activity by a number of departments and agencies, all of which were finding a growing overlap between domestic and international activity. Various departments were setting up special branches to deal with international matters, and a variety of international negotiations and initiatives were being mounted with very little intergovernmental consultation or contact. Often, Foreign Affairs, like a cuckolded spouse, was the last to know. There was a compelling need to get our act together, a difficult task when turf maintenance, featuring solo departmental performances, is a highly developed skill among both bureaucracies and ministers.

One illustration was our efforts to convene regular meetings among ministers and senior officials dealing with Foreign Affairs—myself, Trade, CIDA and the two secretaries of state, five people in all. The intent was simple: to share information, discuss travel schedules and see how on overseas visits we might support each other's objectives. Simple it may seem, but it was extremely difficult to achieve. My executive assistant, Pat Neri, would spend countless hours trying to find a convenient meeting time, work out an agenda, decide which officials should attend. When the meeting finally occurred, usually at a lunch hour just before Question Period, there would be last-minute no-shows, or fifteen-minute cameo appearances by one or more ministers. Very little was accomplished. Trying to bring five ministers together on an ad hoc basis, unless it is to talk about money, is one of the more frustrating Ottawa exercises. And there was no designated cabinet committee to work through. Formal coordination would take place only when a special committee of cabinet was established by the prime minister. In my day that occurred only to manage a crisis such as Kosovo or to examine Canada–U.S. border relations. Far more frequently, it was direct one-on-one personal discussion between officials or ministers that got the job done. One of the tasks of my staff before each cabinet or cabinet committee meeting was to supply me with a list of ministers I had to talk to on the edges of the room or at the coffee urn.

It was through personal discussion with Pierre Pettigrew and his staff (later, with his successor, Don Boudria) that we were able to establish a successful collaboration with CIDA on a program of peace-building that we hoped would set a model for interdepartmental cooperation. The idea began with the recognition that the conflicts we now face are no longer purely military in nature; nor can they be resolved by military means alone. They occur within states, rather than between them, but they tend to spill over into surrounding regions and affect overall global stability. They are characterized by long-term cycles of violence and seriously impede efforts at development or renewal. It was this prevailing pattern of internal, civil conflict, occasioned by the breakdown of state protection for individuals or the attack against individuals by their own governments, that caused us to rethink the notion of security and led to an increasing demand for intervention. But intervention involved more than military action. It involved casting a lifeline to foundering societies struggling to end the cycle of violence. A key requirement was to either preserve or restore civil order by helping build a strengthened infrastructure, or to enable the societies to take charge of their political, social and economic destiny themselves.

This was a departure from normal development practices that require long negotiation and focus on traditional means of alleviating poverty. The peace-building initiative was designed to enable us to respond to risky situations in a rapid, flexible way, drawing on Canadian civil, administrative and governmental expertise. It was to be jointly managed by CIDA and Foreign Affairs, with all projects subject to joint ministerial approval. CIDA budgeted $10 million for direct projects, and DFAIT set aside $1 million to establish the domestic component and to support diplomatic initiatives on conflict resolution.

The peace-building initiative was constructed with direct civilian participation in mind, the idea being to enlist individual Canadians, NGOs and the academic community in an open decision-making process. Indeed, we established an annual consultative forum with the NGO community and a secretariat of NGOs to help select projects and assess outcomes. This citizen involvement has become a lasting element in the structure of peace-building. At the UN General Assembly that fall I announced the establishment of a domestic roster of Canadian experts on human rights and democracy, available for rapid deployment for purposes of monitoring, inspection and election surveillance. (A good example of the application was the monitoring mission to Kosovo.) This inventory of Canadian civilians available for peace-building duties was an embryonic civilian equivalent of our military peacekeeping forces and a prime example of how to capitalize on the skills and motivation of Canadians to do good work abroad.

It was important to give immediate meaning to the peace-building idea. In Guatemala, after the signing of the peace accords in December 1996, we supported the Commission on Historical Clarification's objective inquiry into the human rights violations during the thirty-six-year civil war. We sent a mission to Cambodia to assess how we could assist in the work of the election commission. In the Great Lakes region of Africa our funds supported the work of the UN in trying to broker a peace deal. And in Bosnia they were used to establish a public information campaign promoting the work of the Hague tribunal. Since then the peace-building initiative has supplied a wide variety of projects around the world.

As for the lessons learned on how to cooperate internally, there is still a long way to go. In 1999, a new minister for CIDA, Diane Marleau, decided that the joint decision making with DFAIT should be severed and that the two components of the program would be delivered separately. Although there would continue to be some crossover on the peace-building initiative, the result was a return to the single-silo approach, with its lack of overall planning and delivery. No amount of argument could get the decision overturned.

When there is a crisis such as September 11, the system can be mobilized and a degree of cooperation and integration takes place. But as part of the normal course of business, the rules of departmental competition still apply, and now there is no place or designated authority for managing a comprehensive approach. There is a price to be paid for this fragmentation.

HUMAN RIGHTS

When I arrived at Foreign Affairs, I saw the pursuit of human rights as fundamental to both Canada's international role and the continued articulation of a rights agenda in our own country. It soon became clear that the advancement of human rights was part of a redefinition of the meaning of international security and indeed of international community. But this policy ran counter to strongly vested economic and political interests in the country. It also contended with the policies and approaches of some of our powerful allies and trade partners, and had to be managed with those interests in mind.

My experience in the U.S. during the civil rights era, and my years in government when I was responsible for refugees and women's rights, had given me a grounding. I had also gone through the emotional and excruciating national debate surrounding the Charter of Rights and come to see how instrumental the Charter has been in establishing the framework for a "rights culture" in Canada; we increasingly defined ourselves through the advancement of both individual and collective rights. HRD had taught me to include the economic and social dimensions of rights and about the increasing interdependence of international and domestic rights. Once at Foreign Affairs, I found a tension between the highly visible articulation of trade as the centrepiece of our international role and the increasing demand of NGOs and human rights advocates for a more assertive stand against international rights abuses.

It was a real tension, but not so clearly divided into opposing positions as was often made out by the media or the more excitable advocates of both sides. There was no doubt when our government came to office that the need for economic revival was paramount, and that involved the promotion of international trade: hence the Team Canada visits and the North American Free Trade Agreement with the U.S. and Mexico. Canada was still a leader in the promotion of international women's rights and played a prominent role in the UN Human Rights Commission. Prime Minister Chrétien had played an important role in the Commonwealth summit that passed a far-reaching declaration on democratic rights and suspended

Nigeria as a result of the military takeover and the brutal treatment of Nigerian citizens. Yet the perception persisted that international human rights was not a priority, nor given much concerted attention compared to, say, economic relations.

That was not a totally false impression. There were certainly gaps in our human rights policy. I felt it was important to publicly map out a clear strategy, enlist the help of NGOs, and then take on specific initiatives. The most delicate part was to draft an approach that would be meaningful and reflect our core values as a country without contradicting the broad trade strategy of the government or raising too many red flags downtown.

In the late 1990s, human rights policy had become more germane. One sign of this was that in 1998 John Humphrey finally got the recognition he deserved. In ceremonies honouring the fiftieth anniversary of the Universal Declaration of Human Rights, his own country finally celebrated the role of this distinguished Canadian as a major drafter of the document. The occasion corresponded with a growing realization of the influence human rights has come to play in the conduct of global affairs. A mounting number of international covenants and agreements, spelling out economic and social rights, the rights of women and children and protection against torture and genocide, were being backed up by institutions such as the UN Human Rights Commission and by supportive member states. The Declaration thus gave birth to a body of law and practice that has endowed the individual with basic protection against the worst invasions of the powerful, whether it be an authoritarian state, warlord, terrorist or restrictive religious or cultural regime. It has provided a significant counterweight to the traditional notion of sovereignty.

In addition, a widespread and complex network of NGOs are on the front lines where abuse takes place, corralling evidence and blowing the whistle on the offenders, pursuing changes to the law and the prosecution of transgressions. Some, such as Amnesty International and Human Rights Watch, are worldwide in scope, well funded and with impressive access to the media and government. They provide a regular and authoritative assessment of violations.

In Canada, we have our own unique institution called Rights and Democracy. Established by Parliament in 1988, it works at arm's length from the government, even though it receives its core funding from CIDA appropriations and reports through the minister of foreign affairs. Headed successively by Ed Broadbent, Warren Allmand and Jean-Louis Roy, its job is to support human rights activities around the world and within Canada and it has been especially active on women's and indigenous peoples' rights. It acts as a prod to government. Only in Canada would there be a federally funded institution, reporting to Parliament, led by former politicians, with a world mandate to advocate, organize and agitate on behalf of the powerless against government. Who says we can't be different?

Most of the NGO community is more singly focused, usually concentrating on the violations perpetrated by specific governments against minorities or particular ethnic groups. Often these groups are organized among the diaspora of the cultural group in question, taking on the cause of their homeland in their new surroundings. It leads to the phenomenon of dual loyalty, where a group takes on the rights issue of its native soil and applies pressure through Canadian institutions. This leads to strong domestic influences on which human rights issues a Canadian government will take on in other parts of the world. Canadian society is alive with groups advancing the cause of the East Timorese, Tamils, Sikhs, Palestinians, Somalis and so on, and people attempting to redress old wrongs, such as the Armenians. They often align themselves with members of Parliament from the constituencies where they are strongly represented, and increasingly use the political party nominating systems to gain access and influence. I remember one prolonged exercise with more than thirty caucus members who were pushing for a resolution in the House of Commons on the massacre of Armenians in 1915 by the Turks. We formed a special committee, met numerous times, finally arrived at compromise wording—the word *genocide* carried legal significance that Department of Justice lawyers said would imply direct court action—and introduced it in the House. It was an important effort to acknowledge a serious grievance and bring further attention to the past indifference of the international community to "crimes against humanity." A few weeks later I met with the foreign minister from Armenia at an international conference and told him what we had done. He looked at me quizzically and said that was nice, but Armenia was more interested in immediate support from Canada in its struggle to survive as a newly independent state and survive the conflict taking place with Azerbaijan.

Canada's cultural interest groups and NGOs have come to be key influences in making foreign trouble spots and human crises part and parcel of the domestic political scene. Given the increasing pluralism of our society, they are a major factor in setting our foreign policy. It is part of our distinctiveness and our strength, though we haven't quite figured out how to take full advantage of the influence and resources of our diaspora communities and their communication networks around the world.

Within government it is, nevertheless, a constant struggle to prevent human rights from becoming submerged. This is a particular problem since September 11. There is a constant trumping of rights in the name of counterterrorism: the Geneva Convention on war prisoners is flouted, basic domestic rights such as the prohibition of indefinite detention of suspected security risks are ignored, and allies in the battle against al-Qaeda are given full licence to continue repression of their own populations, such as we see in the Russian treatment of the Chechen people or the flagrant abuses in Uzbekistan. The 2002 Human Rights Watch Report made this assessment: "Leading members [of the anti-terrorist coalition] have violated human rights principles at home and overlooked human rights transgressions among their partners. Whatever its success in pursuing particular terrorists, the coalition risks reinforcing the logic of terrorism unless human rights are given a far more central role."

Despite this, I believe the trend is towards a universal system of rights. That became clear as we set about making the treatment of human rights a priority. Nowhere was the traditional notion of state sovereignty more directly challenged. Nowhere was the intersection between civil groups and foreign and trade policy decision makers more evident. But with the help of some long-time advisors and friends, I began to map a framework. One extra-valuable factor was that at the time my wife was director of communications at the Canadian Human Rights Commission, which, under its chief commissioner, Max Yalden, had begun a series of projects to advise foreign governments on establishing human rights programs. It was a prime example of how we could use the well-developed institutions and highly experienced practitioners of our legal, judicial and human rights systems to promote good practices in other countries.

We called our initiative Principled Pragmatism. It involved bilateral engagement with selected countries where Canadians did business but where the human rights record was poor. Candidates that readily came to mind were China, Cuba and Indonesia. Rather than skirting around the fact that these were places for investment and trade, the idea was to use the access that such contacts afforded to see if we might graft onto the relationship an engagement on human rights. It would involve building up the capacity of local organizations and rights-based institutions, and it would involve direct discussion and dialogue on human rights issues, including raising specific cases of abuse. I proposed that rather than seeing a dichotomy between trade and rights, we make the two policy thrusts reinforce each other. Business interests might benefit from a surer sense of rules and the application of impartial law. Rights issues could be promoted with economic benefits as a sweetener. Initially it was a hard sell to skeptical NGOs. It did, however, begin a serious debate with human rights groups, one that needs to be continued today and into the future.

The first opportunity to put the policy to work was with Cuba. In the fall of 1996, the U.S. Congress passed the Helms-Burton Law, a blatant incursion of American extraterritorial jurisdiction into other countries' economic relations with Cuba that subjected non-American companies doing business in Cuba to legal penalties in the U.S. We stood up to American demands and in fact led the international fight against this attempt to impose U.S. policies on the rest of the world. As could be expected, our efforts didn't go unnoticed in Havana, and I received overtures from the Cuban ambassador to the effect that the Cuban leadership would like to open an exchange of views on our relationship. The first meeting took place in a private dining room in an airport hotel just outside Heathrow. My dining companion was Carlos Lage, the Cuban vice-president for economic development. It was clear that his objective was to increase Canadian aid and assistance to his country. My pitch was that any new economic program would have to be part of a package that included human rights. It turned out to be a fascinating afternoon in the fake-Tudor surroundings of a commercial British hotel. Lage defended his government's use of police power as protection against American efforts to dislodge the regime, while I argued that joining international covenants on human rights and opening up political space for Cuban society was a better way to preserve their position. It was to be the first of many similar discussions I was to have with a variety of Cuban ministers and with President Fidel Castro himself over the next four years. Eventually, a combined economic aid, commercial assistance and human rights agreement was struck.

The prime minister was supportive of this initiative, seeing both economic and political benefits. We also kept the State Department apprised. While not wildly enthusiastic, the Americans didn't exercise any heavy pressure. In December, the PM authorized me to go to Cuba in early January, the first high-level visit since Trudeau's era. It was a trip that attracted a great deal of interest, especially from the right wing in both Canada and the U.S. The agreement that Foreign Minister Roberto Robaina and I signed contained provisions for joint meetings on children's and women's rights, specified a commitment by Cuba to explore the signing of the UN covenant on economic and social rights and established clear rules for the international funding of Cuban civil groups. As a sidebar to the visit, I had the chance to watch Fidel Castro in action. Over a very late dinner, he shared with me his favourite recipe for vegetable soup and his encyclopedic knowledge of political polling in the U.S. and Canada. At the end of the dinner, in a private moment with the president, I raised the cases of several political prisoners, including one of a Cuban writer who was later allowed to come to Canada. It was a controversial but, I believe, useful first test of the engagement strategy.

China followed soon after and was much trickier. There was a host of concerns about the state of rights in China—the lingering aftermath of Tiananmen Square, the treatment of Tibet, the suppression of religious freedom and the arrest of political dissidents—and continuing pressure from the rights community and the media because of our highly visible efforts at trade promotion in China. At the same time, we were wrestling with the impending transfer of Hong Kong to the People's Republic of China. Canada is home to many citizens with Hong Kong roots and has very close economic ties with the island. A number of thorny issues were at stake, dealing with right of abode and citizenship and the preservation of the rule of law in the former British colony. The Chinese leadership was at great pains to give assurances and made special efforts to meet Canadian concerns.

This resulted in the visit of Quian Quichen, the Chinese foreign minister, to Ottawa in the fall of 1996, mainly to discuss Hong Kong. To the idea of our pursuing a more explicit one-on-one exchange on rights issues as applied to Hong Kong and broader human rights topics, he reacted with caution, but not rejection. After this overture, we sought a regular structured dialogue on rights with the Chinese. In April I visited China to put these propositions before the Chinese leadership. They agreed, and in fact suggested that our two countries jointly sponsor a regional symposium to debate whether universal human rights was a Western-based value as opposed to a universal value. This was the first time the Chinese had agreed to this kind of structured dialogue.

It wasn't without a price, however. At the 1997 spring session of the UN Human Rights Commission, the customarily proposed resolution condemning Chinese rights practices began to come apart, with the Germans and the French indicating they would no longer sponsor the resolution. As one of the traditional co-sponsors, Canada was faced with the choice of backing a resolution that now appeared doomed to fail and thereby putting our newfound bilateral initiative at risk, or withdrawing our sponsorship. During my trip to Beijing, it had been made clear that our positioning on the resolution would have a bearing on Chinese cooperation. On my return I spoke to the prime minister, and we decided to opt for the bi-lateral agreement we had just negotiated, seeing the other option as a lost cause. We still voted for the resolution condemning abuses in China, but our absence as a sponsor was widely noticed and the subject of much criticism from the human rights community.

The same critique was made of our approach to Indonesia and the Suharto regime's ruthless treatment of the East Timorese. In 1997, I visited Indonesia and began discussing with Foreign Minister Ali Alitas an agreement launching a bilateral dialogue on human rights. We offered aid from our peace-building fund to convene a roundtable on East Timor, provided $500,000 directly to human rights NGOs and helped the Indonesian Human Rights Commission with technical assistance. I met with a number of Indonesian NGOs who were insistent that we stay engaged in the country, especially in support of the locally based Human Rights Commission. They made the telling point that because of the backing of Canada, Indonesian authorities would be chary of closing it down.

But many Canadian-based and international groups were much more interested in persuading us to publicly condemn Indonesia or impose sanctions. At the APEC meeting in Canada in 1997, some protesters claimed that my trip had been designed to appease President Suharto so that he would come to the meeting in Vancouver. They wouldn't accept that the purpose was to ratchet up our support for the locally based civil rights groups that were contending with abuses. It wasn't the first time that I noticed a disparity between such views at home and the views of activists in another country who were anxious for the presence and support of a credible outside party like Canada. Judgment calls on which approach is right, or how to balance the two, are among the toughest a foreign minister must make. To get it right requires a constant update on human rights conditions in various countries and a continuing exchange with civil groups, tasks handicapped by limited resources available for a comprehensive rights program. It is another example of where our suit is too tight because we don't make enough cloth available.

Clearly, the strategy of bilateral engagement is not an easy one and is derided by those who think that the only way to deal with human rights abuses is by mounting the barricades or the docket.

Engagement emphasizes building from within, enhancing the capacity of local civil society, establishing dialogue with the government in order to pressure and persuade, and pushing the acceptance of international rules. It is often difficult to prove that it works and it certainly doesn't have the satisfaction level of ringing critiques or oratory. But the calculation is that in certain circumstances such an approach gets results.

In Cuba, the outcome was mixed. At the outset there was enthusiastic participation, and we were able to mount a number of useful forums involving Cuban citizens and government officials on women's rights and drug trafficking. The Cubans showed an early interest in signing the UN covenant on economic and social rights, and we won a hard-fought battle to have outside funding approved for distribution to civil groups. We held serious discussions with the Cubans on helping their re-entry into the Organization of American States. In a high-profile visit, the prime minister made our policy of engagement a clear alternative to the embargo policy being followed by the Americans.

Then, in 1998 after the visit of the Pope, the tide began to turn. The Cubans became deliberate and implacable foes of initiatives on human rights and human security, and slowed down any domestic progress. We continued to run up against the core refusal to subject the police power to scrutiny or restraint. The Cubans were anxious for more economic assistance but refused serious examination of broader rights activity. A real break point came in 1999, with the imprisonment of a number of dissidents and the imposition of harsh sentences. The prime minister announced a freeze on all new programming, and relations remain cool to this day, although fundamental Canadian policy still holds that it is preferable to engage than to isolate. What the Cuban case shows, however, is that the policy must be adaptable, with pauses and alterations depending on reciprocity.

In Indonesia, we had barely started our program of human rights meetings before the internal combustion took place that led to the fall of Suharto and the liberation of East Timor. It is important to note that the Indonesian Human Rights Commission that had been one of the prime recipients of our support played a crucial role in the anti-Suharto movement. Many of the East Timorese groups we had worked with also became key players in the reconstruction of the country. We helped mobilize support for international intervention, and Canadian troops became part of the peace force. Apparently the new East Timorese leadership still speaks of the constructive role that Canada played in helping them gain independence.

China is still an unfolding story. After our initial foray into bilateral discussions, many others, such as the European Union, followed; it became a virtual parade. We were granted permission for a commission of Canadian religious groups to visit and report on the treatment of religious minorities. We also mounted an inquiry group that visited Tibet. In 1997 CIDA started a major program that offered aid for the training of rural women in addressing local community problems, support for advancing democracy at the local level, training of judges and lawyers in legal aid, and help for Chinese NGOs to attend international meetings on governance and democracy. The Chinese also lived up to their commitments to jointly sponsor symposia on universal human rights versus cultural relativism. This is not the stuff of headlines, but it does illustrate the continuing effort to help create reform from within.

In recent years China has made a discernible shift towards involvement in multilateral organizations, especially in Southeast Asia. It has signed the UN covenant on economic and social rights, is committed to signing the covenant on political and human rights and has made dramatic changes to its criminal code. Its accession to the World Trade Organization is bringing about even greater adherence to international rules and laws and will require significant changes in opening the Chinese economy and Chinese society to international influence—another example of trade as a complementary agent of political change. At the same time, the continued suppression of political dissent and the repressive treatment of the Falun Gong shows that the human rights struggle is far from over. The blanket of secrecy that covered up the early stages of the SARS epidemic reminds us that the Chinese leadership still operates a closed system, one that in this case endangered global public health. These are good reasons for continued and more creative engagement.

Bilateral engagement, whatever its vicissitudes, has proven, I believe, to be a useful and distinctive approach for Canada and a pragmatic policy for human rights promotion and protection. In a period when military force and big-power bluster are seen as the primary tools for dealing with "rogue" states, it is worth remembering that a constructive engagement policy can be an alternative.

It is not the only way, however, and in fact should be seen as a complement to promoting basic rights at the global level and strengthening transcendent laws and multilateral institutions to enforce them. The issue of our time is how to keep on building a system of rights that encompasses the complexity of the contemporary global order. The rampages of powerful but irresponsible political leaders, the lawlessness of non-state actors and the transgression of rights are global problems and cannot be met by states acting in isolation, or by separating consideration of human rights from questions of peace, security, trade and development.

Using Canadian civil organizations for ideas, advice and action not just in peace-building but in the international human rights arena became one of the most important lessons we learned. Such human resources are not generally counted in the calculations of national power. They don't carry the same weight in traditional measurements as guns or the GNP. Yet this pool of civilian talent, this well-endowed civil network that we possess, is one of our real assets internationally. It gives us the capacity to carve out special niches of global activity, such as peace-building and human rights work, where we can put our social capital to work on global issues. It is how Canadians of various backgrounds and interests can apply their talents, exercising the responsibilities of global citizenship. Adding to that our ability to work with other countries without arousing suspicion as to motive or intent, our experience in peace-keeping, a skilled diplomatic team and a parliamentary-cabinet system that can make quick decisions, we began to see how we could play an activist and innovative role.

"Soft power" became the shorthand term for this approach that sought to use our advantages of wealth, good education and a generally secure, stable society. It drew upon the culture of compromise we use to govern a vast, diverse, multiracial, bilingual country.

And it relied upon the skill and talent of Canadians to negotiate, advise, organize and create, solve problems peaceably and look for practical solutions. We have all the assets needed to make a value-added contribution. We don't have to ride in the slipstream of other nations, or simply play deputy sheriff to the actions of the U.S. marshal.

That doesn't mean that we eschew military commitments or fail to cooperate with allies when there is a common threat. It doesn't mean paying less attention to our economic relations, for without a strong economy our ability and will to perform as a consequential global player are handicapped. The key questions are how best to use our assets; what initiatives lend themselves to our particular strengths; when do we simply go along and when do we strike out on our own?

All these questions are affected by the realities of our coexistence in North America with the world's most powerful state. And it is to relations with the U.S. that I now turn.

PART III

Border Choices

CHAPTER 4

How to Make Love to a Porcupine

═══════════

ON A BLUSTERY, COLD MID-NOVEMBER DAY IN 2002, A LONG BLACK limousine was seen pulling up to the front doors of the Pearson Building and out stepped one of the most powerful men in the world, U.S. Secretary of State Colin Powell. He had come calling on the Canadian foreign affairs minister, Bill Graham, to line up support for the Bush administration's policy of intervention in Iraq. After a six-week negotiation, the UN Security Council had finally adopted a resolution requiring Saddam Hussein's government to comply with strict measures for disarming what American and British authorities claimed was a growing arsenal of weapons of mass destruction, and a UN inspection team was being mobilized to monitor compliance. While some Security Council members held that any breach of these measures would require another decision by the council to determine the extent of the transgression, President George W. Bush, fresh from victories in the mid-term congressional elections, said that he reserved the right to assess any breach and if necessary send in the troops. In his Ottawa press conference, Secretary of State Powell said that the U.S. would want Canadian support for whatever was decided. A letter to Graham soon followed, outlining the shopping list of troop contributions the Americans would expect.

A few days earlier I too had pulled up to the front doors of the Pearson Building (in a Blue Line cab—a five-dollar fare from the Château Laurier hotel) to attend a conference organized by the Parliamentarians for Global Action at the behest of Minister Graham. The aim was to mobilize support for the International Criminal Court and discuss the recommendations made by the Canadian-inspired International Commission on Intervention and State Sovereignty. This discussion centred on new international efforts at collaboration to fight global crime and insecurity. As the day proceeded, I had the chance to exchange views with former colleagues from both Parliament and the ministry, and the common thread running through the conversations was a sense of dismay at the prospect of having to go to war in Iraq.

In the space of a few days, two very different meetings, two very different agendas, two very contrasting sets of choices. For those on the tenth floor it was another test of how to tread a path between being a good ally and joining in the fight or following our own lights in trying to create an international system that controls the use of force and advances the rule of law. It is symptomatic of a constant state of tension and sometimes torment caused by the unique position Canada occupies as the North American neighbour of the U.S., especially at a time when the U.S. administration expects total fealty from its friends for its international adventures: "You are either with us or against us."

That wasn't the only dilemma facing Canadians during those grey days of November. Foreign Affairs was trying to negotiate with the U.S. on increasingly stringent border examinations that saw Canadians, primarily those of Middle Eastern origin, being denied entry or subjected to fingerprinting and profiling. At the same time officials were preparing the position papers for the prime minister, Bill Graham and Defence Minister John McCallum as they prepared to set out for a NATO summit meeting where they could expect U.S. pressure to increase military expenditures and join in an American plan to revamp NATO as a rapid-reaction force to fight global terrorism.

On the economic front, more demands. Scan the business pages of the *Globe and Mail* for November 20, 2002. A prominent oil executive threatens to move a billion-dollar investment to the U.S. if Canada ratifies the Kyoto Accord, citing the disparity in costs as a result of the U.S. not joining, while assuring us that "he is not un-Canadian." The chief executive of a major U.S. forestry company offers what he believes is a truce in the softwood lumber dispute between the two countries: a 20 per cent border tax on Canadian imports in return for Canada withdrawing its appeals to the WTO and NAFTA trade panels claiming that the U.S.'s imposition of a 27 per cent duty is illegal. (Whatever happened to our free trade arrangement?) The U.S. International Trade Commission rules that Canadian wheat imports are injurious to American farmers. The object of their ire is the Canadian Wheat Board, a venerable Canadian institution that has the audacity to market grain on behalf of all farmers, not through private grain companies, clearly not in keeping with the Americans' view of free-market principles. And, perhaps most noteworthy, our industry minister announces parliamentary hearings to examine how to loosen foreign ownership restrictions on Canadian telecommunications companies, to increase their capital pool, while critics warn of a further hollowing out of Canadian industry. All this in one day's business news!

Our proximity, friendship and interdependence with the U.S. creates a relationship of incredible diversity, complexity, prosperity and security, but it also causes an unremitting torrent of pressures, which has the cumulative effect of calling into question our ability to choose the shape and contours of our own community and how we relate to the rest of the world. As much as we share geography, values and many common interests, we also cherish quite different views about the nature of our society, the way we do business and what we believe to be the appropriate role of government. A public health system, gun-control laws, producer-controlled marketing boards, a CBC, public support for bilingual education and multicultural groups—all these are examples. We have neither the world-straddling military obligations nor the hubris of a great power, but we do see an active role for Canada in promoting disarmament, international collaboration, institutions based on the rule of law, the Kyoto Protocol, the International Criminal Court, the land-mine treaty—all in contrast to U.S. positions. Resolving these differences, protecting our distinctive institutions and keeping in check those Canadians belonging to the Team America cheerleading squad who push for greater integration is a never-ending task that becomes increasingly problematic as the Americans assert a right to be an unrestrained dominant power and eschew most forms of collaborative engagement—except when they expect compliance by way of a coalition endorsement.

The invasion of Iraq by U.S. and British forces in March 2003 brought to a head the dilemmas faced by Canadian decision makers. The Canadian government decided not to participate, citing the lack of a UN mandate for the use of force and mindful of the strong public opposition to a war seen by many Canadians as unnecessary. Behind all this was a loss of public trust in the Bush administration's leadership on matters of security and a growing suspicion that the purpose of the war was not so much to disarm Saddam Hussein as to fulfill a new U.S. strategic vision devised in the mid-1990s by a group of national security hawks, including Vice-President Dick Cheney and Under-Secretary of Defense Paul Wolfowitz.

The September 11 terrorist attack gave them the opportunity to transform their ideas into action. The American people were deeply traumatized by this breakdown in security and the tragic loss of life. The public's prevailing fear of further incursions created a receptive environment to promote an aggressive military strategy. Even while the campaign to snuff out the al-Qaeda network was underway the terrorist threat was linked to Iraq and the argument was advanced by the hard line neo-conservatives in the administration and their allies that deposing Saddam Hussein would have a domino effect leading to democracy and stability in the Middle East and serve as a warning to everyone that the U.S. would use its military machine to pursue a mission of salvation without the niceties of restraint by treaties or rules of law.

These hawks agreed to refer Iraqi compliance on disarmament to the UN only because Colin Powell said this was a way to gain legitimacy for a war that had been planned for over a year. When it looked as if the inspectors might actually succeed and that the UN was contemplating more robust actions to achieve disarmament, the plug was pulled and the war of "liberation" was launched.

If we had participated in the war, we would have been caught in the same trap as Tony Blair—signing on to a doctrine that repudiates principles that have slowly become the standards of global society—restraining the use of force, resolving conflicts peacefully when at all possible, using institutions such as the UN to share in collective responsibility and establishing rules of law to protect the rights of individuals. The Canadian position was challenged by the U.S. ambassador to Canada, Paul Cellucci, who in a speech to the Empire Club in Toronto expressed his government's displeasure and hinted that some form of blowback could be expected. This undiplomatic intervention touched off a major debate in the country, fuelled by a hyperventilating Alliance opposition, business lobby and right-wing media that used Cellucci's hectoring as a way to attack the Chrétien government.

This pressure had the desired effect. Within weeks the price of atonement for Canadian apostasy in the Iraq war became known— the Canadian cabinet began shifting its position on the very controversial U.S. program of missile defense systems (MDS). Various ministers trotted out explanations about changed strategic conditions citing the threat of terrorism to continental security. (If there was a change it was to make missile defense less relevant or necessary.) Paul Martin and John Manley, two out of the three Liberal leadership candidates, espoused the MDS as a way of signaling their priority of establishing closer ties with the U.S. What began as honest difference of policy with our neighbour over the use of armed intervention has turned into an act of capitulation on the altar of preserving good continental relations.

What this portends for the future is deeply troubling. As long as the U.S. government persists in following the radical doctrine of pre-emptive intervention, Canadians will be faced with a serial set of unpalatable decisions—standing up for principles of international cooperation and thereby invoking the wrath of the U.S. administration or giving in to the political pressure of those in Canada who counsel succumbing to continental comity, either because they support the U.S.'s ideological stance or because they are petrified by the threat of U.S. retaliation.

This is a tightrope walk for any foreign minister. It is a central fact in calculating our foreign policy, and is increasingly difficult to manage. Furthermore, the events of September 11 and the search for security have spawned a Medusa-like outgrowth of U.S. agencies dealing with military, intelligence, police and immigration matters, each of which entwines Canadians in a closer continental hug. The increasing importance of continental energy and water resources compels even further connections. NAFTA on its tenth birthday is showing signs of wear and tear, in spite of the claims of its advocates. It is time for some new thinking.

How to Make Love to a Porcupine

Sitting across the table from me in a huge, ornate hall in Kiev in the fall of 1996 was the newly elected president of Ukraine, Leonid Kuchma. When I asked him how best Canada could aid Ukraine's efforts at building an independent state out of the wreckage of the Soviet Union, the president answered without hesitation, "Can you send someone who will tell us how to live next door to a very large, powerful neighbour?"

Who better to ask than a Canadian? But whom to send, considering how divided opinions were on the subject among the various factions and forces in DFAIT, to say nothing of the government as a whole or Canadians in general? What passed through my mind was the answer to the classic Canadian question of how to make love to a porcupine—"carefully." I refrained from offering that particular piece of advice.

I wasn't quite so cautious a few years later during an exchange at a university in Taiwan. In my new role as a lecturer, unbound from the restraint of departmental briefing notes, I responded to a question about what advice I might have for the Taiwanese in dealing with China, based on my experience with the U.S. I offered my advice on connubial relations with a porcupine. The next day, as I attended a breakfast meeting with Taiwanese businesspeople, I noticed some reservation among the group. When I asked my host if I had committed a protocol error, he replied that it might have something to do with the account of my speech in that morning's newspaper. It reported that when asked what I would advise as an action in dealing with a powerful neighbour, I had said, "It should be like making love to a concubine." Take it as a variation on the debated use of hard vs. soft power.

Back to the question posed by President Kuchma, which, for as long as I can remember, has been at the heart of Canadian public debate and decision. Much of my own political history has been wound around this central issue. I recall lining up at the microphone with my brother Tom at a Liberal Party policy convention in 1966 to support Walter Gordon, then minister of finance, in his motion to limit foreign ownership in Canada. Those were the days when the party actually had such debates even while in government. Some saw the takeover of Canadian industry as a threat to our independence in decision making; others, as a source of investment and economic growth. This is the same fundamental debate that played itself out before the 1988 federal election over free trade with the U.S.—economic advantage versus control of choices on how we define ourselves.

The free trade debate caused great soul-searching in Liberal ranks, as traditionally we were the party of free trade. We had been strong advocates of multilateral trade liberalization under the General Agreement on Tariffs and Trade, whose broad-based rules applied to everyone. And there was no denying the attraction of a continental policy that could only facilitate what had already become a close and active Canada–U.S. market.

What was of major concern to us was the kind of pact being negotiated by the Mulroney government. There was not any effective dispute-resolving mechanism to protect Canadian industry from the marauding tactics of U.S. businesses using their political clout in Washington. In 2003 we continue to see how this major omission results in big problems for key sectors of the economy, most notably in the softwood lumber dispute. There was also a fear that under the agreement we would lose control of institutions essential to Canada, such as health care, culture and, on the resource side, the sale of fresh water.

We were at pains to point out that Liberals weren't against the concept of free trade. Our problem was with this particular treaty. We argued instead for an updated multilateral round of negotiations where Canada would not be so vulnerable to the weight of U.S. power, and where the dispute-resolution system wasn't grounded in national trade law. Yet this wasn't a debate about specific trade options; it was about closer ties with the commercial business system of the U.S., even though the message of the advocates of the deal was all about job creation and improved standards of living.

It was a fierce battle, and we lost. We were up against a very powerful business lobby led by the Business Council on National Issues (now the Canadian Council of Chief Executives), who mounted a highly successful public relations campaign to discredit the Liberal position. I well recall a meeting I had with John Turner shortly after he had taken a skiing holiday in Collingwood, a favourite spot for many of the Bay Street businessmen he knew well from his law-practice days. He was clearly shaken by the experience, saying to me, "These guys don't believe in Canada any more."

The 1993 election carried forward the trade issue, this time over a new, improved pact—the North American Free Trade Agreement of 1992. NAFTA was more acceptable to the Liberals, especially under the leadership of Jean Chrétien, a strong advocate of free trade, in part because it included Mexico. Having a third player and a potential partner meant that some semblance of a multilateral system was in play. We promised that once elected we would seek amendments that would recognize labour and environmental concerns. On becoming the government, we struck side deals setting up separate commissions in these areas with the right to hear grievances and undertake studies—not the kind of teeth being asked for by labour and environmental groups, but the start of a trilateral process. Particularly troublesome in granting final approval to NAFTA was Chapter 11, concerning discriminatory investment rules in host countries. Assurances were given by our trade experts that this was similar in intent to other bilateral agreements over the years. But the NAFTA negotiators quietly introduced new wrinkles, in particular one giving corporations the right to sue governments for perceived loss of profits from investments affected by government decisions, which has become a vexing challenge. I think of the backtracking our government had to do on the control of a major gasoline additive, MMT, because of the threat of a lawsuit from the manufacturer. An American company, Sunbelt, is challenging B.C. legislation that limits the bulk export of water. Even the Americans are becoming worried about the impact of Chapter 11. The Canadian company Methanex has sued California for passing regulations limiting the use of a gasoline additive believed to cause cancer. Here is trade and investment law being used to trump public efforts at environmental and health protection. Deep in the voluminous pages of trade documents, obligations can be infiltrated that may appear innocuous on the surface but are potent in application. I trust our negotiators on the proposed trilateral free trade agreement for the Americas have learned their lessons and will reconsider any such provisions.

NAFTA AT TEN

In December 2002 there was a gala gathering of the original signers of NAFTA—former presidents George Bush Sr. and Carlos Salinas, and former prime minister Mulroney—to celebrate its tenth anniversary. People were full of congratulations for the great success of the treaty. And certainly there is a welter of statistics testifying to increased trade flows and consequent economic payoffs. Moreover, NAFTA appears to enjoy broad public support in all three countries, although the numbers are coming down. In Canada, a poll taken in late 2002 shows support of NAFTA now evenly split, though it remains an article of faith with the business community and most economists.[1] Much of our economic interplay is now structured north–south, and NAFTA is seen by other regions as a model to be emulated. In fact, regional and bilateral trade deals are proliferating in every part of the globe.

Around the same time as the proponents of NAFTA were waxing eloquent I attended a meeting in Mexico City of the Commission on Globalization, where trade and social equity were on the agenda. In the previous few weeks, elections of left-wing governments in Brazil and Ecuador had caused tremors for free trade devotees. The elections were viewed in much of the Americas as a reaction against the policies of trade liberalization and the free market. That view was strongly presented by an economist working for the UN Commission for Latin America and the Caribbean. She asserted that free trade had failed to deliver on its promises of job creation and that in absolute terms poverty had increased in the Americas, including Mexico. With all agricultural tariffs removed on January 1, 2003, and massive subsidies both old and new flowing to American agri-industry and creating cheap farm products, the rural areas of Mexico will be severely affected. And on Canada's West Coast I hear the lament that NAFTA hasn't been much help in keeping the lumber mills open in the face of a prohibitive 19.3 per cent countervail duty and a 12.57 per cent anti-dumping duty from the U.S. government.

What was also striking were the concerns raised by the president of a large U.S. environmental organization, one of the few that originally backed NAFTA, who pointed to the increasing use by private companies of Chapter 11 to weaken environmental-protection legislation. A consultant for the International Labour Organization also criticized the lack of any effective application of basic labour standards, especially as they applied to female workers. In other words, many of the concerns that had supposedly been answered by the inclusion of environmental and labour clauses were in fact a festering problem.

In his spirited defence of the trade pact, Luis de la Calle, a former deputy trade minister from Mexico, rightly pointed out that it should not be considered the sole source of severe poverty problems, nor should it be seen as a silver bullet, the solution to all problems. From the Mexican point of view, NAFTA had opened up access to a huge market and had given a degree of certainty to the business environment. But I left the meeting with a sense of problems that still needed to be addressed and a nagging feeling that perhaps the economic benefits had been oversold and the social fallout minimized.

Changes are required. But the chance of doing that in today's political context is slim, especially given the present degree of aggressiveness in Washington. Any attempted change might prove disruptive. Nevertheless, that is why I think it is important to look at how to revamp the North American partnership, broaden the NAFTA arrangement to incorporate other continental issues and see how fair practices on labour and the environment can be built in. We need to gain a better hold on the way decisions are made on the management of our common property in North America. Integration is broadening in scope, but the institutional base to manage it is not in place. We need an effective political strategy to stake out our own political and economic space in North America.

SEPTEMBER 11 AND CANADIAN CHOICES

Nothing dramatized more for me the crucial responsibility that elected representatives have in defending Canadian values, institutions and programs than the experience over free trade. Along with others, I was vilified in the big business community for my opposing position. Later, when I considered running for the Liberal leadership, it was obvious from the start that I was being blackballed in my fundraising efforts because of my opposition to the Mulroney Free Trade Agreement. Ever since, I've been labelled anti-American, a charge I reject. It is not anti-American to be pro-Canadian on issues on which our national interests diverge. Nor is it anti-American to take a pro-Canadian stand when many of the ideas, values and institutions we have stood for and fostered as liberal-minded Canadians are under attack by a right-wing administration in the U.S.

However, attacks on the legitimacy of the Canadian nationalist stance involve powerful forces not only in business but in the media and the academic world. Too many in our elite structures define the Canadian interest primarily as following the American lead without question. The stronger the pull towards North American integration, the more insistent they are that we simply bow to the inevitable, ignoring the oft-stated preference by most Canadians for keeping our own identity. Our political system is crucial in counteracting this blind attachment. The onus is on our public representatives to maintain our capacity to act in the best

Canadian interest and preserve our autonomy. This will be put to the test under the Martin government, which promises to work on closer relationships with the U.S. Jean Chrétien came into office vowing to keep a respectful distance. He is leaving office having kept Canada out of the Iraq war, but then feeling compelled to seek a peace offering to the Bush administration on missile defence. It is an example of how our elected leaders are in a constant tug of war in trying to steer a balanced course for Canada between the U.S. push and the internationalist pull.

In the meantime, various academics, think-tank gurus, business leaders, and senior Liberals are calling for even greater continental integration, including a common currency. Wendy Dobson of the C. D. Howe Institute, a pro-business think-tank, recommends that we concede to all demands for "interoperability of defence forces" in the name of keeping the trucks rolling across the border.[2] The CanWest publication empire ran front-page editorials in all its newspapers castigating anyone who has the temerity to question U.S. policy on Iraq and most other matters, arguing that it is un-Canadian to criticize the wisdom and the ways of the Bush administration. The Canadian Council of Chief Executives has established a high-powered action group to push the linkage between economic security and an integration of defence operations.

In light of these constant efforts to acquiesce to perceived American demands, one can't help wondering if we are about to pass the point of no return in surrendering our freedom of action. Borders shape the character of our country, especially in determining who is invited to come and join the distinctive cultural mix of Canada. I agree with Ron Atkey, the former Conservative employment and immigration minister, who once told me that the minister responsible for immigration has a sacred trust to keep Canada's doors open against all pressure to restrict entry. In general, successive governments have striven to attain that ideal, even though many immigration officials are congenitally opposed to open immigration. But under relentless pounding from the right-wing press, and the Alliance Party, especially since September 11, we are now witnessing a change. Refugees have become suspect. Immigrants coming for family reasons will be increasingly scarce. This in a country desperately in need of people to populate our vast land and provide a renewed workforce and which, since the Second World War, has provided leadership internationally on the right of sanctuary for the dispossessed.

Given that so much of our economy is dependent on trade and investment with Americans, it's no surprise that the threat of retaliation in the form of restrictive border measures raises the blood pressure in both federal and provincial cabinet rooms and corporate boardrooms. Shortly after September 11, a respected businessman in Vancouver told me with great conviction that if the Americans wanted perimeter defence then we should give it to them just to keep the border free from hassle. A few days later, in Ottawa, a DFAIT official said to me that there was only one foreign policy that Canada had to follow and that was to keep the Americans happy and show that we were loyal.

Such a stance implies that in addition to giving military support to actions in Afghanistan, muting criticism of the U.S.-led attack on Iraq, abandoning basic positions on arms control, tightening border controls and harmonizing other related policies, we should not take issue with the U.S. government on any of their actions. So if they abandon the Anti-Ballistic Missile (ABM) treaty, set up military tribunals rather than rely on international law, or advance any other form of unilateralism or exceptionalism, nary a cross word should be spoken? In that case, the war on terrorism not only changes the ground rules for Canada–U.S. relations but also impinges on our ability or interest in advancing a distinctive global agenda.

In a speech he gave in 2002 at Cornell University, former defence minister Art Eggleton spoke of his increasing discomfort with U.S. unilateralism and recounted a meeting in which U.S. Secretary of Defense Donald Rumsfeld told him that "the mission defines the coalition" and not the other way around. In other words, terms are to be dictated, not mutually agreed. This approach is repeated in many spheres of our relations with the U.S. and has created a Pavlovian response in many Canadian decision makers, who believe there is no choice but to go along. The fierce response and second-guessing that took place after the prime minister decided not to join in the Iraq adventure shows how prevalent such attitudes are, even amongst Liberals.

This could be tactical and short term, taking into account the public mood of sympathy for the American tragedy of September 11. But it may also reflect a serious calculation that the risk presented by global terrorism overrides other concerns, although, as this book aims to show, it is not the only human security risk. Nor is the predominantly military approach necessarily the best way to respond. There is a delicate and difficult balance to be struck in our relations with the U.S. Tactical and temporary concessions may tip the balance in such a way that we permanently lose precious elements of our independence.

The war on terrorism could clearly be a turning point for the broader international community as well. What we do in carving out a separate, if connected, trajectory from our powerful neighbour has meaning for many others in the world. As President Kuchma's request for a Canadian sage clearly demonstrates, the Canada–U.S. sharing of a continent through an elaborate system of treaties, more than two hundred in number, and an extensive range of contacts and relationships has been seen by many as a model for how to manage border affairs in a peaceful way, and on how to respect differences even when there is a disparity in power. Many other medium-power states feel we have maintained the right balance between our relations with the U.S. and our wider international relations. If, however, the undefended frontier is now to be subsumed into a North American security fortress dominated by the imperatives of homeland defence, then a very different model appears, with sobering lessons for all those countries who are struggling to construct political space for themselves in proximity to bigger, stronger nations—which, in the global system of interdependence, basically means most other countries. Canada is better equipped than most to ride the waves of globalization without going under. If we can't keep our identity, who can?

The key choices we make in answering the Kuchma question are not for the future but are with us now. Will buying into the anti-missile strategy of the Bush administration mean abandoning our long and constructive role in promoting multilateral arms agreements? How will we maintain an immigration policy that remains reasonably open and in fact is one of the few left that recognizes the legitimacy of refugee determination? Is the rush to amend the Criminal Code to give police more power to apprehend terrorists going to affect the protection of Charter rights? What will be the consequence of continued big-business pressure to push us into closer economic dependence? How do we work out an acceptable agreement with our North American cohabitants on vital issues of energy, climate change and water resources? Does being compliant with American international policies mean abandoning a human security agenda?

There have been occasions when we have stood up to the U.S. on matters of principle—when we resisted American efforts to scuttle the International Criminal Court, when we signed the Kyoto Accord or when Prime Minister Chrétien and Bill Graham were strong advocates of having the Iraq issue dealt with by the UN. On the other hand, the decision to proceed on missile defence negotiations and to become part of a joint planning unit on continental defence against terrorism is just a disguised way of setting the stage for a full integration of our land and sea forces, carrying with it major consequences for our own territorial integrity.

Muddling through these issues won't get us very far. And responding in haste to self-interested domestic pressures or American demands real or perceived is a mistake. No, we need a game plan based on public discussion and consensus. The time has come for a clear blueprint for managing our U.S. relations in the context of evolving North American interdependence. Can we build this based on the principles of a community where we share responsibility for decisions on common problems, or do we simply leave it to the market or Uncle Sam to decide?

TREATIES AND TRANSACTIONS: RULES OR POWER

In the autumn of 1997, I asked Paul Fraser, past president of both the Canadian and Commonwealth bar associations, to undertake a study on transboundary relations between Canada and the U.S., with particular attention to how to better deal with disputes. The request was prompted by several developments. One was the stalemate in our quarrel with the U.S. over the Pacific Coast Salmon Treaty. There was no agreement on what proportion of fish could be caught, each country believing the other was abusing its treaty quotas. Here was a scarce resource in danger of being extinguished, with various groups and communities struggling to maintain a livelihood, and with stakeholders all along the coast, commercial and sport fisheries, and Indian bands each vying to catch the maximum. Meanwhile, the governments of B.C., Alaska, Washington and Oregon were all demanding of their respective federal governments that there be no compromise. The treaty procedures for stakeholder consultations and for resolution through meetings of the Salmon Commission ended up in angry and unproductive wrangling. As for the salmon, they didn't care much about border definitions; they swam where the ocean flow and water conditions dictated.

In Ottawa, management of the issue was shared by Foreign Affairs and the Department of Fisheries and Oceans. Fisheries officials, fresh from the success of the turbot war, wanted to be assertive in limiting the passage of American boats in Canadian waters, and the mechanisms in place, especially by the B.C. and Alaskan governments, were based on confrontation, not on finding a solution for the long-term preservation of the salmon stock. At Foreign Affairs we were more inclined to negotiate, reminding the Fisheries folk that the U.S. was not Spain. We agreed to work jointly. Fisheries would look after the science and technical arguments, deal with the Canadian stakeholders and relate to the B.C. and state governments. Our job was to get the attention of the various players in Washington, who, with all the other global matters on their plate, weren't too inclined to view salmon as a high priority. Thus, in my first meetings with Secretary of State Madeleine Albright, the subject of note was not matters of traditional security concerns but how to resolve a dispute over fish, reflecting the growing significance of resource issues in our relationship. It became a constant refrain, to the point that we both vowed we wouldn't eat salmon until the dispute was resolved.

The dispute was difficult and prolonged, exacerbated by an ugly confrontation. In the summer of 1997, angry Canadian fishermen surrounded an American cruise vessel in the port of Prince Rupert, prompting a call from Madeleine Albright as I was attending a street event in my constituency, asking what we were going to do, and reminding me in as nice a way as possible that if this had happened anywhere but in Canada then the Marines might be preparing to go ashore. The immediate crisis was averted, but the incident showed that a more radical solution was needed. Once you dug through the politics and posturing there were some vital matters at stake. An extremely valuable shared resource was in danger of disappearing for lack of stewardship just as we had seen the disappearance of cod off the East Coast. We decided that the normal channels wouldn't work; we had to go outside the system.

The answer was a negotiating process that would carry the imprimatur of both the prime minister and the president and short-circuit the treaty. The Americans agreed to this arrangement, and David Strangway, former UBC president, and William Ruckelshaus, a cabinet member in the previous Bush administration, were selected to represent each government. This eminent-person approach succeeded in bringing more light and less heat to the issue. Strangway and Ruckelshaus cut through the immediate political fray to show that it was basically an issue of conservation, demanding a long-term plan of restoration and careful extraction. Through their sound recommendations, skilful work with the state governments by David Anderson, who became fisheries minister halfway through the dispute, and our moving the matter up to the agenda level of leaders, the dispute was eventually resolved. An agreement setting out certain levels of fish catch was concluded, along with a Canadian commitment to provide funding for seeding the fish stock in the rivers running into the Alaska Panhandle. Madeleine and I were now free once again to serve salmon at luncheon gatherings.

Here was another example, some might say, of successful Canada–U.S. compromise on an ad hoc basis. And it is true that there is a dynamic process of negotiation and adjudication, based on a substantial reservoir of political goodwill, in settling disputes. For me, however, there was something wrong in relying on a reactive, crisis-driven response system to deal with complex cross-border issues. This weakness was highlighted for me during a speaking tour of U.S. cities in 1997, during which I met with a variety of interest groups. In Boston, at the John F. Kennedy School of Government, the topic was defence and security. In Chicago, business executives discussed the problems in transferring people and the need for addressing human resources as a cross-border issue. In Minneapolis, water was one topic of interest, because of the ongoing difficulty with the Garrison Diversion and North Dakota's plans for changing water flows. The other topic was the possibility of constructing transportation corridors that would traverse the spine of North America. Similar interests were expressed in Seattle. In San Francisco, environment was top of mind. And in Los Angeles, culture and communication were the focus. Amongst these various encounters, one in particular comes to mind. At a dinner organized by our consul-general, Kim Campbell, with members of the movie community, I sat next to a young Canadian woman who had a senior position in the Disney organization. She pointed out that many of the best animators in the business were trained in Canada but had to work in the U.S. because of the opportunities there. She made a compelling case to change our approach in Canada from one of protection to one of further developing the Canadian industry, making sure it was tied into the global structure of mega-firms such as Disney. It was a clear articulation of the need for Canada to think in global terms.

The issue of integration is usually expressed in the language of economics. The billion and a half dollars a day of trade that crosses the border, the fact that cross-border trade represents 30 per cent or better of our GNP, and that increasingly the trade is north–south, not east–west—all this certainly signals our interdependence. Yet what came through loud and clear from my discussions was how much more extensive the integration really was. Our folding in to a continental weave was multiple in its strands and complex in its pattern. What was missing was how to ensure that a Canadian design would be part of this evolving North American fabric. Our decision-making system, treaty structure and transactional approach at dispute resolution were inadequate, too old-fashioned for the task.

Under NAFTA there is a system of panels for resolving trade disputes. The lack of an agreed definition of countervail and dumping (common trade violations in which one country subsidizes its products to undercut the price in the importing country) allows the Americans to hammer us on vital issues such as softwood lumber. But at least there is a framework. In many other areas NAFTA has nothing to say; there is only the push and pull of political power, where we are handicapped by an unequal bargaining position. In the crucial issue of culture, for example, when Sheila Copps, our minister of heritage, tried to introduce measures to balance out the major advantage that certain American publications enjoyed, the strong U.S. industry lobbied the Clinton administration, who passed the pressure on to our own government, and the legislation was withdrawn. Since the early seventies my home province of Manitoba has faced efforts by the congressional delegation from North Dakota to build water-control systems that would introduce non-native plants and animals into our waterways. Despite continuous rearguard action by our Washington embassy and provincial officials, the North Dakotan congressional delegation has persisted in its efforts with no regard for our environmental standards or the Boundary Waters Treaty. The Bush administration announced a continental energy policy, which includes drilling in an animal sanctuary off Alaska, with little regard for Canadian environmental interests. These examples touch upon areas that are vital to our quality of life; such issues are becoming more frequent, governed less and less by mutually agreed rules and more and more by unilateral actions by the Americans. Hence, my request to Paul Fraser to help modernize the treaty process of dispute resolution.

An obsolescent legal structure was just one of numerous deep-seated problems. We were caught in a time warp of old debates between protectionists and continentalists, carried forward in their modern reincarnations by Maude Barlow of the Council of Canadians and Thomas d'Aquino of the Business Council on National Issues, one demanding no truck or trade with the Yankees, the other advising that we just lie back and enjoy the pleasures of continental cohabitation. Both arguments had merits, but the absolutist way in which they were presented went overboard. Canadian nationalists are right to insist that we maintain government vigilance and act to preserve Canadian institutions, but there is in some quarters a fortress mentality that ignores how we can make the relationship work for us both economically and politically. On the other hand, the continentalists see no problem in slavishly following the U.S. lead on everything and plump inordinately for any policy that draws us closer together. This historical divide tends to colour the way we all look at Canada–U.S. affairs. One is pro- or anti-American, a nationalist or continentalist, a free trader or a protectionist. Such stereotyping replaces analysis and obscures the search for thinking and positioning that doesn't fall into either camp.

One result is that we fail to fully appreciate the shift going on in the political demographics of the U.S. and how that affects U.S. attitudes not only towards Canada but also towards its international role. Political power is shifting to the south and west of the U.S., bringing with it more conservative politics, less understanding of, or interest in Canada, and certainly an anti-internationalist stance. Underpinning this change is the rise of Christian fundamentalism as a powerful political force, particularly in the Republican Party. The Reagan presidency, the Gingrich New Revolution and the present Bush administration have strong roots in evangelical religious organizations, which pursue their political goals with all the zeal expressed in the old hymn "Onward, Christian Soldiers." The result is an extreme right-wing agenda centred on anti-abortion policies; resistance to anything that smacks of family planning; law and order; corporate tax cuts; and gargantuan military spending. There is strong antipathy to anything that suggests international governance; a deep-seated belief that the U.S. can and should go it alone and not participate in multilateral agreements of any kind; and an attitude, especially prevalent amongst congressional Republicans, that the U.S. can legislate extraterritorially to compel other countries to abide by their decisions. No one epitomized this philosophy more than Senator Jesse Helms of North Carolina, who became a one-man wrecking crew in opposing U.S. participation in the UN, various arms control agreements and human rights commitments. The Helms-Burton Law that he authored on Cuba received congressional support because of the political clout of the expatriate anti-Castro Cuban community in key states such as Florida and New Jersey.

Canada's strong stand against this infringement on our right to decide who to do business with and how to conduct our own foreign policy served notice to our other hemispheric neighbours that we were northern gringos of a different sort and gained us substantial respect in the Americas, where they have traditionally been subject to the U.S.'s extraterritorial bullying.

That was just the beginning of a series of contretemps with Mr. Helms, who was an avowed opponent of many initiatives we took. Under the Bush administration, this aversion to international cooperation and the rule of law has gained the blessing of the White House, which creates a major challenge for Canadians. I had a foretaste of what to expect in an exchange with President Bush when he was still governor of Texas. A Canadian named Stanley Faulder had been convicted of murder and was slated for execution. The Vienna Convention grants foreign nationals charged with a crime the support of their own country and consular services. Evidence came to light that Faulder had been denied these rights. I drew this to the attention of Governor Bush and asked for a review of the case. His response was that he didn't really care if he broke an international covenant even if it was ratified by the U.S.; the Texas court had spoken, and it was the only authority he cared about. Mr. Faulder was duly executed.

Such views have now become an article of faith in the U.S. administration. They have refused to join the Kyoto Protocol, disavowed the International Criminal Court and withdrawn from the ABM treaty with Russia limiting the development of anti-missile systems. As already noted, this last puts Canada in a particular bind. Under NORAD, we share with the U.S. responsibility for surveillance and response against penetration of the continental air space. Now there is an expectation that this role will extend to the proposed National Missile Defense System being developed by the Americans. To join, however, runs against the long-held and well-regarded position Canada has maintained as a major advocate and architect of international non-proliferation agreements. Our adherence would condone the Bush administration's antagonism to arms control agreements in general and runs counter to our oft-stated view that the major nuclear powers must live up to their commitments under the Non-Proliferation of Nuclear Weapons Treaty and work towards nuclear disarmament. In other words, our adherence to National Missile Defense would fundamentally alter our position as a leading nation on the control and elimination of nuclear, chemical and biological weapons and constitute a significant retreat from protecting people against the threat of mass destruction.

DIPLOMATIC INITIATIVES

Anyone who thinks that proximity brings favours or privileges is living in a dream world. The problem we have with the U.S. is not that President Bush doesn't mention Canada in a speech to Congress or in a fit of pique orders his ambassador to act as viceroy reading the riot act to the locals; that's just a symptom. In the changing landscape of U.S. politics and policies, we haven't gained the necessary traction. We rely too often on old connections and our ability to negotiate a crisis, rather than anticipating issues and building a political case in the U.S. to support our point of view.

To begin with, we are not strong on the ground diplomatically. It is true that we have a magnificent embassy building in Washington with a prime location on Pennsylvania Avenue, which affords us good presence. Our officials there are consummate professionals and represent Canadian interests superbly in the day-to-day handling of relations.

Where we go missing is outside the Beltway, where our presence is limited and in large parts of the U.S. non-existent. We have ten consulates, in New York, Boston, Detroit, Chicago, Minneapolis, Atlanta, Houston, Los Angeles, San Francisco and Seattle. Compare that with our other NAFTA partner, Mexico, which has three times the number of diplomatic outposts, many of them in the emerging political, technological and business centres of the south and west, where we are weakest. To use one example, after leaving government I was invited by Duke University, in Durham, North Carolina, to give a series of lectures. The same week I was there, the Mexicans were opening a consulate in Raleigh, North Carolina, the hub of a dynamic area of high-tech industries and major universities, including Duke, which has one of the best

Canadian studies program in the U.S. The Mexicans are now in a position to tap into the knowledge and business strength of that region and make valuable political contacts at the local, county and state levels, which in itself has a bearing on positions taken in Washington. Canada's nearest office is 377 miles away in Atlanta, where our consul-general and staff are expected to cover a seven-state area. Not hard to figure who has the advantage.

We are also absent in other key cities, among them Denver, Phoenix, Nashville and St. Louis, except for periodic visits from Canadian staff located elsewhere. Missed opportunities are the result. We are simply not in a position to develop and nurture American contacts, associations and connections through which we can explain our positions, lobby for our interests and gain allies for our policies. Consulates are traditionally seen as trade offices that also provide assistance to Canadians who get into trouble abroad. In today's world their role is far more complex and political. To handle issues of environment, resources, energy, culture, security, trans-portation and human resources in close concert with the Americans, we need to be well positioned in all regions, not just in Washington. I recall watching Roger Simmons, our consul-general in Seattle, in action. A former MP and cabinet minister with an aptitude for the Rolodex as befits a former Newfie politician, Roger had developed an impressive array of business, university, NGO, community and journalistic contacts, which he used to great effect in promoting Canadian interests and sending back to Ottawa invaluable information. He told me it was often easier and more productive to meet a senator on home ground rather than in the hothouse environment of Washington, or to work with a local public interest group on mis-sile defence and let them lobby their own politicians.

In the 2003 budget the government took some limited steps to invest in an expanded diplomatic network plugged into the regions of growing political, social and commercial importance in the U.S. But it is just a limited downpayment on what needs to be a major investment.

Equally important is the need to reform the institutional frame-work of our border relations with the U.S. This was the intent of Paul Fraser's study. As he stated in the introduction to his report, "An effective dispute resolution system is essential if the two friendliest countries in the world are to have the benefits of a rule-based system instead of a traditional power-based system."[3] But what he found was that few of the more than two hundred treaties between the two countries have any kind of formal dispute mechanisms and there is virtually no provision for identifying emerging problems or for engaging in pre-crisis solutions. He concluded that no form of binding adjudication would sell with the Americans. Instead, he proposed that we begin work on a mandatory process for managing disputes, without requiring a binding outcome, and he called for the two countries to apply ingenuity and will to establish such a process.

The Fraser proposal proved too dramatic a departure for the Americans, and I daresay for many Canadian officials as well. What it did do was help us focus on how to move away from reactive, crisis-management border diplomacy towards setting up mechanisms for proactive planning on common issues with appropriate public input.

The area we picked to experiment with was the hot-button issue of water, and the institution we chose to lead the innovation was the venerable International Joint Commission (IJC). Historically, management of the many water systems we share across the border has been the subject of intense and controversial exchange. The Boundary Waters Treaty of 1909 set up the IJC with reasonably broad judicial and investigative powers, with commissioners drawn equally from both countries. Over the years the commission has confined itself mainly to fact-finding and monitoring functions. This has provided a stabilizing influence on boundary waters management but has not tested the full range of the commission's potential, especially its adjudicative powers.

What made the issue of water so topical and amenable to agreement was the experience both counties had with the devastating Red River flood in the spring of 1997, which soon swamped the dike protection around the cities of Fargo and Grand Forks, then headed for the border into Manitoba. While attending to flood duties there, I still had to attend to foreign minister's business, and out of that came an idea: Why not use the flood as an opportunity to initiate a cross-border water-management system in the two countries? The IJC could be commissioned to look at ways of coordinating remedial measures and begin planning to avoid future damaging floods in the shared watershed. What better demonstration of joint problem solving than to cooperate on flood management through the IJC? The prime minister thought it was a good idea, and so did President Bill Clinton, and in short order we had agreement. Under the guidance of the experienced and creative Canadian chairman, Len Legault, it recommended that the IJC expand its role to include preventative functions. This meant initiating cross-border planning of shared water basins and involving local stakeholders, governments and agencies to coordinate usage and gain maximum benefit. We then reorganized the IJC to give it the flexibility and range of functions originally intended by its signers. When we later discussed rewiring other boundary circuits, we had a live model already up and running. The advent of Herb Gray as Canadian chair will add further heft to the role of the commission.

Canada and the U.S. also agreed on a consultative body that would bring together officials and stakeholders to examine common problems, share information and allow some degree of forward thinking to occur. It was a far cry from a broad, general mechanism for identifying and collaborating to avert disputes, as recommended by Fraser, but it was the embryo of a useful process. In the fall of 1999, when President Clinton came to Ottawa to open the new U.S. embassy, he and the prime minister signed a border agreement formally setting up the Canada–U.S. Partnership Forum (CUSP), a body that now meets quarterly and draws in reputable and knowledgeable citizens from each country for an exchange of views. It is charged with preparing an annual "Report on the State of the Border" designed to pinpoint areas of reform and coordination. The first meetings elicited strong demands for more strategic direction, especially in the problem of enforcement action against terrorism, drug trafficking and other forms of criminal exploitation of the border system.

SECURITY VS RIGHTS IN NORTH AMERICA

Security is a particularly crucial issue now. The September 11 attacks affected the American psyche in very profound ways. Protection of the "heartland" has become a driving force in U.S.

politics. The pressure is on Canada to join in a North American perimeter defence strategy against terrorism. The Pentagon has announced a Northern Command overseeing U.S. forces from Mexico to Canada, and there is strong pressure to have our own forces come under its jurisdiction. A continental anti-missile defence system will further involve Canadians in what military jargon calls interoperability, which is another way of saying "takeover." Duke University Professor Mike Byers spelled out the implications of this increasing military integration: we would lose our capacity to make independent choices on deployment of troops and their uses and find ourselves having to backtrack or renege on various policies and treaty agreements.[4]

A redefining of North American security is necessary. There are different threats, new-style weapons, invasion of our common space by traffickers and terrorists. Unfortunately we have accepted analysis and prescriptions supplied by the U.S. administration instead of engaging in our own assessment of what the serious risks are from our perspective and sharing this Canadian "risk assessment" with our neighbour. Instead of working up a lather about NORAD being threatened if we don't join a missile defence program (a patent exercise in fear mongering), we should be working on recommendations for amending the role of NORAD to give it an updated mission for cooperative continental security in the new century. The most serious problem in meeting post-September 11 security issues is not peremptory American demands but our own lack of creative policy-making and a lame willingness to simply follow their direction without injecting our definition of what would be a good security regime.

The same fault lies in the treatment of civilian border management. The mammoth new Department of Homeland Security, amalgamating many U.S. governmental agencies and organizations that deal with border issues and focused almost single-mindedly on anti-terrorist activities, will increase the demand for closer harmonization of cross-border matters as defined by the terrorist mission. The Canadian government has already signed a comprehensive border agreement that incorporates a thirty-point action plan covering everything from immigration to infrastructure, customs control and schemes for detecting suspicious persons seeking refugee asylum. There is no doubt that some of these measures are necessary. They lead inexorably, however, to a greater harmonization of key policies. And it is fair to say that most Canadians have little knowledge of the nature of the agreements or their implications. Of greatest concern are those dealing with immigration and the joint exercise of police powers. The agreement signed with some fanfare dealing with the return of refugees who claim asylum in Canada to American authorities for processing is a capitulation from our commitments to a liberal refugee policy. As we saw during the eighties, we had very different views from the U.S. on what constituted a refugee from Central America. We were able to give sanctuary to many from that wartorn area who came to Canada through the U.S. Now they would be sent back.

The opaque nature of the cooperation is a worry. Take, for example, the extensive surveillance system authorized under the Homeland Security Act. This is a plan to establish a data pool on a broad sweep of individuals by mining various sources such as credit-card accounts, bank accounts and other confidential files— a version of Orwellian spying that is about to come true. Significant registration and information requirements may well be imposed on Canadians travelling to the U.S. Our new border arrangements could well incorporate cooperation with the Homeland Security Big Brother. In 2003, a Canadian citizen, Maher Arar, was sent by the U.S. to a prison in Syria, and tortured there, without the due process of law. His case raises disturbing issues on how border cooperation may seriously impinge on our Charter of Rights. The government must be far more transparent on the cross-border cooperative arrangements and spell out directly what is entailed.

The call of continental security also has troublesome implications for vital areas of Canadian domestic policy. If we too readily accept American notions of who is a security threat, we could risk undermining distinctive elements of our multicultural society. I say this based on my experience during very tough negotiations with the Americans between 1998 and 2000 over amendments to the International Traffic in Arms Regulations. Since the Second World War, Canada and the U.S. had agreements that allowed for the free exchange of defence-related goods and information. In July 1998, in the wake of a U.S. technology-secrets scandal, with minimal notice and no consultation the State Department advised us that they were changing these regulations and imposing an export licence requirement on Canada. Such sweeping changes coming in such an arbitrary fashion would have put Canadian-based defence industries (a $10-billion annual enterprise) at a severe disadvantage in competing for procurement contracts against their American counterparts.

Shortly after learning of this peremptory move I asked Madeleine Albright for a delay until we could discuss these amendments. There ensued a protracted negotiation. We began by acknowledging that if there was a security risk in transfers of technology information to Canadian industry, then we would fix it, in accordance with our own rules. The American negotiators began with the assertion that they would lift the proposed amendments only if we complied with their conditions, a key one being that any Canadian company receiving classified technology could employ only Canadian citizens. They were totally unmoved when told that this contravened our Charter of Rights that grants equal rights to landed immigrants as to citizens. To State Department officials our Charter of Rights was irrelevant to their security concerns. Irrelevant, too, was the fact that many of our high-tech industries recruit skilled workers from other countries, based on Canadian rules that encourage economic immigration (at least until the latest round of changes that make economic immigration highly selective). Eventually I was able to work out with Madeleine Albright a compromise that would replace the citizenship test with a security-screening system for each company, one designed and implemented by Canadian officials. Even then her officials dragged the details on for several months until agreement was secured.

Politicians and bureaucrats in Washington, as this case demonstrates, have little regard for what we consider our fundamental values, especially when security is at stake. In the absence of clear rules, muscle prevails, and serious damage can be done to our interests. We need to define our own strategy for managing those interests and not just be in a reactive mode. The place to start is by defining the border security issue in the mode of a community, not a fortress.

CHAPTER 5

THE NORTH AMERICAN CONDO

———————

SECURITY WILL BE THE WATCHWORD FOR DEFINING OUR RELATIONSHIP with the United States. What we must do is ensure that the definition of security is one not solely authored by the U.S. but one that reflects the thinking and experience of our own country as we view individuals at risk from a number of global threats.

We also need to conceive this broader concept of security in a North American framework, to escape from perpetually dealing with the U.S. one-on-one. If we persist on a bilateral basis we are in trouble. One of the advantages of being in a framework with Mexico is that it gives us a partner in negotiating with the colossus that sits between us. If you are a 180-pound halfback faced with blocking a 300-pound defensive tackle, you'd better find some help. This idea is still very hard for many Canadians to face. They still nurture illusions about our so-called special relationship, even though it is apparent that Mexico has its own cachet with present-day American politicians based on the growing power of Spanish-speaking Americans. The unseemly preoccupation of Canadian officialdom with whether George Bush would meet first with the president of Mexico rather than the Canadian prime minister was misplaced. There should be far more attention to approaches we could jointly pursue with the Mexicans in our respective encounters with the Americans this would afford both of us greater leverage.

The difficult part is to find the formula that allows the two smaller partners to engage in cooperative relationships and partnerships with the U.S. in the new environment without relinquishing separate political, economic and cultural domains. Most of the proposals currently being discussed are for even tighter forms of integration, usually on the grounds of securing untrammelled border access. Little consideration is given to how to serve mutual economic interests while maintaining Mexico's and Canada's freedom of action.

Instead, the approach should be one of community, not of a fortress or perimeter, a community that would encourage the retention of each country's individuality through structures with set rules and rights. Maybe the model is a condominium, where there is shared decision making on common interests, with the freedom to decorate and manage each unit according to individual taste.

A TEST OF TRILATERALISM

Let's look again, as an example, at water. In the summer of 2000, I flew to Santa Fe for a trilateral meeting of the foreign ministers of North America. Not many knew that such a group existed. Indeed it doesn't any more. I arrived on a scorching day in August as that region was experiencing its second month without rain. Moisture was so rare that, as one local put it, when you spat on the sidewalk you got a medal. I had just left Black Lake in northern Saskatchewan, a seventy-mile-long stretch of pristine fresh water that, as my son, friends and I departed, had at a maximum only ten or twelve other fishing parties on it. The contrast couldn't have been more stark or the look into the future more sobering. Did sharing a continent mean sharing this scarce and increasingly valuable resource, which for many Canadians would be like sharing a birthright? When I sat down for lunch with my counterparts, Rosario Green and Madeleine Albright, I told them that water should be on our political menu, even though it was not on the agenda, in fact was kept off because it was thought too controversial—a defining issue, but one that officials considered too hot to handle. On the edge of the Mojave Desert, in what was once the home of Georgia O'Keeffe, there ensued what was likely the first serious discussion at a senior political level of the freshwater crisis facing North America and what our governments might do. If ever there was a security issue that would affect millions in our baili-wick, this was it. It was amazing to think that discussion was just now beginning to take place at this level, and only because of per-sonal contact and relationships among us, not by any grand design.

Rosario and Madeleine had known each other when they both served at the UN. I had come to know them particularly well through a dinner at the Summit Meeting of the Americas, in Chile, and out of this had grown the habit of getting together periodically to exchange views. Each of us had an interest in exploring new ideas and recognized and responded to that quality in the others. We also found ourselves becoming good friends. It was an unusual trio, and looking back I feel honoured to have been associated with two such accomplished women—Madeleine Albright a sharp and persuasive academic who carried huge responsibilities at the time in trying to craft American policies in the Middle East and the Balkans, and Rosario Green, an elegant and seasoned diplomat who was a strong advocate of the traditional Mexican version of non-intervention in sovereign affairs and an ardent supporter of disarmament. I saw an unexpected combative side of Rosario when I persuaded her to come to a Senators hockey game during a visit of Mexican ministers to Ottawa as part of the Canada–Mexico Commission (another institution abandoned by our successors). She couldn't imagine herself ever voluntarily going to a sporting event but said she would drop in for a few minutes as a courtesy to me. She stayed to the very end, cheering every bodycheck.

Over time our discussions turned towards cooperation between the three countries on continental matters. Attention on econom-ic issues could be gained through NAFTA, but there was at the time no place to talk about drugs, border issues, resource disputes, security. So, informally, we began a dialogue, the three of us and a few officials.

This effort crystallized when we all received invitations to the annual meeting of the North American Institute in the summer of

1998. The institute is a unique organization started by the late John Wirth, a distinguished American historian and one of the few academics in any of the three countries who conceived of North America not as just a slab of geography but as an entity that has woven together many common threads.

Our acceptance of the invitation outed us. Our interest in North American cooperation was now public, and some Canadian commentators had trouble reconciling my interest in it with the conventional wisdom that saw me as an unregenerate Canadian nationalist. What was more difficult was finding the intellectual horsepower to begin analyzing the changing state of North American relationships. At DFAIT, the Trade section could supply a mound of statistics on cross-border traffic flows and import-export figures, but nada on anything else. On the political side, there was literally no one working on the non-NAFTA dimensions of our continental membership. Earlier, we had reorganized the department to set up a division of the Americas. But George Haynal, who provided its very intelligent leadership, admitted to me that when it came to North American expertise the cupboard was bare. The same could be said of the academic pantry. There were mounds of material on U.S.–Canada studies, and scholarship on Canadian–Mexican relations, mainly on aboriginal rights dealing with Chiapas, but only a few crumbs on Canada in North America. The one exception on this barren landscape was the valuable work undertaken through the two NAFTA commissions set up to investigate infractions on environment and labour. (Perhaps they could take on added mandates?) Our intellectual generals, it seemed, were fighting the last war. Once again it became clear that a lack of investment in good analysis and ideas handicaps Canadian policy-makers; given today's complex issues, good scholarship translated into good advice is essential. Without it, all is improvisation.

Another insight came from discussions with Russian authorities about a polar transit link via Churchill, Manitoba. Intrigued by the concept of transportation corridors running on a north–south axis, I saw the chance for what I called a Murmansk to Monterrey link. A study I commissioned had come forward with the novel idea of "green corridors" in North America that would link the three countries by way of information-smart, environmentally sustainable transportation networks that would improve productivity, make border crossings more secure and reduce emissions. It showed the merit of looking at issues through a North American lens.

Human security added further refraction. If we could reorient our thinking on global affairs to focus on threats to individuals, why not examine our role in North America from the same perspective? At the North American Institute I gave the notion a trial run. First, I suggested that within North America there were security concerns derived from shrinking resources, environmental degradation and natural disasters that had to be met through cooperation. Then there were external threats from organized crime, drug trafficking and terrorism, which again could be better dealt with in a cooperative framework. The present institutional structures were not up to handling these new threats, there was little recognition that they were commonly experienced, and there was little opportunity for a participatory process to enlist the private sector or the public. The human security idea struck a chord with this group.

From that point on, a North American policy began to take shape at DFAIT and was reciprocated by the other two foreign ministers. In September 1999, the three of us met to agree on a framework statement. In addition to pursuing coordinated policy in development aid in the Americas, the key sentence was: "All three of our countries face specific problems—such as environmental degradation, climate change, organized crime and narcotics trafficking—that can only be addressed through common understanding and dialogue that will build confidence, foster cooperation and enhance human security."

This agenda widened at Santa Fe the next summer. The three countries established a trilateral Web site to share information with the public. (Strangely, the Canadian portal of this site has subsequently disappeared.) We discussed how to use information technology as a way of linking interest groups in all three countries; we initiated a joint art show that brought together the works of Emily Carr (Canada), Georgia O'Keeffe (the United States) and Frida Kahlo (Mexico) and would tour throughout the continent; began a virtual museum project; supported the North American Youth Conference to be held in Montreal; and looked at how to develop links between North American women. Our lunchtime discussion on water led to an agreement to have it become the focal point of the next agenda.

Then time ran out. Because of my own decision to leave politics and the end of the government terms of Madeleine and Rosario, the trilateral process has fallen fallow. Our successors apparently didn't see it as a priority. Too bad. It was just getting interesting. It had a different footprint than the ideas of union prevalent in Europe. It recognized and respected the integrity, equality and contribution of each of the countries, and it embodied the notion of community building on a continental scale. Recognizing that the role of government has been changing from a traditional command role to one of facilitation, I saw the goal of the trilateral process as stimulating interaction by many players at many levels of government, the private sector and civil society. One of the purposes of setting up a Web site, examining ways to link aboriginal groups, helping to establish a higher education cooperative and setting women's issues as a priority was the need to strengthen the network of associations in North America, to complement the activity of the environmental and labour commissions of NAFTA and the various trade and commercial connections on the economic level.

Such active organizational life between the individual and government is crucial to democracy, but there must also be anchor institutions to provide basic rules and a framework. We hadn't yet looked at a new North American architecture, but issues such as water, resources management and security were of such a broad nature that one was in order. What form of trilateral agreements would lay a foundation for a new North American problem-solving, decision-making system? How would they embody the characteristics of forward thinking, planning and dispute resolution recommended in the Fraser report? Should there be further amendments to NAFTA to encompass a broader range of issues or should there be a separate set of treaties with accompanying institutions to ensure parity and equality of participation between the three partners?

In the book *The New Sovereignty*, Abram and Antonia Handler Chayes point out that treaties have traditionally recorded settlements between states on a bilateral or regional level. In recent decades, however, the focus has swung to multilateral arrangements to address complex social, economic, political and cultural problems. But at the centre, they say, "there is almost always a formal treaty—sometimes more than one—that gives the regime its basic architecture."[1] So what kind of treaty should be considered and how can we engage our North American partners in a joint examination?

The answer is a formal trilateral structure mandated by the three leaders, managed by the foreign ministers and operated through various tri-sectoral arrangements and agreements—an architecture of networks to reach solutions for specific problems.

This is a clear alternative to the present predilection for bilateral negotiation, favoured by the Bush administration, which doesn't like formal agreements anyway and is quite happy with a hub-and-spoke relationship. It makes far less sense for Canada and Mexico, which end up dealing with a powerful neighbour without the advantage of agreed rules and procedures and without the blocking leverage of working in concert. Both governments seem to be relying on some special dispensation from Washington based on close personal ties, acquiescence to American demands or building a special political base amongst Spanish-speaking Americans in the case of Mexico. But trilateral community and network building would be better. In December 2002 the House of Commons Standing Committee on Foreign Affairs and International Trade called for a three-wise-men review of the trilateral relationship. I hope the government will take this to heart.

IDEAS

Let me suggest some ideas that might form the basis for such a review, since for all the concern expressed about North American integration, not too much is done to look at the options. When there is serious public debate, it is usually from a narrow economic standpoint or with a fix-it mentality. Of course there are the radical notions promoting currency and customs union, a sure prelude to eventual statehood for Canada. But the April 2001 meeting between the three North American leaders about continental cooperation, with President Vicente Fox leading the call for closer ties, has shown few results. The trend in these endeavours is towards furthering interdependence without furthering governance that respects the uniqueness of each society. It is a blueprint for a continental commune dominated by a powerful leader. Alternatives are needed.

Let's start with energy security. One lesson arising out of September 11 is the need to lessen dependence on Middle East oil. Developing sustainable energy supplies has taken on increased importance. The Bush administration unilaterally announced an energy policy having major implications for both Canada and Mexico, as it involved tapping energy sources in both countries. It is a deeply flawed approach. The emphasis is on supply, with little focus on conservation. Proposals to drill in the Arctic National Wildlife Refuge and to beef up coal production fly in the face of environmental responsibility. There is also a wanton disregard for anything resembling partnership with the other two nations, each a major energy supplier. For example, U.S. legislation mandated an exclusive routing for a new northern pipeline through Alaska, ignoring other options that might be of interest to Canada.

Prime Minister Chrétien started a dialogue when he suggested that the Alberta tar sands were a potential source of new energy along with our abundant gas reserves and hydro power. But he also made the point that the tar sands development increases our output of carbon emissions, so we should be able to get credit for our efforts to supply the U.S. with clean fuel. This approach has been rejected by the Americans. Mexican officials are talking about a substantial increase in their oil output as one way of meeting U.S. demand and gaining needed cash flow. Thus, Canada and Mexico are in a position to be important partners in meeting American energy needs.

They're also in a position to lever considerations on a broader approach to energy supply. Painfully missing from the American self-sufficient energy policy is the need to incorporate renewable and alternative sources such as hydro power and wind, along with conservation measures to cut usage. There is, however, the Bush initiative to sink millions into research on hydrogen-fuelled cars offering some prospect for the future, and a potential base for trilateral discussions on how to move towards a hydrogen-based economy.

Such trilateral discussions incorporating both supply and demand issues might well lead to a more balanced and sustainable continental strategy in the energy sector. But both Canada and Mexico are nervous about formal arrangements for fear of a takeover. The result is that the planning is being done covertly, with major decisions being taken by Congress without due consideration of Mexican or Canadian interests and with little regard for the environment. Relying on a bilateral approach, cuddling with the administration or lobbying on the Hill, is missing the mark.

Central to any eventual North American strategy on energy is how to cooperate on climate change. Canada has ratified Kyoto, the Americans will not, and the Mexicans as a developing nation aren't required to, although they are eligible to participate in the Kyoto mechanisms for trading—clearly an asymmetrical situation. It is a source of much anguish in our own country, especially among high-intensity users of fossil fuel, who fear that meeting Kyoto quotas will carry additional costs and put them at a competitive disadvantage with American firms. A good part of the government's action plan to implement Kyoto is designed to relieve industry angst. One way forward would be to engage our North American partners in some joint, mutually beneficial initiatives.

Although Washington has reneged on climate-change quotas under Kyoto, the U.S. is still an adherent to the UN Framework Convention on Climate Change of 1991 requiring eventual action on its part. Mexico, while not bound by any climate-change agreement, still has a stake as a major producer of gas and oil. It also has a major interest in investing in conservation and reforestation projects. These varying circumstances need to be reconciled through joint planning, ultimately anchored in an agreement.

It can be innovative. The Task Force on Climate Change that I chaired for the Manitoba government recommended the idea of an emissions trading scheme for North America, using a market mechanism to exchange credits for emissions. Under Kyoto there is room for meeting obligations through "carbon sinks," agricultural land or forest areas that sequester carbon and take it out of the air. That creates a credit. As well, certain emission-reduction measures may take a particular country below the Kyoto threshold. When this happens, a jurisdiction such as Canada, which has a high level of emissions, can meet its obligations by purchasing such credits. Several pilot trading projects already exist in the U.S. and Canada. Mexico has shown an interest in such regimes as a way of raising funds for reforestation and conservation. The U.S. government's hydrogen initiative envisions the need for major investment in sesquetration. The credit scheme could form the basis of a broader strategy of sustainable energy development, with the government to set rules, the private sector to allocate resources and environmental groups to advance the reclamation projects for the purposes of sequestering carbon. Out of this could ultimately come an effective energy-environment strategy involving government, private sector and environmental groups. The North American Environment Commission is already in place. Give it a mandate to bring stakeholders together to work on an emissions trading scheme and related energy-environment proposals, such as hydrogen and carbon storage, and we will have a trilateral vehicle for ideas and innovation.

The same possibility for adapting an existing institution to meet contemporary continental problems is available in the International Joint Commission. How about not only broadening its mandate but taking the bold leap of asking Mexico to become a member? It could begin as an associate and down the road evolve into a full-fledged participant, just as the IJC itself might have to look down the road at its role as a dispute-resolution mechanism. Water will be either a touchstone for cooperation or a tinderbox for conflict among North Americans in the not too distant future. It would be wise to lay the foundation for a system of decision making that is respectful of everyone's interests and not just subject to sheer power politics.

Transportation corridors present a similar opportunity for new thinking. Initially the idea was for smart, green transit systems running north–south. But now border security is the priority. With a Maginot-line mentality, the official obsession following September 11 has been to apply ever greater control on the borders thus impeding the flow of people and goods. It is a daunting task considering the volume of movement and the diversity of transportation modes that need to be carefully monitored. The border becomes a bottle-neck unless ways are found to manage the control without erecting inefficient barriers. Stephen Flynn makes a persuasive case for rethinking the management of borders. He says that "developing the means to manage terrorist threats and other transnational muck that is contaminating the integrative process within the global community is essential, but we need to liberate ourselves from the notion that the border is the best place for accomplishing this. Indeed, an overreliance on the border to regulate and police the flow of goods and people can contribute to the problem."[2] In his view, one important way to control borders is to validate, in advance, those who are of low risk. The other is to develop a capacity to intercept potential illegal shipments of goods or suspicious individuals. This calls for a trilateral approach that builds a North American system of combined transport and intelligence, closely merged into a global network.

Why not combine the various objectives of security and green transportation corridors into a North American infrastructure program? The trick is to make it happen beyond the present piecemeal approach. The federal government has established the Working Group on Trade and Transportation Corridors. The 2001 federal budgets set aside $600 million over five years for infrastructure at border crossings, matched by a U.S.$700-million commitment under the Transportation Equity Act. There is consultation with stake-holders and border communities, yet there is little in the way of a broad-based plan, between the three countries. A series of continental corridors incorporating high-speed rail and highway transport, using the most advanced smart technology, applying energy-saving measures using dedicated trade lanes, could efficiently move goods and people, significantly reduce carbon emissions and ensure effective security control without adding to border checks. Increased security, productivity and economic stimulus all in one go.

The private sectors in the three countries have the most at stake, and could be asked to be part of the financing, much like with a toll-road system. Environmentalists should become part of the process, with the research community providing the green security technology. It's an exciting possibility. A trilateral body under the direction of all three governments and with the full engagement of their respective publics, with a mandate to examine the security-environmental-efficiency possibilities of corridor infrastructure: it could be the remaking of the continent.

What is evident is that to make all these proposals work there must be more equitable and effective financing of joint projects and a serious effort to provide direct assistance to deal with the impact of free trade on people. This will be a particularly difficult problem for Mexico as it tries to cope with large-scale dislocations in the rural areas as a result of the elimination of all tariffs in January 2003 while expensive subsidy programs in the U.S. remain intact. NAFTA as a trade deal never contemplated the kind of development program that is an essential ingredient of the EU's social program to help poorer regions reach some form of parity. The U.S. and Mexico have established the North American Development Bank to help fund environmental projects for a hundred miles on each side of the border. (Canada declined to join, arguing that such initiatives could be funded through the Inter-American Development Bank—simply a pretext for staying uninvolved.) This initial effort at North American development cooperation hasn't exactly been a paragon of achievement or effectiveness. It is poorly funded and poorly supported and hasn't created any impulse for joint efforts to resolve the horrendous cross-border water supply and sanitation problems. But it does provide the germ of an idea for a NAFTA regional development agency, administered along the lines of the NAFTA commissions, that could provide loans and direct funding for cross-border initiatives and help different areas adjust to trade impacts or simply cope with deep-seated poverty.

I would like to see Canada take the lead on such an enterprise. It would show the Mexicans that we are prepared to work at meeting some of the problems they face and it would address head-on some of the more intractable border problems they encounter with the U.S. Such a fund could also be used to develop a network of economic cooperation between indigenous peoples throughout the continent, assisting with technical aid and capital investment to help address the severe poverty in places like Chiapas and Oaxaca. (Such a concept was put forward by Phil Fontaine when he was

grand chief in Canada and was worked on by my advisor on aboriginal affairs, Chief Blaine Favel.) It could also draw in the private
sector to help finance infrastructure projects and enlist the established multilateral financial institutions. As a trilateral fund, it
would help build a sense of community.

This form of economic sharing would help to address perhaps
the most difficult problem facing the continental partnership, one
that will only grow in intensity—the migration of people across
borders. It represents the most serious source of disagreement currently between the U.S. and Mexico. The Mexican government is
becoming disillusioned by the unwillingness of the Bush administration to work out ways to regularize cross-border movement. Jorge
Castañeda, the first Mexican foreign minister appointed by
President Vincente Fox, resigned in January 2003 in protest after
the Americans reneged on promises to regularize the situation of
Mexican guest workers and illegal migrants in the U.S. Meanwhile,
immigration policy is being severely tested by the security requirements being imposed by the U.S. since September 11. Here we
can lead by example. Our farm worker program is a good model for
organizing the flow of workers across borders under proper regulation and control. Equally, the program we developed to give landed
status to family care workers (nannies) after they had lived in
Canada for a set period is an example of a workable program for
granting rights to those who have come into the country to perform a necessary economic function and over time and with good
behaviour earned the right to stay. These programs could become
the grounds for serious trilateral discussion to address the problems
faced by Mexicans without status.

Ideas, though, eventually need to be translated into action. So
the real test of any plan of action for a North American community
will be one of governance—how to get decisions made in a democratic way.

GOVERNANCE

Governing our border relations with the U.S. with skill is assumed
to be a Canadian trademark. President Kuchma's request shows

something of that expectation. But in fact we need to work on some new ideas.

Across the Atlantic there is the model of the European Community, which has evolved into a highly integrated continental union replete with its own supranational institutions, courts, tribunals and parliament that penetrate every aspect of daily life. As it expands its membership and attempts to adopt common policies in defence and foreign affairs, its weight as a counterpoint to North America could become more significant. Even now its members vote together in international meetings, and it increasingly works as a bloc in international relations (Iraq being the exception). There is a growing interest in our own country in following the European model for North America. Might be a good idea—if we didn't have the U.S. as the eight-hundred-pound gorilla in the North American cage. A European-style union including the U.S. would be so imbalanced as to be a farce.

So how do we form a structure of continental governance that serves our ends? What model might serve our needs ten, twenty, thirty years from now?

Let's think of going virtual, of building a North American e-community by creating an on-line democratic decision-making network. What if we jump over the twentieth-century style of centralized, hierarchical institutions adopted by the EU and build a wired (wireless) system to abet a decentralized direct democratic network in North America? At least we need to imagine what such a system might look like before we lock ourselves into the fortress mentality being prescribed by the centurion guards of security orthodoxy.

There are several ways in which the potential of IT might be used here. (Its larger application in international governance will be dealt with later.) First, information can become a prime tool in inducing compliance with agreements and ensuring transparency in managing complex cross-border exchanges and transactions. Too much of our present business gets lost in the murky, bureaucratic maze of intergovernmental relations and negotiations. Citizens are left out, bewildered by decisions that deeply affect their lives or business, whether they are woodworkers on Vancouver Island losing their livelihood because of arcane trade rules set by the U.S. or people trapped by new border security regulations. NAFTA trade panels are closed affairs; border consultations are kept under bureaucratic wraps. Indeed, the attitude in dealing with the public on border matters seems to be the same as for raising mush-rooms—keep them in the dark and sprinkle with fertilizer. This practice will only increase as homeland security requirements kick in and the Bush administration's efforts to curtail personal free-doms become endemic.

Requirements for disclosure and reporting, available through the Web, will be a necessity if we are to keep the system open and expose misuse and exploitation. I think of how public glare focused on the International Traffic in Arms Regulations case might have sped up resolution of that dispute and exposed the attempt to subvert our Charter. It would have been a sobering lesson for Canadians.

By providing instantaneous, comprehensive accounting of deci-sions and rulings, IT takes the regulatory process into the public realm. It can reassure against unfair advantage, and deter non-compliance. It can also allow interactive public input into negotiation and adjudication—a form of electronic town hall. The Web site we thought up in Santa Fe was a first step in trilateral electronic information sharing. It should be restored and expanded. If govern-ments are not interested, then let's look at joint sponsorship by the private sector, universities and the NGOs.

An information highway for virtual education and civic partner-ship, especially among young people, should also be part of North American governance. We need to know more about each other, explore our common heritage as North Americans, discuss shared problems, understand each other's positions and bond in forming consensus on controversial problems. I was on a talk-radio program broadcast out of San Francisco soon after returning from a human-itarian mission on the borders of Afghanistan. The host confronted me with a local newspaper story that cited a Stanford professor blaming Canada for the entry into the U.S. of the terrorists who attacked the World Trade Center and the Pentagon—a prime illus-tration of the ignorance that abounds on border security issues. These misperceptions are going to be clarified not through diplomatic notes or high-level negotiations but through person-to-person contact aided by the magic of the Internet and the multimedia.

A more constructive example took place between a group of schoolchildren in my former riding of Winnipeg South-Centre and a similar group of Mexican children in the border province of Monterrey. They hooked up an electronic exchange looking at the plight of the monarch butterfly, which resides in Manitoba in the summer and in Mexico in the winter—not too different from many Canadians who do the same thing. Unfortunately, the monarch was headed for extinction, because Manitoba farmers were using pesticides and because its nesting grounds in a forest reserve in Mexico were being overrun with tourists. These school kids mounted a campaign on the Internet to alert their respective publics. They even took their show on the road. At the 2000 Organization of American States meeting in Windsor, they showed foreign ministers from around the Americas not only how to save the monarch butterfly through joint action in curtailing the use of pesticides and limiting tourist activity but how young people can come together and mobilize across borders.

The potential for interaction is unlimited, the issues to be discussed manifold. Here, then, is a defining leadership role for Canada in an information-sharing agenda for North America.

In fact we could go one step further and undertake a program of external information to help prevent threats to security from criminals, traffickers and terrorists. The best protection is to enlist allies and associates in broad international networks and judicial systems to suffocate the problems at source. This type of network can be greatly aided by worldwide on-line connections. A vast array of private, non-government, on-the-ground observers can quickly parlay information about potential lawbreakers. One of the most successful projects we sponsored at DFAIT was called Human Rights Internet. It detailed human rights abuses around the world and how the authorities were responding to these transgressions. We also started a hook-up in the Caribbean that linked a number of local organizations that were battling drug trafficking. The effect of sharing resources and information was profound. The closed world of government intelligence, still too often kept cloistered in separate agencies and embargoed between countries, is not the only way of fighting international criminals.

Is this barking at the moon? Are information-based governance systems with electronic public participation, working towards institutional arrangements to manage water, energy, environment, transit corridors and youth networks, at all feasible in today's embittered, hard-nosed ideological straitjacket? Narrow-gauged bilateralism centred on building fences around the continent, bombing perceived foes, suppressing dissent and new ideas, rejecting international agreements and architecture, providing extra resources for police border guards and military hardware—these hardly seem the portents of an era of creative statecraft in ordering our relations with the U.S.

It wouldn't hurt to try, especially when preserving one's freedom of action is at stake. Also, atmospherics change; the overwhelming preoccupations with al-Qaeda and Iraq have a shelf life, and in the meantime thought must go into other pressing issues. At any rate, it's not necessary for governments to be the sole sires of many of these ideas. Setting up a North American Web featuring transparency and participation, for example, is just one project that lends itself to civic diplomacy undertaken by individual interest groups and corporations. Conservation of endangered species by a consortia of private foundations, firms and environmental groups; new partnerships in water between corporations and NGOs; developing global networks to sell organically grown commodities like tea and coffee from poorer regions are all emerging examples of non-governmental community building. What's needed is to break the discussion out of the conventional ruts.

THE MEXICAN CONNECTION

Finally, developing a strong and inclusive partnership between Canada and Mexico is the key to advancing a progressive agenda in North America. The Mexicans have as great an interest as we do in managing continental integration while maintaining their own identity and freedom to act. Fear of overdependence on the U.S. still runs strong in Mexico, along with a recognition—similar to our own—of the advantages of close ties with the U.S. We have a mutual interest in developing common positions.

To make that work, we have to substantially upgrade our work both with Mexico's government and with its various civic and business sectors. This is a country that still doesn't have much visibility for Canadians—except for the 200,000 snowbirds who travel there in winter and see it primarily as a place of warm beaches, hot food and old ruins. There is increasing business activity, especially along the maquiladora, where goods can be shipped duty-free back into the U.S. and Canada after being assembled by low-cost labour. Prime Minister Chrétien has led some high-profile trade missions there, and our embassy has branched out; it is now one of the major diplomatic posts in our system. Generally, however, there is a low level of contact and communication, with virtually no media coverage and limited research or attention.

This is regrettable, as Mexico is going through significant economic, social and political change. The Zedillo government presided over a remarkable reform of its electoral machinery, paving the way for a defeat for the PRI party after generations in power. Under President Vicente Fox, a social transformation is under way in the ranks of Mexican indigenous people. They are migrating in large numbers from south to north, shifting the population base, and there is a growing assertion of rights at the grassroots level. Finally, Mexico's economic dynamism will soon lead it to surpass us as the number-one trader with our mutual neighbour.

My own experience has been that Mexicans at a number of levels are eager to form close ties with Canada. Mexico played a crucial role in many of the initiatives we sponsored internationally, and the new Fox government has been on the cutting edge of North American cooperative activity. Even on aboriginal problems there have been remarkable exchanges. At first the Mexican authorities were extremely nervous at the idea of having Canadian aboriginal leaders visiting their counterparts in Mexico to talk about development and self-government. When they saw how effectively this program transferred skills and lessons, they became enthusiastic backers. The resulting social contacts and economic links have been a two-way benefit.

Mexico and Canada can work well together. Indeed we must, or suffer the consequences of being divided. Each of us has certain strengths to bring to the table. The Mexicans have a better political association and diplomatic presence in the U.S. We have our own contact list, a highly sophisticated population, effective communication talents and the financial resources to be a sponsor and innovator. Our memberships in the G-8 and the international finance institutions are critical to the Mexicans. Increasingly, we share common interests internationally. During the intense UN negotiations over Iraq, Prime Minister Chrétien paid a visit to Mexico and suggested that they, as members of the Security Council, put forward a Canadian compromise solution to break the impasse between the permanent five members. This resulted in closer consultation by our respective UN delegations and warmed up our sense of collaboration. Visiting Mexico in March 2003, I suggested that, because of our increasingly mutual interests, Mexico should become a member of the Human Security Network. If we mesh our efforts, a potent combination can push a North American community agenda. And, where the Americans are not interested or are busy doing other things, there is nothing to stop our two societies from working together on water, immigration, environment, energy and transportation and otherwise forging international partnerships.

GOING GLOBAL

The prescriptions that have been presented here are not enough. This is our holding action; it protects home base. We are still faced with the overwhelming reality of powerful economic forces and compelling U.S. demands for political conformity. There is no need to give in. There is scope for innovation. And it is important to persevere; without such efforts, the sucking sound you hear will be Canada sliding into the great American melting pot. But to break free from the constraints of our geography and the dominance of our friendly neighbour, we need to go global. We need to take full advantage of our assets, our reputation, our smarts as a country to carve out a role in international organizations. It is through these associations that we can enhance our bargaining position in dealing with bigger states.

PART IV

Human Security

CHAPTER 6

THE OTTAWA PROCESS

––––––––

PART OF MY POLITICAL CREED WAS FORGED WHILE PLAYING FOOTBALL for Sisler High in Winnipeg many long years ago. As a fullback I was expected to grind a few yards up the middle and provide blocking for the quarterback. That's a pretty good way of describing the role of a member of Parliament, or even a minister—make a few short gains and protect the leader. But Coach Al Kornberg (who went on to become a distinguished political scientist at Duke University) said to me, "Always look for that rare moment when a small sliver of light appears in the opposing line." Then there is a chance to break into the open field and run like hell. Timing and opportunity are crucial. That is what happened to us in the campaign for a treaty to ban the use of anti-personnel land mines: we looked for the light, saw the opening, did some broken field running and made a score. It's an example of how we Canadians can make a difference.

AT THE STATION

In the downtown core of most Canadian cities, there is usually an imposing, pseudo-Greek classical stone building that once served as the central railway station—a symbol of the dominance once

~ *126*

exercised by the major railway companies in these communities, not unlike today's massive, arching bank towers. Some still perform their original function, but generally they have been converted to a more contemporary use as a shopping mall, gentrified apartments or office space. In Ottawa, a historically conscious Trudeau government redid the space into a conference hall, just a stone's throw from Parliament Hill. Most Canadians recognize it as the site of innumerable federal-provincial meetings, where premiers ganged up on the prime minister. (It will soon become a museum.)

It was here on a Saturday morning, October 5, 1996, that the Ottawa Process on Landmines was launched. The result was a treaty signed by 122 countries—now up to 143—banning the manufacture, use and export of anti-personnel land mines. Promoting, negotiating and implementing the land-mine treaty gave Canada both a new role and a distinctive voice on international matters and helped reshape certain of our assumptions governing global affairs. The old railway station thus stands out as a locale where a threshold was crossed.

The National Conference Centre, as the building is called, became in those mid-autumn days of 1996 the meeting place of representatives from more than seventy countries, a large delegation of NGOs and several officials from the UN and the International Red Cross. The session was unusual, as international meetings go, as each of the participants had equal standing at the table regardless of their status or position. Mine victims sat next to ministers discussing strategy, reflecting an emerging sense of partnership between government and civil groups.

The event had been organized under Canadian auspices out of a series of meetings around the world to mobilize support for a ban on land mines. It had been conceived as a fairly small gathering to promote an action plan. But, as the meeting time approached, momentum grew. It was no longer a low-key undertaking; it had begun to attract the interest of a wide range of countries and NGOs.

Two things had happened to bring matters to a boil. First, the campaign against anti-personnel land mines, begun in earnest in the early 1990s, had by 1996 reached a high level of intensity. The driving force was a powerful amalgam of humanitarian groups that included the International Red Cross, several NGOs interested in both arms control and human rights, and a number of committed individuals, many of them victims of land-mine explosions or the relatives of victims. They came together in 1992 to form the International Campaign to Ban Landmines, directed by Jody Williams, a community organizer from Vermont. She had been hired by Bobby Mueller, the head of Vietnam Veterans of America, to give an international complement to the campaign against land mines that his organization was waging in the U.S.

The role played by the Vietnam Vets in the international coalition highlights a fact often overlooked by those critics of the Ottawa Process who cite it as a cause of friction between Canada and the U.S.: leadership on the issue owed a great deal to many Americans. In addition to Mueller, Williams and other strong advocates such as Areyh Neir and Steve Goose of Human Rights Watch, there was the sterling figure of Senator Patrick Leahy of Vermont, who succeeded in 1992 in getting a moratorium on land mines passed in the U.S. Senate, as well as funding for de-mining. He became a strong supporter of the Ottawa Process and constantly urged his friend Bill Clinton to sign the treaty. Late in President Clinton's term, the senator invited me to his sixtieth birthday party, held at Bobby Mueller's Washington home, hoping we could use the occasion to lobby Clinton to sign on before leaving office. It was a great party, and the president was in an expansive mood and highly complimentary about the success of the land-mine effort. But in Clintonesque fashion he was still not ready to move.

This close association with key American members of the movement is one of the reasons that I tried hard to bring the U.S. onside. I thought the extraordinary effort of these Americans deserved some equal effort on our part to have their country become a signatory. We continue to work together on the issue.

What the coalition managed to do, working in company with a large number of affiliate groups strung across the globe, was earth moving. At the end of the Cold War, land mines were an accepted part of virtually every country's military arsenal, subject to some desultory arms control negotiations but barely on the radar screen of governments. Within a few short years, the combined efforts of various non-governmental groups succeeded in turning it into a humanitarian issue commanding worldwide attention. It was an early demonstration of how civil society can raise the profile of issues and mobilize public support at a global level.

Their strategy was to focus on the risk of these weapons to individuals, thus taking it out of the obscure realm of diplomatic and military arms control language, and homing in on the destructive impact on innocent civilians. They had a good case. Land mines were an invisible killer of non-combatants. Traditionally sown by armies for protection against a foe, they remain on the ground long after the conflict is over, presenting a huge danger to an unsuspecting passersby.

In parts of France, mine ordnance left over from the First World War is still surfacing and being destroyed. The Vietnam War, fought under the glare of global media, drew increasing attention to the destructiveness of land mines for both soldiers and civilians. And in the nasty conflicts of the 1990s, such as Angola, Mozambique, Congo, Uganda and Bosnia, the use of land mines as a weapon directly targeted at non-combatants, as a means of intimidation or control, became all the more apparent.

Statistics told a grim story. The U.S. State Department estimated that in the mid-1990s there were eighty-five to ninety million land mines planted in more than sixty countries.[1] Human Rights Watch calculated between five and ten million land mines were produced a year.[2] The estimated casualty rate of this epidemic was in the order of thirty to forty thousand a year, with the most destruction in Third World countries. Alex Vines, a researcher at Human Rights Watch, calculated in 1998 that in southern Africa alone there were some twenty million land mines.[3] Land mines had claimed more than 250,000 victims in that region since 1961. The cost of cleaning up and de-mining is so high, and the care of the victims so expensive, that post-conflict development in many of these poorer regions is itself handicapped. It is estimated that in Mozambique alone treatment of land-mine victims accounted for 30 per cent of the annual health budget.

Even today, with the treaty in place and the destruction of more than thirty-four million stockpiled mines, and with the substantial drop or complete halt in use in key countries such as Angola and Sri Lanka, the carnage continues. Landmine Monitor, a reporting network set up by the International Campaign, estimates that in 2001 there were still between fifteen and twenty thousand casualties, 70 per cent of them civilians. Increases in death and injury occurred in places like Afghanistan, where the numbers were up from 1,114 in 2000 to 1,368 in 2001; in Colombia, where the casualties more than doubled year over year; and Chechnya, where it is reported that there are thirty to fifty episodes of injury or death a month. Just as serious is the inadequacy of facilities for treatment. Despite the average of $225 million spent each year on various aspects of de-mining assistance and rehabilitation, Landmine Monitor reports some forty countries still don't have the proper facilities to treat victims.[4]

The public's attention was gripped, however, not by the statistics but by the words and experiences of the victims. A unique partner in the coalition was the Landmine Survivors Network, which brings together survivors, their family members and aid workers. They began appearing in front of international bodies, describing the land-mine experience first-hand and making a direct pitch to governments for assistance to victims. Their stories were greatly enhanced for the media by words of support from the Pope and the involvement of celebrities such as Princess Diana. A small, sad footnote to the Ottawa Process was that the day I sent an invitation to Princess Diana to come to the signing ceremony in Ottawa was the day her car crashed in the Paris underpass.

The importance of telling the human story was brought home to me directly during a trip to Lebanon. I visited a rehabilitation hospital, close by the ancient city of Tyre, that specialized in the treatment of land-mine victims. There I met a teenage girl who had lost her left arm in a particularly pernicious way. She had been walking in a tree-covered area of her father's farm when she spied a small, brightly coloured object shaped like a butterfly. She picked it up, thinking it would make a good toy for her younger brother. Inside the plastic cover was an explosive device that was detonated by the heat of her hand. It was a form of land mine that could be dropped in large numbers from an airplane and was clearly designed to entice children, hardly a weapon that could in any way be military in its purpose unless one is evil enough to think injuring or killing innocent children has a military purpose. I imagined my son Steve walking in a field and picking one up.

The doctors at this hospital explained that for the children victimized by these weapons the worst result was not physical. Modern prosthetics could restore most of their physical facility. The most serious consequence was psychological trauma, the aftermath of being suddenly mutilated, of having their lives drastically changed for no reason. This required careful, often prolonged counselling.

The public and policy-makers alike could understand this kind of narrative. The International Red Cross played an essential role in documenting these cases and demonstrating the widespread damage. They pointed out that land mines hidden in the ground or undergrowth of countless terrains prevent any form of development or cultivation. They are thus a serious impediment to economic renewal in wartorn countries. The Red Cross was also able to amass strong testimony from various military experts, including Gen. Norman Schwarzkopf, the U.S. commander in the first Gulf War, about the limited military utility of mines. They simply don't offer much in the way of protection and are, in fact, often a great danger to troops.

Armed with such compelling documentation, the civil advocates mounted skilful campaigns to change the perspective and position of governments. Their approach was to concentrate on a number of targeted countries, mobilizing public support and following that up with direct lobbying. The coalition tried to enlist government involvement through educational conferences and building up close working relationships with sympathetic officials. At international meetings they did not necessarily confront, but used strong pressure in the corridors.

One example of this low-intensity but highly effective approach occurred when I was asked by Mines Action Canada to participate in an event on Parliament Hill at which the empty shoes of land-mine victims were piled in a heap. Pictures of the pile appeared in newspapers across the country. It was a graphic way of getting the message across, and illustrated the tough but non-confrontational style of the NGOs. The later awarding of the Nobel Peace Prize to the coalition and Jody Williams was apt testimony to the skilful role they played.

Governments began to pay attention. In 1992, the U.S. declared a moratorium on the export of land mines, and several governments followed closely with similar export bans. The French government called for a review of land mines at the UN Conference on Conventional Weapons. The Swedish government issued a call for a total ban. The Italian senate ordered the Italian government to pursue an end to the production of land mines, a significant move from a country that was one of the largest suppliers.

In his first speech to the UN General Assembly, President Clinton went so far as to call for an eventual elimination of anti-personnel land mines.[5] The president's groundbreaking statement was followed by a U.S.-sponsored resolution in the General Assembly that urged states to exercise a ban on exports and to undertake "further efforts to seek solutions to the problems caused by anti-personnel land mines, with a view towards [their] eventual elimination"—a significant change in policy for the world's largest producer and user of land mines. Soon after, Belgium and Norway announced total bans on the production, export and use of the weapon. The momentum was building.

A pivotal event took place in June 1995, when the first meeting of any magnitude to deal with the restriction on the use of mines was held in a mine-infested country, Cambodia. Its success in attracting widespread participation from developing countries gave the campaign a big global boost. Having the direct involvement of mine victims counterbalanced the position of countries such as China and India that opposed any limitation on mine use.

Around the world there was growing interaction between governments and NGOs and increasing media coverage. The fax machine and the cell telephone provided the civil groups with powerful organizing tools, and television brought into living rooms the poignant message that land mines were a deadly killer primarily of innocent civilians, not soldiers.

At the same time, however, there was a serious divergence of approach. Increasingly, the NGO activists, strongly supported by the influential International Committee of the Red Cross, took the position that only an outright ban or prohibition would end the suffering of so many victims. A few governments agreed, but the majority wanted to work at amendments to the 1982 UN Convention on Certain Conventional Weapons. The CCW treaty mentioned the need to protect civilians against land-mine destruction, but limited its purview to international, cross-border armed conflicts and had no compliance mechanism. The French initiative to convene a review conference of the CCW was agreed to, but after a series of prolonged meetings among the nation-state members of the UN Disarmament Conference (NGOs were kept outside the room), the CCW review proved a bust. The protocol that emerged was a weak, watered-down document. The UN system of disarmament negotiation, based on achieving full consensus, was, as so often, held hostage to the position of the most recalcitrant members. There was clear blockage by a number of states such as India, China, Cuba and the permanent five members of the Security Council, who wanted discussions confined to a forum they controlled.

Disappointment was high, and so was the level of frustration. There was growing support at the public level and a well-organized campaign, and a number of governments saw the need for substantial change but nowhere to make it happen. It was at this point that Mark Moher, our ambassador for disarmament, announced that Canada would host a meeting in Ottawa to plan follow-up strategy. Our government was eager to be involved. As early as 1994, my predecessor, André Ouellet, had begun to advocate to the defence minister, David Collenette, the idea of declaring a moratorium on the use of land mines by Canadian forces to demonstrate Canadian seriousness.

Our Defence officials didn't like the idea. At one point their response was a somewhat bizarre counter-offer to work on limiting anti-tank mines, but not the anti-personnel kind that maimed and killed humans. Eventually the Department of National Defence agreed to announce a moratorium on the export of anti-personnel mines (APMs).

Ouellet was not satisfied; Canada didn't export mines anyway. In November, he went public with his concerns and declared that Canada should destroy its stockpile of APMs and begin working towards a total ban. This caught a lot of people by surprise, especially at Defence headquarters. More important, it signalled a much more assertive policy for Canada and gave a mandate to Foreign Affairs officials to broaden their approach.

The Ouellet statement had a galvanizing effect on a small but highly involved coterie of officials in DFAIT. It was at that stage that I took over at Foreign Affairs. We began to look beyond the review meetings.

The issue of land mines was not new to me. During my time in opposition I had taken a special interest in the conflict going on in Central America and in several visits had seen first-hand the devastating effect of these weapons. I vividly remember the fear villagers had of stepping off marked paths. And on the outskirts of Managua I went to a small workshop where land-mine victims, mainly children or teens, were crafting from wood their own prosthetics. The sight of these young people struggling to restore some semblance of normalcy to their lives in very primitive circumstances is one that I shall never forget. It underscored how the various conflicts fought out in a variety of poor, underdeveloped places around the world, with weapons whose prime victims are innocent people, were an abomination that needed fixing. In December 2002, Celia Sanchez, a Nicaraguan NGO worker with land-mine victims, reported on the first class of forty land-mine survivors to graduate from a program that prepared them for the employment market, a program I had initiated with the Mexican government after the signing of the land-mine treaty. It was a sweet moment of satisfaction to know that the scene I had found so disturbing and touching several years ago in Nicaragua was now being corrected by a program emanating from the Ottawa Process.

We decided to give top priority to establishing Canadian leadership on the land-mine issue. Michael Pearson, my senior policy advisor, was to work with officials and keep me informed.

We developed a three-pronged approach. First was to give high-level attention to the strategy meeting being planned for Ottawa.

Second, we would step up diplomatic activity at the UN to establish Canadian engagement, and to invite participation in the Ottawa discussions—especially important because the U.S. was, as we have seen, showing a lively commitment of its own on land-mine matters. Third, we would continue working with the minister of defence and his staff to convince them of the importance of getting rid of the Canadian land-mine stockpile. I found David Collenette willing to work with us, and the personal ministerial contact that close proximity in cabinet brings was, I believe, key to gaining the buy-in of the Defence establishment. They went along even though they felt strong counter-influences from the Pentagon.

The announcement of the Ottawa session shifted the bailiwick of the land-mine movement away from Geneva. The battle over strategy was rejoined, with Canada at centre court. Most governments still favoured working through the UN disarmament structures, where the consensus rule applied. But those on the civil side of the movement saw this as a guaranteed recipe for stalemate. In Ottawa, the NGOs would be in the room, able to make their case. We were starting to challenge the accepted conventional procedures by which international decisions are made and to broaden the scope of participation.

When the meeting opened, no one was entirely sure what the result would be; there were just too many wild cards at play. The mixture of NGOs and government proved combustible. Jody Williams, the head of the International Campaign, supported strongly by other civil groups, challenged the view of the U.K., French, U.S. and Russian delegations that any negotiation must be confined to the established channels. Those governments didn't bend on this matter, and suspicion grew that this was a Big Power tactic to deflect serious efforts to achieve a ban. Assessments that I received from the chair of the meeting were pessimistic.

Two competing moods were at play in the corridors of the conference centre—an overwhelming sense of urgency and a growing feeling of frustration. These were feelings that I shared. I was also struck by the number of people not connected to the conference—local residents attending a Mines Action Canada concert—who came over to express their strong desire that we in Canada take a lead. They were speaking, I think, for a significant constituency in the country that believes that it is in the promoting of humanitarian initiatives that Canada can play a constructive role. They are not the wiseacres who write learned commentary in academic journals about how to advance our national interest or who hold forth in editorials on how we should mind our manners in deference to our powerful allies. Nor are they the hard-edged Ottawa thirtysomethings who play at the power game. They are just ordinary Canadians who want to do the right thing.

My own resolve was certainly strengthened by this sign of public support, and enhanced by the experience of trying to answer my young son's question as we toured a mine exhibit: Why would anyone use such weapons to kill children? There was no acceptable answer. But it did raise the question of what we could do. How could we avoid the same cul-de-sac that had stymied all previous efforts? We needed a catalyst. On Friday evening, as the conference began to wind down, I assembled a group of senior officials and staff in my tenth-floor office. The next afternoon was to be the wrap-up to the meeting and I was scheduled to give the benediction. What should I say?

It was then that a senior official—Paul Heinbecker, then the new assistant deputy minister for global affairs—mentioned that the land-mine team at the arms control division in DFAIT had been bandying about the possibility of short-circuiting the conventional process and setting up a separate track leading to a treaty banning mines. This was certainly not the diplomatic thing to do. There had been no time to prepare the groundwork, and there would be opposition from some very powerful players. It would be seen as an audacious, even impudent, step for Canada to take, since we would be breaking the rules of accepted international behaviour and running the risk of falling flat on our face. Yet, in the absence of anything better, it was worth a look. I asked officials and staff to gauge potential support and to draft remarks for an announcement. Then I went home to sleep on the idea.

The next morning we reconvened in an anteroom behind the main conference hall. Sitting around a small table was a crowd of officials, in particular Jill Sinclair, director of DFAIT's arms control and disarmament division, and Ralph Lysyshyn, the conference chair, who had been taking soundings and were confident that we could gain support from the NGOs and, importantly, from the president of the International Committee of the Red Cross, Cornelio Sommaruga. There would also be a core group of states that had been working together on the land-mine issue, even though some of them might resent our taking the lead. Could it succeed, given tough opposition from the large powers? No one knew. But what was impressive was that these officials, usually the voices of caution and prudent counsel, were ready to give it a go.

U.S. President Harry Truman is famous for his saying that "the buck stops here." That morning in the crowded backroom of the old Ottawa railway station, I understood what he meant. There was no one else to pass the decision on to. I said, "It's the right thing. Let's do it."

LEAVING THE STATION

As the session drew to a close on Saturday afternoon, with delegates voting on a declaration and an action plan, I was waiting in the wings to deliver the closing remarks with more than a twinge of nervousness. I knew I would be committing Canada to a course of action that defied traditional diplomatic niceties and procedures and challenged the positions of the permanent members of the Security Council. It would require an enormous expenditure of time, resources and diplomatic capital. Yet, without it, the land-mine campaign was headed towards a standstill.

Some necessary calls and contacts had been made. Peter Donolo of the Prime Minister's Office gave the green light. UN Secretary-General Boutros Boutros-Ghali gave his blessing. A handful of key delegates were given advance notice. But the circle of communication was limited to forestall any attempts to waylay the plan.

Finally, Ralph Lysyshyn asked me to the podium. I went through the normal list of thank yous and words of appreciation, and then concluded: "The challenge is to see a treaty signed no later than the end of 1997. The challenge is to the governments assembled here to put our rhetoric into action. . . . The challenge is also to the

International Campaign to ensure that governments around the world are prepared to work with us to ensure that a treaty is developed and signed next year."[6]

The reaction in the hall was a mixture of surprise, applause and incredulity. The NGO contingents rose to their feet. The representatives of many governments sat in their seats, too stunned to react, several barely suppressing their anger and opposition. In the press conference afterwards, the Canadian media weren't quite sure what to make of it all. They knew that we had stepped out of the box, but they couldn't decide if this was a bold stroke or if I had just lost it. The crucial question was how many countries we expected to follow our lead and show up in Ottawa in just over a year's time to sign a treaty banning land mines.

The simple answer was that we didn't know. We weren't working from a well-developed playbook; it was more like calling an audible at the line of scrimmage. But it wasn't purely impetuous, either. We had the political will to make it work, and the elements for an effective campaign were in place. The task ahead was to meld these elements into a coherent strategy and develop momentum in a very short period. Or, as one official put it as we left the conference centre, "How do we get the train to leave the station?"

Three tracks were laid. First, we had to launch a credible negotiating process among governments. We needed a sufficient number of governments to ratify the treaty to make it an effective international instrument, so we started by enlisting a core group of countries, beginning with Austria, Norway, South Africa, New Zealand, Switzerland, Belgium and Mexico, to act with us as a coordinating team. With them we would host a series of diplomatic sessions that would both shape the elements of a treaty and emphasize the humanitarian, human security message about the damage to people. An appeal to conscience and common sense would put the opponents of the treaty, especially those arguing military utility, on the defensive.

The second track was to develop a close working partnership with the NGOs and international organizations such as the Red Cross that had already displayed an impressive ability to mobilize opinion and pressure governments. Two thousand or so organizations in a coordinated network had brought increasing attention to the problem. Now this network had to be enlisted to focus on a treaty process.

If there was one lesson that I had learned over the years, it was the real power that organized people could exercise in presenting a case and energizing support. But there had to be synergy between the efforts of civil-based groups and sympathetic governmental officials. Only government could ultimately make legally binding decisions. Only government could tap into tax revenues to pay for such decisions. To be effective, government and NGOs had to be full partners.

This wasn't always easy to achieve. Often, citizen-based groups with singular goals get frustrated with what they see as the delaying tactics of government. They fail to accept the need to compromise or to balance competing interests. There is often a suspicion that self-interested economic forces limit the range of political choice and dominate the political game, and of course in this they have a point. As a result, they are often wary of getting too close to government and prefer to play the role of independent advocate and critic.

On the government side there is equal unease and sometimes downright hostility. Many politicians are irritated that people they see as self-appointed spokespersons for specific causes are usurping their role as elected representatives. They smart under the criticisms and resent what is often perceived as a tendency to self-righteousness or ideology on the part of interest groups. In the bureaucracy, there is frequently a reluctance to accept the advice and position of NGOs, simply because the officials feel they know more and don't like to share their decision making. (This bureaucratic view often cuts off politicians as well.) So there tends to be a mutual agreement to keep a distance, operate in different spheres and intersect only on specific issues with a greater or lesser degree of cooperation. With land mines we saw an opportunity to rewrite the script.

The need to fast-track the treaty was a compelling reason to develop a close collaboration, with the NGOs organizing public meetings and mobilizing direct pressure on parliaments and cabinets, while the core group of governments worked the diplomatic circle and funded the NGOs.

Drafting the treaty itself was a fully shared exercise, which led to moments of tension between the partners when it got down to the trade-off between the purity of the treaty and the need to sell it to the largest possible number of governments, especially the U.S. In broad strokes, however, there was a common front. The message here is that in unity there is strength. There is great value in finding the means to cooperate, even though it may require some accommodation of positions, especially on the part of the civil groups, and some flexibility, especially on the part of governments, on matters of status and rank. The reward is an alternative model of problem-solving networks incorporating government and non-government actors that has many advantages over both the present fashion for large-scale world conferences with casts of thousands engaged in a wild melee of activity, and massive protests and demonstrations at every international gathering.

The aim was to influence specific leaders one by one. There were no mass meetings or barricade confrontations. The public pressure was highly targeted, aimed at securing agreement by individual governments to a well-defined objective. One day I received a call from a European foreign minister asking if I could help turn off the deluge of faxes from all over the globe that was flooding the offices of legislators in his country. I told him it wasn't in my purview to do. The message was being delivered.

The third track in our strategy, one often overlooked, was to get the full approval and commitment of our own government. We couldn't play a leadership role if it didn't have full backing within our own political system. This involved getting rid of our own stockpile of mines, recruiting ministers and parliamentarians in the diplomatic process and gaining financial resources to fund a serious downpayment on a global mine-action program. On the diplomatic front, the two secretaries of state, Christine Stewart, who looked after Latin America and Africa, and Raymond Chan, who had responsibility for Asia, were especially helpful, as were innumerable members of Parliament who lobbied their counterparts abroad.

The key to achieving this commitment was the prime minister. As discussed previously, in foreign affairs, prime ministerial approval, or at least acquiescence, is essential. And it is particularly so when cooperation among various elements of the government is required. Fortunately, the prime minister was a backer of the initiative, having first raised the land-mine issue at the G-7 meetings in Halifax in 1995. He pitched the treaty to his counterparts at various international meetings, and later made a special effort to enlist President Clinton during the crucial Oslo discussions. He was also instrumental in securing approval from cabinet for a $100-million special fund to be used as a powerful signal of Canada's commitment. This was not an easy sell at a time when program review was slashing departmental expenditures; it wouldn't have happened without the prime minister's intervention.

The most serious obstacle we had to overcome on the home front was gaining agreement on eliminating our own stockpile of land mines. This was something that had to be worked out with the defence department, and it was not easy. The military had gone through the bruising experience of the Somalia inquiry and were still smarting from cutbacks to their budget. They weren't in a good frame of mind to respond to a request to abandon what many still felt was an essential part of their arsenal, although they hadn't deployed mines since the Korean War. Art Eggleton, the new minister of defence, proved very helpful in bringing Defence officials to an agreement. One of the carrots offered was that part of the $100-million land-mine fund could be allocated to research at the Sheffield testing range in Alberta to look at alternatives to land mines. Another compelling factor was the experience of our troops in the Balkans with land mines. There had been serious accidents; in one case a Canadian soldier, Mark Isfeld, lost his life removing land mines in Croatia. His family attended the October 1996 meeting in Ottawa and made a very moving presentation that struck a sympathetic chord among our own soldiers.

In Canada, our senior officer corps doesn't exercise the same independent political influence in government that the Pentagon does in the United States. Canada's generals have an effective lobby on Parliament Hill, they skilfully fund a network of think-tanks and university centres that help propagate their cause and they rightly enjoy the respect of the public for their peacekeeping and their achievements in response to civil disaster. This gives them a position of substantial influence. But they are still generally responsive to civilian policy-makers and don't have the veto power of their American counterparts. In the land-mine case, the U.S. military establishment joined with conservative legislators to block the efforts of the Clinton administration in pursuing a ban. Many of our senior generals shared the views of their American counterparts but did not stand in the way when cabinet decided to phase out our stockpile, a decision that made our leading role possible.

On November 7, 1997, in a Defence testing range outside Ottawa, the prime minister, Art Eggleton and I, along with Jody Williams and representatives of Mines Action Canada, presided over the explosion of the last remaining land mines held by Canada. We watched the weapons disappear in a whoosh of smoke. It was a major milestone in advancing our case.

On the diplomatic front, after meetings in Vienna to consider the wording of a treaty, in Brussels to enlist commitment to a total ban and in Germany to look at the issue of verification, the various elements of a treaty were in place. Norway agreed to host the all-important negotiating session in Oslo, in September 1997. In all these meetings, a core group of medium-sized and smaller countries with no great-power pretensions worked together with increasing unity of purpose, backed by Germany as a big-nation supporter. We also got lucky with the inner-circle states of the Security Council. The election of Tony Blair's government in Britain and of Lionel Jospin's socialist government in France led to major changes in those countries' positions, and they became backers, unlike their conservative predecessors.

The same momentum was seen in other regions. In February, the South African government unilaterally announced a total ban on land mines, just before convening an NGO conference on land mines in Maputo. This was followed by a similar declaration by the Mozambique government during the conference. These were crucial decisions, coming from countries that were the sites of extensive land-mine pollution. It signalled that this was not to be another

Western enterprise foisted on the developing world. Countries that had provided surrogate conflict zones in the Cold War, and were still on the receiving end of mine weaponry from northern countries, which produced 80 per cent of the world's mines, were prepared to take a lead. Here was a cause that was clearly in the interest of the developing world.

South Africa, under Nelson Mandela, who undoubtedly had the benefit of advice from his partner, and child advocate, Graça Machel based on her experience in Mozambique, went to work on persuading other African states. As a result, forty-three Organization of African Unity members pledged their support. The same kind of regional consensus was forming in the Americas. Again, the experience of living and dying with land mines proved to be a powerful motivation for Central American and Caribbean countries. In the end, from the Western Hemisphere, only the U.S. and Cuba didn't sign. A tougher sell was required in Asia, where there was entrenched opposition from countries such as China, India and Korea, the latter reflecting the strong commitment of both its own government and the U.S. to using mines in the Demilitarized Zone separating north from south.

An important breakthrough was the conversion of Japan to support for the treaty, due primarily to the personal endeavour and political courage of the foreign minister (soon to be prime minister), Keizo Obuchi. We first met at the G-7 meetings in Lyon, where we began to discuss human security issues, including land mines. His own bureaucracy was strongly opposed, but he became a believer and pushed through a commitment for Japan to play an active role. (I will always remember his gracious invitation to my son and me to attend the opening ceremonies of the Nagano Olympics, where there was a graphic and colourful commemoration of the land-mine treaty. I mourn the loss of such a fine statesman.)

The more than ten regional meetings held before the drafting session in Oslo could never have happened without our worldwide network of diplomatic missions. Strained though they were by budget cuts, these offices, housing Foreign Affairs and CIDA officials, became essential links in mobilizing a global effort in a short period. That we maintain connections in all regions of the globe gives us an enormous asset in pursuing significant international activism. If we were to become overly focused on just our own immediate neighbourhood, as is argued by those who see our foreign policy primarily through a North American prism, we would lose this ability to be a global player.

The place where all this preparation would receive its major test was Oslo, where the draft treaty would be negotiated before going on Ottawa for signature in December. The run-up to the Oslo meeting was given a major boost when ninety-seven countries declared at the Brussels conference in late June that they would sign the treaty. A media campaign was launched, using the status of such people as Princess Diana, Desmond Tutu and the newly elected UN secretary-general, Kofi Annan, to raise the public profile of the issue. Intense lobbying continued in capitals around the world.

The major sticking point was the position of the U.S. As we have seen, President Bill Clinton had delivered a stirring call at the UN to end the tyranny of land mines, but his administration was hamstrung by its own domestic political circumstances, which had become increasingly hostile to any great leap forward towards a total ban on land mines. The 1994 election had given the Republicans control of the Congress, and they were dominated by very right-wing, anti-internationalist members drawn from their new power base in the South and Southwest. Senator Jesse Helms had become chairman of the Senate Foreign Relations Committee, and a more implacable foe of arms control, humanitarianism, multilateralism or allowing the U.S. to pay its UN dues would be hard to find.

Helms signalled his opposition to the land-mines treaty in an open letter to the president, and threatened retaliation through various forms of legislative harassment. He was not alone in his party. There was a strong antipathy among many Republicans to any form of international agreement that appeared to constrain the use of any options by the Pentagon. The prevailing sentiment in conservative think-tanks, and among many academics, was that the U.S. was big enough and strong enough to go it alone, and that collective international accords limit the U.S.'s freedom to advance its national interest. Even beyond conservative ranks, there was a general assumption that its status as sole superpower endowed the U.S. with both special responsibilities and special exemptions from international rules.

Buttressing American political opposition was the hard-line position taken by Pentagon officials. They skilfully centred their agreement to any treaty on three main conditions: the exclusion of Korea; an exemption for anti-personnel mines used as protective devices for anti-tank mines; and a delayed timetable for the treaty coming into effect. The Clinton administration was reluctant to take on the senior military over specific items of military advice. As much as there was a general commitment to the idea in the administration, the land-mine issue didn't appear to be worth a confrontation with an antagonistic congressional majority and the Joint Chiefs of Staff.

This was an administration that came into office without a firm set of foreign policy goals or guidelines. The focus was on "the economy, stupid," and the limited effort devoted to international matters was taken up with the deteriorating situation in the Balkans, and with Haiti, both involving the deployment of U.S. military forces against the will of the Pentagon decision makers. The Americans weren't alone in wrestling with the new reality of the post–Cold War world of internal war and humanitarian disasters, yet they were caught in the vise of having the necessary capability to mount international missions but neither the political will nor the support of their military. If there was any foreign policy preoccupation, this was it. As a result, they simply didn't comprehend the head of steam building towards a total-ban treaty and discovered to their surprise in late spring that they were on the outside.

In March 1997, I raised land mines with Madeleine Albright, the new secretary of state, and expressed my hope for U.S. participation in the treaty-making process. At our first meeting, she expressed her own support, but reiterated the standard State Department response that they preferred the Geneva conference route. However, as the Americans became more aware of the progress of the Ottawa Process, she and I initiated talks at the senior officials' level during the summer. In the meantime, however, the Brussels conference had set a high threshold for the treaty, calling for a total ban without exceptions or modifications. This made it very difficult at such a late stage to work out language that might allow the Americans to become part of the process. In a letter to other governments, Madeleine announced that Washington would participate in the Ottawa Process, which was a big step forward, but said that the U.S. would be seeking changes to the draft treaty based on their three main conditions.

The Oslo meeting began on September 1 with eighty-seven full participants and thirty-three observer nations. The dominant undercurrent was the issue of American demands for change, and whether having the U.S. as part of the convention outweighed the consequences of accepting their modifications. The president of the meeting was Jackie Selebi, a highly respected South African diplomat, but not someone who was prone to accommodating the Americans. He shared the view of many that this was simply a U.S. tactic to delay or even scuttle agreement. The civil groups blitzed the media in Oslo, arguing strenuously against any amendment to meet American demands. There were, however, strong advocates for responding to the American position. Japan, Australia and Ecuador in particular argued for the necessary time to get the U.S. on board.

This put us in the centre of a dilemma. We wanted the Americans in, but not at the price of watering down the draft convention. In my speech to the Oslo meeting, I stated that there should be no major exceptions or amendments to the text that had been carefully developed over the preceding eleven months. Where there might be room for accommodation was in the entry-into-force terms, particularly as applied to Korea.

While the negotiations continued in Oslo, the phone lines were busy between Ottawa and Washington. I was conversing with Madeleine Albright and Sandy Berger, head of the National Security Council; the prime minister spoke to the president. We were asking for U.S. flexibility in return for an entry arrangement that would allow them time to make a change in the Korean DMZ. Word of these discussions got back to the meeting in Oslo, and rumours circulated that we were giving in to the entire American demand. When the U.S. delegation asked for extra time, I instructed

our delegation to agree, causing more charges that we were buck-
ling. Despite this rebuff from the NGOs, I still thought it possible
to find a way to bring the Americans in without damaging the
treaty, and that having them as signatories would be a big plus. The
telephone diplomacy continued, with the prime minister and me
on the phone to our respective counterparts well into the late
evening during the last twenty-four hours of the Oslo conference.
We came close to success, but ultimately the major stumbling
block proved to be not so much Korea as the Pentagon's insistence
on retaining an anti-tank mine system that used unconnected anti-
personnel mines as guards, rather than the systems used by other
armies, which wired them directly to the anti-tank device. Our
argument was that the U.S. defence department could use the connected devices. For a moment it looked as if this was going to work.
Sandy Berger called me about eleven p.m. to say that they would
likely be in. I went home, told my wife that we had something to
celebrate and broke open a bottle of malt Scotch. The feeling was
short-lived. At about one o'clock in the morning, I received another
call from Berger to say that the president had finally decided that
the opposition inside the Beltway would be too intense and that the
U.S. wouldn't sign. The malt Scotch came in equally handy after
that call.

The good news was that we had a draft treaty that enjoyed widespread support. Now all we had to do was to hold the coalition of
pro-ban states together with the NGO community until December,
and continue to press reluctant governments to sign. This effort
received a major boost on October 1 when Jody Williams and the
International Campaign to Ban Landmines were awarded the
Nobel Peace Prize for their work. The added attention helped win
over several governments.

BACK AT THE STATION

What a difference thirteen months could make. As I approached
the National Conference Centre in early December to join the
opening ceremonies of the second Ottawa land mine conference,
the place was abuzz with activity, almost a carnival atmosphere.

The cause of the commotion was the arrival of a bus carrying land-mine activists who had crossed several continents to get to Ottawa. In the surrounding crowd, a group of senior-citizen peace activists, appropriately named the Raging Grannies, was holding forth. A horde of media scrambled for a good visual. Passing by the melee and making their way into the hall was a steady stream of delegates, some of the twenty-four hundred participants. It was a far cry from the tense and anxious atmosphere that had filled the air in the small antechamber of the old railway building when we made the decision to launch the treaty process, against what seemed very difficult odds, just a little over a year before.

The ceremony that followed further highlighted the magnitude of what had been accomplished. After strong speeches by the prime minister, the UN secretary-general, Cornelio Sommaruga and Jody Williams—who gave us a stirring reminder that the power of civil society is a form of superpower in the making—my role in the program was to affix the first signature on the Convention on the Prohibition of the Use, Stockpiling, Production and Transfer of Anti-personnel Land Mines and on their Destruction—which I did with great pride and satisfaction.

My signature, on behalf of Canada, was followed by 121 others—an achievement that Prime Minister Chrétien remarked was "without precedent in international arms control or humanitarian law." Beyond the signatures were the endorsement of a major action plan and the pledging of more than $500 million for de-mining and victim assistance, a result of our officials having thought ahead to move implementation of the treaty forward before the ink was dry. The treaty was the framework to compel state compliance and cooperation. The next step was to give it substance. The flow and use of land mines had to be stopped; mines had to be removed; victims had to be rehabilitated, communities rebuilt.

Ratification was of course critical. We established the special office of ambassador for mine action, with Jill Sinclair as the first incumbent, and gave her a budget to support the ratification process. She had been involved from the outset, and her performance was superb. She had the right mix of skills to work with both governments and civil groups. We also established the private

Canadian Landmine Foundation to raise funds from the public for de-mining activity (it has become the sponsor of the very successful Night of a Thousand Dinners, which annually raises tens of thousands of dollars). And we organized a highly successful program of youth ambassadors to work in the schools to keep the issue alive for the next generation. My job was to continue jawboning at every chance I got with my ministerial colleagues, urging ratification. I also went on the speaking circuit in the U.S., where I spoke to international clubs, universities and foreign relations councils. The positive reaction I received demonstrated the value of extending our direct contacts beyond official circles in Washington to informed constituencies in the U.S. and through them to build support for human security initiatives.

Within fifteen months, we had the requisite sixty ratifications; on March 1, 1999, the treaty came into force. By July 2002, the number of states ratifying the convention was 125, with another 18 countries as signatories, bringing the total to 143 countries—three-quarters of the world's nations. In November 2001 the UN General Assembly passed Resolution 56/24m calling on all states to adhere to the Land Mine Convention by a vote of 138 for, none against and 19 abstentions. What is noteworthy about this vote is that twenty-four states that have yet to sign the treaty were among those that supported the resolution. It is also significant that three countries where there has been extensive use of land mines—Angola, Eritrea and the Democratic Republic of Congo—are now signatories.

Treaty provisions ensure compliance and transparency. Each signatory must submit a report that is monitored and verified by a network of NGOs. If one of the signatories believes that another country is cheating, a fact-finding mechanism can be activated. Its findings are submitted to a meeting of the signatory states, who can then authorize a series of enforcement actions, including a reference to the Security Council.

Even for those countries that haven't formally joined, the treaty acts as a regulator—a marker that measures their behaviour and stigmatizes non-compliance. Most noticeably, the U.S. has announced a ban on all exports and said that it will end all use of anti-personnel mines outside of Korea by 2003 and in Korea by

2006, although it must be said that this was a commitment made by the Clinton administration and one that the Bush regime has put under review. Similarly, Russia came very close to signing the treaty after talks between President Yeltsin and Prime Minister Chrétien and did declare a moratorium on the export of mines. Their use of land mines in Chechnya is a retrograde step. Even China has put a moratorium on exports. The annual Landmine Monitor includes assessments of how non-signatory states are meeting the standards of the treaty. Transgressors are named and shamed. This acts as a deterrent for many abusers of the treaty.

The influence of the treaty can also be seen in very practical ways. Casualty rates in Cambodia have dropped by one-third, and more than sixty square miles of land-mine-infested terrain have been cleared. In Bosnia, there has been a steady decline in the number of victims from a high of 625 in 1996. The number of nations producing anti-personnel mines has fallen from fifty-five to fourteen. Most surprising was a joint agreement between Israel and Jordan to begin mine clearance along their border, the only arms-control measure extant in the Middle East. But it isn't just the numbers that are impressive, nor are they the best indicator of the treaty's effect. What is important is that it limits the terror felt by people and communities. The Mines Survey Center believes that the priority for clearance should be based not on the number of mines (as some may be in remote areas) but on the potential impact on people. It then concentrates international resources on eliminating the fear caused by these high-impact areas, forming partnerships with local governments to slowly advance the de-mining into other, less severely affected regions. What is also happening is the increasing incidence of community de-mining. Poor people anxious to secure land do their own retrieval at a cost of very high casualties. Training programs are desperately needed.

There is of course a lot of tough sledding to go before the world is mine-free. De-mining is a costly, slow and dangerous business. Setbacks occur, such as the flooding in Mozambique and Hurricane Mitch in Nicaragua, where mines dislodged by rampaging waters were spread randomly throughout the terrain. With the onslaught of renewed conflict and fighting, there are also examples of recidivism from previous commitments and re-mining activities in places such as Chechnya and Afghanistan. And of course there is still the aberrant behaviour of certain countries that have stayed outside the treaty. In 2001 India laid land mines along a 620-mile border with Pakistan in a region of some half a million people. Already more than a hundred civilian lives are reported lost. Reports were made public that the U.S. stockpiled anti-personnel land mines for use in Iraq, a clear contradiction of the undertakings given by President Clinton that even though they were not signatories, they would abide by the terms of the treaty. Similar reports of the U.S. planting land mines in Afghanistan are now surfacing.

There is also the problem of maintaining governments' commitments to supply resources for ongoing work. With the world now preoccupied with fighting terrorism, money for humanitarian efforts is increasingly in short supply. Landmine Monitor identified $237 million in mine action funding in 2001, a decrease of about $4 million from 2000 and the first time since 1992 that a significant increase has not been registered.[7] It is increasingly evident that at current levels, many mine-affected signatory states will not meet the ten-year deadline for completion of mine clearance. In view of this, it was encouraging to see the Canadian government renew its commitments with the announcement of an additional $70 million for de-mining purposes over the next four years.

So much of the credibility of the land-mine treaty and what it stands for relies on progress and accomplishment to keep the flame alive—and that means maintaining a drive towards universality and continuing to aid victims, destroy stockpiles, extract the mines from the ground and pressure those who continue to use land mines as a weapon of war. It also means assessing what needs to be revised to make the treaty a live document relevant to its times and realities. One of the great features of the Ottawa Process was a willingness to dare, to take chances, to show that the traditional diplomatic refrain copied from J. Alfred Prufrock—"Do I dare disturb the universe? . . . Do I dare eat a peach?"—was no longer the watchword. The treaty can be improved, and its mandate extended into a land-mine treaty part two.

The treaty must begin to incorporate into its provisions the responsibility of non-state groups and hold them accountable for their use of land mines. Opposition rebel groups are reported to have used anti-personnel mines in at least fourteen countries in 2001–2002.[8] In my recent visit to northern Uganda, I saw how devious and destructive the device of booby-trapping people in the displaced persons camps can be; the weapons are used as a tool of revenge and intimidation. Alternatively, or as a supplement to signing the deed, non-state groups should be encouraged to declare their own mine bans.

The 2004 meeting of all those who are signatories to the treaty must also come to grips with such issues as the use of cluster bombs. Cluster bombs are intended to explode once they hit the ground; however, not all do. Similar to land mines, "they kill, maim and make land inaccessible long after fighting has stopped."[9] The NGO community has certainly come to realize the necessity of addressing this issue, and they are again vocal in leading the way: witness their calls for a moratorium on the production, use and trade of cluster munitions. It is time for government to get on with the unfinished business of ridding the world of these civilian-killing machines.

NEW DEPARTURES

As the Ottawa treaty conference came to an end, I sensed that for many participants this was a breakout from the dominance of big-power politics towards an agenda that would put people's needs ahead of the raw power interests of the state. The Ottawa Process had flummoxed the experts who didn't believe there was anything more at stake than the exercise of naked self-interest. But the question was, Did it augur a change in perspective or was it an aberration?

Given the shift away from the pre-eminence of the nation-state, and the transcendence of global economic and social trends, the time seemed ripe to exercise an independent role for Canada in focusing on individual needs. The success of the land-mine initiative gave us a concrete accomplishment in which the theory became practice. (At a university talk, a professor of political science challenged me on the human security idea, "which may work in practice," he said, "but does it work in theory?") We had demonstrated that it wasn't always necessary to have "a dog in that fight," to use James Baker's phrase, in order to motivate the public, civil groups and certain governments to pursue humanitarian policies.

The land-mine experience also showcased the potential for partnerships between governments, NGOs and international humanitarian organizations, where the whole became greater than the parts. The NGOs in particular lost their skepticism about government intentions when they saw that we were prepared to stick out our neck. For our part, it would have been impossible for governments to mobilize opinion and pressure the way the coalition did. The international organizations such as the Red Cross and UNICEF, usually reluctant to get into what is seen as political activity, were essential players in lending their credibility, knowledge and worldwide networks.

Bridges were built between the North and the South, and between governments of states that didn't have great-power status or its pretense. The alliances that were made built up confidence, familiarity, and contact and shared outlooks. The issue did not divide the developed nations against the developing, but in fact brought them together.

It also taught the value of working out these issues at the regional level. One of the difficulties in managing global issues is that we assume that they need to be decided in global forums, which are often unmanageable or subject to bloc political bargaining. The UN suffers from that syndrome, as do the massive environmental and economic meetings. When the land-mine issue got caught up in a UN disarmament forum, we decided to go outside that system. The negotiating and organizing was done through regional bodies that arrived at a global treaty that could then be brought back into the UN system.

For a country like Canada, working with such regional bodies or in organizations such as la Francophonie or the Commonwealth allows us to extend our reach. This is not always possible in large multilateral organizations dominated by bigger powers.

One example of how the land-mine portfolio was an enabling experience came at the first meeting of the state parties to the treaty, held in Maputo, Mozambique. It took place as the conflict in Kosovo was under way. Discussion over lunch turned to the Balkans, and several of the African ministers who had direct experience in such events pointed out that unless there was a crash program of humanitarian de-mining when the war ended and the refugees started heading back in large numbers, the casualties would be horrendous. This made obvious sense and was quickly relayed back to Ottawa for action. An idea generated in a southern African city, by a collection of ministers from North and South who shared a common interest in the issue of land mines, ended up saving many lives in a strife-torn region of Europe. Opportunity presents itself in many diverse ways in today's world.

We also learned something about how to more carefully nuance relations with our American neighbours, recognizing that there are many in the U.S. who are in sync with the liberal internationalist view that we in Canada generally espouse. Interpreting American views purely from a Washington perspective, as too many officials and commentators are apt to do, misses the opportunity to forge valuable alliances with like-minded Americans and tap into the powerful resources of their foundations, universities and civil organizations to apply pressure on Washington and help build worldwide networks. There will always be a degree of tension. They are a superpower, we are not. But I was surprised to find how many Americans respected Canadian efforts to move away from sheer power politics.

Soft power also got a major workout in the Ottawa Process. This concept, first elaborated by Joseph Nye, dean of Harvard's Kennedy School of Government, describes how the instruments of statecraft are not necessarily those of military might or economic heft. In many circumstances, the ability to influence the behaviour of others comes through persuasion, communication, negotiation or organization. No proposition of mine garnered more derision among the chattering classes than my advocacy of soft power—until the Ottawa Process showed that it worked. No one was threatened with a bombing. No economic sanctions were imposed.

No diplomatic muscles were flexed by the treaty's proponents. Yet a significant change was achieved in the face of stiff opposition.

Soft power cannot always work: the harsh realities of living in a tough, global neighbourhood sometimes require forceful measures. But using human security as a concept and soft power as a tool kit had produced a treaty that set out global norms for the protection of people. Could this lesson be translated to fit other global challenges?

Above all, the Ottawa Process was an act of exploration in a dramatically altered global landscape—searching for a new pathway to save lives. Before the Ottawa treaty, circumventing traditional diplomatic channels was not a viable option. From the nineteenth-century Concert of Europe to the present-day veto-wielding Security Council, the great powers have always occupied a place of privilege in international affairs. In the case of land mines, the one instrument we had on hand to execute a ban—the UN Conference on Disarmament—also happened to be the campaign's most stubborn barrier. The only way to move beyond the "lowest common denominator" approach was to walk a different path.

That walk began with citizens' groups. They were the ones who eventually yanked politicians and officials out of their comfortable chairs and forced them into stride. Focusing on the humanitarian impact of what had hitherto been strictly seen as a disarmament issue helped give the campaign the emotional force that it needed. And this was done by the power of people working in a global network.

CHAPTER 7

CHRONICLE OF A DEATH FORETOLD

THE LAND-MINE CAMPAIGN WAS A PATHFINDER. MANY OF US ON THE tenth floor of the Pearson Building began to see how to use the methods of the Ottawa Process to shift from traditional national security concerns towards ways of protecting the security of individuals, and we began to translate the lessons of land mines into other initiatives.

There was no lack of opportunities. Government tends to be pragmatic, the natural inclination is to work at discrete projects. So initially we focused on specific efforts to limit risks associated with conflict—treaties on small arms, protection of children in war and against nuclear proliferation. At the same time we were beginning to gear up an election run for a non-permanent seat on the UN Security Council. Protection of individuals was an obvious policy to put at the centre of our campaign. Various representatives approached me to see if we would take on other causes. One of the most compelling was the case for us to become an active champion of the International Criminal Court.

We wrapped all these files under the rubric of human security. By now other countries were beginning to buy in and use the human security template, if not the specific language. Encouragingly for us, the need for a small arms treaty and for the protection of children was becoming part of the international agenda. Given this growing interest, there was a need to call on the best thinkers in the department to flesh out the full meaning and potential of human security. But it wasn't to be an academic exercise. Events in the Balkans, most specifically in Kosovo, brought to a head the crucial decision of international humanitarian intervention. It was to be a catalyst in prompting a serious assessment of the meaning of human security. It came down to this question: If this new norm of humanitarian protection of people was to become a prime responsibility, and when necessary trump the long-held principle of national sovereignty, then was international military intervention justified to enforce this standard, and if so, under what conditions?

The effort to answer that question occupied a good part of my attention and interest during my last year at Foreign Affairs. I held discussions with the secretary-general of the UN, who expressed strong concerns on the intervention issue, and concurred on the need to set up a body to examine the question. That led to the establishment of the International Commission on Intervention and State Sovereignty, one of the last and most important of my initiatives. This body of fifteen experts, sponsored by Canada, granted resources by major U.S. foundations and enjoying the blessing of the secretary-general, spent more than a year in worldwide consultations and issued a report called *The Responsibility to Protect* in December 2001.[1] It is in many ways a revolutionary document and I shall refer to it frequently in the rest of this book. It advances the idea that sovereignty is based on the ability and willingness of governments to accept the responsibility to protect their own citizens. Failing that, the international community has a right to intervene. The report outlines criteria, conditions and strategies. It gives a strong intellectual base to the notion of the right of people to live with freedom from fear. It marries ideas to action.

The "responsibility to protect" idea soon showed that it has application beyond the realm of humanitarian intervention. This fundamental shift of perspective to that of the victim, not the intervener, has particular relevance to the war in Iraq. One of the most far-reaching and provocative positions of present U.S. policy-makers is to assert the right of pre-emptive intervention at a time, place and target of their own choosing—contrary to the precepts of basic international law. The commission report sets out tests to determine when and how intervention is justified, tests that can be applied to interventions proposed by a great power for its political aims as well as to those of a humanitarian nature. It thereby works as an accountability check on the pre-emptive strategy of attacking self-defined entities of evil.

The commission findings can lead to a much broader strategy on how to ensure the prevention of conflict and the protection of individuals. Work is underway to have the report appear as a UN General Assembly resolution. This would give the Assembly the power to direct the Security Council to meet cases of serious crimes against people in a timely and effective fashion. In an earlier era, the General Assembly defined the rules governing self-determination and colonial trusteeship, which set a clear protocol for the Security Council to follow. The same could happen here. The adoption of such a resolution to protect individuals will require a great deal of effort and persuasion, but it offers an opening for a process of renewal that would give much-needed energy and credibility to the UN.

Later we will see how the "responsibility to protect" idea can be extended to enforcing standards of democracy, to countering risks of an economic or environmental kind and even to protecting citizens from weapons of mass destruction. For now, though, I want to examine the controversial area of "hard"—that is, military—intervention.

RWANDA

In his novel *Chronicle of a Death Foretold*, Gabriel García Márquez tells the story of how the people of a town in Colombia stand by and do nothing while two brothers plan, proclaim and carry out the murder of a man they believe has defiled their sister. Everyone knows it is coming but is either indifferent or indolent in offering any help or protection until it is too late.

The events leading up to the unchecked genocide in Rwanda in 1994 and the tragic conflict in Kosovo in the spring of 1999 can also be seen as chronicles of deaths foretold. Many observers and commentators sounded dire warnings, but little was done. Rwanda, Zaire, Srebrenica, Sierra Leone, Kosovo, East Timor and Chechnya all stand as stark reminders of how in the last decade of the last century so many innocent people were murdered, maimed or abused because the international community failed to act.

One night, soon after becoming foreign affairs minister, I came up from the House of Commons to my fifth-floor office in the Centre Block for a short rest before going back to what promised to be a long evening of voting on opposition amendments. Lying on the meeting table in my office was a colourful boxed set of reports, put there by Lea Attrux, my secretary, before she left for the night. I had come looking for some reading material to keep me occupied for the ordeal ahead, so pulled out the slimmest of the volumes, bound with a bright orange cover and carrying the title *The International Response to Conflict and Genocide: Lessons from the Rwanda Experience.*[2] It was a stunner to read, making an impact that I still strongly feel.

Prepared by a group of experts from the OECD, the Red Cross and Red Crescent movement, and five international NGOs, this report and the other four volumes set out in meticulous detail the inception and implementation of the mass murder of more than 800,000 Rwandans, mainly members of the Tutsi tribe, by their fellow citizens, while the rest of the world stood by. It chronicled the warning signals that appeared in reports from UN officials who witnessed preparations for mass exterminations, the virulent hate messages spewing from the government-controlled radio and the refusal of the Security Council to heed any recommendation to beef up the meagre UN force on the ground or to give it the needed resources or necessary rules of engagement to permit the protection of those who had been targeted. The language of the report was calm and measured, but the effect was incendiary. It was hard to comprehend something so horrendous.

Back in 1994, I had read the newspapers faithfully and kept up-to-date, yet I didn't recall any sense of outrage at this case of monumental inhumanity. Not until that evening, reading a report that happened to arrive on my desk as part of everyday reading matter, not because of any policy brief or special presentation or even my awareness as an elected public official, did the import of the massive communal killing take hold. I'm sure there were many who were deeply disturbed by the Rwanda experience. We have since learned of the emotional trauma experienced by Canadian Gen. Roméo Dallaire, the commander of the UN Observer Mission at the time. But my own failure to appreciate what had happened was perhaps symptomatic of the general inattention to and lack of full understanding of just how murderous our age had become, and how selective the international community was about whose lives mattered.

I thought back to when our government committed early on to a peacekeeping role in Bosnia, how discussions in cabinet and Parliament had increasingly focused more on the risk to our own forces there than on the atrocities that took place daily. A sense of relief had greeted the replacement of our own troops by Dutch soldiers in Srebrenica just before the massacre of seven thousand men—another case of the UN standing by. Even in cabinet, I never felt the weight of the immoral events taking place in the Balkans.

As a young person, I was deeply affected by stories of the Holocaust. Reading *The Diary of Anne Frank*, I had been introduced to the horrific treatment of the Jews during World War II. And the killing fields of Cambodia had been a focus of interest in my teaching days. But, along the way, those feelings had become muted, disconnected from my everyday work as a practising politician.

No longer, I decided that night as I read other parts of the report that presented ways such catastrophes could be averted if only there was political will. Here I was, the foreign minister of a significant, respected country that could make a difference in protecting people against a massive assault on their personal security. The Rwanda report became for me a template that would guide my four and a half years in Foreign Affairs.

The events it portrays of murderous intent and international neglect haunt me even today. During a trip to Rwanda in the late fall of 2002 I met Manuel Murangira, a soft-spoken guide and interpreter at a partially built genocide museum just outside the southwest market town of Gikongoro. He began his presentation to a group of us from the MacArthur Foundation, there on a fact-finding mission, by pointing to the indentation on his upper left forehead to show where the bullet that saved his life had struck. Saved his life because, while only a surface wound, it was sufficient to make the assassins who eight years ago stormed the Catholic schoolyard where we now stood think he was dead.

He was the exception. Along with three others, he is a lonely survivor of a massacre that took the lives of some fifty to sixty thousand Tutsi men, women and children, including all of his own family. The perpetrators were Hutu genocidaires (a term used to describe the armed groups of Hutu youth who carried out much of the killing in Rwanda), many of them from the same towns and villages as the victims, spurred on by their own government, which had embarked on a diabolical plan to eliminate the Tutsi.

The story of the genocide that wreaked havoc in this very poor, small east African country just a little less than a decade ago was there to see in simple, stark, horrifying terms as Manuel opened the door to one of forty-eight huts at the back of the main school building: limed-over skeletons of victims laid out on row after row of pallets in silent, macabre witness to the night of madness that took their lives.

I could see the countless skulls of young children cracked open by the blow of a machete. The remains of a nun with the rosary still clutched in her hands, her neck bones severed by similar attack, was a figure of great poignancy, because the Tutsi had sought sanctuary in a church just half a mile away, but after two days of waiting were sent by church authorities to the schoolground where they were attacked. Another sight of dramatic irony was a tattered blue tarpaulin with the UN insignia framing a window below which lay the grisly human evidence of how the Security Council, following the dictates of its most powerful members, refused General Dallaire's request to send additional troops to help protect helpless civilians from being murdered.

The people of Rwanda are still struggling to come to grips with the enormity of what happened in Gikongoro and countless other killing fields around the country. An ad hoc UN tribunal is hearing cases against the ringleaders. The government of Rwanda is setting up what is called the gacaca system, a form of traditional justice meted out through community courts. Accusers get to name the accused in front of locally chosen judges who then decide on the severity of the involvement and whether the suspects should go on to trial in the regular legal system. It is a remarkable experiment in community-based justice.

Everywhere, one gets a sense that, while normal life goes on, below the surface is disbelief that something so inhumane was ever allowed to happen. What potent mixture of hate propaganda, political fanaticism and intolerance could have brought this about? Wresting some closure to the guilt in this society will take a very long time. How the rest of us can begin to make some restitution for our failures is still an issue.

What happened in Rwanda led me inexorably to my decision to support military intervention in Kosovo launched to stop what had become a massive case of ethnic cleansing of the majority Muslim population. The intervention was not without controversy, because NATO, not the UN, made the decision and carried out the operation, but it was nevertheless motivated by humanitarian concerns: the need to protect human beings from a ruthless government bent on displacing an entire community of people from their ancestral homes. It sparked serious debate on the rules justifying the overturn of principles of sovereignty in the cause of defending people against state terrorism. And in many ways it is one of the most important debates of this new century, with far-reaching implications for the way global society is to be governed in the years ahead.

A Cautionary Tale

Kosovo was not my first opportunity to take part in a form of international intervention. Early in my Foreign Affairs tenure, Canada led a humanitarian mission to aid refugees in Zaire (now the Democratic Republic of Congo). While it was a bold initiative, it illustrated the difficulties encountered in mounting such a mission with tepid support from the U.S., gaps in our own capacity, and inadequate international or UN machinery to manage the enterprise. It demonstrated an ongoing inattention to the human dimension of conflict and it also shows the consequences of the international community's failure to carry through on preventative action.

The Zaire crisis in the fall of 1996 was a direct outcome of unsettled business arising from the Rwandan genocide and the general state of instability in the Great Lakes region of Africa. The estimated one million Hutu refugees who crossed the border into Zaire to escape Tutsi reprisals in Rwanda had been settled into camps nominally run by the UN High Commission for Refugees but in fact controlled by the Hutu genocidaires, many of whom had infiltrated refugee ranks. Their presence brought them into conflict with the local Tutsi tribes that inhabited eastern Zaire, who themselves were in a constant state of siege with contingents of the Zairean army. The new regime in Rwanda was a provocateur in this mix, as was the army of Uganda. Adding to the combustion was a rebel force led by Laurent Kabila, who was out to unseat the Zairean government (using the term loosely) of Mobutu Sese Seko. As the fighting intensified into October, the situation in the camps became untenable and thousands of refugees were forced to flee.

As we see so often today, conflict visits helpless, innocent people, not combatants, with the heaviest price. International humanitarian organizations began to raise the alarm of mass starvation, disease and slaughter in Zaire. Because of the fighting, with its risk to aid workers, they were forced to withdraw their services to the refugees, thus leaving them totally deprived of any support or protection. Another humanitarian disaster was in the making, and the international community was faced with the quandary of what to do.

In late October, UN Secretary-General Boutros Boutros-Ghali asked if Canada would nominate a special envoy for the region to see whether the conflict could be ameliorated. We put forward the name of Raymond Chrétien, our ambassador in Washington and a highly experienced diplomat who had extensive knowledge of the area from previous postings and, needless to say, enjoyed a special relationship with the prime minister, his uncle. We supplied Ambassador Chrétien with a plane, staff and on-the-ground logistical support. There is no question that his involvement was a major factor in Canada's taking a lead in Zaire.

It was the prime minister, however, who made it happen. As he himself has said, watching the unfolding tragedy on television he decided to pick up the phone and call other leaders to see what could be done. The answer, as one might expect, was that if we were so concerned then Canada should take the initiative in mobilizing international action, specifically some form of multilateral force to guarantee the safety of the refugees and help secure safe routes for aid delivery. This set off a period of intensive diplomatic activity on a number of fronts, and military preparations to intervene.

The involvement of the Americans was deemed essential, as they alone possessed the means of transporting people there, to say nothing of the need for their approval at the Security Council. Discussions were started between senior officials to work out arrangements for U.S. participation with a very reluctant Clinton administration still smarting from the debacle in Somalia. Calls were made to other states in Africa and Europe to enlist support, and work was undertaken at the UN to secure an authorization from the Security Council. On November 14, President Clinton announced his conditional agreement to involve one thousand U.S. troops in a humanitarian measure. The following day the Security Council passed Resolution 1080, giving Canada the lead in a multinational force to last four months, with contingents to be drawn from South Africa, Malawi, Senegal, Denmark, Belgium, France and the U.S., with several other countries offering assistance. Gen. Maurice Baril of Canada was given command, and a steering committee of participating countries was set up to coordinate efforts and provide political direction.

As these arrangements were being cobbled together—remember that the UN has a limited in-house capacity to organize such deployments—the situation on the ground began to deteriorate. The fighting dislodged the control exercised by the Hutu genocidaires inside the refugee camps and humanitarian organizations withdrew their support. The result was a massive deluge of refugees out of the camps, seeking some place of security. Kabila and the Rwandans then rejected any notion of UN involvement; after all, they were winning and didn't want interference from an international force.

The original consensus began to break down, especially with the Americans, strongly supported by the British, arguing that deployment was no longer necessary, that the refugees could be looked after once they reached Rwanda. The Europeans, on the other hand, claimed that large-scale abuses were taking place and that many refugees were heading into the jungles of Zaire, not to the border. The aid organizations tabled reports of large-scale suffering and harassment.

We argued that, at a minimum, air drops would relieve some suffering, although I was of the opinion that we should establish an airlift capacity, and on November 28, the minister of defence, Doug Young, and I announced the establishment of a multilateral operation in Entebbe, Uganda, to help humanitarian organizations, gather information on the whereabouts of the refugees and, if needed, begin air drops. Canadian troops were deployed to Uganda to set up the base of operations.

Then the wheels began to fall off the mission. Intelligence reports provided to us exclusively by the British and by the Americans, who were lukewarm at best and certainly didn't want to see any American GI or British Tommy put in harm's way, began to show a surprising disappearance of refugees; it was believed they were all heading for home in Rwanda. That assessment was strongly disputed by the humanitarian groups, who insisted that many thousands of refugees were still trapped between the warring parties and in dire need of help. Neither the UN nor we had independent means of checking these contradictory claims, although I had my suspicions about the veracity of the American and British evidence. On the other hand, Canadian Defence officials placed great stock in U.S. and U.K. reports, reflecting the increasingly cold feet our own officials at Defence had for the mission.

General Baril visited the area to meet Kabila and came back convinced that the refugee crisis was not severe and that any intervention would be met with opposition. In early December, he presented a report recommending that we stand down the force, since the refugees were going home. On December 13, our chairman of the steering group announced the end of Canadian participation over the strenuous objection of many of our European and African partners and the aid groups who argued for a continued international presence in the area. All Canadian troops were gone from Uganda by year's end. In his New Year's wrap-up, the prime minister declared the mission a success because it had woken up the international community and set the conditions for the refugees to return.

What if we had stayed? What if the original plan of putting international troops on the ground had gone ahead and they had established a buffer between the contending parties, a base to work out diplomatic solutions, a supply point for humanitarian aid? We know what has happened since. Zaire became the Congo, Kabila overthrew the Mobutu regime, and that region has been convulsed ever since in a vicious war involving six other African countries that has taken countless thousands, maybe millions, of innocent lives. The UN Security Council has been unable to mount an effective international force to secure a ceasefire, let alone a permanent peace. The killing, raping and despoliation of the land and its people continue.

During my trip to Rwanda in the fall of 2002, I was involved in a meeting between Jonathan Fanton, president of the MacArthur Foundation, and Rwandan President Paul Kagame. The president spoke with deep feeling of being abandoned by the international community. Across his border with the Congo, the Interahamwe, the same group responsible for the deaths in Gikongoro, still roams free, engaging in civil war with other factional armies. A Security Council resolution ordered him to withdraw his own troops, which he had just done. But nobody is willing to fill the vacuum that has been left, the killing goes on, and the infiltration of the genocidaires into Rwanda remains a threat. This was no idle claim. On the morning I was to leave Rwanda, I attended a meeting of people trying to save the precious parklands that straddle the Rwanda–Congo border, home to many rare species, including the mountain gorilla. One group of conservationists were late in arriving, held up by the fighting going on between Congolese forces and fighters reported to be a smokescreen for the Interahamwe. No international presence was to be found; no one was on the ground trying to keep the peace. Everybody was too busy preparing for war in the Middle East to care about the hemorrhaging of lives and security in eastern-central Africa, even though Amnesty International warns that another genocide is in the making.

If we had persevered in our original plan, rather than withdrawing precipitously, might we have been able to exercise a restraining presence in the region? The reality is that we couldn't do it; we didn't have the wherewithal to launch and maintain a multilateral force on our own, or in the company of a few other smaller states. We were totally dependent on intelligence from sources that had their own reasons for wanting to halt the mission. In the past, I had argued that we could make a real contribution to UN peacekeeping efforts by using the satellite-sensing capacity developed by a Canadian firm, MacDonald Dettwiler of Vancouver, for surveillance of international hot spots and early warning. UN officials thought it was a terrific idea, but we would have to pay for it, and we couldn't find the funds.

We were also limited by our inability to deploy rapidly. We and other smaller states simply didn't have the necessary transport to get people to conflict zones. The UN had limited capacity to do the planning and so arrangements had to be on a fly-by-the-seat-of-your-pants basis. The assumption of our military planners was that we could rely upon the Americans—except when the Americans were not so disposed. When they were not so disposed, we shouldn't be either, or so the reasoning seemed to go. I cannot recall ever receiving from Defence a strong case for enhancing our transport and supply systems, just lots of pressure to join anti-missile defence. These lacunae in our capacity for fast, flexible, mobile forces should give some pause to the advocates of closer integration with a U.S. defence system. The real need is to enhance our own ability for more rapid deployment.

Finally, there is the question of political will once we see that the Americans aren't interested or are opposed. The defence department view that we shouldn't proceed without U.S. blessing and participation had a dampening effect on the political decision makers. There wasn't much sense at that time of the larger stakes at play. Humanitarian intervention was not a concept that had been given much thought, and with the breakdown of agreement from other countries, plus the confused situation on the ground, the

Zaire mission lost its allure. But the question of intervention wasn't about to go away. It would appear time and again as we faced similar demands in Kosovo, the Central African Republic, Congo, East Timor and Sierra Leone. It will appear time and time again in the future.

A pattern is emerging, especially among our military and their political and media supporters, to be very reserved about commitments to situations in developing countries where there is a crisis involving huge loss of life. Lack of resources and the high risk are cited as reasons. But the same people are enthusiastic about engagements undertaken in collaboration with the U.S., or within NATO, where there is a feeling that we are acting with the big players. This attitude inhibits our playing a more distinctive role and limits us from taking more active leadership—witness, in contrast, what the Australians did in East Timor.

This situation is especially galling when we can see—as we did in Zaire—that Canada possesses a strong international convening power. In a short time we were able to organize a credible coalition of countries and to mobilize the Canadian government. One key to that is the extraordinary position our prime minister has in our present parliamentary system to initiate action, command resources and have an international reach. There are few limitations on his or her power, which endows the PM with some form of imperial authority. In the field of foreign affairs this can be a distinct advantage, giving Canada a capacity to act decisively and with dispatch. What is more problematic is the ambivalence of many decision makers in Ottawa about playing an activist role, especially in responding to humanitarian crises, which results in a lack of strategy, the lack of a rationale articulating why it is in our interest to respond and the lack of an appropriate allocation of resources. Consequently, the ability to act that is a prime advantage of our system is not often employed. Preparation and planning of our military capacity is rarely designed in a way to enhance humanitarian intervention, yet there is a case to be made for upgrading transit, intelligence and mobility for quick humanitarian intervention missions. Interestingly, two military scholars, Joel Sokolsky and Joe Jockel, have written that in fact the human security strategy gave the Canadian armed forces a fresh rationale and basis for renewal.[3] Evidently, the military has not picked up the ball. Their clear predilection is to eschew peacemaking missions and to be part of the fighting force of the "empire."

THE BALKANS, 1996

In March 1996, seven months before the Zaire crisis, I left on my first extended overseas trip as foreign minister. Destination, the Balkans; purpose, to gain a sense of what was going on and what role Canada might play in the post-conflict period, especially in promoting reconciliation and peace-building. We had committed troops as part of the force to supervise the Dayton Peace Agreement in Bosnia, but our role on the civil side wasn't so clear, and our diplomatic involvement wasn't particularly proactive. The U.S., Great Britain, France, Germany, Italy and Russia had formed an informal cabal called the Contact Group that appropriated decision-making responsibility on Balkan issues. Other countries that were expected to contribute to the various Dayton tasks didn't have much of a say, a matter of no little irritation to Canadian officials. So my trip was designed as a search-and-discovery mission in pursuit of a more clearly defined Canadian role.

When we arrived at Zagreb, Ambassador Graham Green met us on the Tarmac. He pointed to a gaggle of unmarked planes parked nearby—suppliers of weapons to Muslim and Croatian factions in Bosnia, even though under the Dayton Peace Agreement there was supposed to be an arms embargo. From there we went to his office in a downtown hotel, our embassy being one of the satellite operations set up as a way of gaining representation on the cheap. Later came meetings with President Franjo Tudjman of Croatia and members of his government, held in his palace on the hilly outskirts of the city, reached by a winding road with no other inhabitants along its course. The road was a metaphor for the discussion that ensued with the president, as we were given a long, discursive history of the conflict between Islam and Christendom with the fault line running substantially to the south of the Croatian border. President Tudjman took seriously his responsibility as a defender of the Christian faith and made no secret of his belief that the Dayton agreement's working premise of shared government between Croats, Muslims and Serbs was not set in stone. It was a chilling encounter with a person whose mindset saw the world so neatly divided into two warring camps, with religion as the root of difference.

It was, however, a good primer for the next major engagement of the trip, an audience with Slobodan Milosevic in the ornate presidential palace in Belgrade. Watching him now perform his bravura act of outraged victim in front of the judges at the Hague tribunal takes me back to my own face-to-face meeting and the feeling I had from the beginning that I was being conned. He was flush with his success at Dayton, portraying himself as a man of reason, open to a peaceful solution, and thereby deserving of reward by way of a release from sanctions. In the same breath, however, came the denunciation of all things Muslim, a repetition of the holy war thesis that we had heard in Zagreb. I don't know how much of the Tudjman performance was belief, how much expediency, but in the case of Milosevic I had no doubt that his crusade against the Muslims was essentially the work of a cynic. He was a smart man, but also a dangerous one who rode the winds of extreme nationalism and religious holy war for political gain. He would not be won over by blandishments from the West.

The desperate situation of the people in Serbia, however, gave pause for thought. Theirs was not the violent turmoil experienced by the Bosnians, or the expulsion and killing that would be the lot of the Kosovars. Their pain was one of deprivation, isolation and a soul-destroying barrenness in material goods. It became a reason to consider relieving the impact of economic sanctions against a whole population. But how could we do that without giving succour and support to the leadership of the country that would exploit such a move to reinforce its own position? There had to be a way of targeting those at the top without damaging unduly those at the bottom. One way was through "smart sanctions," targeting restrictions at the governing elite of a country. The other way, and one that began to take on increasing relevance as I became more familiar with the Balkans, was to use criminal proceedings against the leadership. Break impunity; hold them accountable. Milosevic would become a test case for that proposition.

A helicopter flew staff members and me from the Canadian base at Coralici, in Bosnia, to an open field near Omarska. We were met by Canadian forces in armoured vehicles ready to escort us to the former iron mine complex that had been turned into a concentration camp by Serb militia—the site of some of the worst atrocities committed against civilians during the three and a half years of conflict. Driving along the roads towards the Omarska complex, I was struck by the checkerboard pattern of destruction. Burnt-out housing shells and razed farm buildings once owned by Bosnian Muslims were interspersed with neat little houses and well-kept gardens with Serbian women hanging the wash out on clotheslines. It was vivid testimony to the selective surgical precision of the violence that had taken place.

At the mine entrance a local Serb commander, whose forces still occupied the premises, met us. He and his soldiers were not pleased to see our delegation, but a young Canadian lieutenant reminded him of the weapons inspection provisions of Dayton and we were allowed to enter. The Serb captors had killed an estimated two thousand Muslim prisoners; constant beating and torture were the fate of the others. More than two hundred women brought to the camp were subject to rape and violation. As I walked around the buildings where these atrocities took place, observing the still-bloodstained walls of the small rooms where people had been crammed together awaiting their fate, the enormity of the crimes was palpable. It was as if the ghosts of the victims were speaking out from the nearby graves, demanding justice.

The call for retribution came the next day in conversations with survivors in and around the town of Gazin, part of the patrol territory for the Canadian peacekeepers. Accompanied by Brenda Cupper, an experienced child worker from CARE Canada, we met with several groups to discuss efforts at rehabilitation. One obvious problem was the large-scale physical destruction. Next was the danger from land mines. Then there were the deep scars left from watching friends and relatives marched away, never to return; the shock of seeing neighbours who had lived next door and shared in family celebrations and community events turn into killers or jailers without remorse. Saddest of all were the children who had spent their young years cowering from gunfights, traumatized by the bloodshed they had seen, left with little but the support and affection offered to them by the aid workers.

At a cluster of huts perched on the side of a hill, we were introduced to a bright-eyed, slightly built seven-year-old girl named Ajla Sabanagic. She had lost her parents and was being looked after by an elderly couple who had lived next door. Throughout our conversation Ajla sat on the floor nearby, clearly trying to figure out just who these people were who had shown up with armoured escort. I asked her some questions about her hopes and she immediately answered that she would like to go back to school. The Bosnian care worker, who was translating, said that would be difficult because she would need supplies, clothes and some initial fees—none of which the foster couple could afford. As we were leaving, we asked whether we could take some pictures, at which point young Ajla turned on a warming smile.

When I got back to Ottawa I showed the photo to my wife and son and told them the story of Ajla. They decided that we should pack up school supplies and other necessities to send to her. Over the next few years we continued to be in touch and sent packages and gifts. A good friend of mine, Gerry Robinson, was working in Bosnia as legal counsel to the Organization for Security and Co-operation in Europe and promised that he would periodically visit to see how Ajla was doing. I returned to Bosnia a few years later and went back to the village to find Ajla, now eleven, doing well in school and still interested in her Canadian friends. For all of us who came in contact with her it was a reward to see her make her way back from the dark days of the war. It was also a welcome antidote to the hateful and deceitful leaders we encountered in various political meetings in the Balkans who were the cause of so much suffering because of their nationalist adventures. Once again the need to find ways of differentiating between the leadership of these countries, whose bitter emotions and vicious crimes had so poisoned the region, and the general population who suffered the consequences became apparent. There had to be more skilful ways of holding the perpetrators responsible while pursuing peace and starting the rebuilding.

The final stop on this early odyssey to the Balkans was Sarajevo. I was there to open a new Canadian embassy and meet with members of the new tripartite government of Bosnia-Herzegovina. The embassy was a long, narrow structure, wedged into a small side street just off a major thoroughfare where only a short time ago sniper attacks had been a daily occurrence. Close by was the bluff across the river where Serb gunners pinpointed deadly artillery, mortar and rifle fire. It was hard to imagine a full-scale war being fought in such close quarters. The absurdity was dramatized during a visit to a land-mine site painstakingly being cleared by a Norwegian NGO. They described how in this particular neighbourhood the line separating Bosnian and Serbian forces had shifted back and forth several times in the course of the fighting. Each time, the retreating troops would lay down a string of land mines in whatever available space they could find, often set up as booby traps. Now, the area was layered with various depths of mines, like some archaeological dig, presenting the returning residents with a dense matrix of hidden killers. I watched with great trepidation as three small boys bounced a soccer ball just a few feet away from a yard marked with the telltale yellow tape denoting a mine area.

The meeting with President Alija Izetbegovic didn't vary much the diet of political sermonizing on the history of ethnic division, religious intolerance and calumny of the other side. Only this time it was the hard-line Muslim inveighing against Croats and Serbs. At the time this litany of religious hostility seemed just part of the historical legacy of the region. Since September 11, however, it is easier to see it as part of a larger pattern of religious absolutism— a clash of religious fundamentalisms that is having a profound effect on politics around the globe. Whether one looks at Islam, Hinduism, Judaism or Christianity, the resurgence of extremism in beliefs is driving conflict and suppression of basic rights. My trip showed me how the fundamentalists' expressions of religion were a growing threat to diversity of thought and belief in a world ever more interdependent, and how promoting democracy as an antidote had even greater significance. It is a conviction that grows stronger as each day brings another example of religious zealotry as a disruptive and destructive force. Sitting in the dark, gloomy offices of President Izetbegovic, fending off his request for a relaxation of the weapons embargo so he could equip his forces and listening to his bellicosity was a depressing reminder of just how difficult a peace process this would be.

An exception to this constant refrain of political intransigence was Foreign Minister Jadranko Prlic, who struck me as someone who wanted the Dayton arrangements in Bosnia to succeed. I was to encounter him many times in the future and found him prepared to work on rebuilding. He became one of the most active supporters of the land-mine treaty and saw to it that Bosnia became one of the first signatories.

The other impressive person I met in Sarajevo was Carl Bildt, an austere Swede who, as UN high representative, was charged with implementing the civilian side of the Dayton agreement. He had what most people thought was an impossible task in trying to physically rebuild the country while forging some form of working political system among the fragmented and fractious warlords who were clearly reluctant to give up their power and spoils. When we first met, in the cramped quarters of the UN in downtown Sarajevo, he rattled off a list of desperately needed supplies and resources that had been promised by the international community but were lagging in delivery. Exasperation was mixed with exhaustion as he outlined the multiple tasks confronting him. Planning for elections, restoring a wartorn infrastructure, constructing rudimentary public services and administration, trying to coordinate the various international organizations and agencies—all the time having to herd unruly and combative politicians who wouldn't work together. It was a Herculean task, testing not only the makeshift international administration but in the end the will and resources of the Dayton partners to show that they could rebuild a nation. International managers like Bildt are a sterling example of global citizenship.

And while it wasn't pretty, one could say it was a success. As is said about a dog walking on its hind legs, it may not be elegant, but it walks. The foundations laid in those early post-Dayton days by Bildt and all the others who toiled in that harsh environment, supported by a dedicated NGO community and aided by peace-building resources from donor countries, have slowly garnered results. Two sets of elections have been held with political parties that increasingly downplay the old violent nationalisms. A degree of social and economic normalcy is returning, and along with it a sense of stability and hope. The ingredients of a working democratic state are beginning to emerge. The deep divisions along ethnic lines are beginning to heal.

Central to this development has been the continued presence of an international force of peacekeepers, the establishment of a new system of policing based on respect for civil authority, and the arresting of war criminals. As we've watched pyrotechnics over Iraq, and a huge arms buildup in the Middle East, attention has been focused on the war-fighting capacity of various armed forces, including our own. Countless journals and commentaries laud the new "smart" way of waging war. Forgotten in this wave of adulation over the use of force is the just-as-crucial role that the military play in keeping the peace once the conflict is over—a lesson that the U.S. is painfully learning in post-war Iraq.

In Bosnia, as I travelled with Canadian forces on patrol, and watched them negotiate with local Serb militia, undertake risky mine clearing and help rebuild a school, I was continuously impressed by their proficiency in performing the practical functions of rebuilding. The Canadian soldiers were also the most visible representatives of the international community and its standards. To the ordinary people, whose lives had been racked with turmoil and threat, they were protectors. To the criminals and combatants, they were the policing authority. When I returned to Ottawa, I persuaded CIDA that a portion of our assistance to Bosnia should be channelled through our soldiers. These funds enabled the peacekeepers to add to their portfolio of community activities and play a more direct role in reconstruction.

The most difficult task asked of the international peacekeepers was to act as a police arm for the International Crime Tribunal for Former Yugoslavia, a Security Council body charged with prosecuting war crimes. The then foreign minister of Germany, Klaus Kinkel, had first suggested the idea of a tribunal for Yugoslavia in

1992. It was picked up by the Clinton administration in 1994 and was strongly advanced by Madeleine Albright when she was U.S. ambassador to the UN. Albright's became a dominant voice expressing outrage at the atrocities that had been committed, in particular violence against women. She successfully rounded up support and overrode objections from more conventional UN diplomats. The tribunal was set up under Article Seven of the Security Council that authorizes mandatory measures to deal with international peace and security. In addition to providing protection for investigators, who had begun the grisly job of exhuming gravesites to gather forensic evidence, there was the expectation that the peacekeepers would seek the arrest of those named by the tribunal. Many military commanders were reluctant to get involved, fearing reprisals against their troops, and not accepting this as a proper task for soldiers. The tribunal prosecutors complained about the lack of cooperation in seeking out criminals.

This took me back to the feelings I had on first reading the report on Rwanda. There had to be a way of intervening to prevent crimes against innocent people, but there also had to be a way of insuring justice for the victims, their families and the community being violated. The role of the tribunal in Bosnia marked for me the emergence of criminal law and justice as an effective instrument of international action. It meant giving resources, supporting the work politically and taking on the responsibility for either urging a robust role for the military or creating specially trained police units to act as the implementing arm. We took this policy to the NATO council, and it became a building block in defining our human security strategy. Our exposure to the cunning of people like Milosevic and other Balkan leaders in manipulating the emotions of nationalism and religion to gain power, and using the trappings of sovereignty to protect their cruel actions, were lessons too. It was an eye-opener into the saga of Kosovo that would follow two years later.

Leaving Sarajevo was symbolic. The Challenger pilots had to use the high acceleration of a power takeoff to get us quickly over the hills before the plane hit the storm clouds coming in.

CHAPTER 8

RESPONSIBILITY TO PROTECT

A FULL ACCOUNT OF THE CRISIS IN KOSOVO COULD BEGIN ANYWHERE on a historical spectrum going back to 1389, when the Muslims defeated the Serbs at the battle of Kosovo, an event held sacred in the long memories of many Serb nationalists. A more recent trigger was the rescinding, in 1990, of the special educational rights and governing powers Tito granted to the Muslim population in Kosovo in the days when Yugoslavia was seen as a model of tolerant federalism. The author of this reversal was Slobodan Milosevic, who had ridden to power as Yugoslav president on a tide of strong nationalist appeal. Resentments grew among the Kosovars, but in large part there were peaceful protests led by Ibrahim Rugova, a man steeped in the philosophy of Gandhian non-violent resistance.

Then two events dramatically changed the situation. The Dayton meetings, convened to find a resolution to the conflict in Bosnia, did not include any mention of the increasing tension and level of government abuse in Kosovo. None of the participating leaders from the former Yugoslavia wanted Kosovo on the table, especially Milosevic, who claimed it was purely an internal matter. To keep him onside, Kosovo was ignored, and in fact Milosevic was rewarded with promises that the sanctions imposed on Yugoslavia would be lifted. The fallout was fateful for the cause of peaceful resolution. The message conveyed to the Muslim community in Kosovo was that they were being abandoned.

Meanwhile, in the neighbouring state of Albania, a pyramid financial scam led to a breakdown of the government and with it any semblance of security. One of the consequences was that armouries went unguarded, resulting in the large-scale pilfering of small arms and anti-tank weapons, many of which found their way into the hands of elements in Kosovo that rejected the moderate approach of Rugova. Financed by the Kosovo diaspora, these younger nationalists, calling themselves the Kosovo Liberation Army (KLA), now mushroomed from a small group of militants into a fighting force of between fifteen and twenty thousand combatants. By 1997, they were engaged in a series of raids and attacks against Serbian police and army units, who retaliated with accustomed ferocity. The long-simmering pot of religious, ethnic and political dispute in Kosovo had begun to boil.

In the meantime, the international community had difficulty getting its act together. "Too many cooks spoil the broth" perfectly describes the overlapping and often competing initiatives of various agencies and states trying to concoct the right recipe for the looming Kosovo crisis. The self-appointed six-nation Contact Group that had formed during the Bosnia crisis met regularly but without much effect. There was a clear division between the Americans, led by Madeleine Albright, who took a very hard line against Milosevic, the Europeans, who preferred quiet diplomacy, and the Russians, who thought the Contact Group was stacked against them and who counselled cooperation with Milosevic, fearing a domestic backlash against any intervention against the Serbs. Milosevic interpreted these mixed signals as a licence to continue his crackdown on the KLA and any civilians who happened to be in the way. In February 1998, the situation turned particularly ugly after a KLA attack on units of the Serbian police brought about a vicious response involving the killing of more than a hundred people and reports of a major uprooting of civilians on the border area with Albania.

In NATO, the escalating violence was seen as a source of major regional instability. Not only had NATO invested a substantial stake in the peaceful development of Bosnia but also the displacement of Kosovars across borders and the threat of fighting on the frontiers was a threat to Macedonia, Albania and even Greece. The NATO council began to churn out a stream of declarations calling for ceasefires and border stability. More to the point, they began to seriously consider military contingencies as a way of persuading Milosevic to moderate the reprisals and begin negotiating on the future of Kosovo. The inside debate, however, was how far NATO could go in military action without some form of mandate from the UN Security Council, not an easy call because of the threat of veto by Russia and China.

This was where we concentrated our efforts. In the summer of 1998, we undertook our own diplomatic initiative to have the UN become the forum of discussion and decision. In early August, I publicly called for a more active involvement of the United Nations in the deepening crisis. I then followed up with Russian Foreign Minister Yevgeny Primakov to see if there could be flexibility in the Russian position, urging them to take leadership in the council and with the Yugoslav government. The Russians had been bruised by the somewhat peremptory tenor of NATO expansion into Eastern Europe, and had to deal with a strong pan-Slav sentiment in their Duma. But they also had the capacity to intercede with Milosevic. It was therefore important to recognize their value as an interlocutor.

One arena in which the Russians felt comfortable was the G-8. Started primarily as a forum for economic discussions, it had increasingly taken on a political agenda. In the spring of 1998, G-8 foreign ministers discussed the Kosovo situation and imposed limited sanctions with Russian approval. It was also a place where I felt that Canada could exercise a useful role, especially in acting as a bridge between American, European and Russian interests.

The same could not be said for the UN Security Council. While response from the elected members on the council was generally positive, the permanent five members couldn't agree on a course of action that would directly involve the UN. In particular, the U.S. felt that NATO should be the prime agency for action, and they didn't want to risk a veto that would preclude future initiatives. It was an indication of just how hamstrung the Security Council had become in coping with crises arising from internal conflicts. The veto might have made sense in the early years after World War II, and even during the Cold War to counter cross-border aggressions. But it makes increasingly less sense when the conflicts involve internal and civil strife.

To show just how the Security Council's ability to preserve peace can be hijacked by the special interests of the permanent five, consider what happened to the UN Preventive Deployment Force (UNPREDEP) on the Kosovo–Macedonia border. Its mission was to limit refugee flows arising out of the turmoil in Kosovo, a threat to the delicate ethnic balance of Macedonia, and to control the movement of arms the other way. It was a classic example of how to use an international preventative instrument. In the deteriorating situation inside Kosovo, it gave the Macedonians a degree of security and it could also be a potential base for future operations in the effort to restrain Milosevic.

But it was not to be. The Macedonian government had accepted direct aid from Taiwan in exchange for supporting them in their efforts at international recognition. China's government was understandably upset and, unfortunately, took out its ire by refusing to renew the UNPREDEP mandate. At a critical time, the UN lost an important perch from which it could intercede. It is hardly surprising that Milosevic and his cohorts thought they could continue getting their way.

By September 1998, the humanitarian situation had become desperate. Serbian troops and police had pushed back a summer offensive by the KLA and were engaged in a major uprooting of people and mass arrests of key Kosovar community leaders. The UN High Commission for Refugees reported more than 200,000 displaced persons. There were continuous reports of attacks against villages and communities resulting in numerous civilian deaths and disappearances, and intelligence assessments suggested that this was part of a well-designed plot of ethnic cleansing. Events were inexorably leading to a decision on intervention, but the diplomatic minuet had first to play out. No one on the side of the NATO countries wanted to take the plunge. At the end of

September the Security Council finally passed a resolution condemning the violence, deploring the humanitarian crisis and recognizing that the conflict in Kosovo constituted a threat to regional security and stability. But support for intervention could not be mustered.

The Contact Group authorized Richard Holbrook, the impresario of the Dayton accords, to go to Belgrade and negotiate some form of ceasefire agreement with Milosevic. Milosevic, ever the master at playing for time, agreed to the Holbrook conditions and allowed a verification force into Kosovo to monitor the supposed deal. This project was managed by the Organization for Security and Co-operation in Europe (a regional security organization with a membership of fifty-five states, including Canada, dedicated to preventative diplomacy and election monitoring), bringing yet another international player into the arena. The OSCE issued an emergency call for member states to ante up money and personnel to go to Kosovo as verifiers. It was a tricky call for us to make, knowing the precariousness of the situation and the risk that international personnel would be under. But there was little choice if we were to be consistent in the commitment to protect helpless people in Kosovo and be serious about responding to humanitarian crises before they got out of hand.

One advantage we had was a ready-made roster of skilled experts. Our organization of civilian peacekeepers was now fully functioning, so we simply had to choose from a list of former diplomats, RCMP and military veterans and NGO personnel, all well versed in difficult overseas duty. It was a useful test case of the value of having a rapid-reaction team for civil peace missions.

Unfortunately, the verification group didn't have long to prove its mettle. The very shaky agreement, which at best was only tolerated by both sides to the Kosovo dispute, was soon eroded. Cease-fire infractions were frequent, and it was increasingly apparent that Milosevic was simply using the time to build up his police and military forces. Matters came to a head early in the new year when Serb militia massacred civilians in the town of Racak. The head of the OSCE mission, William Walker, arrived on the scene the day after the killings and denounced the action as a crime against humanity. The Milosevic government retorted by asking him to leave. Another effort in trying to avoid a major confrontation was doomed. At the end of the month the NATO council passed a resolution authorizing any steps necessary to avert a humanitarian disaster. Planning for air strikes was accelerated.

Before taking that decision, the Europeans insisted on a final diplomatic play. The Rambouillet conference, held in a chateau outside Paris, was the Contact Group's last hurrah, a final stab at bringing the protagonists together. Except they never met face to face—all the discussions were through third parties. The conference failed, illustrating the inadequacy of last-minute, ad hoc diplomatic efforts undertaken without the proper representation of interests. This badly managed diplomatic manoeuvre underlined for many of us the reactive nature of the international community to humanitarian crises. The failure of the UN Security Council was exacting yet another toll in human lives. The fact that Milosevic had far exceeded in his brutality any right to claim impunity from international action should have been recognized and acted upon by the Security Council, which effectively abdicated its role as the central agency for protecting people. By the middle of March it was clear that NATO was the only game in town. Using previous UN resolutions as a mandate, the decision was taken to intervene militarily.

I can think of no more difficult decision than to go to war, even a limited war fought for humanitarian principles. As foreign minister, it was my responsibility, along with the defence minister and ultimately the prime minister, to advise cabinet and Parliament on Canada's participation in the air offensive against Yugoslavia. Even though intervention had long been in the offing, when the moment finally came, it was a cause of personal soul-searching.

First, there was the realization that such a decision would put Canadian men and women in our armed forces in harm's way. Then there was the issue of the use of force itself as the arbiter of the dispute, and what damage and loss of life it might cause. I had always had an aversion to military action. Growing up during World War II with a father and several uncles overseas, I had learned early of the personal tragedies and suffering caused by war. My religious beliefs, though not pacifist in nature, led me generally to prefer peaceful means of resolving disputes. The policies that I espoused were founded on the premise of protecting people against violence and force. Yet it was those very principles that impelled me towards accepting the need for military action as a last resort. It was evident that "hard power" might have to be used to protect against the abuses and atrocities that had become so endemic in the Balkans and elsewhere. If you are going to have standards and laws to protect people, then there are times when such laws have to be enforced.

Shortly after the inception of the air campaign, I talked about these feelings with the minister of my local United Church, Jim Christie. He is a man of great faith, with an astute sense of how it applies in daily life. We spent the best part of a Saturday afternoon ranging over the questions I found troublesome while I tried to reconcile the responsibilities of exercising power with what I believed were the tenets of my Christian beliefs. Was this a just war? Had all other recourses been tested? Did the international indifference to the Rwanda genocide provide a lesson? Finally, it simply came down to what I felt in good conscience—that without the ultimate willingness to use military power to enforce the rule of law, there could be abuses that would violate many innocent people.

That certainly didn't imply that such force should be used without conditions. One of the most important functions foreign ministers collectively had to perform during the eighty-some days of bombing was to set limits on targets in order to keep civilian casualties to a minimum and ensure that the military action kept on track with the continuing diplomatic efforts. It was undoubtedly frustrating for the military people to be under such restraint, but necessary as one of the defining elements of a humanitarian intervention. The object was not overwhelming victory or the destruction of an enemy; it was to stop the crimes against people from being committed. Many commentators who later decried the time it took, or the awkwardness of having a constant political oversight by the NATO council, miss the point that an intervention undertaken to promote humanitarian values must have its own distinctive rules of engagement that reflect those values. The bombing of the major Serb television station was a case where I felt NATO overstepped the mark; the idea of deliberately attacking journalists was highly questionable.

What that attack illustrated was the strategic importance of communication as a weapon of war in Kosovo. The TV station in Belgrade was the broadcast centre for a constant stream of reports highlighting NATO bombing indiscretions. These reports, some from Canadians invited by the Yugoslav government as their guests, would then find their way onto the networks of NATO countries; as well, they were the only staple for consumption by the people of Serbia. I recall my distress at watching an extensive CNN interview with Arkan, a Serb paramilitary leader who was denouncing NATO attacks against civilians. The report never mentioned that he had already been indicted as a war criminal for his notorious killing of civilians in Bosnia. Needless to say, the openness of Western media was not reciprocated inside the territory controlled by Milosevic.

Indeed, NATO's countervailing communication plan was inferior to that of Milosevic. He understood much better that in this kind of conflict soft power could be an invaluable tool, while the rest of us had to learn on the job. Michael Ignatieff, in his book *Virtual War*, observes that "Milosevic could afford to lose military assets because he was not fighting NATO in the air, he fought NATO on the airwaves. Propaganda has been central to war since the dawn of democracy, but it took an authoritarian populist from the Balkans to understand the awesome potential for influencing the opinion base of an enemy, by manipulating real time news to his own advantage."[1] Milosevic later used the same tactics in his defence before the Hague tribunal. The muted response of the prosecutor's office shows that the champions of humanitarian causes still have important lessons to learn in executing similarly skilled presentations of their case.

Unfortunately, if Afghanistan is anything to go by, the lessons drawn from Kosovo on how to handle communication in the era of virtual war have been the wrong ones. There, the notion seemed to be to severely control the media, totally limit access and occasionally disguise and omit facts in reporting. Our government's downplaying of the humanitarian crisis in Afghanistan further strengthened this impression, as did the misleading reports on civilian casualties. The view of the military still seems to be that it is best to curtail public understanding of the realities of conflict. The "embedded" journalism of the Iraq war was a variation of the same theme. Here it appears that being ensconced in a combat unit will ensure sympathetic reporting. There is a blurring between combatant and journalist.

Hiding the facts will eventually prove self-defeating—witness the missing weapons in Iraq. So it is better to adopt an open approach. In our case we constantly informed Parliament, as the most appropriate and effective vehicle for enforcing accountability, and also held a daily press briefing, often attended by the defence minister and myself. This was important to counter the criticisms coming via the Yugoslav media or from critics inside Canada, especially the Serb-Canadian community, who opposed Canadian intervention.

The role of the ethnic diaspora, as I've said, increasingly influences Canadian foreign policy decisions, and this was certainly the case in Kosovo. Legitimate questions were raised by representatives of the Serbian community. There were also personal attacks and allegations against many of us in the government about our motives, suggesting this was a plot against the Serbian people. What was most distressful was a general unwillingness amongst Serbian Canadians to face the fact of the Milosevic government's campaign to ethnically cleanse Kosovo of its majority Muslim population. In one incident in Ottawa I was out on a bicycle ride with my family when a number of Serb Canadians who had been demonstrating on Parliament Hill turned ugly with both verbal abuse and physical threats, not exactly the kind of experience you want to share with your wife and son. Cooler heads soon prevailed, but it was a reflection of the depth of their feeling and loyalty to their homeland. Such sentiments make it all the more important for governments that undertake a humanitarian intervention in another country to present their case openly. The diaspora can aggravate a conflict by advancing hard-line attitudes or giving direct aid to combatants. They can also play a very useful role in helping to resolve conflicts in their homelands. This latter potential is still not very well developed as part of our foreign policy calculations.

Kosovo proved an opportunity to substantially advance the credibility of the concept of human security. In the past the notion of protecting individuals from new global threats had usually been seen in the light of the Canadian practice of doing good works. So-called hard-nosed critics had seen us as being nothing more than an international do-gooder. Kosovo changed that. The ultimate test for a human security policy was a willingness to exercise military force to uphold the principles of protection—an argument we were able to advance day after day in Parliament and the media.

Kosovo also brought out the best in the Foreign Affairs ministry. An outstanding group of officials brought intellect and commitment to the task of defining the concept of humanitarian intervention and formulating a far-reaching definition to respond to internal violations of human rights. Their arguments influenced discussion on how to gain a peace settlement in Kosovo based on the same principles. We were attempting to refashion the global security paradigm.

At first, it was thought that the bombing would quickly bring Milosevic to the bargaining table. But Kosovo wasn't Bosnia. There was a lot more at stake for Milosevic and, furthermore, he believed his clever media campaign could break NATO solidarity. Once it was obvious that there wouldn't be an immediate capitulation, efforts turned towards finding a resolution. The Russians got involved, with Victor Chernomyrdin, the former premier, as special envoy. The Americans recruited President Martti Ahtisaari of Finland to team up with the Russians in an effort to engage Milosevic in discussions. They became the crucial conduit to the Yugoslavs.

Just as important was the emergence of the G-8 Foreign Ministers group, which began drafting the principles for ending the war. This led to some hard bargaining at the May meeting in Cologne. The major hang-up was over the kind of international force that would be acceptable in Kosovo after the conflict. There were those who held out for a pure NATO operation, a position strongly rejected by the Russians. The Canadian delegation found itself playing middleman in drafting an acceptable compromise, conveying to the Security Council the need to have a resolution enacted immediately and at the same time getting the message to

Milosevic that this was a united position to which the Russians subscribed. It was an amusing tableau to see the G-8 ministers sitting around the conference table, each with a cellphone to the ear, instructing their UN ambassadors in very undiplomatic language to get a resolution drafted and accepted post-haste. Resolution 1244 was passed thirty-six hours later and became the framework for the Kosovo settlement—an unprecedented exercise in multilateral diplomacy with the purpose of saving lives.

The Cologne G-8 meetings were also crucial in the development of the International Criminal Court. I shall return to the court in the next chapter, but it is worth considering here how it can play a role in affecting the outcome of deadly armed conflicts. At Cologne, we were told that the chief prosecutor for the Hague tribunal, Louise Arbour, was about to lay down indictments of Milosevic and six of his confederates. Some of the ministers expressed dismay, believing that this would derail the delicate negotiations under way. Arbour went ahead nevertheless, and only a few days later Milosevic, who up to that time had been quite intransigent, agreed to the conditions that eventually became the basis for Resolution 1244. I'm convinced that the indictment swayed him. I believe it sent a strong message to others in the Serb leadership, who began to distance themselves from their president. Naming him a war criminal isolated and shamed him, with a consequent loss of political stature and power. The fortunate timing of Louise Arbour's move strongly buttressed the case for juridical means as an important tool in deterring state violence and gaining compliance to international norms.

Our delegation at the G-8 meeting also drafted a protocol that outlined the clear responsibility of KFOR, the international body policing the Kosovo settlement, to cooperate with the international tribunal to avoid the ambiguities and obstacles that had plagued the investigation of war crimes in Bosnia. When KFOR troops arrived in Kosovo they were accompanied by tribunal investigators, properly funded and supplied with useful intelligence information. Very soon they uncovered sixty-three mass graves of ethnic Albanians, dramatically bringing to light the kind of atrocities the intervention was designed to stop. The ultimate vindication for the tribunal came when a new, democratically elected government of Yugoslavia delivered the deposed President Milosevic to The Hague for trial. This one man who had brought such suffering to the people of the Balkans was, at last, to be held accountable for his crimes.

NATION BUILDING

The end of the fighting did not mean the end of interest or attention. The most immediate need was to establish basic security and sustenance. Aside from the expected problems of restoring a wartorn community, the situation in Kosovo was complicated by the unplanned return of hundreds of thousands of refugees, forcing authorities into a crash program of de-mining and rehousing. Canada responded immediately with money for a land-mine program and to repair the electrical generating plant just outside Pristina. When I was in Kosovo later in the year, I visited a school that had been repaired by Canadian craftsmen from Montreal after our soldiers had cleared the land mines from the schoolyard, a great example of civilian–military cooperation.

The second complication was the presence of armed members of the KLA, anxious to undertake reprisals against Serbs remaining in the region. After meeting with KLA leaders, it was obvious to me that reconciliation was not on their minds. Seeing that they were quickly disarmed would be a priority. I resisted strenuously the idea being proposed by the Americans, among others, that the KLA be given responsibility for policing duties. That would be putting the fox in charge of the chicken coop. The alternative was to organize an international police contingent. We contributed more than two hundred police officers—an ability that once again highlighted the need to always have a pool of talent and experience available for international peace-building. In fact, through CIDA programs, we took major responsibility for installing a proper prison system, using the expertise of officials from Corrections Canada. One sad moment during my trip was a memorial service for a young Canadian man from the Correctional Service who had died in a plane crash while serving in Kosovo, a reminder that risk is always part of these overseas missions. We should be enormously grateful to those civilians who take on the task. Someday, perhaps, we will erect a monument in Ottawa to honour our civilian peacemakers similar to the one we have for our military peacekeepers.

The task of post-conflict rebuilding and reconciliation is as much a part of the international responsibility as are prevention and intervention, though it rarely garners the same interest and certainly not the same resources. Conventional aid programs usually don't build conflict into their calculations. Fortunately, Kosovo was an exception, and we won a commitment from cabinet for civilian peacemaking comparable to the money being spent on our military contribution. Nevertheless, it is an area that deserves a lot more focus, for it is a function that Canada is ideally positioned to perform.

Post-conflict management in Kosovo was assigned to the UN, a job it is becoming increasingly good at since Secretary-General Kofi Annan's reorganization established the Office for the Coordination of Humanitarian Affairs. Under this office, the UN had to coordinate the myriad international organizations and NGOs, liaise with the military commanders of KFOR on security and work with the local political bosses and groups towards elections—not an easy task considering the degree of enmity and hostility that had been generated. But there has been slow but steady progress in stitching together a new political fabric in Kosovo and restoring a sense of order. On November 19, 2001, the first parliamentary elections since 1999 were held, fairly and with generally positive, if not unalloyed, results. For the first time in a decade Albanians and Serbs will sit in the same assembly. The new government, headed by Ibrahim Rugova, while still espousing independence from Serbia, is seen as moderate. Kosovo has a long way to go to become a stable, democratic state, but it has begun the journey with the help of the international community. Nation building is never easy, nor is there a quick fix. But it can be done.

SOVEREIGNTY: THE RESPONSIBILITY TO PROTECT

Kosovo raised difficult questions pertaining to humanitarian interventions and the meaning of sovereignty. While there was strong endorsement of the need to intervene to protect people from the widespread abuse, there was equally strong criticism of the way the actions in Kosovo contravened fundamental articles of national sovereignty without explicit authorization from the UN Security Council. The time has come to face these issues. Death and destruction from internal armed conflicts had become a scourge of the last part of the twentieth century and things look no better for the new century: 310,000 casualties a year is a current estimate of the human cost.[2] The ripple effect these conflicts have on disease, poverty, environmental degradation and overall instability is equally damaging. The case can be made that internal, civil conflicts can be the seedbed for the development of terrorism. Martha Crenshaw of Wesleyan University at a symposium at the International Peace Academy provides the following analysis, "International terrorism in the twenty-first century is the result of a spillover of civil conflict rather than the clash of civilizations or a generic reaction to modernization or globalization—campaigns of terrorism involving a multinational mix of targets, perpetrators and sites have roots in local grievances."[3] All the more reason why means of preventing and containing civil conflict is an imperative. At the G-8 Foreign Ministers meeting in the spring of 1999, I said: "Non-interference remains basic to international peace and security, so the intervention in Kosovo must not be held up as a precedent to justify intervention anywhere, any time or for any reason. However, in cases of extreme abuse, the concept of national sovereignty cannot be absolute. . . . The UN Security Council cannot stand aside in the face of outrages we have seen in a variety of violent disputes."[4]

How do we bring about such change? Powerful forces were opposed. P-5 members, such as Russia and China, didn't like the idea of condoning international oversight of human rights violations because of their own blemished records. The U.S. had reservations about any broadening of collective action by the UN, because of its financial arrears with the organization and because, as the primary hegemonic state, it didn't want to be encumbered by group decisions. Many Southern countries, especially in Asia, had legitimate concerns about big powers using humanitarian intervention as a cover for a new form of imperialism. And there was the usual cast of characters from the Right who generally discounted any form of humanitarian response in international affairs and from the Left who saw a conspiracy to advance the free market Western system.

We nonetheless believed that the issue of intervention needed to be addressed so that next time there would be a road map to follow. We had a strong ally in Kofi Annan, who is a consummate diplomat well schooled in the "get-along philosophy" of the UN secretariat, but also a man of conviction and courage, not afraid to speak out. At the General Assembly meeting in 1999, he said the challenge to the UN was to stand behind the principle that massive violations of human rights should not be allowed to happen, even if this meant redefining the notion of sovereignty. We also could count on like-minded individuals from key countries, in particular Robin Cook, the British foreign secretary, and on many human rights activists.

What we needed was a way to initiate a far-ranging look at the issues. Don Hubert, senior policy advisor at DFAIT on Human Security, and Jill Sinclair, now director-general of the Global and Human Issues Bureau at DFAIT, put forward the idea of an international commission of respected experts and experienced politicians to undertake a year-long study of the intervention/sovereignty conundrum. The proposal had merit, but to be effective, it needed serious political sponsorship.

I discussed the matter with Kofi Annan, who was very supportive but didn't think it would work under UN auspices. He encouraged Canada to be the sponsor. What he did guarantee was important: his own endorsement of the initiative and a commitment to personally receive the report.

Designing a process that would be open, inclusive and participatory meant appointing people who were representative of different regions and perspectives and who would undertake widespread consultations. The commission could not appear captive to either pro-interventionist views or a Northern Hemisphere perspective. For travel and research we needed help in funding. Fortunately, this was forthcoming from the MacArthur and other U.S. foundations, with the Canadian government paying for administration and further donations coming from the Swiss and U.K. governments.

Now came the difficult task of choosing commissioners who would bring both knowledge and legitimacy to the table. We were fortunate in attracting a talented group, led by two experienced and able co-chairs, Gareth Evans, the head of International Crisis Group and a former foreign minister from Australia, and Mohamed Sahnoun, special advisor on Africa to the UN secretary-general.[5] Prime Minister Chrétien launched the International Commission on Intervention and State Sovereignty in his speech to the UN Millennium Assembly in 2000. It then began a unique exercise in global brainstorming, holding hearings around the world.

On December 17, 2001, the committee handed its final report, *The Responsibility to Protect*, to the UN secretary-general.[6] Attention was scant at first, since the intervening period had seen the al-Qaeda attacks on the U.S., and like many other pressing matters, the issue of intervention to protect human rights was put on the back burner. But the significance of the commission's findings is now beginning to resonate in political circles. The Canadian government is resuming its stewardship of the report after a hiatus and working to bring its findings into the public realm. Quietly, word is getting around that an important set of ideas has been born.

In essence, the commission crafted a definition of sovereignty centred not on the prerogatives of the state but on its primary responsibility to protect its citizens. If a state legitimately protects its citizens, then it is in full right of its sovereign power. If it fails to do so, or is the perpetrator of a massive attack on the rights of its citizens, then the international community must assume the function. To quote from the core principles set out in the report: "Where a population is suffering serious harm, as a result of internal war, insurgency, repression or state failure, and the state in question is unwilling or unable to halt or avert it, the principle of non-intervention yields to the international responsibility to protect."[7]

This international responsibility comprises three tasks: prevention, reaction and rebuilding. The commission stresses that "prevention options should always be exhausted before intervention is contemplated. And should always involve less intrusive measures before coercive measures are used." A high threshold must be met, such as large-scale loss of life or ethnic cleansing, before military action is warranted. Military intervention should be seen as a last resort, and the minimum force necessary should be used. The commission comes down squarely on the need to work through the Security Council, but suggests that the veto should not be used by the P-5 unless their vital interests are at stake. If the council stalemates, there should be recourse to the General Assembly.

This is the gist of the report: sovereignty is not a prerogative but a responsibility. It is a way of coming both at the tyrants who hide behind the walls of sovereignty and at those states that can't or won't protect their citizens, without usurping the right of those states that exercise their sovereign duty to care for their people.

Shifting the onus from the rights of the intervener to the rights of the victim also establishes a series of tests to assess the claims of states or international organizations that want to assert their military will against others. So at a time when we have been witnessing the blustering and bombing intended to prove who is the toughest nation on the block, it offers a much-needed alternative to the U.S. anti-terrorist policy, which asserts the right of preemptive intervention.

Listen to the voice of victims as expressed in a survey conducted by the International Committee of the Red Cross. In twelve wartorn countries, 66 per cent of respondents supported more international intervention on behalf of threatened people, versus only 17 per cent who were against.[8] The problem is that this was an *ex post facto* reading. How can such a survey be done before an intervention takes place? What are the tools to assess the "interests of victims" before they become victims? It's a different and sometimes difficult test to use in determining the use of force, but it nonetheless could have averted the tortured evasions of responsibility that we saw over Rwanda and Bosnia by members of the Security Council.

Let me ask, therefore, whether the case was made against Iraq by proponents of intervention. Were they arguing from the view of the intervener—that is, the Bush administration—or from the point of view of the victims, primarily the Iraqi people who faced double jeopardy, from their own government and from the U.S.? So far as I could see, the Iraqi people weren't given much consideration;

nor did we know much about their perspective on the impending attack. Instead we had protestations of what we thought was best—a dressed-up, modern variation of the nineteenth-century ethos of salvation that I thought had been superseded by tenets of international agreement and collective security. The American administration and their supporters claimed this intervention was to save the world from the threat of weapons of mass destruction, and to promote human rights in Iraq. A favourite thesis of the new apostles of pre-emptive strategy in Washington is that getting rid of Saddam Hussein through military intervention will result in the establishment of a fledgling Iraqi democracy and that this in turn will have a domino effect in bringing about similar changes to other autocratic regimes in the region. This is part of the new American "internationalism"—using the preponderant power of their military to shape the world to their liking.

If one wants recent proof of the problems with this approach, just look at what has happened in Afghanistan, where the warlords reign supreme, the populace is faced with constant threats to their security, development is stymied and the export of heroin is setting new records. I hold no brief for the deposed Taliban government; they were a cruel and intolerant regime that harboured terrorists and applied the most vicious kind of religious discipline, severely suppressing the human rights of women. During Canada's tenure as president of the Security Council, in 1999 we devoted a full-day session to the humanitarian abuses in Afghanistan, followed by the passage of a presidential statement condemning Taliban actions, and we later supported a limited sanctions program against the Taliban leadership. But it is important to note that it was difficult to engage the major powers on the Security Council on the human rights issues and get them to agree on countermeasures. In effect, one of the Intervention and State Sovereignty commission's tests for dealing with the need for preventative action was not met. The commission report applied in hindsight to Afghanistan would have prescribed a far more robust role for the UN.

I also accept the decision to intervene in Afghanistan after the September 11 attacks as authorized by the Security Council. At the time I hoped this would lead to a collective effort to deal with terrorists in a comprehensive way. Unfortunately, the U.S. government doesn't practice a policy of collective, cooperative action for dealing with terrorism. By building a coalition with the local warlords, it missed the opportunity to build democracy. It was certainly indifferent to the serious humanitarian need for food and shelter. Wesley Clark, the U.S. general who commanded NATO forces in Kosovo, has written: "The lesson of Kosovo is that international institutions and alliances are a form of power. Kosovo also suggests a better way to win the war against terrorism: greater reliance on diplomacy and law and relatively less on the military alone."[9]

The Americans were not the only ones to disregard these lessons in Afghanistan. U.S. allies and UN Special Envoy Lakhdar Brahimi acquiesced, and went along with the decisions to give the warlords their sway and limit the international peacemaking presence to the capital, Kabul. Promised humanitarian aid simply did not materialize. On returning from a mission for CARE to the region in 2001, I tried to make the case for some form of direct protection of humanitarian groups for their efforts to deliver needed foodstuffs in remote regions of the country. I also tried to express what I had heard from these groups, mainly younger Afghans who had been risking their lives under the Taliban to support democratic elements in the country and wanted an application of international law to their country, in particular the establishment of a tribunal to prosecute crimes against humanity. I received a polite hearing from my own government, and even had the chance to present the argument to Secretary of State Colin Powell. But the prevailing notion was that all effort had to go into defeating the Taliban and eliminating al-Qaeda. This extended into very questionable military practices, including the use of cluster bombs, which continue to take a toll on civilians in the region.

Belatedly, the U.S. is now recognizing the need to expand to some degree the international force and Canada is now sending troops to be part of the security contingent that guards Kabul, the capital. But these efforts will be severely handicapped by the entrenched position of the warlords.

As a result, the task of rebuilding in Afghanistan has been made more difficult. The place is fraught with insecurity, and the dominant warlords continue to tyrannize many ordinary people. A November 2002 Human Rights Watch report describes widespread intimidation, arrests and torture by police forces in western Afghanistan under the authority of the local political boss, Ismael Khan, along with "severe forms of discrimination against women, comparable to practices under the Taliban." The report makes this stark assessment: "Far from emerging as a stable democracy, Afghanistan remains a fractured, undemocratic collection of fiefdoms in which the warlords are free to intimidate, extort and repress local populations, while almost completely denying basic freedoms. Afghanistan, a textbook definition of a failed state under the Taliban, now runs the risk of becoming a state that fails its people, except this time on the international community's watch."[10]

It's the last statement that is most poignant: "this time on the international community's watch." The hardscrabble of nation building was ignored not just by the Pentagon and the White House but by decision makers who should know better, at the UN and in countries like Canada. This is where the International Commission's report can be of real value, for it outlines criteria for post-conflict rebuilding under international auspices that keep the rights of the victim in mind. The difficulties encountered in Afghanistan will only be compounded in Iraq. There is nothing like the degree of consensus on the legitimacy of the case for intervention. The commission's criteria ensure that the cure is not worse than the ailment.

No one argues that the Iraqi government wasn't one of the most diabolic and anti-democratic in a world where there are many claimants for such distinction. I saw for myself the degree of repression when I spent ten days there negotiating the release of Canadian hostages in the early nineties. I've never been in such an ominous place, where fear was the method of population control. But the present Washington position on controlling the reconstruction does not inspire much confidence in those who want to build a system rooted in law, rules and acceptable practices. U.S. protestations that they are interested in securing rights and democracy ring slightly hollow when measured against their indifference to such issues in Afghanistan, their present consorting with undemocratic regimes in the name of anti-terrorist solidarity, and the increasing restrictions on rights in their own country. Their professed conversion to precepts of nation building doesn't mask the reality that it will be a complicated and risky undertaking. Contending forces of Kurds, Shiites and Sunni factions will compete for power and turf. There will have to be a long term security presence, engendering hostility from the populace, and the reaction in surrounding countries is more likely to be increased anti-Americanism, not a flourishing of pro-democracy spirit. There needs to be a broadening of the present limited role of the UN. As a recent report of the Carnegie Endowment for International Peace concludes, "The idea of an instant democratic transformation in the Middle East is a mirage."[11]

The commission's recommendations can be of great importance in setting the right parameters for intervention, beginning with the fundamental of securing a mandate from the UN Security Council, the only body under the UN Charter authorized to endorse the use of force. Barring agreement there, the commission recommends that the General Assembly should be brought into play. As I'll discuss in a later chapter, I don't believe the Security Council is a paragon of democratic decision making, but right now it's what we have and it must be the central institution in deciding on the rules of intervention. This is particularly acute at this juncture to prevent further "pre-emptive" initiatives.

We must find ways to pre-empt the pre-emptors. The hawks in Washington are already setting their sights on new targets: North Korea, Syria and Iran. Before that happens, there must be effective international action to address threats that the rearmament of those countries poses to security; we must find ways of putting a prophylactic on any potential transfers to extremist groups. The UN has shown it can mount a robust system of prevention, inspection, containment and disarmament when given the appropriate mandate. These are the lessons arising from the commission's report, lessons that must be applied, and soon, if we are to avoid a replay of the military invasion of Iraq in other parts of the world.

Whether the UN will continue to operate as a forum for international decision making; whether there will be proper tests applied to assess the risk to civilians with an appropriate level of intervention; and whether there will be cooperation in establishing a nation-building strategy—these are all questions begging answers. How they are answered will have a strong bearing on the future course of global probity and protection. As John Lloyd wrote in the *Financial Times*, "Intervention has become a fact of life. Its future as international policy—and the future of the majority of the world's poor and struggling peoples—will depend on the articulation of rules and practices that command wider assent than at present."[12]

The next vital step is to generate support for the report and its findings, which define those very rules and practices. Defining sovereignty as the responsibility to protect must become accepted international behaviour. It must be seen as a tool not for the powerful but to protect the interests of the weak. The operational principles of the Security Council and other international institutions will need to be reformed as the idea is translated into action.

But passage of such a resolution by the General Assembly will require like-minded countries, committed NGOs and international institutions to work in concert. Most important, it will take an act of political leadership to make it happen. This is the choice that Canadians must make. Are we ready for such an undertaking?

To do it means breaking away from the present obsession with terrorism; not abandoning engagement and involvement or letting our guard down—indeed, the challenge of terrorism is part of the human security threat to our global community—but shifting attention and resources from the bilateral preoccupation with security towards a broader international view. The commission's reforms can improve the protection of people, prevent atrocities and establish a policy of intervention against predatory warlords and governments who terrorize their people. Working under "responsibility to protect" guidelines, the world would also be substantially less safe for terrorists.

For Canada, leading such a reform movement means shaking up global institutions and structures. It is a demanding task, calling for independence of mind and a willingness to take risk, probably at even a higher level than on the land-mine treaty. Do we have the will in this country to undertake such a task?

Kosovo was a chronicle of death foretold. The suffering there could have been prevented, certainly minimized, at several crucial junctures. It was a unique, complex and torturous situation, but all too familiar in its mass victimization of innocent people. It showed the world that international institutions could not deal with such ruthlessness until it was too late. But, in the end, Kosovo was a place where the international community took a stand. Today there is relative calm in Kosovo, a democratically elected government in Belgrade, and Milosevic is on trial.

That is a lesson that must not be lost. The International Commission's report tries to ensure that there will not be another Kosovo or Rwanda. The harsh reality of communal violence and civil strife is not about to go away. From northern Uganda and eastern Congo to the high plateaus of Colombia to the streets of Tel Aviv, the slaughter of defenceless men, women and children goes on, whether by a tyrant's torture, a terrorist attack or a cluster bomb dropped from a great height. The force of intervention can be used for both good and bad; it depends on the rules and practices that apply. As Kosovo shows, and the recommendations of the commission prescribe, there is a way to begin bringing this chronicle of death to an end.

CHAPTER 9

A New Court for a New Century

⸻

The e-mail I received on the morning of April 11, 2002, was cause for quiet satisfaction. It announced that the sixty-sixth ratification in favour of the International Criminal Court had been received at UN headquarters in New York, surpassing the necessary threshold of sixty. A new international institution of justice anchoring the expanding sphere of a global rule of law had been born. And Canadians had played an instrumental role in its birth.

The idea of an international criminal court has been around for a long time. In the nineteenth century, various moves to establish international criminal norms to hold individuals accountable for crimes of war led to the elaboration of the Hague system of codes of behaviour. At the end of the First World War the Treaty of Versailles contained provisions for prosecuting German officials for war crimes, but setting up a tribunal was too big a step for statesmen of that time. The breakthrough came at the end of the Second World War with two major developments.

The first was the establishment of two war crimes tribunals, one at Nuremberg to try Nazi war criminals, and a similar one for Japanese war criminals. While it has been acknowledged that these tribunals were at heart cases of victors' retributive justice, nevertheless they established the fundamental right to hold individuals directly accountable for egregious acts of barbarism. Individuals could not hide behind the wall of national impunity, claiming to be in the service of the state. It was a declaration of the right to try people, not nations, for breaking norms of international law based on humanitarian principles.

The second landmark was the passage of an international convention making the crime of genocide a matter of universal jurisdiction. Raphael Lemkin became a one-man moral force in advancing the concept of genocide as an international crime. He had left his native Poland in the thirties and settled in the United States, finding refuge on the campus of Duke University. In 1943 he published the first book to reveal the extermination of the Jews in Nazi-occupied Europe, long before any political leader was ready to admit that a "crime that knows no name," to use Winston Churchill's expression, was under way. Lemkin embarked on a personal crusade to enlist support for having genocide included at Nuremberg as a crime. His crowning achievement was the passage, at the UN General Assembly in 1948, of the Convention on the Prevention and Punishment of the Crime of Genocide.

The senate of his adopted country refused to ratify this treaty, and the onslaught of the Cold War put its direct application into deep freeze. Lemkin died in 1959, a disillusioned man. Yet his idea of using an international legal instrument as a civilizing tool lives on today in the expanding body of international criminal law and in the Statute of Rome that established the International Criminal Court. He is an inspiring example of how individual human spirit can move the mountain of inertia and opposition. He is both a pioneer and a hero of the human security ideal.

While the exigencies of the Cold War diverted attention from this movement towards an international rule of law, it wasn't totally forgotten. The idea was kept alive at the UN, which often shelters good ideas and projects while nations play out their hostilities or when the attention of member states is consumed by some crisis. So, even though hostility between the Soviet bloc and the Western powers had eviscerated the primary role of the UN in the field of security, the General Assembly authorized the International Law Commission to begin drafting a statute for an international court.

Complementary work by such organizations as the World Federalist Association and the Parliamentarians for Global Action helped sustain the idea.

As the late eighties and early nineties brought a thaw in the Cold War, interest in an international court regained momentum. In 1996 the General Assembly announced a major conference in Rome in 1998 to decide on a statute for an international court.

Canada immediately took a leading role in the preparatory meetings. Especially important was our chairmanship of like-minded countries that constituted a "friends of the court" group and eventually numbered more than sixty participants. We prodded them to take on a substantive role and to establish "cornerstone positions," such as having an independent prosecutor, ensuring the court was not subordinate to the Security Council and establishing inherent jurisdiction over crimes against humanity, war crimes and genocide. Canadian officials persuaded the group to accept the important principle that crimes against humanity needn't be committed only during wartime.

Working in tandem with this group was an international coalition of NGOs led by Bill Pace of the World Federalists. Working in similar style to that of the land-mine coalition, hundreds of civil groups from around the world organized themselves into a highly coordinated network running worldwide campaigns.

In early March of 1998, a delegation led by Bill Pace came to my tenth-floor office to make a pitch. Concerned that pre-Rome negotiations were bogging down over technicalities, they asked if the Canadian government would take on the role of catalyst. It seemed to me a natural and obvious choice.

We employed the same modus operandi as in the land-mine campaign. At the outset we enlisted the support of the prime minister and other ministers to set the subject as a diplomatic priority. The PM, especially, could be of real value by advancing the court during his various summit encounters. Using our own diplomatic net, and employing special envoys and members of Parliament, we made representations in many national capitals, supported regional seminars and sought endorsements at international gatherings. I undertook a series of conversations with other foreign ministers, we ran a public campaign involving speeches at such places as the Kennedy School of Government at Harvard, and we set up a trust fund to help pay for poorer countries to travel to the Rome conference.

As the Rome session approached, the chairman of the body charged with negotiating the details of the treaty took ill, and Philippe Kirsch, the senior official in DFAIT responsible for our effort on the court, was nominated as his replacement. It was a fortuitous choice. Ambassador Kirsch was a sophisticated international lawyer who had spent most of his diplomatic career at the UN. He was savvy in the ways of multilateral negotiation and well versed in the subtleties of treaty language. His role and that of his legal team at DFAIT in forging compromise on language without giving in on principle was an essential ingredient in bringing the diverse views of different countries into line behind a common text.[1]

This chairmanship proved a real test of our soft-power capacity, putting us in a strategic position, especially on the crucial issue of the court only taking jurisdiction if national systems were unwilling or unable to do so. We felt that this point was essential to overcome fears of a transnational takeover of national criminal proceedings. We also held out for maintaining the independence of the prosecutor from Security Council control, believing that the court's credibility would be severely tarnished if subject to a veto by the permanent five.

The serious test, as in the land-mine campaign, was in trying to keep the U.S. in the fold. The irony was that the U.S. under President Clinton had been one of the most ardent backers of the International Criminal Court (shades of the early going on land mines). Once into the negotiations, however, they found themselves bracketed by opposition from the U.S. military, who were concerned about their soldiers being prosecuted, and from the right-wingers in Congress. With the Republicans in control of the senate, the chairman of the Foreign Relations Committee, Senator Jesse Helms, was exploiting his power to hold up appointments and determine budgets in order to blackmail the administration on crucial issues, especially multilateral ones. For him the idea of a UN-based criminal court was anathema. During several discussions with Madeleine Albright, herself a strong supporter of the court, I agreed that we would make every effort to meet U.S. concerns. In particular, we advanced the need for safeguards in the role of the prosecutor, ensuring against frivolous investigations by requiring a panel of court judges to approve any inquiry. Some demands, however, simply could not be met without distorting the integrity of the court. We couldn't accept an exemption for U.S. servicemen, for example, even though their own court system would have prime jurisdiction, nor could we accept a court that would be limited to cases referred by the Security Council.

As negotiations proceeded, the U.S. became increasingly isolated. I believe that the chief political figures in the administration were not well served by their negotiating team, which didn't really seek solutions and gave back to Washington a less than accurate appraisal of the state of play at the conference. In the last few days of the Rome meeting, Philippe Kirsch made a bold decision to forgo the normal UN practice of working from a bracketed text that delegations could haggle over and presented instead a take-it-or-leave-it package that addressed a number of reservations coming from recalcitrant delegations. My job was to help sell this package to the NGOs and to those governments that had reservations. Sitting in a hallway a few hours before the vote, I reached Secretary Albright on a cellphone to tell her of the package approach. I stressed that it met many of the American concerns and that I detected a strong movement of support. She heard me out, but said her own reports were that the package would fail. Having already counted the votes, I said that the U.S. could find itself in a very small bloc of opposition, which would be most regrettable considering how she and the president had played such an important role in giving momentum to the idea. I didn't prevail, and the U.S. found itself in the company of Libya, Iraq and Cuba in opposing the cause of stronger humanitarian law and practice. To his credit, President Clinton eventually signed the Rome treaty, one of his last acts before leaving office. But President Bush has since renounced that U.S. commitment and has launched a campaign to destroy the court.

When the final vote was tallied, 120 countries were in favour, 7 against. (By the end of 2002, 139 had signed and 89 of them had ratified.) It was an overwhelming, and somewhat surprising, margin of victory. A wild celebration erupted in the conference room as usually reserved diplomats along with many NGOs broke into sustained applause and much hugging and congratulations. It was a sweet moment for all those who had struggled so long to create this unique international institution for global justice. When the prime minister called later that evening to congratulate Philippe and his team, we all savoured the moment, realizing that we had been part of a historic undertaking. To use the phrase of Dean Acheson, it was good to be there "at the creation."

The Rome Statute established an International Criminal Court with jurisdiction over genocide, war crimes and crimes against humanity. With support from Canada, amongst others, the definition of these crimes was substantially broadened to include the plight of women and children in armed conflict, with recognition that sexual violation was a war crime, as was the use of children under fifteen in armed conflict. Individuals would be held responsible for their crimes and could not plead immunity. The court was to be a permanent institution, with its judges elected by the ratifying countries and with an independent prosecutor. At the same time the prime responsibility to prosecute would remain with national courts. The international court would be the residual jurisdiction, a court of last resort. Although the Security Council could refer cases, it could not block court inquiries or decisions. And safeguards were built in against the court being used for political purposes.[2]

The Rome Statute is by no means a perfect document and it will need a great deal of refining in the years ahead. But it was a giant step towards applying the rule of law to global behaviour and promoting human rights. "We stand at the edge of invention," I said in my speech to the Rome convention, "a rare occasion to build a new institution to serve a global need."

Inventions, however, must be patented, developed and turned into real objects. The court still had to lift off the pages of the Rome Statute and become a functioning body. The next major task was an international campaign to secure the necessary ratifications. Although the minimum requirement was sixty countries, the goal was to make the court as universal as possible. Again we turned to the same model of campaigning used for land mines, but this was a more difficult task, with complex issues. Many countries in the South simply didn't have the governmental or legal resources to analyze the requirements for ratification, especially the changes needed in their own criminal codes and justice systems. We provided manuals and technical advice to these countries, drawing upon legal centres at the University of British Columbia and McGill University and our own government lawyers. It was a further example of how important it was to have this kind of soft-power expertise in Canada.

Having to meet the domestic requirements for our own ratification gave us an opportunity to build a model on which other countries could pattern their own changes. In drafting Bill C-19, which was eventually named the Crimes Against Humanity and War Crimes Act, we opted for a comprehensive rewrite of our Criminal Code and associated legislation, rather than just barebones enabling legislation. It was a combined effort of the Department of Justice and DFAIT and was followed with parliamentary consultation and input from a variety of civil interest groups. The rationale was to embed the principles of the Rome Statute right into the heart of our own criminal law so that international crimes would be an inherent part of our core national justice system.

One of the reasons for developing global laws is to internationalize the internal codes of conduct in nation-states. It is a matter not simply of having to adhere to an external set of rules but of building into the domestic structure of law and practice the discipline of meeting universal standards. The Crimes Against Humanity and War Crimes Act achieved that purpose in a number of respects, most notably in the case of prosecuting war criminals, which had been a long-standing, unresolved and contentious issue in Canada. Many of my constituents in Winnipeg during my years in Parliament could never understand why it seemed so difficult to bring to justice Second World War criminals who had immigrated to Canada.

In one landmark case, in 1994 the Supreme Court acquitted Imre Finta, a Canadian citizen from Hungary, saying that our Criminal Code required prosecutors to demonstrate that an offence had been committed under both international and domestic law. They also accepted the defence argument that Mr. Finta was simply obeying orders in organizing the deportation of Hungarian Jews to Nazi Germany. In fourteen years of attempted criminal prosecutions, not one was successful.

Bill C-19 changed all that. First, Canada could turn war criminals found in our country over to the International Criminal Court. Second, the bill explicitly legislated against the use of the "obedience to superior orders" argument as a defence. Third, by obliging the Canadian government to try cases under international law, it took away the double-jurisdiction argument put forward by the Supreme Court. We are now in a position to exercise universal jurisdiction without impediment and still have recourse to the ICC if we wish. War criminals will no longer find sanctuary or escape punishment in Canada, as long as the government is prepared to use the new provisions. The law is there. Now it is just a matter of political and bureaucratic will to make it work.

So far, though, that will has been lacking, and several prime opportunities have been ignored. It is well known that Canada harbours Rwandans suspected of complicity in the genocide in their home country. Our Justice officials have not used the new law to prosecute. Why not? This is not to our credit. And in the aftermath of the defeat of the Taliban in Afghanistan, Human Rights Watch made it known to Canadian officials that certain prisoners being held by northern coalition forces could be brought to Canada to be tried under the new legislation. This could have been a demonstration of how judicial means could be applied in the anti-terrorist campaign. It certainly would have been a contrast to the American incarceration of prisoners in Guantanamo Bay. But nothing was done; the opportunity was missed. This reveals either timidity—perhaps an ingrained resistance to applying international law to individual cases—or simply a reluctance to take the lead without American approval. Whatever the reason, it is a retrograde step for a country that took such an activist position in establishing the ICC. It also speaks to the continuing problem of integrating the agendas of various departments. While DFAIT is taking one position internationally, their colleagues in Justice are on another tangent.

With the ICC now a reality, implementation becomes all the more essential. The court is still a fragile newborn and could die young without a concerted commitment by its friends and supporters. It will need a great deal of support from friendly governments in the start-up phase, with serious work required to implement its machinery, cope with its growing pains and provide research, analysis and policy. Some of the most important first steps, electing judges and officers of the court, have been encouraging. Eighteen judges were elected in February 2003, representing a cross-section of skilled international jurists from different regions, with a reasonable balance between women and men (seven women, eleven men). Philippe Kirsch will reside as President of the Court. In April 2003, a distinguished Argentinian prosecutor, Luis Moreno Ocampo, was chosen by consensus. He is known for his role in prosecuting the military junta that terrorized the civilian population of Argentina in the 1980s. The court is now well positioned to achieve the objectives of those who spent years creating it. With judges, a prosecutor and some staff, the court will shortly be ready to pursue its first cases. When the prosecutor arrives in the Hague, it is likely that that over two hundred and fifty potential files will be on his desk. They will be from most of the world's human rights hotspots: the Democratic Republic of Congo, Cote d'Ivoire, Colombia, Afghanistan, perhaps even Iraq. These cases are extremely complex, with many witnesses, with many victims and vast amounts of evidence, both reliable and not, from all over the world. Administrators at international courts, including the ICC, estimate that complicated international criminal cases might cost U.S.$150 million from beginning to end to prosecute the first three to six cases. That is probably a conservative estimate when taking into account the vast resources that may be required to compensate victims of international crimes: victims, which could number in the millions. A particularly important task will be to connect the court in a complementary way to the many initiatives under way to use traditional forms of justice and reconciliation. In such places as Sierra Leone, Rwanda and Uganda, these are seen as the means of combining the need to bring the community back together after conflict and the need to hold criminals accountable.

The ICC can be an influential partner in these forms of community justice.

There will have to be continued efforts to expand the membership of the court and counter the efforts of its opponents, including the U.S. administration, to degrade its value. The new court will be located at The Hague, but Canada should become its intellectual and political home, committing energy and motivation to make it a significant tool in the building of an international justice system. What is lacking right now is a sense that the ICC is an anchor institution in an international justice network with many components including international tribunals such as the International Criminal Tribunal for the former Yugoslavia, International Criminal Tribunal for Rwanda, Sierra Leone, truth and reconciliation commissions and national criminal legal systems. But there is no framework for treating and embracing all these individual elements as a whole. There are no networks to collaborate, strategize, exchange resources and personnel, formulate policy, undertake research and educate the world community (governments as well as the people on the street or in the villages) about what international justice is about and what it can achieve.[3]

This is especially true as individual countries wrestle with the interplay between the ICC and their own interpretation of the law. The Pinochet case dramatically illustrated the reach of the law when it is used by individual states—in this case Spain—to go after alleged international political criminals. There is talk of trying Henry Kissinger for his role in the bombing of Cambodia. Belgium attempted to use its universal jurisdiction to go after Ariel Sharon. The ICC cannot try these cases because there is a clear rule against trying crimes committed prior to the ICC being established. What they show, however, is that impunity for the powerful is no longer assured, and that decision makers now know that they will be held responsible. When we wrote the Crimes Against Humanity and War Crimes Act, we did not include the right to pursue suspects beyond Canadian borders. We preferred to rely on the International Criminal Court as the best means for bringing individuals to trial for international crimes, although we would hand them over to the court if they arrived in Canada. In retrospect, that looks like a prudent move, and it is a compelling argument why countries should become parties to the Rome Statute, especially those now opposed whose nationals could be subject to a variety of ad hoc investigations and charges. They could provide better protection for their citizens within the jurisdiction of the international court, with its safeguards and prescribed procedures, than they would find under the somewhat indiscriminate and capricious system of various nation-states making up their own lists of whom they want to go after.

An even more demanding challenge is how to use the embryo of the new international justice system to set up a truly global network of intelligence sharing, investigation, police power and judicial treatment to address the new criminal threats to human security, including terrorism. September 11 has prompted a primarily military response from the U.S., and military retaliation has spawned aggressive use of force around the world as other governments follow the American lead. Michael Howard, the Oxford military historian, warned in *Foreign Affairs:* "The use of force is seen no longer as a last resort, but as a first resort and the sooner the better."[4] Yet the effectiveness of military power as a primary tool can be questioned. The terrorist network still exists. Afghanistan is racked by continued violence and insecurity. Invoking the word *terrorism* seems to cut off rational consideration of foreign policy options.

Two years after the attacks in New York and Washington, I have to wonder if the world is a safer place. The alternative is to see the terrorist attacks as the work of vile criminals, part of the global underworld populated by arms traffickers, drug traders, human smugglers, religious and ethnic extremists, local tyrants and other forms of low-life predators. They are all connected. They must be seen as criminals and confronted by global cooperation and effective transnational agencies that amass information, investigate, arrest and bring to trial. Targeting and murdering civilians is a violation of international criminal law. It is a crime against humanity. Although the court will not have jurisdiction over the events of September 11 since the court did not then exist, it can assume jurisdiction over other acts of international terror committed by groups or individuals.

It is time to take the issue right to the centre of the battle against terrorism and show that the ICC can be one of the most effective and appropriate antidotes—and deterrents—to extreme acts of terrorist criminality, one that relies not just upon force of arms but on a clear and comprehensive legal and juridical system. Article 7 of the Rome Statute states that "a crime against humanity is a crime such as murder, extermination or torture . . . when committed as part of a widespread or systematic attack against any civilian population, with knowledge of the attack." Aren't the events of September 11, the Bali bombing and other similar events around the world crimes against humanity? They contain all the elements as defined in the Rome Statute. And if they are crimes against humanity, then there is already an international structure available to deal with them—fairly and swiftly. The ICC should be seen as an integral part of an international campaign against terror.

Following September 11, many countries have created their own counter-terrorism legislation. Cases are now being brought before national courts to test these new laws. Indonesia is testing its own legal system and its resolve to deal with the high-profile case of Abu Bakar Bashir and all its political and religious tensions. While the ICC cannot handle all cases dealing with allegations of international terrorism, it can play a useful role in prosecuting cases that individual countries could not handle: their resources being too thin and the political tensions too explosive. The ICC can also play a role in distinguishing between the activities of political foes and those who commit acts of international terror, which are truly crimes against humanity. These are important issues for the international community, not just individual states.

All the complicated teething problems of the court are made infinitely more difficult by the ongoing efforts of the U.S. to emasculate it. The campaign began in the summer of 2002, when the U.S. threatened to withhold support for the UN peacekeeping force in Bosnia unless their troops were granted immunity from the court—a form of blackmail that was beaten back at the UN. The U.S. tactic is now one of persuading individual countries—and

I use *persuading* in the broadest meaning of the word—to sign bilateral agreements exempting Americans from the court's jurisdiction. Human Rights Watch spells out the import of this: "By signing an impunity agreement with the United States, states parties and signatory states would be endorsing a two-tier rule of law: one that applies to U.S. nationals; another that applies to the rest of the world's citizens."[5] Already several European states have caved on this principle, and the battle to limit the damage continues.

What is ironic—or cynical, depending on your point of view—is that a nation such as the U.S., steeped in the practice of the rule of law, is using its formidable power to attempt to destroy an institution whose purpose is to advance a global rule of law. It makes the president's rhetoric about battling terrorists to preserve principles of justice ring a little hollow.

The concerted counterattack to the U.S. position has to start in the U.S. itself. We have to provide information to overcome the distortions put forward by Washington's spin machine. I believe most Americans would be dismayed to know what their government is trying to do. We should be working with those in the U.S. committed to the court—and there are many—to get out the message that the court is a welcome addition in the battle against terrorism.

The other way to counter the opposition, skepticism and inattention is to persuade by achievement—to make the court work. One means to give the court some zing is to begin bringing charges in cases affecting women and children, crimes specifically included in the Rome Statute. At a UN conference on child protection, held in Tokyo in January 2003, delegates were lamenting the lack of any serious progress in applying the many conventions and protocols on children's rights that have been passed in the last decade. Why not use the court as one way to gain a win and show that transgressors can be brought to justice? The court can deal with the war crimes and crimes against humanity committed by regimes or groups who use and abuse child soldiers, such as has been happening in the Democratic Republic of Congo or Colombia. The UN Committee on the Rights of the Child monitors states' compliance with the 1989 Convention on the Rights of the Child. But monitoring compliance is futile without a recourse for non-compliance. Why not expand the mandate of the committee to include the clauses on child protection in the Rome Statute? The decision by Luis Ocampo to move indictments to more violators of children's rights in the norther Uganda conflict is a welcome decision. Such initiatives would help put an end to the carping. Opponents such as the Bush administration and the governments of India and Cuba would be hard pressed to state why they object to an institution that tries to protect kids.

The mandate of the court is large. The possibilities for the court are enormous. And so too are the challenges. The extent of support from the international community will determine the fate of the court, as will its first cases. The building blocks are in place. It is now crucial that the architects of the court are strategic and steadfast in their commitment to the court and that its opponents are proven to be on the wrong side of history.

By taking on the court as a continuing priority, Canadians will significantly help protect the rights of persecuted people around the world, the UN will gain strength and the global rule of law will be enhanced. These are important steps towards creating the conditions for true global citizenship.

CHAPTER 10

THE CROWDED GLOBAL VILLAGE

THE GLOBAL VILLAGE IS BECOMING A TRIFLE OVERCROWDED. THE streets teem with close to 190 nations. The big and powerful strut and swagger at centre stage while the poor and small are shuffled to the outer edge. Others are states in name only, presiding over a presidential palace while a group of warlords control the hinterland. Yet national sovereignty is still acknowledged to be the right of each villager, even though the reality is that all the inhabitants find their fortunes and futures intertwined.

The Westphalian nation-state system has been around a long time and is a deeply entrenched belief in most corridors of power and in the mindset of most people. And for good reason, as over the past two and a half centuries it has been, by and large, an effective system for managing affairs, getting rid of pretensions of world empire, and serving people's needs. In the lexicon of political science, it has been an appropriate level of governance. Nor has it been static. After the Second World War, there was a creative period of institution building where a whole raft of political and economic intergovernmental agencies and organizations were established to order the increasing interdependency. More recently we have witnessed the World Trade Organization and the emergence of regional groupings, with greater or lesser degrees of integration, such as the European Union. Of course we also see the increasing power of other players. Some are influential international organizations in the humanitarian field, such as the Red Cross, but the most notable are the global corporations. Multinational corporations bestride a global marketplace, serviced and supported by a plethora of international consultants, rating agencies, lawyers and accountants.

There is, too, a dark underside of this system, one which shows that modern tools of global management, finance and organization can be used to exploit and to murder and to traffic in drugs with worldwide efficiency. The globe is becoming more corrupted and terrorized. It is also home to increasing numbers of the dispossessed, those who have no home, standing, privileges or rights. These are the refugees, the displaced, the victims of illegal migration, the unemployed youth, the young children deprived of parents and community by the ravages of war, AIDS or natural disaster. They are forgotten, ignored and often exploited by the global elite.

On the plus side, global civil society has multiplied into thousands of NGOs, wired together, joined by a proliferating number of associations and multilateral institutions addressing worldwide or regional issues, drawing all the other villagers into an ever changing galaxy of networks and connections. Marshall McLuhan would be impressed. This village is more democratic, in many places more prosperous and healthy. There is the embryo of international governance, and the information revolution promises to bind people together and make control by elites more difficult. These efforts add to the complexity of interactions and connections between the various occupants and add to the overriding of nation-state distinctions. "Community" might well be a better way to understand what is going on.

But we continue to organize around the nation-state as a fundamental premise. Sovereignty remains an article of faith for those who have enough power to believe they can go it alone, for many former colonial states that often suspiciously see international efforts at cooperation as plots to restore Western control, and for many dictators who hide their authoritarianism and violence behind the wall of sovereignty. But many states that are less ideological or self-interested, while they would agree that the nation-state system has been the way of doing business for a long time, and it generally works so why try to fix it, are nonetheless open to alterations on the edge, and it is on this basis that the shift to a human security model is taking place. There is a search for more effective ways to govern the complexity and interdependency of our lives.

Robert Cooper, a British scholar, has put forward an interesting typology to describe the principal categories of nation-state today. First are modern states, where there is a close coupling of the sovereignty of a state and the way in which the individual citizen constructs his or her own identity; the U.S. and China are good examples. Second are the postmodern states, where identity is decreasingly tied to one's state citizenship and people are increasingly more cosmopolitan in what they believe in; Western Europeans and to some extent Canadians fit this description. Then there are the pre-modern states, where individuals inhabit informal economies or groupings and there is little state loyalty because there isn't much of a state; Somalia is a prime example.[1]

On January 10, 2002, a *Globe and Mail* headline read: "Canada Jumps in Ranking on Globalization." In an assessment by *Foreign Affairs* magazine of the world's most global nations, Canada had jumped three places to rank no. 7 overall among those societies that were adapting best to globalization, outscored by Ireland and Singapore, but ahead of the U.S. and France, to name just a few. It would be easy to dismiss this as yet another artificial index of global comparisons, but a closer look at the study points to an interesting measure of what it takes to be successful in the global village. The criteria used are simple but telling: the degree of economic integration, the level and frequency of political engagement, personal contact with other people, and use of technology, especially the Internet. These are seen as indicators of a capacity to manoeuvre and manage in a global context, of street-smart societies dexterous in navigating the global landscape. This is not just a function of economics or technology but of political and social strengths as well.

I have made the case when discussing Canada–U.S. affairs that the best strategy for us is to avoid whenever possible governing our relations one-on-one. Building a North American framework, including Mexico, was one antidote. On a much broader plain is the potential to become a global player, using our resources, our reputation for honest and constructive intentions and our capacity as a joiner and builder of multilateral, perhaps supranational bodies, to exercise influence, gain stature and set agendas. The surge of globalization has opened new avenues of endeavour for us to play an activist role. Let's tap into the globalizing instincts of Canadians, our desire to move and shake abroad. Let's extend our appetite for being wired into an international society.

Make the village our turf—that is what the global index is telling us. Working through the UN, the Commonwealth, the G-20 or any number of other regional, economic or environmental institutions is where Canada is most effective.

Paradoxically, the more governance we apply to global developments, the greater our potential for exercising a distinctive role and operating according to our own coordinates and not just in the slipstream of the United States. This is not supposition. Recent experience shows it can be done.

In this chapter I will look at some instances of "soft" intervention to enforce standards of democracy—international suasion aimed at changing the course of a nation-state with the goal of protecting its citizens. Regional organizations are becoming increasingly involved in enforcing standards of democracy and responding to conflict. As we shall see, the Organization of American States mission to Peru (and now Venezuela) and the Commonwealth missions to Pakistan and Nigeria are examples of an emerging pattern of soft international interventions at a regional level seeking compliance with new standards.

PERU

The crisis in Peru arose when President Alberto Fujimori tried to steal an election. This enigmatic man had presided over an erratic and contradictory government, combatting the terrorist activities of the Shining Path, presiding over the storming of the Japanese embassy to release hostages, presenting the image of a modern economic manager and condoning, if not directing, an increasingly corrupt and repressive regime dominated by the secret police and military headed by Vladimiro Montesinos, a true political Svengali. By the time presidential elections were due in the spring of 2000, Fujimori was in deep trouble, challenged by a coalition of workers, women and the underclass led by a populist economist, Alejandro Toledo. With signs of election fraud and manipulation in the air, the OAS dispatched Eduardo Stein to chair the Electoral Observation Mission. Stein was the recent foreign minister of Guatemala and a man of great integrity who had been involved in the democratization in his own country. In a hard-hitting report, he concluded that the Peruvian election had been a fraud. President Fujimori defiantly refused to agree to a new election. This apparent election steal ran counter to recent declarations at both the OAS and Summit of the Americas meetings enunciating principles of democratic rights and the need to protect against takeovers or corrupt elections. The U.S. tried to mobilize collective action against Peru, including the threat of sanctions. But some delegations, especially Mexico and Brazil, saw this as going too far in interfering in another country's internal affairs.

Finding a resolution to the standoff was crucial. To push for high-powered intervention would break the consensus that had been forming in the OAS under César Gaviria's leadership for the advancement of democratic principles, but to do nothing would set back the progress that had seen democratic regimes established after a long history of military dictatorships and authoritarianism. Canada, as chair and host that year of the OAS General Assembly to be held in Windsor, Ontario, faced a special challenge to find a solution.

Being in such a pivotal position in hemispheric affairs was reasonably new for Canadians. We hadn't even been members of the OAS until 1990, though we had subsequently helped establish the Unit for Promotion of Democracy and taken our stand against the Helms-Burton Law. Underlying our efforts was a deliberate strategy to strengthen our connections in the Americas as a way of offsetting the predominance of the Canada–U.S. relationship. Jean Chrétien had promoted a hemispheric approach, including an emphasis on regional free trade, partly with the purpose of recasting the Mulroney government's overkill of continentalism. In 1998 the prime minister had offered to host not only the next Summit of the Americas but also a major meeting of trade ministers to launch free trade negotiations and the OAS General Assembly in Windsor in 2000. We were stepping out onto the Americas' stage in a big way. We were also applying the concept of human security to an issue of central importance in the region— drugs. We proposed the Dialogue on Drugs, at the foreign minister level, aimed at viewing the problem from the perspective of the victims of the drug trade and looking for solutions through multilateral cooperation and community action, mobilizing local civic groups in the fight against the traffickers. Shifting the focus away from the hub-and-spoke system of American strategy had its appeal, and the OAS formally endorsed the Dialogue.

Coming into the Windsor meeting, then, we had a lot at stake, much of which could be derailed by a bust-up over Peru. Already, Windsor had been targeted by the anti-globalization demonstrators, and the breakdown of democracy in Peru was an obvious *cause célèbre* that would fuel their fury.

After the opening ceremonies, we quickly moved to set time aside for a special debate on Peru, allowing everyone the opportunity to vent their feelings and highlighting to the Peruvian delegation that there was an intense amount of pressure for action. At the same time, we began behind-the-scenes negotiations with the Peruvians, the Americans and other key delegations. The U.S. made it clear from the outset that they would defer to us in these negotiations, recognizing that their previous tough stand precluded them from gaining the confidence of the delegations opposed to overt intervention. On the other side, Brazil and Mexico accepted that some form of action was necessary and would consider a reasonable proposition as long as Peru agreed. So there were many long sessions with the Peruvian foreign minister, Fernando de Trazegenies, who was under strict orders to limit any outside involvement. As happens often in such negotiations, it came down to finding the language that allowed everyone to have a slice of the pie. Fortunately, we have in the Canadian foreign service creative wordsmiths as well as persuasive diplomats.

A consensus eventually emerged around the idea of a high-level mission to help strengthen democracy in Peru. In a cramped little room off the main meeting area, we basically told the Peruvian minister that if there was no agreement here, his country could face sanctions or other strong measures from the U.S. and perhaps the European Union. After long haggling over words, he finally agreed, on condition that we not propose that Peru hold new elections.

We then took the proposal to the General Assembly. The new foreign minister from Argentina, who had been one of the most outspoken proponents for a tough stand on democracy, accepted our proposal and helped sell it to the other Latin American ministers. With the exception of the minister from Uruguay, who held forth for an interminable period on the philosophy of non-intervention, everyone agreed and a motion was passed setting up the mission. OAS Secretary-General César Gaviria and I were to lead the mission, and it was up to us to give definition and substance to the deliberately vague mandate of "strengthening democracy."

Two weeks later, six of us were sitting in a Challenger some thirty-five thousand feet above the southern Caribbean, heading for Lima. We had left early in the morning from Ottawa (myself, Assistant Deputy Minister George Haynal and my staffer, John Clarke) and stopped in Washington to pick up Gaviria, his chief of staff, Fernando Jaramillo, and Peter Boehm, our OAS ambassador. During a refuelling stop in Barbados, Peter and I went for a walk to stretch our legs. Peter had been to Lima the week before and he warned that we would be stepping into a highly polarized and volatile community that had high expectations for the mission. It was obvious that we needed a plan. Once the plane took off we spoke to the secretary-general and agreed that we should begin drafting a specific blueprint. By the time we headed in for landing later that evening, we had come up with a list of twenty-nine reform measures as the basis for discussion and an agreement that we would pursue a broad-based, open, inclusive consultation. It was the beginning of an intensive three days of what Canadian political scientist Andrew Cooper has called "just-in-time diplomacy," and of intervention to promote democratic reform unprecedented in the annals of the OAS.

Driving in from the airport to the centre of the city after mid-
night, we were greeted at virtually every street corner by armed
contingents of soldiers or police. Around the hotel were thick cor-
dons of security personnel, and access routes were blocked to ordinary traffic. Our ambassador, Graeme Clark, told us that in expectation of mass demonstrations by the opponents of President
Fujimori who were demanding new elections, the government had
deployed some twenty thousand troops. From wheeling and dealing in hotel corridors and conference rooms at Windsor, we were
now suddenly in the arena of the street, in the midst of a country
polarized and on the brink of violence. It brought home that this
mission's mandate went far beyond the ambiguous wording of the
resolution. We were at ground zero of a political crisis.

Next morning we started consultations, meeting everyone from
trade unions and civic groups to the president and his cabinet. At
the session in the presidential palace—which was surrounded by a
large and boisterous demonstration—we presented the plan of
action conjured up during the flight. I had expected a feisty
response from the president, knowing his reputation as a combative, take-no-prisoners type of person. But he was eerily muted, sitting at the end of a long table in a high-ceilinged, dimly lit room
accompanied by key members of his cabinet. After the presentations and some desultory and unprovocative responses, the president said that he would authorize his ministers to participate in
consultations with the opposition parties, unions, NGOs, the business community and the media to discuss our reform agenda. We
then went back to the other political players to see whether they
would sit down with the government. All agreed, except Alejandro
Toledo, who said we should be demanding an immediate overturn
of the election. However, he eventually consented to have his associates participate while he stayed removed. Apparently, Toledo initially told his close advisors not to join in, but they did anyway
because our mission held out the best hope of avoiding violence in
the country—a crucial and courageous step in giving the initiative
credibility. What we set up became known as "la mesa de diálo-
go"—the table of dialogue. It brought together a cross-section of
Peruvian political society to discuss reform of the judiciary, the

electoral system, the constitution, the media and—the most delicate area—the role of the police and army. To aid in the process, we announced that we would establish a permanent OAS office, funded by Canada, to ride herd on the "mesa" process. And in the background we beefed up our embassy staff with experts in constitutional law, election procedures and so on. Our peace-building fund came in handy once again.

After three days our mission had put in place a mechanism for political bridge-building, with a general agreement to foster real reform. Through the table of dialogue the various parties worked out their differences and built confidence in one another. In the words of Andrew Cooper: "Although it continually had to be rejigged with each wave of events, the mesa process possessed considerable entrepreneurial and problem-solving capabilities."[2]

It had been a tricky game. The wily President Fujimori was no pushover, but this time he was facing the censure of his peers. He had underestimated the strength with which the principle of democracy was beginning to outweigh the principles of sovereignty and non-intervention. With a major Summit of the Americas meeting about to take place—one where there would be a commitment to establish a charter of democracy—he was being seen as an embarrassment.

We also initiated a little back-channel diplomacy. I asked Madeleine Albright, the Japanese foreign minister and representatives of the European Union to apply pressure on Fujimori, who found himself faced with a formidable common front. I believe that some of his fight had gone, that the odds were catching up with him. Just before I left Lima, I received a call from the president, who was cruising on a Peruvian naval ship off shore. At the end of the conversation I took the opportunity to pass on advice from one old politico to another. I said, "Mr. President, if you want to survive and help your country, you have to get rid of your secret service chief, Montesinos." After a long pause he simply said: "Thanks for all your advice." A few months later, an incriminating videotape showing the security chief trying to bribe a Peruvian congressman set off a national storm, forcing the president to fire Montesinos, who then fled the country. He returned later in the fall, to be met with further calls for his prosecution.

Then on a visit to Japan, Fujimori sent a fax to the congress, announcing his resignation and his intention not to return to Peru. In the ensuing election Toledo was elected president, and Peru began the delicate task of building a renewed democracy. Throughout this period of turmoil, the mesa played a crucial role of filling a political void. It reached agreement on sixteen of the twenty-nine items on its agenda, including the independence of the judiciary and electoral reforms.

Little attention was paid to the success of the mission. At home only Paul Knox of the *Globe and Mail* showed any interest. And while the Quebec Summit passed its declaration on democracy, it made no effort to establish a mandate for OAS ministers to watch over democracy in the Americas, nor did the leaders provide resources for continuous third-party facilitation of democratic development. In fact, the budget for the OAS Unit for the Promotion of Democracy has had to be slashed for lack of donations. However, the precedent-setting nature of the mission has not been forgotten. It still stands as a model for moderate, legitimate intrusion—or multilateral "non-intervention intervention." And certainly many Peruvians have not forgotten.

If one wants to chart a manual for Canadian foreign policy, the Peru mission is a good place to start. Carried out under the auspices of a multilateral, regional organization, it focused on areas where Canadian diplomatic skills and resources could effectively be deployed. We had in the Peru crisis an opportunity to fill a role that wasn't within the ken of the United States but enjoyed their support, demonstrating that one can often be a good ally by playing an independent role. We did some impromptu open field running, but we also had a game plan for the long haul. And it was a team sport, not an individual test of strength.

DEMOCRACY AND THE COMMONWEALTH

It doesn't pay to make Nelson Mandela mad. That is the lesson to be drawn from Nigeria's close and exceedingly fractious encounter with the Commonwealth heads of state that led to its suspension from the club during its meeting in Auckland in 1995.

As the story is told, President Mandela had received assurances from Gen. Sani Abacha, the military dictator of Nigeria, that he would begin to mend his ways. Abacha had seized control of the country in 1993, declaring invalid the presidential election. The civilian candidate who had won the election, Chief Moshood Abiola, was thrown in prison, where he remained until his death in 1998. The military government of Abacha then began a regime of repression and corruption, with particular severity visited on the Ogoni people of the Niger delta, the huge oil-producing region of the country. The Ogoni engaged in various protests and acts of civil disobedience in an attempt to wrest some share of the revenue coming from the oil developments and to arrest some of the environmental despoliation of their land. Abacha had the army and police suppress the protests, for which it is widely reported he was well paid. A more unsavoury example of personal avarice and anti-democratic government would be hard to find. But Mandela endeavoured to extract commitments that Abacha would move toward constitutional reform and ease up on the strong-arm tactics.

Then, just as the Commonwealth leaders' meeting got under way, the brutal executions of Nigerian dissidents, including the well-known writer Ken Saro-Wiwa, were reported. Mandela, feeling betrayed by Abacha, used his personal prestige and presence to push through the immediate suspension of Nigeria under the terms of the Harare Declaration, which forbade military takeovers in member states. The decision on what steps to follow was turned over to a special group of foreign ministers called the Commonwealth Ministerial Action Group.

CMAG was a small but significant group assigned responsibility to implement the Harare Declaration in between summit sessions. Its members come from Africa (Ghana, Botswana), the Caribbean (Jamaica, Barbados), North America (Canada), Europe (Great Britain), Asia (Malaysia) and the Pacific (New Zealand). One couldn't find a more diverse group, yet it is bound together by intangible Commonwealth ties and a common interest in making preventative diplomacy, or soft intervention, work.

When I took Canada's seat in the spring of 1996, CMAG was undecided how far to apply punitive measures against Nigeria with the aim of reintroducing civilian rule. Nigeria was an important, influential country in Africa. It had oil. It was the most influential member of the Economic Community of West African States. It was, to its credit, playing a peacekeeping role in Sierra Leone. Understandably, African members of CMAG were wary about going too far in condemning Nigeria, urging dialogue instead. Not surprisingly, the British government, still Tory at that time, was equally reluctant to move, given the substantial British economic interest in Nigeria. (This position changed with the election of the Labour government.)

My position was that we certainly needed to engage the Nigerian government, but there also had to be a strong signal that there would be a price to pay for their behaviour. I felt that Canada was in a position to lead on the issue because we weren't encumbered by the restraints of other CMAG members. But senior DFAIT officials took a different tack: because we had no vital interests, why stick our neck out? Why not stay comfortably and quietly within the minimalist CMAG consensus? I disagreed, and I announced that Canada would put in place its own sanctions, using the Harare Declaration as a base. Our sanctions were not extensive, aimed mainly at the prerogatives important to the Nigerian leadership, such as travel and sports events. We also asked Canadian oil companies to restrict imports of Nigerian oil, and discussed with them a code of conduct for their operations inside Nigeria. Finally, we began a plan of direct support for Nigerian pro-democracy groups outside Nigeria, providing resources for information programs to be beamed back to Nigeria and stepping up pressure for the release of political prisoners. This is how we came to be closely connected to the current president of Nigeria, Olusegun Obasanjo, one of those in jail at the time whose cause we championed.

These actions had two results. First, they angered the military government of Nigeria, which started a media campaign blaming Canada for what were in fact dissident groups' bomb attacks in the country. They closed their high commission in Ottawa and harassed our officials in Nigeria, to the point that we withdrew our personnel for safety reasons.

Second, these actions helped to galvanize a more proactive response from CMAG. The Nigerian government was invited to

London for talks on whether they should be expelled from the organization—in effect a hearing on the legitimacy of their state. On our suggestion, CMAG also invited Nigerian dissident groups, especially those from the Ogoni region and NGO groups such as the Commonwealth Bar Association, to give testimony.

It was a stormy session when we sat face to face in the ornate, gilded meeting room in Marlborough House with a large Nigerian delegation wearing flowing, colourful robes and casting baleful glances at the Canadian representatives. I was reminded of the old saying "If looks could kill." The Nigerian foreign minister, Tom Ikimi, went through a long and at times abusive presentation, with most of the venom directed at yours truly. But as I listened to the twists and turns in his argument, one central element emerged— the Nigerian government was very anxious to retain membership in the Commonwealth. Status, credibility, belonging to the club, were important to them; they strenuously objected to being blackballed.

Valuing membership in international clubs is common to many regimes and governments; they want to be part of international organizations. Witness the eagerness of Central European countries to join Western-based organizations once they were freed of Soviet domination. Being a member endows one with presence, some prestige and some practical benefits, such as increased security and economic access to other states. Therefore, the threat of isolation is a powerful one. Even the mighty U.S., when it looked as if it might have its voting rights in the UN General Assembly suspended, went into overdrive to get congressional funds released to pay its dues.

Much as they desired to be restored to good standing, the Nigerian group would not commit to a timetable for enacting a new constitution, restoring political rights or freeing prisoners. They also faced damning testimony from many civil groups representing persecuted Nigerians. (Canada provided resources to help the civil groups do their investigations, travel to the meetings and make their case.) In the end, CMAG reached consensus on the failure of the Abacha regime to demonstrate any progress towards democracy and condemned its harsh rule. The recommendation to the leaders of the Commonwealth was to maintain the suspension and adopt a limited package of sanctions aimed primarily at the leadership.

The decision opened up an activist phase for CMAG, and the group became heavily involved in trying to restore legitimate government in Gambia and Sierra Leone. Through these CMAG meetings I was exposed to life-and-death struggles taking place around the world, and I grew increasingly frustrated as I saw countless countries that should have known better condoning or outright supporting arms sales—the top five countries for conventional arms sales are the U.S., the Russian Federation, France, the U.K. and Germany—or exploiting the resources of poor countries. After some special sessions of CMAG or missions to places embroiled in violence or extreme instability, I would return to Canada dismayed at the indifference of the public, the media and the government, or the pompous editorializing of right-wing commentators against being a do-gooder and straying too far from the position of our "big" allies, even though these allies were often the reason why there was no international action on humanitarian issues.

In June 1998, General Abacha died under somewhat mysterious circumstances. His successor, Gen. Abdulsalam Abubakar, moved quickly to respond to the Commonwealth conditions. He released political prisoners, established a timetable for constitutional elections the next year and dispatched his new foreign minister to discuss how CMAG could help in the transition to democracy. Canada responded by re-establishing our diplomatic presence and offering assistance. CMAG recommended Nigeria's readmission to the Commonwealth, and in 1999, General Obasanjo, whom we had supported during his period of exile, was elected president. When he visited Canada in the spring of 2000, he recognized the role we had played in promoting democracy in his country and our stand against the military rule. We had a clear bond with the new government and had helped define a creative role for the Commonwealth.

PAKISTAN

One of the most interesting of the missions I was involved in was leading the Commonwealth group that went to Pakistan after the military takeover in October 1999. CMAG had immediately suspended Pakistan from the councils of the Commonwealth, one step short of outright suspension, and I was asked to head a delegation of foreign ministers to discuss with the military regime their intentions in restoring democracy and their treatment of the imprisoned members of the previous government.

We arrived in Islamabad on October 28. Our reception in the Pakistani capital was a combination of studied politeness from the new government, apprehension from the traditional political class of powerful bureaucrats who had governed for decades, and very intense and critical interest from the media. The most surprising reaction was from members of deposed Prime Minister Nawaz Sharif's own party, who advised a go-easy policy by the Commonwealth in recognition of the parlous state of the country. Even many NGO and civil groups, who one would have thought would be strongly opposed to a military regime, asked us to moderate our stand and give Gen. Pervez Musharraf a chance to restore some order to the country and deal with rampant corruption. They described a society dominated by a hundred wealthy families who had used government to further their personal gain. In a foretaste of events that have unfolded in that region since September 11, 2001, we heard of power being amassed by fundamentalist groups and their threat to secular government in Pakistan. Hanging over all these discussions were the stirrings of the nuclear competition with India and the volatility of the dispute over Kashmir. The issues we uncovered in our short stay were much more complicated than the immediate crisis of a military coup.

That was brought home in our meeting with General Musharraf, which took place in an army compound outside Islamabad. Travelling on the Grand Trunk Highway, dodging the large craters in the concrete surface, we had a fleeting chance to observe the panorama of life in Pakistan. One striking and sobering sight amid the roadside dust and confusion was an imposing, pristine madrassa, an Islamic school for boys and a hotbed of recruitment for the fundamentalist movement.

The session with the general, in a room that was clearly that of a proud military man, decorated with flags and insignia and the trappings of various commands, was equally sobering. Dressed in starched army khakis, he was a man on a mission, clearly in charge, and seeing it as his duty to save his country. His sternness, sense of rectitude and diplomatic skills were evident—despite how he liked to describe himself, he was no simple soldier. But he was unyielding in not granting much of a timetable for democratic reform. He agreed on certain milestones, beginning with the holding of local elections, but I had the sense that restoring civilian rule was not his top priority.

As I continued to push him on the need for a specific time frame for restoring democracy, he responded with a revealing story. He told of visiting the southern Pakistani city of Lahore a few days earlier, travelling without escort or guards, being one of the people. As he stopped at a red light, people looked into his car, recognized him and broke into applause. "What more democracy do you want than that?" he asked me. I didn't have time to explain that the immediate adulation of the crowd doesn't quite add up to a democracy where a constitution sets restraint on leaders, people have a right to peacefully change leaders and human rights and basic freedoms must be honoured. What his comment showed was just how shallow the understanding of democracy can be in the military caste of Pakistan, if Musharraf is taken to be typical, and I daresay in many other places as well.

What his story also demonstrated was that we were faced with a dilemma. Our mandate was to promote restoration of civil rule and democratic practices. Yet there was strong evidence that General Musharraf enjoyed widespread popular support, and that the previous regimes, while civil and democratic in name, were really oligarchic and increasingly under the sway of fundamentalist forces in the country. Underlying Musharraf's support, however, was the hope that the general would live up to his commitment to build the foundations of a true democracy.

That sentiment formed the gist of our report back to the Commonwealth Heads of Government. We acknowledged the appetite for change that gave some credence to the new government, but emphasized that military rule should not be a permanent state. It was up to the Commonwealth to keep the pressure on and apply every effort to move the regime towards democratic reform.

I also tried to enlist support for an international campaign to promote democracy in Pakistan. As I stated in my letter to Madeleine
Albright, "General Musharraf feels little external pressure to
restore civilian government. This could lead the general to the mistaken belief that a relatively peaceful and well-intended military
coup is more acceptable than a violent and unpopular one." Not
much resulted from my effort. There were too many other considerations of a military and economic nature.

Looking back, I wish there had been more time, or perhaps inclination, to pick up on the signs and portents in Pakistan. Here was
a society under stress: extremes of poverty and wealth in a region
of instability, drought and intrigue; an overburdening debt; huge
outlays for the military; minuscule expenditures for education or
health; Islamic extremism on the rise, infiltrating the army and
intelligence service; a dangerous border conflict with India, made
all the more treacherous by a nuclear arms race. Offering advice
and registering admonishment on a military takeover was too narrow an approach. CMAG should have discussed a broad plan of
action with the Pakistanis.

Since the mission, Pakistan has experienced some significant
post-September 11 developments: Musharraf became a staunch
supporter of the U.S.-led coalition against al-Qaeda and the
Taliban, transforming Pakistan in the eyes of the Western world
from pariah to partner. He installed himself formally as president,
with formidable powers over the government, in what virtually all
observers saw as a rigged election. In national and provincial elections in October 2002, a hard-line Islamic coalition gained control
of the legislatures of the two northernmost provinces, and the dispute with India over Kashmir continues at a high state of sabre rat-
tling. Terrorist attacks against foreigners are increasing, and Taliban
and al-Qaeda insurgencies in the northern provinces continue to
threaten stability in the region. Musharraf claims that the cause of
stability requires a strong man at the tiller and heavy military and
secret police activity. In the meantime, the social and economic
condition of the country goes unattended and Muslim fundamentalism, still aided by influential officers in the army and the secret
service, is on the increase.

If I were to pick an area of real risk in the world, a source of instability and insecurity, it would be Pakistan. To use the old Asian expression, Musharraf is riding a tiger—astride a country that can in a second turn on him. Yet paying lip service to the fight against terrorism takes precedence over improving living conditions, advancing democratic rights or resolving the Kashmir dispute. The key player in this equation is the U.S. But a stronger Commonwealth presence could play a crucial role.

The irony is that at the time of the Pakistan mission we were involved in discussions on how to broaden the mandate of CMAG to give it more scope and capacity to respond in a proactive, preventative way. But some influential Commonwealth leaders saw this goal as too energetic and active. A leader in waylaying the initiative was, not too surprisingly, Robert Mugabe of Zimbabwe.

This didn't stop the Commonwealth from becoming engaged with Zimbabwe over the next year. In March 2002, after receiving a report from a Commonwealth observer group on the fraudulent elections that returned Mugabe for a fifth term, an ad hoc group of heads of state, composed of President Obasanjo of Nigeria, President Thabo Mbeki of South Africa and Prime Minister John Howard of Australia, ordered a temporary suspension of Zimbabwe. Discussions with Mugabe's government simply didn't go anywhere, and the expectation, especially in light of the increasing violence, was that the Commonwealth would move on to full suspension, as it did with Nigeria. But in September the same group of three backed away from full suspension and gave Mugabe another six months without setting any conditions. Clearly the two African leaders in the troika didn't want to move against a peer, while John Howard of Australia wants tougher action. Matters will come to a climax at the Commonwealth heads of government meeting in December.

Despite such setbacks, CMAG remains a useful instrument of soft intervention in the protection of people, in this case protecting their democratic rights. The UN system has deferred leadership on these issues to common-interest or regional organizations like CMAG and the OAS.

These organizations are not paragons. Their soft interventions go only as far as the political commitments of leaders will allow. A lot depends on who those leaders are and the kind of leadership shown. The difference between a Mandela and an Mbeki is obvious; the ascension of a Labour government in the U.K. changed the dynamics of CMAG's handling of Nigeria. But those who say the actions of such groups as the OAS and CMAG don't matter are missing the fact that membership in such bodies is conditional on good behaviour and there are mechanisms to hold member states responsible for their actions, and subject them to such penalties as sanctions or suspension. Here is a model for emerging associations such as New Partnerships for Africa's Development. It also reveals, by way of contrast, the weakness of regions where such mechanisms don't exist. The absence of effective collective standards or security institutions in, for example, Southeast or Central Asia is reflective of that problem.

The same potential exists in la Francophonie, where we have great and comparable advantage as a French-speaking country; the Group of 20, where we have taken a lead in trying to reform international finance; in NATO where we can help in searching for a renewed transatlantic partnership; and in various organizations dealing with environment, health and labour practices. The drawback is that each of these initiatives is the consequence of individual leadership from an individual minister or ministry; it is not part of a Canadian government policy, properly funded and supported. Without such a coherent framework, the vagaries of events and pressures can push us off course, as we have seen in the neglect that our multilateral participation suffered after September 11, and in our less than modest efforts on, for example, Uganda and the Ivory Coast. Unfortunately, much of our time and energy is expended in dealing with the U.S. border and the washout from U.S. adventures against the "axis of evil."

PART V

The *United* Nations

CHAPTER 11

REWIRING THE UN

THROUGHOUT THIS BOOK I HAVE PRESENTED THE UNITED NATIONS IN both positive and negative lights. Sometimes it cuts the Gordian knot. Sometimes it ties it tighter. It's time to address the UN's role in the world, and Canada's position within the UN. This is especially important in the wake of the role played by the UN during the Iraq imbroglio, a time when many of its basic tenets were put to the test.

In the walk-up to the military invasion of Iraq, the UN was at global centre stage. The debates at the Security Council were the stuff of great drama, as contending views on how to achieve disarmament in Iraq were duked out by foreign ministers. The goings, comings and pronouncements of UN weapons inspectors were followed minutely by the global media. The U.S. hurled about charges of irrelevancy, countered by claims for the legitimacy that only the UN can endow to any use of force.

Our UN ambassador, Paul Heinbecker, was a regular feature on Canadian newscasts in his role as the carrier of a compromise solution to the permanent-five divide, and our prime minister took a principled stand against Canadian participation in the invading military force because of the lack of a UN resolution—a position endorsed by the majority of Canadians but severely attacked by various editorialists, politicians and certain business community representatives, a debate that again revealed the ongoing tensions inherent in trying to travel a distinctive Canadian path.

The aftermath of the Iraq events created doubts about the UN. In a survey taken in twelve countries six months after the terrorist attacks 94 per cent of Canadians, the highest number of all those polled, expressed believed that the UN could have a major or moderate role in making the world a safer place. In fact Canadians were the only national group where a majority (52 per cent) believed it could make a significant impact.[1] The Iraq war shook those beliefs. In a global survey conducted in June 2003, only 43 per cent of Canadians considered the UN important in dealing with international conflicts as compared to 50 per cent who said it was no longer so important. Even at that we were still ahead of most other countries where perceptions of the value of the UN were much lower.[2]

These poll results show that many Canadians like others around the world are questioning the validity of our UN role which has been a mainstay of Canadian foreign policy. For more than fifty years we have rightly bought into the case made at the end of World War II that there had to be a multilateral approach to preventing aggression, preserving security and promoting widespread international cooperation in social, economic and health matters.

The poll numbers also show that multilateralism, at least as represented by the UN, is an increasingly harder sell. The UN is not the shining beacon on the hill that it once was. One of its chief founders, the United States, is governed by an administration that sees it as an expedient to be used only when necessary and isn't too eager to pay its bills. Even those who believe in the institution sometimes see the UN as mired in bureaucracy, a hothouse talk shop dominated by special interests.

This tarnish puts a special onus on countries like Canada. We must do what we can to make it an effective place for the meeting of minds, the resolution of disputes and the advancement of hope. We must also recognize that the UN is *vital* to Canada, affording us a place in which we can exercise influence, lessen our dependence on bilateral relations and help establish policies and practices consonant with our values and interests. The urgency and necessity of this commitment has become all the more apparent as the world tries to pick up the pieces after Iraq and bolster the capacity of the UN to meet the challenges of today's conflicts and the hostility of the world's superpower to using the institution, except as a necessary handmaiden to clean up post-conflict debris.

There have been many permutations in both the nature of international issues the UN has considered since its inception and the way it has responded. Cross-border aggression has been displaced by internal wars as a major source of conflict. These conflicts are the seedbed that spawns disease, drug trafficking and terrorism around the globe. The new threat of a network of terrorists who call no territory home poses a particular challenge to the fundamentals of the UN, which bases its security rules on nation-states. How to respond to aggressors and their threats when they occupy no territorial base will require a much stronger UN role in mobilizing a multilateral anti-terrorist campaign.[3]

The UN's original campaign to end colonialism has been replaced by the battles to control AIDS, develop market economies and build stable democracies. Strict adherence to the notion of state sovereignty has been challenged by the growing ramifications of international human rights and humanitarian law. Powerful forces of global integration, both positive and negative, are also altering traditional governance. Throughout, Canada has been steadfast—at least until recent days—in its attention and interest, making a variety of contributions to UN operations, paying our bills on time and, in the instance of Lester Pearson's historic initiative on peacekeeping, playing a vital and innovative role in shaping UN action.

This is a role we must continue to play. For all its flaws—and there are many—the UN system is essential to world peace, justice and progress. After being awarded, along with the UN, the Nobel Peace Prize for 2001, Secretary-General Kofi Annan captured the essence of the argument for the UN when he addressed the General Assembly: "The Nobel committee has used this prize to, in its own words, proclaim that the only negotiable route to global peace and cooperation goes by way of the United Nations. In a world that is growing ever more interconnected, and is yet still torn by brutal conflict and cruel injustice, it is more important than ever that humanity travel that route, and that all of us work hard to pave the road ahead of it." The UN thus acts as a pathway away from dominance by one superpower or a return to international anarchy. To continue in this role, the UN needs the strong involvement of key member states like Canada.

Canada also needs a strong UN. It is the cornerstone of a network of rules, institutions and practices that restrain the unilateral use of power by states that wish to rule by might. It is emerging as a seedbed for increasing democratization and, through the International Criminal Court, for holding individuals accountable to a rule of law. It is the crucible for formulating collective action to meet global challenges ranging from the global digital divide to the chasm of world poverty.

The human security approach is a natural fit with an activist role for Canada in the UN system. While it was true that to achieve a treaty banning land mines we had to short-circuit the UN Conference on Disarmament in Geneva, an institution persistently paralyzed by consensus decision making, the broad sweep of the land-mine campaign fully engaged many other agencies and people in the UN network, including two secretaries-general. More important, it provided the tools and techniques to create the International Criminal Court.

Our championing protection of civilians at the UN has also established Canada's presence. The crucial choice now is how to fashion a continuing role for Canada in the UN that enhances those initiatives. To see how easy or difficult that might be—and to offer some insight into how the UN works—it's worth seeing what happened when Canada last served on the Security Council from 1999 to 2000.

ON THE SECURITY COUNCIL

The campaign Canada launched in 1997 to win a non-permanent, two-year seat on the Security Council demanded some tailoring of techniques to meet the unique political customs of the UN.

First, we had to perform the distinctive dance steps of a diplomatic minuet, both in the corridors of the UN building in New York and over seven-course meals in various ambassadorial residences around the world. It takes not only a strong set of kidneys but also the fine art of subtle persuasion. The internal politics of the UN are organized around an elaborate set of groups and caucuses for which, each year, candidates are put forward by the respective blocs. Some blocs—the Africans and Latin Americans—are quite disciplined and offer only two candidates for election as Security Council members. The final vote is then taken by the full membership of the General Assembly. Unfortunately, for historical reasons, Canada belongs to the Western European and Others Group, twenty-seven members increasingly dominated by the bloc voting of EU members, or would-be EU members. WEOG doesn't formally designate its candidates, relying instead on informal agreements. Often, agreement is hard to come by, especially if a non-European member such as Canada, Australia or New Zealand wants to contend. In the 1998 election, our competition was the Netherlands and Greece, both of whom mounted strong efforts. We could not count on much voting support from the Europeans.

What we had going for us was a very strong base in the Americas and in Africa. Over the years our aid efforts and our membership in the Commonwealth and la Francophonie had brought us into close contact with nations in those areas. Some political analysts have commented that Canada is a regional power without a region. But the Security Council race, and our other international campaigns, tends to refute that thesis. There are a number of Southern countries who see us as part of their region as long as we work with them and help on their issues. Staying engaged and well represented in those areas is thus a requisite to building Canadian influence on the international stage.

By way of contrast, the year before our election, Australia had been resoundingly defeated in their bid for a council seat from the Western European and Others Group. They were certainly affected by the EU bloc voting, but in addition, they hadn't built up bases of support. Australia's foreign policy specifically focused on their own region of the Pacific, which led to their having little credit in other regions. To ensure that we didn't take this Southern constituency for granted, we organized a program of special envoys, employing the talents of current and former members of Parliament and former diplomats, all of whom had special knowledge or contacts in various areas. At times, DFAIT had a sales force that would have made Amway proud.

Horse-trading skills also came in handy. Bargaining for votes is a well-honoured practice in the UN, just as it is in any domestic legislature or cabinet room. I found having been the regional minister for Manitoba for several years a useful preparation for exchanging with fellow foreign ministers their promises of support for a Security Council vote for Canada against our future consideration of their countries for other international posts. The hard-slogging, door-knocking, numbers-crunching exercise that is part of any well-organized electoral campaign proved of immense value, except that the potential voters were the 185 members of the General Assembly and the turf to be covered ranged from South Sea atolls to the Organization of African Unity meeting in Ouagadougou. In campaigning for the Security Council, the old political adage that you must press the flesh meant whirlwind tours to several countries in the space of a week. If this is Wednesday it must be Latvia, Lithuania and Estonia . . .

Being an impresario helps. Events designed to impress upon potential supporters the quality of one's national character and cultures are a must. One of our European competitors—the one with a beautiful archipelago of islands in the Aegean Sea—staged a history tour for UN permanent representatives and their spouses. We countered with a Cirque du Soleil performance in Lower Manhattan and a seminar on the new UN security agenda in the Gatineau Hills. While not quite so scenic, I think we came out ahead.

Ultimately, though, as in domestic politics, the real judgment is of the credibility, reputation and performance of the candidate. What you stand for and how you comport yourself as an international citizen is the real litmus test, at least for a country running without the luxury of a guaranteed vote from its own group. We had to earn our votes. From the outset, it was clear that Canada carried a good brand name in UN circles. Our UN ambassador, Bob Fowler, was highly respected by other permanent representatives in New York, and our UN delegation was seen as effective and creative. The presence and personality of Ambassador Fowler and his team brought great credibility to Canada's candidacy. But as we sized up our chances in late 1997, we felt those assets weren't enough. We needed to present a winning case—to spell out the specific priorities Canada would pursue if elected. It was issues politics at the global level.

We came up with a three-pronged commitment. First was to make the work of the Security Council more open and participatory. Smaller states were complaining about the increasing secrecy of the council and the closed-shop approach of the permanent five, or P-5, members. Along with others we had experienced the unpleasant situation of having the council make decisions on peacekeeping missions without ever consulting donor countries. The bypass on Bosnia still rankled. Rarely were heads of UN agencies or outside experts asked to speak to the council on matters where their special knowledge would be of great use.

Second was to reassert the role of the Security Council as an active player in global security. We wanted to restore the integrity of the council in exercising its prime mandate: deciding on and initiating multilateral responses to acts of violence and conflict. From its period of activism in the early nineties, the council had become a reluctant dragon, tarnished over Rwanda and Bosnia, subject to squabbling over mandates and money, offloading its responsibilities to coalitions of the willing and setting up trust funds to pay for peace missions as a way of avoiding adding to the dues of UN members. Clearly, the efficacy of the council had become a problem. The secretary-general had already emphasized to me the need for the council to have a much stronger grasp of the challenge presented by internal wars. Helping restore the council's effectiveness, we decided, was a noteworthy aim.

One way was through the human security agenda, our third prong. I felt this was an ideal opportunity to put front and centre our views on how the UN Security Council should become far more aware of the need to protect individuals. P-5 members were notorious for defending nation-states' sovereign rights unless it was in their interest to intervene. In the meantime, though, the toll on civilians in internal conflicts was mounting. Particularly galling were the memories of UN peacekeepers standing by in Srebrenica while innocent people were taken away to be murdered or abused. It was important to find ways for the council to broaden the mandate and meaning of security.

We packaged these three ideas together, gained cabinet approval and launched a highly visible platform of reform. It was a winner. Many members who felt excluded, who resented having their interests ignored or who shared our concerns about the conservatism of the council responded with enthusiasm and with their votes.

On October 8, 1998, I sat in the assembly chamber with Ambassador Fowler and other members of our UN delegation awaiting the results. As the afternoon wore on, tension started to eat away at our confidence.

Being inside the General Assembly, with its vast tier of seats occupied by delegations large and small from every corner of the globe, dominated at the front by an imposing black-and-green-marble speaker's dais, always filled me with a mixture of awe and reverence; it is as close as we have come to a world forum for decisions affecting the grand sweep of peace, security and well-being. The opening words of the UN's Charter, "We the Peoples of the United Nations," carry meaning and consequence. In one of those rare moments of reflection when the treadmill stops, I realized how fortunate I was to be sitting there waiting for the decision of the world's representatives on whether they would support my country to act for them over the next two years in what is in effect the cabinet of the UN.

When the votes were announced it was a moment of surprise and delight. We won with 75 per cent of the vote, far ahead of any other candidate, and clearly a strong endorsement of our platform. For the next two years we would be able to put many of our ideas to work. As various delegates and ambassadors came over to offer their congratulations, it struck me just how heartfelt many of the good wishes were.

We now needed a strategy that would give us the scope to fulfill our commitments within the limits that we faced as a non-permanent member of the council. There is nothing equal about Security

Council membership. There are the P-5, who were seen as the dominant powers at the end of World War II, and then there is everybody else. And members of the P-5, just like any unelected elite, defend their prerogatives and privileges—namely their veto—with fierce determination and guile. One of the constant refrains on UN reform is the need to expand the number of permanent members to reflect changing global politics. Asians, Africans and Latin Americans claim they are under-represented; the Japanese and Germans argue they have economic power. My thought is, and always was, that the veto should be abolished and that it would be much better for the UN if everyone had to stand for election. The council could then be expanded to include more Southern members. There could be a variation on the period of election, with staggered terms, allowing certain countries longer terms. Direct accountability to the membership, however, should be the basic principle. Of course, that is not about to happen. For now we are stuck with two-tier membership.

Nevertheless, there are ways to parlay the position of an elected member. I liked to remind the P-5 representatives that we had received an overwhelming vote for our platform, and our UN diplomats were assiduous in keeping in contact with the constituency who voted for us—nations from the South—briefing them on council business, insisting on their right to appear before council on matters of interest and constantly decrying the P-5's habit of holding privileged, secret meetings. As one somewhat exasperated P-5 ambassador remarked to me, he thought that Ralph Nader was our strategist.

Another tactic was to use the post of president of the council to full advantage. The presidency is a rotating position, with each member holding the chair for a month. With a fourteen-member council, we could expect to hold the presidency twice in our term. During each of those periods we would have control over the agenda. There would be the necessary grunge work and the crises that were the commonplace of an unsettled world. But the presidency also opened the opportunity to bring forward topics of our own choosing. The trick was to introduce a broad enough program during our first turn at the chair, and then attempt decisions or resolutions in the second round fourteen months hence.

The choice we made for our first presidency was to promote the physical protection of civilians. With the memory still fresh of UN peacekeepers standing by in the massacre at Srebrenica and the genocide in Rwanda, we were determined to ensure that any UN action would incorporate a mandate to protect civilians in times of conflict. This included humanitarian aid workers and child soldiers, as well as the millions of displaced persons uprooted by internal wars. To add substance, we took the unprecedented step of inviting the president of the International Committee of the Red Cross, Cornelio Sommaruga; the president of UNICEF, Carol Bellamy; and the UN Special Representative for Children, Olara Otunnu, to appear before the council. They gave powerful testimony on the condition of civilians in conflict and the need for international military intervention. A few weeks later we invited non-council members to make similar presentations. More than twenty member states responded, adding validity to our argument that member states would respond on substantive issues when the council opened its procedures to broader involvement.

This first foray into the protection agenda worked well. I issued a presidential statement detailing the severity of the problem and asked the secretary-general to present a report to the council within six months containing recommendations for action. A working group chaired by Canada was set up to help prepare this report. This was all done with the full approval of all members of the council. The initial acceptance of our proposals, however, depended on more than just the persuasiveness of the arguments. A good deal of time and effort had been spent in behind-the-scenes diplomatic discussion. In this we were helped greatly by the election of the Blair government in Great Britain and the arrival of Foreign Secretary Robin Cook, who had declared his own version of human security in calling for an ethical foreign policy. Madeleine Albright and Russia's Yevgeny Primakov also instructed their UN delegations to be helpful.

One of the most important issues at the time was sanctions. As a tool for enforcing international decisions against states that break the rules, sanctions are far less drastic than military intervention, but severe enough to impart seriousness of intent, and so potentially can be very effective. South Africa is one obvious example. But the use of sanctions had increasingly fallen into disrepute. There was growing concern that economic sanctions restricted the flow of basic necessities, so that the suffering fell on a country's general population and not on its leadership. That was certainly the argument against the sanctions that had been imposed on Iraq. At the other extreme, there have been far too many examples of the Security Council deciding on sanctions and then never properly implementing them. Either way, most people agree that sanctions are not a silver bullet. More often than not, they amount to doing peace and security on the cheap in places where troops and aid are considered too costly.

As a new member on the council we were offered a choice of chairing either the committee overseeing the sanctions in Iraq or the one overseeing Angola. We chose Angola as holding greater prospects for results, since Iraq was hung up in a tortured back-and-forthing among the P-5. Angola presented the sorry state of an incredibly rich country impoverished and devastated by thirty years of war, its population decimated by the profusion of land mines and small arms imported by the Soviets and Americans to support their surrogate armies. As the Cold War ended and the big powers withdrew their patronage, the vacuum was filled by the purveyors of arms. It has been estimated that in the 1990s the rebel forces—UNITA, led by Jonas Savimbi—received between U.S.$3 and $4 billion from diamond trafficking, a healthy source of revenue with which to purchase weapons and keep the troops happy. The war went on.

Beginning in 1993, the Security Council had introduced a series of resolutions setting out sanctions against UNITA, the first time such measures had been taken against a group other than a state. The embargo first applied to arms and oil and later targeted the leadership of UNITA. It was our task to monitor their application and effectiveness. There wasn't much to do, as the sanctions were a joke, a paper commitment that nobody took seriously. Ambassador Fowler set out to change that. He travelled to Angola to gather evidence on who was breaking the sanctions program, and the council approved a group of experts to evaluate the complex relationship between the trade in diamonds and oil and the arms trade. Even the diamond-trading industry realized that the heat was on and began taking steps to curtail the purchase of "blood diamonds," as they were becoming known, from Angola.

As the work progressed, the reports coming across my desk began reading like a Le Carré novel. Private-sector involvement in civil armed conflicts makes for an underground world where multinationals of international repute, airlines, arms traffickers and shady financial brokers find themselves mixing with corrupt political leaders and mendacious warlords in an economic network that exploits divided communities for profit and greed. As Don Hubert, one of DFAIT's insightful policy advisors, has observed, "the accumulation of wealth seems to be at the heart of many contemporary conflicts."[4] But this economic dimension is not generally given much consideration. It doesn't fit the conventional notions of war as aggression between nation-states and it involves private, non-state actors. One of our primary goals was to strengthen the UN's capacity to deal with the cause of internal wars, and Ambassador Fowler's findings helped reveal the growing nexus between conflict and commerce.

Iraq offered another window into the complicated workings of the council and the problems associated with sanctions. Another failed opportunity to resolve a festering source of disruption and confrontation that finally resulted in a major armed attack by the U.S. and the U.K. against the regime of Saddam Hussein, and the consequent "regime change."

I had already been exposed to the Byzantine politics of Iraq under Saddam. In late November 1990 I had joined two other members of Parliament in a mission to attempt to negotiate the release of a group of Canadian oil workers held hostage by the Iraqi government—"detainees," to use today's euphemism. It was a strange ten-day odyssey, with official minders constantly on watch, bugged hotel rooms, long days waiting in elaborate government reception rooms for audience with Iraqi leaders, and the omnipresent visage of Saddam Hussein smiling from a plethora of billboards and murals. It was a country ruled in large part by fear, ravaged by the exhausting and disastrous war with Iran, defiant in its attitudes towards the West. After several days of badgering, we finally obtained the release of the detainees. I returned to Canada with the chilled feeling of having witnessed a truly oppressive regime. So I had no illusions about the ruthlessness of the Iraqi leader or about his absolute control of the country. He was certainly capable of developing weapons of mass destruction, an assessment later reinforced in briefings I received from Richard Butler, then head of the UN weapons inspectors in Iraq, who laid out the harsh reality of the tricks Saddam Hussein was capable of using to avoid compliance with UN resolutions requiring full disclosure and disarmament dating back to 1991.

I had, however, questions about the sanctions policy that was being applied. Evidence was mounting of the severe hardships being experienced by the Iraqi people and the breakdown in the basic infrastructure. All too often it is the people who pay for their leaders' sins. With that in mind we used our best efforts to unstick the stalemate between, on one side, the U.S. and Great Britain, who favoured resuming inspections and maintaining harsh sanctions, and, on the other side, China, France and Russia, who opposed a return to a comprehensive inspection regime. We held out against both positions and suggested that the degree of sanctions should be tied to the acceptance of inspections. As compliance improved, sanctions would be lifted; there could be complete rescinding with full compliance. Since several other council members agreed with this strategy, neither side of the P-5 division could gain a sufficient majority of votes to win the day.

We were under some considerable pressure, especially from the Americans and the British, to accede to one of the polarized positions, but we continued to push back. Finally, Madeleine Albright and I struck a deal during a meeting of the Association of South-East Asian Nations in Kuala Lumpur. She agreed to lighten the sanctions criteria and allow the freer exports to Iraq of medical, pharmaceutical, educational and agricultural products, along with machinery and steel pipe to repair the oil fields. It was not all that we wanted, but it was a concession that would result in less restrictive impositions on the Iraqis. We agreed to become a co-sponsor of a resolution and brought with us several other council members. We then framed a resolution that, while it would not command the outright support of the Russians, Chinese and French, would avoid a veto. Those three countries abstained when an omnibus resolution was passed in December 1999 (resolution 1284, December 1999).

At the time it looked as though we had played a useful role in helping to shape a solution that gave more direct aid to the Iraqi people. But in retrospect, I believe we made a mistake. I wish we had held out longer. We could have committed more time and greater diplomatic effort to seek a deal with real "light at the end of the tunnel" provisions. It might have worked. As it was, the Iraqi leadership spurned the UN move of 1999, the inspectors stayed in New York and the American administration has waged a major war unseating Saddam, repudiating fundamental principles of international behaviour, and embarking on a major test case of their doctrine of "pre-emption." A little more time and perhaps more stubbornness on our part might have paid a real peace dividend.

There was some redeeming benefit to our efforts in Iraq. In our exchanges with the P-5 we advanced our ideas on civilian protection and sanctions. As Kosovo began heating up, we put forward the case for UN humanitarian intervention, and we later played a strong role in mobilizing support for a UN force in Sierra Leone, including a clause requiring the UN peacekeepers to provide protection for civilians. We did the same for the UN resolution on East Timor. "Never again" was our constant refrain.

All this was important to give us a strong position from which to present a series of proposals in April 2000, the next time we would hold the council presidency. We orchestrated various measures on sanctions and civilian protection and recruited an impressive line-up of notable international figures to appear. We planned an initiative to follow the experts' report on Angola, held an open session on the human rights situation in Afghanistan and Sudan and responded to the report on Rwanda. By that time cabinet had approved a $10-million human security fund. Having money to fund projects appropriate to these issues was a good way of showing we were serious.

Secretary-General Kofi Annan and the secretariat provided a major boost when they tabled, in September 1999, their report on the protection of civilians in conflict, with forty detailed recommendations. It was a well-argued document, expressing the secretary-general's own deep commitment. Having that kind of backing gave weight to our arguments on everything from preventative peacekeeping to direct intervention to stop serious human rights abuses.

Why is all this manoeuvring important to mention? It shows that Canadians can make multilateralism work. It is a special kind of vocation, requiring a variety of skills and resources. Forming alliances, negotiating deals, constructing proposals, coordinating between home office in Ottawa and the delegation in New York, having our diplomatic posts abroad work their counterparts in national capitals, changing attitudes and behaviour through influence and persuasion—these are the much maligned but highly effective attributes of soft power. It requires a good game plan, carefully watched over by the prime minister and endorsed by cabinet. We also made an effort at consulting the Canadian public through the UN Association in Canada, and as always sought cooperation with key NGO groups.

One example of how this diplomatic activity can connect directly to Canadians came about as a result of a meeting I had with Sally Armstrong, then the editor of *Homemakers* magazine. Through her magazine, she had mobilized a petition of ten thousand signatures protesting the plight of women in Afghanistan under the Taliban. It struck me that this kind of public commitment by individual Canadians should find expression directly in the council, so we organized for April a full day's treatment of the issue, highlighting the involvement of tens of thousands of Canadian women in making this a matter of international priority. Besides broadening the range of security issues to be treated by the council, it demonstrated how the council could be made more accessible to a concerned public.

In the end, however, it all comes down to performance, and in April 2000 we were on centre stage in New York. Not really a stage but a horseshoe-shaped table in light Scandinavian wood with slightly frayed blue upholstered seats in the middle of the brightly lit council chamber. There is a well-worn protocol to Security Council sessions. The elaborate use of exalted salutations—"the distinguished representative from Slovenia"—is all carefully scripted by a UN secretariat official and neatly typed in a binder so that the untutored chairperson won't stray from the prescribed order of things.

A foreign minister presiding as a president, which I did on six occasions in April, is greeted by the regular attendees with some suspicion, especially by the P-5 ambassadors, who wonder what devious scheme brings an elected politician to these sacred sur-roundings. It does serve to signal, however, that any item on the agenda is not just another stratagem from the permanent delega-tion but carries the weight of the government in question.

The debate on any one item follows no particular order of prece-dence. Most statements are designed not to change minds but to establish markers for future positioning. Where the bargaining goes on is in the little anteroom behind the council chamber assigned to the president for the duration, in the corridors or delegates' coffee lounge or over the very elaborate lunches between one and three-thirty every day. It is here that the real discussions take place and support is solicited. We would meet with countries that supported our initiatives, along with key NGO representatives, to plan strategy and discuss the contacts we thought crucial. The mem-bers would then fan out to take their calls, as they say in the sales business. Key to this operation were the skilled Canadian foreign service officers, such as David Angel, Elissa Goldberg, Andras Vamos-Goldman and John Holmes, who kept an eye on the various UN committees and so knew the players, what their interests were and what kind of approach had to be made. Before I went into a meeting with another foreign minister or an ambassador from a country that needed courting, they would hand me a short note with all the pertinent information and relevant advice.

It was a success. During the one month of our presidency we constructed a package of measures, proposals and public debates that focused on the need for the Security Council to shift its per-spective to the security interests of people, not just states. Central to this was Resolution 1296, on civilian protection, which established a clear responsibility and guidelines for the Security Council to act against crimes against humanity and committed it to respond to violations against humanitarian personnel, displaced persons or refugees. Its call for mandates for peacekeepers to ensure protection for civilians under "imminent physical threat" was a direct response to the failure in Bosnia and Rwanda of UN peacekeepers to act against crimes against people due to vague instructions, inadequate resources and an absence of political will. Resolution 1296 was an important addition to the rules that define international accountability for human security. It doesn't ensure that this will always be honoured. Political calculation by member states is still the ultimate determinant. But weaving such principles into the institutional fabric of the Security Council creates a better-defined framework for humanitarian intervention.

Sharpening the tools for that intervention is also necessary if international action is to be effective, which is why we focused on improving sanctions. First, we tabled a report on sanctions prepared for us by the International Peace Academy. Second, we gained approval for wide-ranging recommendations on how to make the sanctions regime against UNITA effective. A month earlier, the panel of experts on sanctions against UNITA (set up by our original resolution) had published a dramatic report on how the flaccid sanctions could be made far more robust. The findings included naming President Blaise Compaoré of Burkina Faso, President Gnassingbe Eyadema of Togo, the deposed leader of Zaire, Mobutu Sese Seko, and certain leaders in Congo-Brazzaville as being complicit in trafficking arms to the rebels in return for payment in diamonds. It also pointed out that some Eastern European countries (Bulgaria was the prime suspect) were too lax in their export controls, allowing arms traders to use their territory, and criticized the diamond-marketing system based in Antwerp for its use of "blood diamonds." This bold naming and shaming was a fist into the solar plexus of the genteel world of UN diplomacy, occasioning many disclaimers and howls of protest.

The New York Times ran a story based on the report before its official release. Within minutes after the story appeared, my phone began to ring with calls—not always polite—from ministers whose countries had been singled out. But the evidence was there, and my retort was, "Show us to be wrong by curtailing the practices." The diamond industry went into immediate damage control by offering remedial measures. Just as important, the report propelled the Security Council to condemn the sanctions busters and set up a monitoring mechanism on Angola sanctions.

Angola has now entered a new and, I hope, more peaceful stage. Savimbi is dead, killed in a fight with government troops, the rebellion has come to an end, and there is a chance for peace to be restored. For the first time in a long time, Angolans are without immediate fear of violence spawned by war, even though the after-effects of the war—a destroyed economy, a land corrupted by land mines, broken lives and limbs—remain. Reconstruction will be a massive task, with international assistance much needed. There will still be the question of how to turn the wealth of Angola into benefits for its entire populace, not just for the elite and their multinational corporate partners.

It is fair to say that the effort Canada made, focusing international attention on ways to end the conflict, helped bring about change. Certainly, one result was a substantial limit on the material support that the rebel forces could derive from diamond trading. The naming exercise, and the subsequent monitoring, also placed a damper on Savimbi's political connections; it wasn't convenient to be seen as a friend of UNITA.

Since the Angola report, many more steps have been taken to address the role of private players in conflict situations. Various extractive industries are beginning to formulate codes of conduct for their members. The secretary-general's initiative, the Global Compact, which brings together major corporations to examine their responsibilities to promote human rights and environmental good practices, is being mirrored by similar efforts by the World Bank and the OECD. The U.S. and Great Britain have agreed to establish guidelines for corporate investment abroad, and DFAIT has established a unit dedicated to corporate social responsibility.

What is still missing are the lessons from the Angola report: that naming and shaming works, and that there must be a regime for enforcement and judicial action against individual transgressors. There are still too many predators, public and private alike, who prey upon the riches of the many poor countries, exploit and foster conflict to fill their pockets and contribute to depths of human misery. One only has to look at continuing conflicts in Colombia and the Congo to see such avarice at work.

WHAT NEXT?

The Security Council and the International Criminal Court are just two among many of the platforms within the UN system where Canada has shown its ability to make things happen. In the aftermath of September 11, Canada's UN role has been downplayed, in some ways underplayed—regrettably so, since our period on the council, and the efforts by Canadian ambassador Paul Heinbecker to try to broker a compromise on the Iraq resolution, shows that the UN is a good place for us to exercise our talents for creative diplomacy. The emphasis by the Canadian government, however, has been on anti-terrorism measures, and contending with pressures for greater integration with the U.S. And since we left the council, our government has not paid much attention to following up council initiatives launched as part of our human security agenda, nor to taking leadership on UN-related issues. As one senior UN official commented at a public conference, "Canada seems disengaged from the UN." This may change now that Bill Graham, a knowledgeable internationalist, as foreign affairs minister appears interested in promoting *The Responsibility to Protect*, the report of the International Commission on Intervention and State Sovereignty.

The recent tabling of this report offers an opportunity to mobilize the General Assembly. One little-used power the assembly has is to direct the Security Council through resolutions. Such resolutions are not binding, but do carry weight. For example, the General Assembly set terms on carrying out the UN's policy on decolonization, even though the Security Council ostensibly had the authority. Our emphasis should be on gaining strong assembly endorsement for this principle of reorienting the definition of sovereignty and for the commission's recommendations for reform of the UN to meet the needs of a more robust interventionist mandate.

Indeed, the reform of the UN is a natural and necessary corollary to a human security agenda. While on the council, we pushed for greater accountability, transparency and participation from both non-council members and non-state actors. The push for openness should be continued, and extended beyond the council to all other UN venues. The UN still has trouble dealing with civil groups. There is a tendency to keep them at a distance and not invite public involvement. This may be one reason for the decline in the UN's credibility among the public at large. Our efforts to work with NGOs and our innovations in designing multilateral forums should be a priority for Canada at the UN.

The time couldn't be more propitious. The anti-globalism movement has created a demand for more accountability from global institutions. There is a scramble to find means of giving individuals a sense of being involved in decisions that affect them but which are made by seemingly unreachable international bodies dominated by faceless international bureaucrats or blocs of countries intent only on defending their prerogatives. The giant global conferences organized by the UN are becoming more unmanageable as they are overtaken by special interests or become the battleground for clashes between competing ideologies of a cultural or religious kind. The wrecking-crew strategy followed by the U.S. and the paralyzing tactics of countries like Cuba in defending the status quo are two reasons why there will have to be reform.

REWIRING THE UN

Present efforts to reform the UN either are of the housekeeping category—better use of resources, effective coordination (both useful up to a point)—or consist of regional powers importuning to become permanent members of the Security Council. Neither really gets to the nub of the problem: the flawed nature of a multilateral body designed around power alignments and policy ideas stemming from the Second World War. One of the most egregious of these leftovers is the secretive and exclusive exercise of power by the five permanent members of the Security Council. They have too much power, the members of the General Assembly too little. As we have seen, this leads to stalemate on issues of special interest to any one permanent member, or the abuse of their joint position as they collude behind closed doors.

Some political scientists argue that this situation only reflects political reality, but this is a hard case to make given that Britain and France are members, but not Germany, Japan, India or Brazil, to name just a few qualified contenders. It makes even less sense when you consider the dominant position of the U.S. relative to all the others, and the increasing importance of regional bodies. The European Union is a full participant in the G-8 but is represented on the Security Council by only two of its members. Anger over European opposition to the U.S.'s war on Iraq has resulted in the U.S. asserting the need to kick France off the council, to be replaced by a more compliant Japan. The right wing is even suggesting that the U.S. should leave the council altogether.

All this brings to the fore the central role of the Security Council. Its legitimacy and credibility are under attack. Its usefulness is marred by the present makeup of the P-5 and the provision of the veto. If it is to have a future as a significant place of decision making, it must become both more representative and democratic and subject to more direct scrutiny and accountability to the General Assembly.

It is too much to expect the present membership to give up their privileged position. But it is possible, as Canada tried to demonstrate, to make the council more responsive and open. It would also be possible to develop a membership formula based on varying terms—from four to eight years—that would be served by members of different regional groups—larger, more significant members serving for the longer term but without the veto. Personally, I would like to see the veto abolished. But that may be for a future generation to achieve. For the immediate near term the power of the veto needs to be circumscribed so that it can be used only on specific issues of peace and security, such as an action under Article Seven, authorizing robust peacemaking missions or mandating regional groups to exercise an interventionary force. This is an immediate

requirement. In order for the UN to be truly effective using intervention based on "responsibility to protect" principles, the General
Assembly should take on a decision-making role.

The other serious consideration is how to apply certain basic tests
of membership—a question that runs throughout many of the
organs and agencies of the UN. Should a member state be allowed
to take a seat endowing certain responsibilities, especially in the
Security Council, if it is in flagrant violation of a UN resolution, has
refused to pay its membership dues, is governed by a military dictatorship, and is under inquiry for suppressing the rights of its own
citizens? Tricky questions, particularly since some of the P-5 may
have trouble passing the bar. Yet many other multilateral organizations
are establishing codes of conduct for their members. It's time the UN
examined its criteria, not so much for belonging to the organization
but for being given seats of responsibility and decision making.

The principle should be carried over to the General Assembly
and its committees. Greater democratization would give real heft to
enhancing the scope of the assembly's powers. The most obvious
move, much debated in NGO circles, is some form of People's
General Assembly, modelled after the European Parliament, that
would serve as a second chamber of the General Assembly. Direct
election to a global body, bypassing governments, is an idea whose
time is surely coming, however much it would be opposed by big
countries who ignore the UN or use it only when it serves their purpose. Trying to sell the idea of direct election to the U.S. Congress,
the Russian Duma, the Chinese Politburo, the Indian Parliament
or to Fidel Castro would need divine intervention. Nevertheless,
presenting the proposal as a legitimate long-term plan would bring
some needed zest to the institution. In the meantime, there is
nothing to stop individual member states from experimenting by
some form of direct election of their representatives.

Such reforms would enhance the assembly's overall credibility and
be the grounds for giving it a more active overriding authority. The
General Assembly could expand its responsibility to the protection of
civilians during peacemaking missions; it could be prepared to act
when the Security Council freezes on an issue. It would be able to
deal assertively with terrorist threats. Policy-makers in Washington

shouldn't be the sole authors of the UN's response to terrorist threats. A multilateral response, based on law and full cooperation, will in the long run be a better antidote than a unilateral military strategy. The General Assembly has passed several important anti-terrorist conventions. It now needs to think operationally.

If this change is to take place, there will eventually have to be a standing UN constabulary that can move quickly on preventative missions and be the beachhead for larger peacemaking missions, provide an investigative enforcement arm for the International Criminal Court, and be available for robust duty in protecting UN humanitarian workers or seeing to the dismantling of arms systems in compliance with disarmament resolutions. Right now there is limited capacity at the UN for a rapid response to security crises, and all previous efforts to establish some form of standby force or to have a UN constabulary have been rejected or ignored. In this respect UN members are mired in the status quo, unwilling to challenge the big powers who want to keep the UN emasculated, and reluctant to put up the money and commit the resources. But why is it all right for the European Union or NATO to have a rapid-reaction force, but not the UN? The only reason is that the EU or NATO is where the bigger powers can exercise control. It's imperative that the UN have the ability to act effectively, whether in offsetting a killing spree in a member state, ensuring weapons inspections in a place like Iraq or protecting UN activities.

One little-known organization that Canada participates in is the Stand-by High Readiness Brigade, made up by ten (with another eleven observer nations) countries that have standby units available for UN duty. Their last exercise was to head up the UN mission in Ethiopia and Eritrea. They could be the embryo for a more expansive UN capacity to directly serve UN needs. Canada chaired the group in 2003, putting it in a prime spot to begin working on a plan for a UN force that can react quickly, without too much delay and red tape. What is disappointing is how little was done during this tenure in pursuing a more up-to-date peace role through a standby force, whether through the Stand-by Brigade or a more expansive UN gendarmerie. There is a distinct lack of initiative on how to advance the concept of peacemaking, especially in light of the turbulent conditions we live in. Nor has there been serious political development of coherent approaches to what modern-day peacemaking requires in the way of training, resources or commitment. This is another failure of living the unexamined life in terms of global responsibilities.

The Geneva-based UN Disarmament Commission, the UN Commission on Human Rights, the UN High Commission for Refugees—each in its own way suffers from sclerosis and needs fixing. Countries whose prime motive is to stall action and prevent any worthwhile initiative seek membership in these bodies. The disarmament agency has ceased to play much of a role and needs a new assignment. The human rights group is discredited by indulging in the worst kind of political horse-trading. The refugee organization is dismally underfunded and hasn't taken on the politically difficult issue of dealing with internally displaced persons, or environmental refugees, even though in numbers and degree of suffering they weigh equally with the plight of conventional refugees. Nor is it tackling the problem of national governments restricting acceptance of conventional refugees. In fact, there is a complete absence of international institutions to deal with the growing number of cross-border migrants.

In each of these cases, traditional sovereignty gets in the way; too often there is implacable hostility or outright bullying from the strongest members and defiance from many of the smaller outlaw regimes and their criminal allies. All these UN organizations are in need of a spark, something to break the ritual dance. The "responsibility to protect" principle could light a fire of real reform by establishing a new, modern standard by which the behaviour of states is measured.

It can also take us beyond war, conflict and criminal activity into a basic rethinking of the ways in which the "responsibility to protect" must be applied to economic and environmental dangers—disparity, drought, disease and degradation of scarce resources. As we shall see, there is a fundamental economic inequity based on a trade and investment system that is discriminatory and insensitive to local efforts towards growth. Yet any notion of developing some form of global-based source of revenue, such as a transaction tax, in which revenue is derived from taxing international currency transactions (the Tobin tax), is discarded out of hand, and there are constant efforts to keep labour and international environmental institutions ineffective.

There is a plethora of ideas on how to restructure existing international organizations and build new ones.[5] Joseph Stiglitz, the Nobel laureate and former chief economist of the World Bank, has provided a number of useful suggestions, including an international bankruptcy court, more frequent use of standstill provisions (an insurance system to help mitigate risk) and altered voting systems in the IMF and World Bank to ensure more inclusive representation. George Soros, the international financier, has a good idea in establishing a system of global drawing rights that would give developing countries greater liquidity and limit the role of the IMF. Everyone from the anti-globalists to the World Economic Forum is looking at new forms of global governance, and there is no lack of creative combustion. What it comes down to is a need to change the nature of who makes decisions and in whose interests. It is the classic question of all political systems—who governs?

If we want the UN to be the governing body for so many of these issues, there is much work for Canadians to do to help transform it into a more credible institution for the twenty-first century.

CHAPTER 12

REBIRTH OF A COUNTRY

EARLY ONE APRIL MORNING IN 2002 THE PHONE RANG AT MY HOME on Vancouver Island, coaxing me to leave the comforts of my bed, where I had been applying myself intermittently to the *New York Times* crossword. On the line was Chris Child, a senior official from the Commonwealth Secretariat in London. Would I be prepared, he asked, to serve as the head of the observer mission being organized for the May 14 election in Sierra Leone?

At first, it seemed an offer I could have and should have refused. Three weeks earlier I had returned from a long trip to China, and had spent the previous week in Washington and Ottawa. It seemed I was on the road more now than when I was foreign minister.

Over coffee, I discussed the offer with my wife, Denise, and the conclusion we reached was that I couldn't say no. What really swung the balance was the memory of my last time in Sierra Leone, just about two years ago to the day. Sierra Leone was then a devastated country, destroyed by years of war and the most extreme brutality. It was full of people mutilated in the attack on the capital city of Freetown and camps of former child soldiers living with the recent experience of being violated or being forced to murder. A government that had no visible authority, propped up by an ill-equipped and poorly trained UN force, was faced with the immense tasks of reconstruction.

What took me to Freetown in 2000 was the plight of war-affected children. Earlier that year, negotiations in Geneva had produced a UN protocol that held transgressors accountable for employing children as warriors. At the time, the atrocities in Sierra Leone were receiving worldwide attention. The sight of children being used as human shields and the mutilation of children's arms and legs by the rebel group the Revolutionary United Front brought home to the world just how diabolic the use of children in conflict is.

At a meeting organized by Canada and Ghana of foreign ministers of ECOWAS—the Economic Community of West African States—there had been a strong plea for quick action. I flew to Freetown as part of a delegation carrying a message to the rebel leadership that there should be an immediate release of the several thousand children, mainly girls, who were being held by rebel groups in the country.

Three things stand out in my memory from that brief visit. First was meeting the victims of the atrocities. It is hard to describe the shock of encountering a large group of young people whose limbs have been brutally amputated not because the children were in any way involved in the war but simply because the RUF saw this as a way of instilling fear into the local population. That sense of inhumanity was compounded during a session with repatriated war children in St. Michael's Interim Care Center, a camp outside Freetown, painfully making their way back from their days in the bush as marauding warriors. A Canadian-supported pilot project designed to aid in the demobilization and rehabilitation of former young warriors, St. Michael's was a stirring example of the creative use of our foreign aid.

There was poignancy in this encounter with children who yearned for some normalcy after the various violations they had suffered but had little opportunity under the circumstances. One young girl, when asked what she would like most, replied, "To go to school," echoing the plea of Emma from Uganda. Unfortunately, there were virtually no public schools in the country, just as there was little in the way of any public services, even though Sierra

Leone was a country rich in resources. The diamonds, though, had become the spoils of war and gone into the pockets of the corrupt rebel leadership, their allies like Liberian president Charles Taylor, and the arms traders and diamond companies. Money was not available for schools or hospitals.

The second memory is of my session with Foday Sankoh, the head of the Revolutionary United Front. Under an agreement to end the fighting, signed the previous summer between the RUF and the government, Sankoh had been brought in as a member of the new coalition government. Ironically, he was in charge of mineral policy, meaning that he could continue to control the flow of diamonds to his ally Charles Taylor in neighbouring Liberia and receive guns and money in return. He wouldn't come out of his fortress compound on the outskirts of Freetown for a meeting, so we eventually confronted him in his den. Again, it is hard to find words to describe my reaction on meeting someone who is truly an incarnation of evil, even though in appearance he was not very prepossessing. My first impression was of an unkempt, grizzled man, looking nervous, tired and scared. He sat behind a small desk in a tiny room full of the most modern communications equipment. Crammed into the back of the room and bunched outside the door were his personal guards, those responsible for the many machete-inflicted atrocities that had been committed in the attack on Freetown. It was a daunting and depressing atmosphere in which to present demands for the release of children fighting with or being held by his forces. As could be expected, Sankoh denied all knowledge of any children being held, and said he would issue orders that if such a practice was by some mistake being followed by his lieutenants, it would cease. When I challenged him to join me in making a public statement to that effect, he quickly demurred and let loose with a rant against all those who tried to sully his reputation, particularly the malicious international press.

It was a hopeless exercise, but one that had to be carried out if for no other reason than to let him know that his actions were being monitored and he wouldn't be able to mask his guilt forever. We told him that he would be held responsible, and now he is. He died behind bars awaiting trial for his war crimes.

Third, I learned a lesson about just how risky and primitive is the business of carrying out international humanitarian missions, however right the cause. The morning we arrived at Freetown airport, the Tarmac was full of Nigerian troops leaving after having served as front-line peacekeepers for ECOWAS. They had had to withstand the assault on Freetown a few months before, taking heavy casualties and facing the tough dilemma of whether to fire on the advancing ranks of child soldiers, some as young as eight and ten, being used by the rebels as human shields. To say that they looked relieved at their departure was an understatement.

Peacemaking in the era of messy internal wars is a dangerous business. The Nigerians had suffered hundreds of casualties, but from many accounts had been pretty brutal themselves at times. A UN-sponsored force had now relieved them. We would soon witness a cruel irony. The new UN commander told us he was reasonably upbeat about restoring order in the country, saying that UN soldiers had advanced out of Freetown, were establishing control in the countryside and might soon move into the diamond-producing area held by the rebel groups. That was on a Saturday night. Sunday night, the RUF started a counteroffensive that had clearly been in preparation when we were talking with Sankoh (still ostensibly a member of the government, if not for long). The UN contingent was soon in deep trouble, with several soldiers being killed and many kidnapped. It emerged that many of the UN troops were poorly trained, poorly prepared and poorly equipped to take on the hardened warriors of the RUF, many of them the very child soldiers that Sankoh disavowed knowing about. Once again there was fear that the capital would be overrun, an event forestalled by the immediate dispatch of a contingent of British paratroopers who were training in the area.

Mobilizing an effective force to undertake the tricky and sensitive task of military intervention in tragedies brought on by others is not easy. It was recognized that the government of Sierra Leone didn't have the capacity, and the ECOWAS countries were no longer willing to carry the burden alone. The Security Council had authorized a force with a specific mandate to protect civilians, but it was difficult to recruit forces, especially from nations with well-

equipped professional troops. Mandates are one thing; being willing to deliver is quite another.

Politicians and military advisors are increasingly reluctant to
risk their own forces as international policemen in faraway, dangerous places. Countries find it difficult to mobilize resources and
support for the UN so that it can be in situations on time, with
good equipment, good intelligence and clear instructions. Not
only is there reluctance to become involved, there is greater reluctance to pay the price in lives or money, especially among the
Western countries, who are often the best equipped. In Canada,
Sierra Leone was a tough sell. We had major commitments at the
time in the Balkans, and there was little appetite to go into such a
messy situation—a view shared in most other capitals. There was
a growing aversion amongst our senior soldiers to being seen as
peacekeepers: they wanted to be fighters. So, in 1998, while the
UN Security Council dithered and Western governments, including Canada's, demurred, it was African countries working under an
authority from ECOWAS who had originally intervened, carried
the costs and suffered serious casualties. Later UN forces were
primarily from Asia. Increasingly, it is the Southern countries who
keep the peace.

With all these vivid memories in mind, I found it impossible to
say no to the Commonwealth observer mission two years later. The
night before I left Freetown in 2000, I had been sitting with Olara
Otunnu, the Ugandan who was the UN Special Representative for
Children and Armed Conflict, on a veranda overlooking Man of
War Bay comparing notes on our mission to free the child soldiers.
We talked about the unimaginable horrors we had seen first-hand
and wondered what could ever become of a place that had gone
through such profound collapse.

Yet two years later Sierra Leone was holding democratic elections. Foday Sankoh had been jailed, a special court had been established to try war criminals, and the UN had bolstered its peace
force and given it a stronger mandate. It was a country coming
back from a man-made hell, trying to install a governing society. It
was a story of rebirth, a human story too hard to resist. I wanted
to witness this rebuilding. Many of the ideas of international

peace-building, protection of civilians, rights of war-affected children and international criminal law that I had cared about as foreign minister were being played out in this small country on the west coast of Africa. It was my chance to see the treaties and agreements we had fought for translating into action. Most important was the effort of a weary, war-racked people to find stability and security in their lives, aided by an international community—the very essence of the human security ideal. I wanted to find out directly, not filtered through news reports or briefing notes, how and why this had happened.

As the plane from London made its descent through bumpy skies towards the airport across the bay from Freetown, I wondered what changes I would find. Some were immediately apparent. I was aboard a Sierra National Airlines 757, operated by a British charter company on a twice-weekly schedule, crowded with Sierra Leoneans returning to vote and a large contingent of election observers from the EU and the Carter Center in the U.S. On landing we pulled up to a partially completed modern terminal, crammed with people hustling for their luggage and lining up in a long queue at customs just as at any terminal in a North American city.

Two years earlier, arriving in Lungi on a Canadian military Challenger, I had been greeted by a strong security contingent. The terminal was rundown and seedy. The only other plane on the Tarmac was a transport craft loading the Nigerian troops. Civilian observers and election experts were a much healthier omen than weary troops anxious to leave a scene of threat and uncertainty.

I saw other positive signs as I made the rounds of Freetown that first day. Many of the bombed-out buildings downtown were being repaired or replaced. Houses were being constructed. There was liveliness in the streets, markets were crowded, and there were fresh vegetables for sale. The upbeat sense was emphasized by the finance secretary, a young Sierra Leonean with a Ph.D. in economics from the University of Wales, Bangor, who proudly showed us a graph demonstrating how the finances of the country were coming close to meeting the conditions laid down by the IMF and the World Bank (not without a cut in salaries for teachers and health workers), meaning that Sierra Leone could soon be eligible for debt relief.

The same pride was expressed by Walter Nichol, a former policeman who now found himself in the hot box as chief commissioner of the National Election Commission. When we caught him at the end of a long day, he offered us a beer and described the scramble to get ready for the election of a president and a new Parliament only four months after the war had officially come to an end. It wasn't until January 17, 2002, that President Ahmad Tejan Kabbah had declared that rebels and pro-government militias had completed the disarmament phase of the peace process. This had opened the way for an election on May 14.

Walter Nichol was especially anxious to point out that his commission was impartial and independent and had taken special pains to preclude fraudulent voting. All voters had to be centrally registered with a photo ID, everyone who voted would be stamped with indelible ink, and there were transparent ballot boxes supplied by a Canadian company to ensure against ballot stuffing. With only five days to go until the election, 2.3 million people had been registered out of an eligible 2.7 million, and the atmosphere had been remarkably free of serious violence or disruption. I was surprised to see the RUF on the ballot, their candidate a respected former diplomat.

As we left Nichol's office, climbing down unlit stairs, being jostled by a stream of election observers collecting their certification, a great commotion erupted on the street. I thought, This is it: all the plans for an orderly election are about to come apart. Instead, it was trucks arriving, under heavy escort by UN troops, laden down with the see-through ballot boxes carrying votes cast early by the army, police and election workers who would be occupied on election day. It was a cause of great excitement for the people congregated around the dilapidated election headquarters. The voting had begun. The country was thirsting for a new beginning.

The next morning we set out for the regional centre of Makeni, once the headquarters of the RUF in the north. To avoid congestion from election rallies, our driver took a route through the hills surrounding Freetown. As the Land Rover bumped its way up and down a red dirt road that made an Olympic mogul course look tame, the reality of what ten years of war had brought to Sierra Leone was all too clear. While Freetown had a certain air of optimism, the countryside revealed the true level of devastation. Houses in ruins, villages bombed and burnt, schools and hospitals destroyed, basic infrastructure shattered. Alan Doss, head of the UN Development Fund in Sierra Leone, told me that he estimated that 80 per cent of schools and hospitals had been completely destroyed. In 2001, Sierra Leone was at the very bottom of the UN Human Development Index—the same measure that Canadians like to look to with pride when we are ranked first.

As we made our way north, weaving between massive potholes and axle-breaking ruts, some of the traffic on the road was the ever present white patrol or supply vehicles of the UN. The remainder were dilapidated cars or small vans loaded down with yellow canisters sticking out of the windows or piled on roofs. These were people going in search of scarce and widely dispersed water supplies.

Along the way there were camps for displaced persons, ex-combatants, war-affected children, war widows and refugees. The signs outside each of these settlements offered a veritable who's who of international humanitarian organizations, NGOs and development agencies, all in the business of feeding, rehabilitating and caring for the victims. In 2001, two-thirds of the government's budget came from donations or loans from the World Bank or the African Development Bank. The big UN agencies and various bilateral programs have delivered fully U.S.$120 million in humanitarian aid. The British have made the biggest commitment, spending £8 million per year on various relief and rebuilding programs. Canadian contributions have amounted to about $6 million a year, mainly for humanitarian supplies and support of child-protection activities, funded on a project-by-project basis through NGOs.

One such group is CAUSE Canada, started up by an Alberta couple, Bev and Paul Carrick, who have lived in Sierra Leone since the mid-eighties. I had first come across their work in 2000 when I visited the Murray Town Amputee Camp, in Freetown. CAUSE Canada at that time was involved in providing teaching and therapy to the victims. On this second trip I learned of their work with young girls who had been captured by rebel groups, forced to become their "bush wives" and to suffer through endless violations, not unlike Emma. As part of the peace process, these girls now faced the difficulty of reintegrating into their communities and restoring some sense of security to their lives. CAUSE Canada, in partnership with a Sierra Leone women's organization, was helping with their counselling and training. One of their most serious hurdles was overcoming the stigma of "being rebels." This required intensive mediation with family and the community.

This particular project involved some five hundred young women and girls, with a budget from CIDA of $2 million. To put this in perspective, Sierra Leone must cope with some seventy thousand ex-combatants, seven thousand of them former child soldiers, all needing some form of assistance. The National Committee for Disarmament, Demobilization, and Reintegration is responsible for destroying their weapons, finding them shelter, keeping them fed, training them for new occupations that don't use a gun and trying to give them back some standing in their community, all on a budget of $34 million from the international community. As I write, there is a shortfall of $13 million in those donations, and the largest shortfall is in the area of reintegration. The constant scramble for money is a major part of rebuilding after a conflict.

Arriving in Makeni brought me face to face with the reality of having large numbers of former warriors in your midst. The ex-combatants were threatening to disrupt the election unless they were paid the settlement money owed to them. Part of the deal to end the war was a government commitment to pay the combatants the equivalent of $30 a month living allowance while they were going through adjustment programs. The money hadn't arrived. The local chief of police, who went by the nickname Sisko and proudly told me that he had studied for an M.A. in mathematics at the University of Ottawa in the seventies, made it clear that he was prepared to take on the protestors. Everyone in Makeni was extremely nervous about the impending showdown as election day drew near. The former combatants ended up occupying the local national election office, but left when some of them received their stipend, taking with them only a few light bulbs. There wasn't much else to take.

What came out in my conversation with Chief Sisko was the resentment that many Sierra Leoneans feel about the training and support given to ex-combatants when their own situation is so dire. They see this as coddling a group of killers who once terrorized the country. Along with the deep desire for peace is a suppressed outrage, a feeling that some form of justice, perhaps retribution, is needed. It is one of the most acute dilemmas facing any society that has gone through the torture of a civil war.

I got to meet first-hand the targets of the chief's anger when I sat down with the newly minted political organizers of RUFP, the new political wing, many of whom were former commanders of the RUF. In 2000, I had been repulsed by the brutality and terror tactics of the RUF. In Makeni in 2002, and later the next day in the town of Kenema, another RUF stronghold, I began to understand a little more of why they had started on a road to violent conflict, how diamonds had shaped their rebellion and why such an effort was being made to reintegrate them into the society.

DIAMONDS ARE A REBEL'S BEST FRIEND

University students protesting against corruption, inequality and authoritarianism, hallmarks of the Sierra Leone government in the early nineties, were the original instigators of the civil war in Sierra Leone. Inspired by the revolutionary agenda of Col. Muammar Gaddafi of Libya, the students were able to recruit support amongst the villagers and miners in eastern Sierra Leone who resented the dominance of the local tribal chiefs, the economic and political elite of Freetown and the corrupt government of the time.

The whiff of this early political protest agenda still permeates the rhetoric of RUF adherents. Sitting in a large room upstairs from RUFP election headquarters in a rundown house on the outskirts of Kenema, I was treated to a long treatise on the need for justice and equality by a very angry young man in a stylish pair of black jeans and a turtleneck and wearing an expensive gold watch. He was a former senior commander in the rebel forces; he was perhaps seventeen or eighteen. As he proceeded with his denunciation of the evils of the ruling forces, the young men and women who ringed the room paid rapt attention to their leader. The organization still works in a strict hierarchy, and the former commanders are still very much in control. For many young RUF followers, this is the only association they have. It is their extended family, and they belong here because it is so hard to return to their previous life.

As the RUFP district leader continued his litany of concern for the poor and oppressed and his feelings of betrayal by the government, the UN and anyone else he could think of who was part of the international conspiracy, I had a chilling sense of something missing: no remorse for all the innocent lives he had destroyed, not the slightest tinge of guilt. That is part of the harsh reality of trying to come back from ten years of war.

Where had all the idealism and legitimate aspirations of the first student revolutionaries gone wrong? The answer lies with the cupidity of two men, Foday Sankoh and Charles Taylor, and the corrosive effect of diamonds.

First, there is the central, corruptive role of Sankoh. A British-trained corporal in the Sierra Leone army, he became involved in the Liberian civil war, where he picked up the skills of guerrilla warfare and formed a strong attachment to Taylor, who succeeded in overthrowing William Tubman's government. Back in Sierra Leone, Sankoh became a photographer, then instilled himself with the student radicals as a military expert, organizing the movement along highly disciplined lines while retaining the revolutionary *esprit*. Along the way many of the student leaders found themselves victims of the same murderous tactics that Sankoh later used on a much wider scale. The idealists lost control to a cunning, ruthless man with decidedly strong leadership qualities. In 1991 the RUF was formed and began a major insurgency.

Then came the diamonds, found plentifully in the eastern region. Sankoh and his followers, with the help of the Liberian army, were able to use force of arms to secure control of the diamond fields. A flourishing trade began across the Liberian border involving the RUF, Taylor and a network of diamond merchants who were only too happy to cream off their percentage from this illegal trade. From the trade came the supply of money to buy copious amounts of weapons on the black market, mainly out of

Eastern Europe, and the sophisticated communications equipment and ground transportation that gave the RUF mobility and speed. The money also found its way into the hands of the RUF commanders, who not only profited personally but could buy loyalty from a lot of people and drugs for the young men and women kidnapped to be fighters and kept in a semi-comatose state of induced obedience. Keeping control of the diamond areas became an overriding objective of what had once been a movement for social justice. The irony is that the method of control was to decimate those areas and terrorize the population. In 2002 in the Kono region there was barely a house standing, all the schools, hospitals and government buildings were rubble and most of the people had been displaced and were only just beginning to return.

Diamonds made the RUF capable of a full-scale attack on Freetown in January 1999, and able to surprise, kill and take hostage a large number of lightly armed UN peacekeepers in May 2000. I recalled the room in Sankoh's bunker full of elaborate radio equipment, undoubtedly used to keep in touch with his field officers as they planned the attack against the UN troops who were getting too close to the diamond fields. In this respect, Sierra Leone suffered the same fate as Angola and many other African states—its mineral riches are a curse rather than a blessing. That is why the initiative that Canada took at the UN in tackling the connection between the trade in arms and diamonds in Angola has had major repercussions throughout Africa. The Kimberley Process, set up to register legitimate diamonds and thereby identify illegal, or blood, diamonds, is having its hoped-for outcome. Political leaders can no longer hide their complicity, traders are now subject to scrutiny, and the host country can begin to again enjoy revenue that previously went to criminals and warlords. In a two-year period the government of Sierra Leone went from a little more than $1 million in revenue from the diamond fields to in excess of $26 million.

But the illegal trade continues, producing double the revenue garnered by the government, much of it still going into the hands of RUF supporters and across the border into Liberia, with some also going to the pro-government paramilitary groups that fought against them. On the main street of Kenema, the only buildings that looked in reasonable shape were the multitude of shops of the diamond merchants owned by members of the Lebanese diaspora in Sierra Leone. The government still finds it difficult to apply any comprehensive control on the mining fields and at the border. Indeed, a senior UN official told me that there will never be any control in the region unless the whole area is sealed off and mining turned over to a few key legitimate concessionaires. In a further twist, a report from the Human Security and the International Diamond Trade in Africa project, conducted by Partnership Africa Canada, pointed to a connection between the illegal diamond trade and global terrorism, it is yet another example of how internal conflicts feed terrorist organizations and why a multilateral response to civil conflict is so important.[1]

To add to the precarious situation, Liberia has continued to be a source of arms and a receptacle for diamonds. Although with Charles Taylor now in sanctuary in Nigeria after a bloody civil war, things might improve. Who knows what other factors could destabilize Sierra Leone, to say nothing of the entire West African region. The outbreak of civil war and the attempted coup in the Ivory Coast also trace their roots to rebel groups operating out of Liberia. The abuse of rights continues, civil war goes on, cross-border incursions increase, refugees flee from one temporary sanctuary to another, and children are still dragooned as soldiers. This is another tragedy foretold, and one typically given short shrift by the rest of the world.

It comes back, again, to how and with what means does the international community step in to forestall the actions of a national government that creates misery and conflict for its neighbours. Sierra Leone is struggling to form a peaceful democracy while Taylor of Liberia has nothing but trouble and diamonds on his mind.

If the test is to be human security, rather than national sovereignty, then Liberia is a prime candidate for a far more active form of international involvement. Taylor has been indicted by the Sierra Leone special court. The time is ripe for a sustained international strategy on reconstruction and a much tighter monitoring of countries and companies that aid in the pillaging of resources. To make it work will require a concerted partnership between developed countries and ECOWAS. Following the NEPAD initiative, Canada set up a $15-million West Africa fund. Its application to Liberia's situation would be a timely and necessary investment. Support would be especially effective for the UN-sponsored tribunal that charged Taylor in June 2003 with war crimes.

BLUE HELMETS AND WHITE TILLEY HATS

What is keeping the situation stable right now in Sierra Leone is the "blue helmets." After the UN's humiliation in May 2000, the Security Council decided to get tough. Canada played an important part in revamping the UN role in Sierra Leone and giving the revised force ample powers both to protect itself and to protect citizens. As I write, the UN Mission in Sierra Leone—UNAMSIL—a contingent of more than seventeen thousand troops with civil backup, is omnipresent throughout the country. Drive to any town and you will pass a UN checkpoint properly armed and watchful. As the election proceeded, the UN was called upon to use its helicopters to deliver ballot boxes in remote villages. Its troops are involved in building schools, delivering water and sponsoring human rights education in the schools.

UNAMSIL's primary task, however, is maintaining security, and since 2000 it has achieved that. Sierra Leoneans, including some in the RUF, speak with admiration of Kenyan Gen. Daniel Opande, the force commander, and of his skilful negotiation in getting the RUF to lay down their arms. The surrender by forty-six thousand combatants, handing in 15,840 weapons and 1.3 million rounds of ammunition, is one of the most successful disarmaments of small weaponry in modern times. To put this accomplishment in perspective, think of how difficult it has been to begin a handing over of weapons in Northern Ireland and the fact that no disarmament has taken place in Afghanistan.

Perhaps the ultimate tribute to the UN was contained in a poster I saw in Makeni. It was in support of the re-election of President Kabbah and proclaimed, "Kabbah go, then UN go, white man go, money go"—a clear pitch that Kabbah's victory would mean the UN would stay. Kabbah won an overwhelming majority. When was the last time the UN was a major issue in a Canadian election? Maybe it's one example that refutes President Bush's claim of UN irrelevance?

The UN is now staging down its commitment. UNAMSIL's mandate was renewed in September 2002, but with the understanding that some three thousand troops would be withdrawn over the next year and further downsizing would take place into 2004. The present force costs more than $700 million a year, so the reluctance to maintain that level of commitment is understandable. And the international community is notorious for pulling out once a crisis is over, believing the job to be done. What happens when the UN goes is a matter of serious concern. When and how to exit is one of the trickiest judgment calls. If the basic security blanket is pulled before there is an effective replacement, then the rebuilding is put in peril. Haiti was a textbook case of premature withdrawal and its accompanying headaches.

Efforts are under way to develop a homegrown security capacity. Although the British have taken on the training of the Sierra Leone Army, the public is still highly suspicious of the SLA, who have a long history of overturning civilian governments.

Similarly, the Commonwealth and U.K. government are sponsoring training programs for the police force (and also helping to set up a countrywide radio system). Here, too, there is a long way to go before the national police are capable of keeping civil order. Adrian Horn, a big, burly cop from Birmingham who heads up the Commonwealth Community Safety and Security Project, said that when they started the program the local police were demoralized, corrupt and ill trained. He feels there has been significant headway since. But does he think the police are ready to take over many of the security functions now provided by UNAMSIL? Not by a long shot. If nothing else, their complement is still three thousand short of what is considered necessary to effectively staff stations throughout the country and provide investigative services. So far, pledges of assistance to make up the shortfall haven't been forthcoming.

Even if the police are brought up to standard and sufficient numbers, there will still be the problem of ensuring a fair trial and finding facilities for incarceration. The legal system is close to collapse, with only thirty-five lawyers in all of the country in 2002, the rest having fled the dangers of war. The few judges are in desperate need of training to meet contemporary standards. And virtually all of the country's jails have been destroyed. When I met President Kabbah after the election, he asked if Canada could send—urgently—judges and lawyers to work in Sierra Leone.

It isn't easy rebuilding a country after war, especially if the colonial powers—in this case Great Britain—leave without having bothered to develop a skilled, literate population. The illiteracy rate in Sierra Leone today exceeds 70 per cent. Add to that years of government corruption and a resource-based economy either fleeced by exploiters or discriminated against by a trade system that favours the developed nations. Then mix in ten years of vicious warfare that savaged what services there were and scared away the small coterie of well-trained professionals. Rebuilding is a monumental task.

ELECTION DAY

They made a good start on election day. Hours before the seven a.m. opening of the polls, long lines began to form, and it stayed that way for most of the day. Many people had to wait several hours under a sweltering sun to cast their ballot, an ordeal borne with remarkable patience, good humour and determination. One elderly gentleman I spoke to at a voting station in Freetown—an open-air cabana on a beach—told me he had been there for five hours, but was going to stay as long as it would take because, he said, "It is my right." In the areas most severely touched by the war, voting took place outside or in the shells of buildings without benefit of shade or respite from the heat. Election officials performed their duties without complaint. There was no sign of any intimidation or harassment, remarkable considering the history of election violence in Sierra Leone.

Counting the votes at the end of the day was a display of transparency that makes Canadian elections look like a closed shop. There were nine parties competing for the presidency and ten for parliamentary seats. At one polling station, in the Murray Town Amputee Camp, the presiding election officer began the proceedings with a prayer, read out all the rules and then, as each ballot was counted, showed it to each of the agents of the parties and to all the observers. It took two hours to complete the first tabulation of the presidential results, which amounted to slightly more than five hundred ballots. At another poll, in the far northern area, one of our observers reported that a large number of schoolchildren were present at the counting and were also shown every ballot as it emerged from the see-through box.

There were, of course, irregularities. All parties had registered some underage voters, and there were often mix-ups as to which voters should vote where. But, given that this was an election held four months after war's end, in a very poor country with a limited history of democratic practice, and that it involved setting up more than two thousand polling stations in diverse, mainly rural, locations with a fractured transportation system, it was a test of huge proportions—and one successfully met. And the reason was that it was seen as a crucial step in rebuilding the country. Not for these voters the easy option of indifference to elections that seems increasingly to pervade better-established democracies. This election was one way for them to show that they wanted a new deal for themselves. It was a collective statement that after ten years of war they had a chance to vote for peace.

Just as the UN peacekeepers and aid officials are important to Sierra Leone, so are the many international democracy builders. This community of election advisors, experts and observers engaged around the world in reforming government, holding elections and building democratic institutions is part of an evolving global citizenry who do not limit their activism inside national frontiers. In 1996, we established our roster of skilled Canadians available for nation-building activities. CIDA funded a program of election advisors, and Elections Canada supplied skilled experts. It was just one of those things that Canada had committed to internationally, and that, as foreign minister, I had taken for granted. Chairing the Commonwealth observer mission changed that for me.

My first meeting with the team was at seven on the morning of my arrival, since several had to depart to take up their posts "up country," as they liked to say. We were all given our election uniforms of blue golf shirts and white Tilley hats carrying the Commonwealth insignia. We were an interesting, disparate group: a political scientist from Tanzania, a law professor from Nigeria, an election official from Belize and one from Great Britain, and a woman who looked familiar, the reason being that she was from Winnipeg and had resided for many years in my old riding. Judy Thompson had once been a member of the Elections Manitoba Commission, but for the last ten years had been travelling to hot spots like Cambodia, Palestine and Zimbabwe monitoring and observing elections—just one of many people who criss-cross the globe, wherever election action calls.

Backing up this team was a highly skilled group of Commonwealth Secretariat officials, headed by Chris Child and Dr. Ade Adefuye, a Nigerian academic. They and their staffs were veterans of a wide variety of missions, many of which I had had a hand in authorizing through the Commonwealth Ministers' Action Group. Now I could see for myself how these missions actually worked and the value they brought. It was an impressive lesson. These were real professionals, with a wealth of understanding of how elections could be conducted even under the most trying of circumstances. Their presence usually helped ensure that whatever system was put in place met basic standards of openness and fairness. Where it didn't—as in the notorious case of the presidential election in Zimbabwe in 2002—they were there to blow the whistle.

It is not an easy occupation. There is nothing glamorous about spending months or weeks in substandard accommodation, in difficult climates where malaria, intestinal upset and parasitical infections are common, and often at personal risk. Chris Child told of being picked up by helicopter during the 1996 Sierra Leonean election to escape an advancing rebel attack.

The coterie of democracy builders comes from far and wide with an array of sponsors. The former president of Togo and a former

American ambassador were in Sierra Leone on behalf of the Carter Center. A member of the European Parliament headed the EU delegation. A former ambassador from Ghana was there for the Africans. We found a lot of common ground in our analysis of events and began to share our findings and information. In addition, funded by the Westminster Foundation for Democracy in the U.K. and the National Democratic Institute, some twenty-five hundred Sierra Leoneans had been recruited and trained, along with party agents and election officials, to supply the basic election infrastructure. Meshing these locally based groups with the international teams established a broad web of supervision and support able to cover the entire country.

When I arrived, I had started out questioning the value of such large and extensive international contingents of election monitors and experts. Were we being too intrusive? Was it just a showcase that didn't have lasting value? But I was soon surprised by how much Sierra Leoneans welcomed the international involvement.

Three reasons were given. First, it was a way of putting restraints on abuse or mischief by governments or politicians. In this age of instantaneous global information, it is important to have an international seal of approval. Without it, recognition is withheld, aid and investment are hard to come by. When it is flouted, as in Zimbabwe, a big price is paid. Second, it was an affirmation by the international community that the election mattered, that indeed Sierra Leone mattered. It was important to have the country's activities validated both by observer teams and by international and local media. Third, it was a way of transferring skills and human capacity, perhaps the most essential ingredient for a poor country.

Before too long, Sierra Leone will be in a position to conduct its own elections without a great deal of international participation. This will especially be so if groups such as the Commonwealth allocate funds for extensive training and to supply necessary facilities and equipment to the locally based organizations for good government.

BLUEPRINTS FOR NATION BUILDING

President Kabbah won a majority of the vote, his party a near majority in Parliament. He has been given a mandate to build on the peace he had brought to the country.

It is a daunting challenge, made all the more so because the expectations are so great and the hurdles so high. The people want jobs and improved income. They want continued security against any further outbreak of dissension or insurgency. They want a government prepared to tackle corruption and improve representation, especially by women, young people and the "up country" regions hitherto excluded by the elite. They also want justice for the egregious crimes committed during the war and reconciliation of the disaffected. This is an awesome agenda.

What are the omens for success? Who has the blueprint? Before leaving, I posed those questions to a number of people. Let me recount some of the varied responses I heard.

The morning after the election, I received a call that Ade Adefuye and I should come to the administrative offices of the president, located on a hillside overlooking Freetown. President Kabbah was dressed in a long, flowing traditional African garb of yellow silk. Looking tired, but energized at the same time, this former UN development official clearly understood the challenges ahead. After welcoming me back to his country, he began a precise description of what needed to be done, putting the emphasis on two things— investing in the economy and developing human resources. He was hopeful that Canada could assist with supplying technical skills in public administration and in legal assistance and asked about the possibility of obtaining training for his civil servants in how to deal with trade law and regulation. He said that Sierra Leone simply didn't have the skill base necessary to operate in a global economy.

I asked what he was proposing to do to find a place in the society for war-affected children and young ex-warriors. I could see that he was troubled by the question; it was perhaps the most complicated issue he faced. He talked of the need to give them a stake in the country through infrastructure projects, or cleaning up abandoned palm oil plantations to develop an export crop.

Immediately afterwards, I went to a lunch hosted by our high commissioner, Phillipe Beaulne, where a number of people involved in child protection echoed the concerns of the president that the issue of reintegration of combatants must be tackled as a first priority. Many of the rehabilitation camps had been closed, and the emphasis now was on returning the children to their families and their villages. Keith Wright, from UNICEF, made the point that for this to work there had to be a restoration of local governments, with better control of services at the local level. Here was the rub, however. Donor countries and agencies weren't too interested in reorganizing local government or in long-term investment in such basic services as education and health. Donor money was project money, with short time frames and specific, limited goals. It was okay to fund a two-year trauma-counselling program, but no one would fund broad-based education upgrading over a multi-year schedule. Serious restoration would require a comprehensive and holistic approach to aid, a move away from the project orientation of so much international development.

The next morning I had breakfast with Frances Fortune, a Canadian from Burlington, Ontario, who had married a Sierra Leonean and stayed in the country during the war, working on a variety of resettlement programs. Our discussion was repeatedly interrupted by people coming over to the table to speak to her, set up meetings or ask her views on the election. She was clearly an active force in the community. I could see why. She had wonderful warmth as she delivered a candid appraisal of what needed to be done. The NGO she directed had won great plaudits during the election for sponsoring an independent radio station using young ex-combatants as investigative reporters, giving election information through drama and music. They had a call-in program called "Talking Drums" that provided one of the few ways that ordinary people from every region could be heard on problems common to them all. She reminded me that this initiative was first funded from the DFAIT human security fund—one of the better investments we have made.

Her latest idea was to set up a youth corps for Sierra Leone that would put young people to work on various projects but in a setting where they could acquire a sense of belonging and self-esteem. She told me the best thing that ever happened to her was serving in Katimavik, the innovative youth employment scheme started by former Sen. Jacques Hébert, where she was able to gain skills, confidence and pride in belonging to a group that had a constructive philosophy. She sees the young ex-combatants who served in the RUF as lost souls, with no one to give them guidance or direction. It won't be enough just to give them short-term employment, as the president suggested. They need to be part of a peer group that has purpose and meaning.

I thought back to my days at Human Resources, where we had sponsored youth service corps as a way of addressing problems of employment and disaffection, and of the success it had in instilling a sense of achievement while producing useful work. Such programs have fallen out of favour in our own country under the onslaught of neo-conservative criticism and budget restraints. We've lost much of our commitment to producing public goods, and find market mechanisms the preferred expedient. Perhaps it is time to revive these notions as a way of meeting the demands for an effective youth response in Sierra Leone and other African states. Thank goodness people like Frances Fortune still believe in the positive force of government initiatives.

There are signs that governments both in Sierra Leone and internationally are heeding the call. In November 2002, Kabbah's government presented a plan of action on recovery and development to a group of donor countries in Paris. In early 2003, the African Development Bank approved U.S.$20 million in loans for education and justice. The government is restoring the Paramount Chief system of local government to oversee local development and justice.

But more than jobs and education are needed. If there is not some way of coming to grips with the aftermath of the horrendous crimes committed and the deep rifts riven into the society during ten years of war, then the country will remain unable to turn the page. That was the message from Yasmin Jusu-Sheriff, executive secretary of the country's Truth and Reconciliation Commission. A native Sierra Leonean who practised law in London, England, she has returned to direct an effort to give voice to the victims and their families, particularly the amputees, the war widows and the child soldiers. In her view, this commission is part of the traditional way of dealing with guilt, built into the tribal culture of the country, and helps to create a climate of acceptance for those involved in the conflict.

There is also the Special Court, set up after arduous negotiation as a joint undertaking between the UN and the Sierra Leone government. It is thus a hybrid, different from the tribunals established for the Balkans and Rwanda, both entirely UN managed. But it certainly fits into the remit of the International Criminal Court. It is here that top leaders of the RUF and the heads of the paramilitary organizations will be tried. Between the court and the commission, it is hoped that the fundamental cycle of impunity that historically has allowed many of the elite in Sierra Leone to commit crimes will be broken and the concept of justice will be rejuvenated.

A small, depleted country on the west coast of Africa has had the courage and wit to combine elements of justice as part of a peace settlement. While some states, particularly the U.S., India, Cuba and Iraq, have set themselves in opposition to developing such means, Sierra Leone is willing to innovate. Perhaps it takes years of suffering to understand that peace is more than the absence of war and that without justice being applied there can be only a hollow peace.

There is one worry. A significant element of that search for justice will involve scouring out the rampant corruption that exists as part of the historical legacy of the country. Nothing saps efforts to rebuild more than a spoils system. The government has set up the Anti-Corruption Commission and given it wide powers to investigate, but not to prosecute, and recent reports from journalists suggest that the commission's inquiry into the dealings of senior civil servants and ministers is being frustrated. Unless this is corrected, the donor community and the people of Sierra Leone could lose faith in the new government. Here is a true test for the birth of a new Sierra Leone—and for the international community. Promoting reconciliation and accountability as a way of restoring societal trust has lessons that apply far beyond Sierra Leone's shores.

Tackling the pervasiveness of corruption, much of it tied to the international diamond trade, will require tightly coordinated efforts, accompanied by constant surveillance by the government and interested international partners.

Returning from the mission via London, I picked up a copy of the *Guardian* and read of the enormous problem presented by Afghani refugees flocking to Kabul because it was the only place where there was a UN security force to provide protection. I thought of the refusal of the coalition decision makers and the UN envoy in Afghanistan to pursue disarmament, democratic development or any form of justice system to hold individuals accountable. Instead of support for dictators being extolled as part of the battle against terrorism, here is a place where it might make good sense to look at what is being attempted in Sierra Leone.

My short time in Sierra Leone gave me a strong reminder that democracy both within countries and at the global level is a base value upon which a sustainable social and economic order must be built. By contributing to serious nation building anywhere, we are investing in the future. But the structural engineering must be combined with an attention to the plumbing—making sure that broad principles are applied, practically and in detail, at the local, regional and national levels. There is a direct link between passing a resolution at the UN to limit the diamond trade and then ensuring that resources are dedicated to stopping the flow of the precious stone across the Liberia–Sierra Leone border. To slightly paraphrase Tip O'Neill, all global politics are local.

Canada can be proud of the help it has given the people of Sierra Leone in their quest for security, democracy and prosperity. But there are flaws in our approach, stemming from inconsistency, limited resources and the lack of a coherent approach. We pushed for a strengthened UNAMSIL, but didn't make a significant contribution to it. Our military doesn't like peacemaking missions much any more, especially in Africa. We give short-term grants for child soldiers, but won't consider a long-term commitment to help rebuild an educational system. We are leading the way on a G-8 strategy for Africa, but are not prepared to actively promote trade strategy that counters discrimination against exports from poor countries such as Sierra Leone. If we expect to punch above our weight, which we are perfectly capable of doing, then we must develop a much better double-punch combination.

Without significant international support, there is no guarantee that the rebuilding of Sierra Leone will be a success. The International Commission on Intervention and State Sovereignty's report reminds us that being involved in acts of prevention and of post-conflict rebuilding are as much a part of the international collective responsibility to protect as any acts of direct intervention. It points out why it makes moral, financial and national-interest sense to meet those tests in a place like Sierra Leone.[2] First, there is the simple moral imperative to alleviate the suffering. Second, the costs of mounting another intervention to deal with renewed conflict if the rebuilding fails far exceed the cost of reconstruction, to say nothing of the expense of supplying basic humanitarian assistance to refugees and displaced persons. Third, the possibility of cutting off supplies of diamond money to a global trade network that fuels criminal activity and may channel money to terrorists abets the security of us all. A recent report of the World Bank reinforces the point that because of the negative spillover effects regionally and globally, the international community has "compelling" reasons to prevent such conflicts.[3]

The difficulty is in translating such a sense of responsibility into political will. It is such a contrast to see the billions of dollars being funnelled into military and border-security expenditures as part of the anti-terrorist campaign while paltry sums are allocated for prevention and peace-building investments in areas where human security is at risk. As I wrote this book, the estimated cost of the war in Iraq was U.S.$60 to $100 billion; the costs of rebuilding, even more. What if even half that sum had been allocated to deal with immediate problems in the Middle East of poverty, refugees, water shortages and settling disputes. Perhaps there would be a very different political climate, one in which the threats posed by Osama bin Laden or Saddam Hussein might have been met by a cooperative regional effort. Viewing issues of intervention from the perspective of victims is being far more pragmatic than the war planners who believe the only solution comes from the pointed end of a gun.

Sierra Leone in one way, however, has been fortunate. At least its conflict and the attendant abuse eventually caused a blip on the screen of world attention. Perhaps it was the sight of mutilated children on television newscasts, perhaps the increased focus on war-affected children, perhaps the special interest of the U.K. government that served to move it into a position where the Security Council took the matter seriously and authorized a robust involvement. By comparison, other regional tragedies, such as those in Liberia, the Ivory Coast, Uganda and the Congo, have received token treatment. While some hot spots become the object of international care and concern, others are allowed to languish and fester until they become such a crisis they can't be ignored. In this there is a definite weakness in the machinery of early detection and a lack of equity in the attention given to communities in trouble.

Sierra Leone shows that there can be a resurrection of a failed state and a crucified population. Now it is a question of how to make this the rule, not the exception.

PART VI

Environmental Security

CHAPTER 13

THE MACHINE IN THE GARDEN

———

MONGOLIA IS A PLACE THAT CONJURES UP VISIONS OF THE PAST glories and conquests of Genghis Khan and his Golden Horde riding fearlessly out of the vast steppes of Central Asia, sweeping before them the great powers of the day, presiding over one of the largest empires of the ancient world.

Today, I would hazard that few Canadians know much about what is now called the People's Republic of Mongolia, a large, lightly populated, landlocked country nestling uncomfortably between the contemporary political heavyweights of Russia and China. To many Canadians, myself once included, its best-known feature is likely the fact that Ulaanbaatar, its major city, vies with Ottawa for the title of "coldest national capital in the world." Gaining its independence in 1921 from Chinese rule, but soon absorbed into the orbit of the Soviet Union, Mongolia was largely ignored by the rest of the world until 1990, when it emerged as an autonomous entity. It is now engaged in a massive political, economic and social transformation as it moves from authoritarianism to democracy, from a nomadic herding society to a modern, urban-based economy.

At Foreign Affairs I came to admire its efforts to carve out an independent, pro-democratic stance. I learned about its struggles with a crippling drought that was destroying much of its livestock and about its interest in building relations with Canada. In 1998, Canada and Mongolia signed a declaration on friendship and cooperation, committing us to work together in multilateral organizations on disarmament issues and on combatting organized crime and drug trafficking.

I twice tried to visit the country on ministerial missions, urged on by Madeleine Albright, who spoke to me in glowing terms of its people, its landscape, its efforts to form a viable democracy and the acquired delights of fermented mare's milk, the national drink. But on both occasions, pressing business in Ottawa intervened. I was therefore delighted, after leaving government, to receive an invitation from the Mongolian government to come there in my new academic capacity to talk about security issues. I was particularly intrigued because in 2000, the new government under Prime Minister Nambar Enkhbayar had passed a Good Governance for Human Security Program, the first time to my knowledge that a country had officially set out human security as an across-the-board strategy for analyzing issues and setting priorities. Having used the concept for foreign policy, I was interested to see how the Mongolians were using it for domestic policy as well. Could this be a model for other nations to follow?

What I found was a country wrestling with a series of difficult human security issues, not the problems occasioned by violence and conflict that had been my focus at Foreign Affairs but issues of economic and environmental insecurity. The people of Mongolia were facing serious dislocations and uncertainties. The transition from a centralized command-and-control economic regime to the vagaries of the market economy, with the accompanying stringencies imposed by the international financial donor community, was one shock to the system. It was compounded by a deteriorating environment caused by a mixture of the dubious legacy of Soviet-style industrialization and global climate change. Economic and environmental security bring in their wake the same risks to personal rights, well-being and safety that others face around the world. My visit would help me to see that the responsibility to protect can also be applied to a rethinking of economic and environmental risks. In both cases the global architecture is non-existent, archaic, underfunded or discriminatory; yet, as we know, the magnitude and the impact of climate change, poverty and AIDS—to name just a few pressing global issues—is staggering.

Arriving in Mongolia in the summer of 2002, my wife, Denise, and I were struck by the beauty of the grassland setting and the strong attachment all the people we met had to the land. On our first day we were invited to join the minister of industry and his family on a visit to the countryside to watch the preparations for the horse races that would soon take place as part of the national day of celebration, Naadam. After bumping over twenty miles of rutted pathways, we dipped into a lush valley in the rolling steppe and were greeted by a spectacular sight—hundreds of horses spread throughout, being groomed and exercised, all under the watchful eyes of shrewd trainers who dedicate themselves to this annual equine extravaganza.

Scattered among the various staging areas for horses were gers, the traditional homes of the nomadic families, rounded abodes of wood and felt that can be erected or dismantled within an hour. We were given a lunch of traditional Mongolian food, mainly meat, yogurt and cheese, including of course a bowl of fermented mare's milk. In appearance, smell and texture it is not unlike cow's milk. Being cautious, I ventured a slight sip, until advised by a diplomat beside me that politesse dictated nothing less than a healthy slug. Taking courage in hand, I gave it a full swallow, resulting in the strongest involuntary pucker of my life. Fortunately, this met all the protocol requirements, because what followed was an entrancing interlude of a father and son playing traditional Mongolian music. As we departed in early evening, our last sight was of the two musicians serenading some of the horses with their fiddles. The horses' trainer explained that music was good for their souls and part of getting them ready for the race.

Forget the Kentucky Derby or the Queen's Plate, with their manicured raceways and mannered procedures. You've never seen horse racing until you've witnessed hundreds of short, sturdy Mongolian horses with six- to eleven-year-old riders on their backs, scornful of saddles, storming across the countryside at breakneck speed, followed by a careening caravan of four-wheel drives carrying trainers, owners and speechless-with-fright observers such as our-selves. Horsemanship is still highly honoured by Mongolians, who cherish this bonding with nature and animals.

With all the talk of globalization, with all the homogenization of culture, media, politics and business, there still exist throughout the world wonderful epiphanies like this—myriad outpourings of individual spirit and celebrations of difference and diversity. Here I could sense the deep harmony between animals and humans, steeped in tradition and embedded in a rich natural environment.

But across the highway, not too far in the distance, was another side to present-day Mongolia. Standing stark against the wide sky were three huge smokestacks bellowing heavy black emissions. They were part of a massive coal-fired power plant that supplies the energy needs of Ulaanbaatar and feeds current into a national power grid that supports the burgeoning mining industry. Built in the Soviet era, upwind from the city, it is a pollution nightmare that spreads deadly toxins into the air and into the lungs. It is the proverbial machine in the garden, symbolizing the dilemma faced by all communities, but especially those in poor developing nations—how to balance the demands of economic growth, com-pete in a global economy and try to meet the need for jobs while preserving a unique lifestyle, nurturing long-established traditions and maintaining a distinctive, healthy ecological setting. It's not a new dilemma. Thoreau and other transcendentalists of the nine-teenth century lamented the coming of industrialization and the consequences it would have for the natural rhythms of life. But in Thoreau's day the pace of change was much slower and its impact far less threatening to human existence.

That point was vividly brought home to me a few days after leav-ing Mongolia, when I attended a forum on globalization sponsored by the World Federalist Association. In London, England, the Natural History Museum was hosting an open-air exhibit called "Earth from the Air," a series of aerial photos taken by the Frenchman Yann Arthus-Bertrand showing how the face of the earth is being dramatically altered by resource exploitation, overuse of agricultural land and urbanization. I was struck by these images of what we are doing to our world: a lone "tree of life" standing in a vast expanse of arid wasteland in Kenya; the Arizona desert filled with hundreds of B-52s (another machine in the garden) like some ancient burial ground; a tentacle of polluted waste emanating into the Persian Gulf from a water desalinization plant in Kuwait; the heart-shaped bareness of an over-salted patch in the mangrove swamp of New Caledonia.

The photos were accompanied by simple figures. Between 1990 and 1999, worldwide GDP grew from U.S.$21 to 30 trillion. In the same period, more than 100,000 square kilometres of deforestation took place every year. Today the world uses in one and a half months the amount of oil we used in a year in 1950; the use of fossil fuels has multiplied by five in the past fifty years. The result: four tons of carbon emissions are produced *per person* every year.

The exhibit made the further point that most of the deterioration takes place in Southern countries while the wealth production is concentrated in the North. The share of world trade for the fifty poorest countries dropped from 4 per cent to 2 per cent in the last decade of the twentieth century, while the OECD countries alone share 67 per cent of this commerce. Forty-seven per cent of the world's population lives on less than U.S.$2 a day, while the total wealth of the two hundred richest people exceeds U.S.$1 trillion. More than a billion people in developing nations have no access to drinkable water. The average Kenyan uses 4 litres of water a day; the average New Yorker, 680 litres. Only thirty thousand people out of thirty million afflicted by HIV/AIDS in sub-Saharan Africa are being given anti-retroviral drugs that are readily available to those similarly affected in Northern countries.

The exhibit painted a vivid portrait of a global system heavily weighted towards economic development that benefits a minority of people and brings heavy costs to natural life-support systems. The result is that hunger, poverty, disease and disaster become the everyday lot of most of humankind; their security is as imperilled as if they were in the midst of a violent conflict. The means of managing these threats fall far short of providing adequate protection.

Mongolia's efforts to grapple with these dilemmas illustrate the difficulties that so many poor countries face, made all the more pointed because of its stated intent to provide a human security

approach to finding solutions. The Mongolian political and business leaders and the NGOs I met in projects supported by Canada
Fund resources described for me a precarious economic situation,
exacerbated by a rigid set of conditions laid down by the international financial community and a deteriorating environmental and
social setting—a position shared by many other developing
countries.

When the Soviets left Mongolia in the early nineties, the country lost its guaranteed markets and its social subsidies, especially
in the agricultural sector. The new Mongolian government
accepted the advice of the free-enterprise U.S. think-tanks that
had sprouted up during the Reagan administration and engaged in
a crash program of market reforms, privatization, deregulation, job
cuts and severe cutbacks in health, education and social security.
It was an avid disciple of what has been called the Washington
Consensus view of economic development, which sees free-market
capitalism as the way to prosperity. There was a big price to pay for
this rapid restructuring: high unemployment, falling enrolments in
schools and universities (this in a country that had a 98 per cent
literacy rate) and reduced health coverage.[1] It was a severe shock to
the system and resulted in a slew of unintended consequences—the
payback that often accompanies hastily devised and ideologically
imposed solutions.

One consequence was an accelerated move into Ulaanbaatar of
large numbers of rural people, creating in this sparsely populated
country an urban crisis. Although the official population figure for
the city is 700,000, it is estimated that upwards of 150,000 to
200,000 occupy space on the perimeter. Having lost their livelihood and access to services, like many around the world they
headed for the big city and became squatters. Living in their gers,
generally without water or electricity, they find little or no employment; their children, deprived of the social support of the nomad
existence and its various functions tied to husbandry, become
street kids, captives of a dysfunctional way of life that leads to
crime, violence and a breakdown in community values.

Miro Cernetig and Josh Freed, in their powerful documentary
Juggling Dreams, depicted this breakdown in their look at the

"sewer" children of Ulaanbaatar. These young boys' families couldn't keep their children in school, and the attractions of the street took over—except the street in Mongolia in winter is a very cold place, so the children sought refuge in the underground sewers, where the central heating pipes gave off enough warmth to survive. Life in the sewer was hard; disease, crime and extreme vagrancy were prevalent. Children losing their economic and community security is another example of how the most vulnerable pay the price for the global community's inattention to the "responsibility to protect."

Denise and I saw some of these children in a happier context when we accepted an invitation from Chris Johnstone, our Canadian honorary consul, to visit a summer camp for street kids, a project receiving a modest dollop of support from the Canada Fund that he administers. (The Canada Fund gives a small amount of money to embassies to invest in local projects. It has the advantage of being very flexible and discretionary, with decisions made by local staff rather than in Ottawa.)

Arriving at a small enclosure situated in a pretty river valley about eighteen miles from the city, we were greeted by the sight of about sixty children, ranging in age from about five to seventeen, practising a medley of circus skills—tumbling, juggling, acrobatics and rhythmic dancing. There was a special level of concentration because the children were preparing to give a performance in a nearby town as part of the Naadam celebrations.

At the centre was Cecile Truffaut, a vivacious Quebecker from Cirque du Soleil who from one minute to the next was teaching, cajoling, encouraging and hugging the children as they tested their abilities. She had been coming here for the last three years, as part of a program that the circus undertakes around the world for children who need help. Learning circus skills is a way of gaining self-confidence while having fun. Along with the skills come schoolwork, joining in preparing meals and cleaning up the camp, and coming back into contact with the steppes, so important a part of Mongolian culture. The purpose is not necessarily to train future performers, although some do have the ability and ambition to follow a career. The real aim is to restore pride in accomplishment and motivation to go back to school or find a job. We could see for ourselves in the faces of the children and their eagerness that the project was making a difference in their lives. But this circus group's few weeks of play and education out on the giant steppes can handle only a small percentage of the children of Ulaanbaatar. Most are left with the hardscrabble of eking out a daily existence.

Equally serious environmental problems match the social ones. The smokestacks that so dominate the Ulaanbaatar skyline are not the most damaging environmental degraders. In winter the emissions from the hundreds of thousands of coal-fuelled stoves used in the gers surrounding the city for heat and cooking cause huge accumulations of smog and toxic emissions (concentrations of sulphur dioxide and nitrogen dioxide have doubled since 1996). Furthermore, the move of so many nomad families and their livestock close to the city is creating a severe problem of overgrazing and a water shortage—all the makings of an environmental morass around the capital. The government recognizes the problem and has elaborated plans for regional decentralization. But it is fighting against strong market forces and doesn't have the funds to provide the necessary public goods—education, health and a clean environment.

Mongolia is certainly not alone in contending with the fallout of global urbanization, probably one of the most significant phenomena to affect life in the twenty-first century. It is estimated that by 2030, as many as 60 per cent of all the world's inhabitants will live in urban areas. A million people a week become urban dwellers, according to a National Geographic report.[2] In 1995, the number of megacities—those with more than ten million people—was fourteen. By 2015 there will be twenty-five, most in the developing world. This trend will severely strain the resources, infrastructure and governance of cities worldwide.

One consequence of this floodtide was highlighted in a story in the International Herald Tribune, which begins, "Southeast Asian mega cities are drowning in a sea of trash." It goes on to describe how in Manila, a city that soared over the ten-million mark in the early 1990s, some 5600 metric tons of garbage are hauled away each day to landfill sites, still leaving 30 per cent of the total to clog up waterways and vacant lots.[3] On July 11, 2000, a dump in the Payatas area of Manila collapsed, killing 218 squatters living in shanties at the bottom of the site; another 300 were missing under the piles of rotting garbage. As a UN report on the incident concludes, "The tragedy of their burial underneath the trash of a world city, off its edge and in the darkness of night, symbolizes the invisible, daily plight of innumerable people in today's globalizing world."[4]

Yet human ingenuity is coming through with an answer. Two young Bangladeshi engineers were awarded a prize from the UN Development Programme for their work in setting up an NGO called Waste Concern that turns pollutant waste into fertilizer. The garbage pickers of Dhaka, where 4000 tons of garbage is produced daily in the city of 5.4 million, have been trained to separate waste by type. It is then turned into compost at a waste centre, whose promoters estimate that if this process was applied across Bangladesh, some ninety thousand jobs would be created. They are now shopping their model to other Third World cities.

I came in contact with another side of the urban tragedy during a trip to Rio de Janeiro while working on our strategy for a drug dialogue in the hemisphere. In this beautiful city of beaches and mountains are dark alleyways where gangs of young children, part of the drug distribution system, have taken control of many of the shantytown areas, where police are afraid to intervene and the deaths from guns exceed those in many combat zones around the world. Almost three thousand people a year are shot to death in this city of 5.8 million. Many of the gang members who control the shantytowns are ten or twelve years old, and they use weapons more sophisticated than those possessed by the police. They have supplanted any form of local government. When the UN General Assembly adopted a resolution in August 2001 solemnly asserting, "We also pledge to strengthen the institutions and legal frameworks that assist and allow broad-based participation in decision-making and in the implementation of human settlements strategies, policies and programs,"[5] I don't think they had the children's street gangs of Rio in mind.

Our drug strategy in the region attempted to set up an alternative approach that would centre on tackling the drug problem at the community level, as opposed to the region-wide programs of military interdiction that were failing miserably. But, again, the lack of resources for serious follow-through frustrated the initiative. All we could muster was some Canada Fund money to support local clubs for young drug victims, obtain volunteer time from our young embassy staff and begin an information network linking several community-based projects in the Americas to train street children in computer use and begin some virtual advocacy. It was one small way of trying to respond to the shared problems that put young people at risk, since urban areas are fertile ground for global drug exploitation, from the shantytowns of Rio to the East Side of Vancouver.

Considering how vital urban issues are to the lives of so many worldwide, they have remarkably little visibility on the agendas of global institutions, and there is virtually no mechanism for coordinated global action. There is some help from international funding agencies, and there is the UN Human Settlements Programme (recently converted into UN-HABITAT), with a governing council of fifty-eight members reporting to the Economic and Social Council. But its prime task is to organize meetings and prepare reports—there is no resource for direct funding of the kind of projects that will help make cities viable. To say that there is anything approximating a global urban strategy is illusionary.

Interestingly enough, this looming problem is beginning to attract the attention of the international private sector. I acted as national chair of a committee overseeing Canada's winning entry from Vancouver in an Urban Olympics competition held in Japan in 2003. Sponsored by the international gas industry, the purpose was to choose from a selection of world-class cities the best proposal for achieving sustainable development through planning, technology and alternative fuels. The success of the Canadian submission testifies to the skills we have in this country for dealing with urban issues.

It's fascinating, and encouraging, to see how much innovation and inventiveness there is among Canadians in designing urban areas to meet the crunch of population pressure and a shortage of fossil fuels. The new mantra in Canadian cities is that they can be the incubators of smart growth, where solutions to many worldwide urban problems can be hatched. The trick is sharing that ingenuity with the rest of the world. It is a sign of the times that one way global cooperation on the urban issue is taking place is the networking of specialists in various cities from both North and South, under the auspices of a private-sector association. It shows how the arena of global governance is moving beyond traditional national governments. City and regional groupings are becoming increasingly important. Academic, professional, business and civic groups are now working in concert. This could lead to a more comprehensive approach to the worldwide urbanization crisis involving a more varied coalition of committed private players and local governments.

This is not to forswear action by national governments and multilateral organizations. If we are to come to grips with the unprecedented global nature of economic and environmental security issues, cooperative action backed up by serious enforcement measures will be needed. That is shown in another of the problems experienced by Mongolia, one with worldwide significance. The Gobi Desert that occupies 41 per cent of southern Mongolia and a significant chunk of northern China is on the march, encroaching on the grasslands, and accelerating. China's Environmental Protection Agency reports that between 1994 and 1999 the Gobi Desert expanded by 20,240 square miles. Climate change is the primary culprit; the average annual temperature is estimated to have increased about 1.5 degrees Celsius since 1950. Overgrazing that took place after the Soviet departure, as herds of sheep and goats were vastly increased to compensate for loss of income, adds to the degradation.

The economic impact of lost grazing area is obvious. Even more serious, Mongolia has experienced severe droughts in the past several years, causing an enormous loss of livestock and agricultural income.

Massive sandstorms now sweep out of the desert areas; there are four times the number of dust storm days as in 1960. These carry across eastern and northern Asia, clogging the nostrils and creating a severe health hazard. Visiting China in April 2002, I asked about the dense yellow screen that hovered over the landscape. Gobi sand was the answer. The dust bowl now being formed appears to be an ecological disaster. But before the eyes glaze over at another environmental meltdown somewhere in the far reaches of the earth, we should take note that we are not immune. Evidence of murky dust arising from the Gobi area reaching the western shores of North America has appeared these last few springs. The four countries most affected—Mongolia, China, Japan and Korea— signed an agreement in 2001 to coordinate information and efforts, but so far little has been done. It's not because there is no under- standing of what to do: a complex combination of remedial initia- tives involving reforestation, pasture management and water is the answer. The problem is the lack of money, commitment, cross- border organizations and political will, especially on the part of the international community.

How does a poor country like Mongolia mount a major effort to push back the desert, or control air pollution, when one-third of its people live below the most minimum of poverty levels and the health care system is substandard, while world commodity prices for its copper and cashmere have fallen by 10 per cent and it is being hounded by international lenders and donors to keep expen- ditures low and create an attractive climate for foreign investment by cutting taxes? The answer is, it doesn't.

Environmental security is inevitably trumped by economic exi- gencies. The imperative is maximizing growth to keep pace with the population increase, and ideally to generate some improvement in the standard of living. Sustainable development in a place like Mongolia is a long-term objective; the immediate pressure is to avoid bankruptcy, and so avoid the wrath of international financial institutions.

The Mongolian government has passed all the right legislation and set out the right targets for sustainable development, but how can they pay to implement pollution regulations, train skilled staff to do environmental assessments or undertake reforestation? In 1998, as the government faced a financial crunch, the environment ministry's budget was cut by 48 per cent, and it is yet to be restored. There is no allocation for industrial pollution abatement or solid waste management. The only hope is contributions from donors, and here the level is, to say the least, modest: U.S.$20 mil- lion between 1993 and 1999. Some of the projects are worthwhile.

The Danes and the Dutch are supporting a management plan for a few major rivers; the UN Development Programme pays for some planning and assessment of climate-change problems; and CIDA/IDRC, from Canada, covers some costs for natural resource development and environmental regulation. But the reality is that while donors talk about the environment, the paucity of money belies their words. That's true in all parts of the developing world.

In fact, contradictions tend to be the norm, not the exception. For example, under the current economic development plan in Mongolia, the World Bank is funding the building of three new coal-fired power plants, primarily to supply energy for new mining developments, including a major Canadian investment. This in a country where the impact of climate change, a direct consequence of carbon dioxide emissions, is becoming devastating. But coal in Mongolia is cheap and plentiful, the mining industry is key to development, and there isn't time—or at least commitment—to try to develop alternative sources of energy. Will these power plants meet new emission standards? Will the new mines honour sustainable practices of waste control? Proper monitoring and enforcement of the very good rules the government has on the books could secure that, but fiscal restraint doesn't allow the government to implement the rules.

The New Priesthood

What's happening in Mongolia is a prima facie case of the need to link environmental security to economic security. Unless there is significant progress in alleviating poverty, there can't be any improvement of environmental standards. At the same time, if plans for development ignore the environment, then the consequences of unmitigated growth will undo the well-being of the human community. Such convergence is certainly the watchword at various international meetings and in the public relations bumph of development agencies and donor organizations. Poverty alleviation is the rhetorical marching song. But when it comes to what is actually happening on the ground, there is still a fundamental disconnect between the calls for alleviating poverty and saving the environment.

That fatal flaw was made clear to me as I sat in on an international donors' session in Mongolia. As foreign minister I had some familiarity with donors' gatherings—representatives of developed states, aid agencies and international financial institutions convene to decide how much money to donate to a respective demandeur, be it an individual country or an international agency promoting a worthy cause. These sessions are part of the emerging global rigmarole of international fundraising, comparable to a charity auction or a United Way appeal. They are a substitute for a global scheme of raising revenue for development purposes, and they give to the providers enormous leverage to set conditions and establish priorities—as in the days of Lady Bountiful giving charity to the deserving poor.

I had always wondered what the effect of this curious and decidedly ad hoc system of international decision making would be on the actual issues faced by developing countries. I got one answer in Ulaanbaatar. It was like a Puritan-style New England town meeting presided over by a stern group of elders who oversee the individual members of the congregation, ensuring their strict adherence to the covenants of economic orthodoxy and to obeying the word of such supreme beings as the World Bank and the International Monetary Fund. The donors protect the faith, and the individual supplicants testify to their experience of "grace." It is the new economic fundamentalism of our day.

At the front of the ornate meeting room decorated with Soviet-style flair sat the prime minister and the finance minister, each testifying to the sanctity of their economic program and the need to receive additional help to fight poverty. Stretching down the room were delegates from the various banks and donor countries, desks stacked high with yellow-jacketed reports outlining blueprints for development, infrastructure and macro-economic planning copiously prepared by a legion of international private consultants as offerings to these assembled elders. The response on behalf of the elders came from a representative of the Asian Development Bank who paid opening lip service to the new buzzword of poverty reduction and then proceeded to reel out all the conventional nostrums of today's international economic theology—macro-economic financial stability, the private sector as the engine of growth, regulation to promote transparency, restraint on government spending, export trade expansion. It was an all too familiar liturgy.

That was the puff piece. The tough love came later from the IMF representative, a mid-level technocrat who delivered the hard message: recent decisions by the Parliament and government to provide pension increases to former civil servants should be rescinded. Never mind that because of cutbacks in services and inflation these people were facing serious deprivation. Clearly, for this international banker, the reduction of poverty that was the focus of the meeting did not include the poverty of pensioners; their needs were not in the same league as tax concessions for foreign investors. It was a display of impudence all too common in the management of international finance and the determination of development assistance. A new global economic priesthood stands in judgment of mere elected politicians who stray from the path of righteousness and break the covenant of economic orthodoxy.

This was not an isolated, aberrant performance but one that happens all too often around the world. In Malawi, the World Bank and the IMF insisted that the agricultural sector be restructured, demanding an end to subsidies and controlled prices for local farmers, the application of market principles and the reduction of tariffs. The result was a 400 per cent increase in food prices between October 2001 and March 2002, and the hoarding of foodstuffs by private grain traders that added to the shortages caused by drought. Where once the old system was able to provide a basic supply of foodstuffs, the so-called reforms have contributed to a food crisis.

In Colombia, the government agreed to orthodox market-based reforms in exchange for a structural adjustment loan. The result is the devastation of a once vital agricultural sector that not so long ago met Colombia's needs and exported a surplus. The country now imports more than six million tons of food a year while two million acres of arable land lie idle.

When Brazil hit a financial crunch, with the threat of a massive pullout of investors who feared a default, the IMF came forward with a U.S.$30-billion bailout package. In return, the outgoing government had to agree to a strict set of conditions, including rigorous budget measures that would constrain efforts by the new government of Luiz Inácio Lula da Silva to introduce social measures to alleviate poverty. As quoted in a *New York Times* story, the chief economic advisor to President da Silva said the IMF was trying to confine a Workers' Party government "in a plaster cast."[6]

Each of these cases—and there are many more—illustrated the critique that Joseph Stiglitz, a Nobel laureate in economics and former head economist of the World Bank, has levelled against the international financial institutions and their efforts to manage the development agenda of poor countries. He argues that this kind of micromanagement doesn't work because it discounts the unique circumstances of countries, doesn't allow for much individual tailoring of solutions and is highly undemocratic. It is also the source of much of the resentment in many parts of the world against what is seen as an overbearing, censorious attitude, strikingly reminiscent of the Puritan Fathers.

At dinner one night, a former senior politician in Mongolia, one of the early reformers who fought against the Soviet system and believed in market reform, spoke heatedly about the stringency of the structural reforms imposed on his country and the dominance of outside advisors. In good Mongolian style he was rueful in his humour about the role of international consultants. (Who was the first international consultant? Christopher Columbus, because he made a big mistake in thinking the West Indies was India, and was then sent back again with a bigger contract.) But along with the jokes was a distinct feeling of his country's having lost the ability to make choices rooted in their own culture and based on their own sense of priorities. Everyone recognized that international aid comes with conditions, that a country like Mongolia can't do it on its own, needs development assistance and needs to belong to global institutions for trade and investment. The issue was whether the theology that was being preached was the best way to proceed.

It is not a one-sided case. There is more than enough evidence of development assistance being swallowed up in corrupt, bureaucratic systems, or disappearing into Swiss bank accounts. There are also many cases of poor financial management and an overreliance on government to spur growth, leading to serious inflation and balance-of-payment problems. Kenneth Rogoff, the IMF research director, points out that even with all the chafing that developing governments face under IMF rules, they still wish to liberalize their capital markets and need an institution like the IMF to give advice, even out exchange imbalances and help ward off national bankruptcies.[7]

Equally important is the need for coordinating the various donor contributions. When each development agency works in isolated splendour, then duplication and waste result. This is particularly so the more the development objectives get into tricky fields of democratization—governance, environmental repair and conflict management. So oversight and joint planning make sense. What is more problematic is why it is the IMF and the World Bank who have increasingly assumed the leading role.

Under the Bretton Woods agreements, signed by forty-four nations in 1944, setting up the IMF and the World Bank, these institutions were primarily to be money managers, their present role far exceeds that mandate. One might make the case for the World Bank in a more expansive development role, but the IMF has been afflicted with a mammoth case of mission creep. It now plays a dominant role in determining development policy and has become the apostle, the high priest and the arbiter of the market. In recent years both the World Bank and the IMF have centred their activity on managing a Poverty Reduction Strategy, which includes UN agencies, regional banks and individual donor countries and, especially, the large bilateral aid agencies from the U.S., the European Union and Japan. The aid is highly conditional: structural reform (i.e., liberalization of markets) and acceptance of global rules of trade, investment and intellectual property are the standard requirements.

The international financial institutions (IFIs) are creatures of the finance departments of the big economic powers and they have shaped the international system to gain full advantage and profit for the constituency of global capital and rich countries. Gus Speth, the former head of the environmental think-tank World Resources, has said that the rising tide of economic growth has lifted all yachts. A report released by Oxfam in 2002 said that the current round of liberalization in trade is highly biased against poorer countries.[8] Restrictive tariffs and subsidies in the wealthy countries work against them on their basic commodity products, textiles and clothing, and cost them about U.S.$80 billion in lost revenue, far more than was transferred in direct aid. In *Kicking Away the Ladder* Cambridge economist Ha-Joon Chang claims that the failure of free trade globalism to materially help developing countries in recent years is because of deliberate decisions by the rich nations to lock in their present advantages and deprive poorer countries of the policy tools—such as protecting infant industries and poaching patents—that they themselves used in their early years of development. He calls it "kicking away the ladder" so that others can't climb. Chang cites the very high tariffs used by the U.S. between the 1860s and the 1940s to protect their manufacturing base. Only when they became the leading manufacturing country did free trade become the gospel.[9]

Recently, there have been efforts to lighten up the obligations. The World Bank, under its president Jim Wolfensohn, has engaged civil groups in an advisory capacity and attempted to involve NGOs in consultations. In many cases the bank has funded environmental assessments and monitoring, and there is a growing willingness to support social infrastructure. The deputy managing director of the IMF, Anne Krueger, has acknowledged that the classic intervention in market crisis may not always be successful, and has put forward proposals on how to better manage failing economies. But these are only partial and limited solutions. The flaws in the system are deep and abiding.

The orthodoxy I witnessed at the donors' meeting in Mongolia and the top-down formulae that ignore local conditions and needs are an affront to principles of democracy. The UNDP Human Development Report for 2002 comments on the alarming slippage in real democracy from a few years ago, when it looked as if democracy, along with capitalism, was on the march. Might one reason be that so few people have seen dividends from democracy in the betterment of their own lives? When duly elected governments have little clout in making choices for themselves and their people, some of them naturally react against the theology of the market and see elections as a sham. John Atta Mills, the former vice-president of Ghana, has called this the new colonialism and he suggests it is a major factor holding Africa back. If you take away people's right to make decisions, then you take away responsible decision making and weaken the credibility of elected, democratic systems of governance. The human development report comments that, in implementing the poverty-reduction strategy, only "in rare cases does interaction involve the kind of collaborative planning and decision making envisaged in the description of shared control over decisions and resources."[10]

Another side to this global "democratic deficit" lies in the developing countries' lack of power and influence in the global financial institutions. They are basically disenfranchised. Eight countries (Canada, France, Germany, Italy, Japan, Russia, the U.K. and the U.S.) control almost half the voting power in the IMF and the World Bank. The eight largest developing countries (Bangladesh, Brazil, China, India, Indonesia, Mexico, Nigeria and Pakistan), who represent 52.8 per cent of the world's population, have a voting power of just over 10 per cent. And although membership in the WTO is supposed to be equal, the deals are basically struck, once again, by a small coterie of rich countries in the "green room"—the small group meetings convened by the director-general and heavily influenced by Canada, the European Union, Japan and the U.S. Most developing countries are usually excluded. Board meetings and panel decisions of the global economic institutions are closed shops; transparency and accountability are still at a primitive stage. Even in the developed, well-to-do democracies, there is a distinct opaqueness when it comes to these institutions being connected to the elected members of Parliaments and assemblies.

There is a backlash to the reign of the new priesthood. In Latin America, people are electing left-wing politicians who promise to turn the clock back on the market philosophy. Respected leader Fernando Henrique Cardoso, the outgoing president of Brazil, at a meeting of South American leaders decried U.S. unilateralism and irresponsible global money managers. "They talk of integration, but they practise exclusion," he said, lamenting that the result of their dictates was not "the democratic world for which we prepared for so many decades."[11] The people of Cochabamba, Bolivia's third-largest city, rose in revolt against the privatization of their water system and the higher prices that went with it, and drove the mighty Bechtel corporation out of the country. The widespread hardship caused in Argentina by the collapse of the financial system after the "dollarization" experiment failed has resulted in their rejecting the market solutions that had been imposed, and North American bankers have been charged with criminal neglect. In Mongolia I sensed growing frustration and an increasing longing for the good old bad old days of the Soviet system, when there was at least adequate health care and education.

Much has been said about the anti-globalization protests that have forced leaders to hole up in mountain retreats and spend vast amounts of money on security arrangements. There is a strong strain of rebellion, especially among young people, against what they see as the inequities of globalization and the control of the market capitalists. They were the first wave of protest against the system. What's happening now is that the revolt is spreading to the very people the fundamentalist theology of global market liberalization was supposed to benefit. They are tired of being fooled and are anxious to see a greater sense of choice restored to them. The Washington Consensus is beginning to come apart.

It isn't just trade and investment rules that are at fault. Aid budgets are down across the board, and when it comes to spending money on public goods, less and less is available. World Bank vice-president J.-F. Rischard reports that between 1990 and 2002 "rich governments reduced their aid to the fifty or so least developed countries, mostly in Africa, from U.S.$17 billion to U.S.$12 billion."[12] It is a selective approach: the spoils go to those who are most compliant and where the chance of success in meeting the market tests is greatest. Who privatizes fastest, deregulates the quickest and cuts corporate taxes most expeditiously becomes the favoured son. The Ugandan government of Museveni is seen as a success because of its rapid transfer to an open economy. That there is a vicious war being fought on the northern border with the slaughter of hundreds of children, or that intervention into the bloody conflict in neighbouring Congo garnered rich resource concessions for friends of the government, didn't seem to affect Museveni's poster-boy status. In fact, by joining the war on terrorism as waged against the Lord's Resistance Army, both he and the Sudanese government have enhanced their credibility. Never mind that the dispute could have been peacefully resolved.

A country-by-country strategy—avoiding the regional and sub-regional nature of economic and especially environmental and health-related problems—is an impediment to progress. The drought, aridity and desertification that is driving the dust storms of Central Asia's hinterland, including the Gobi Desert, cannot be met on a country-by-country basis; it needs a combined effort. Yet that is not the way development assistance is structured in either the funding institutions or the aid agencies. The country desk is still the centre of the development machine, and issues that cut across boundaries or don't fit the neat bureaucratic definitions of poverty reduction receive marginal funding.

Reform is long overdue. The spell of the new priesthoods must be broken and the system of decision making must be democratized if global economic and environmental security is to be improved. There are signs that this change may now be coming about.

At the Millennium Summit of the UN, in September 2000, world leaders pledged to meet concrete development goals by 2015:

1. Cut by one-half the number of people living on U.S.$1 a day. (Today, more than a billion people subsist on that amount.)

2. Target universal primary education for all children. (Today, 113 million children do not go to school.)

3. Eliminate gender inequalities in education. (Two-thirds of illiterates are women.)

4. Reduce by two-thirds the mortality rate of young children. (Every year eleven million children under five die from preventable diseases.)

5. Reduce by three-quarters the number of women dying in childbirth. (In the developing world the risk of dying in childbirth is one in forty-eight; in North America it is one in 3,700.)

6. Halt the spread of AIDS. (Forty million are now infected, twenty-eight million in Africa alone.)

7. Reduce by half the number of people without drinking water. (Today, one billion people don't have access to safe drinking water.)

8. Develop an open trading system and debt relief. (Most developing countries spend more on debt servicing than on health and education.)

These were noble undertakings, which set measurable standards by which progress could be gauged. Taken at face value, they are a call to action, setting out a road map towards redistributing resources to overcome the inequity between North and South. But are they goals that will be acted upon, or is it just another masquerade?

After the summit, it looked as if these goals were being taken seriously. At the Doha, Qatar, meeting of the World Trade Organization in November 2001, the discriminatory trade system was addressed, and emphasis was placed on making the meeting a "development round of negotiations," trying in particular to change the subsidy regimes of North American and European agriculture, which distort the price and market for developing nations' commodities. Of course, just a few months after these bold steps were announced, the U.S. introduced a huge new farm-subsidy program, in the realm of $18 billion, throwing the Doha good intentions into disrepute. In late 2002, U.S. negotiators threw another wrench into the trade works by refusing to make concessions that would have allowed generic licensing of drugs in poorer countries, a stand silently supported by Canada's own negotiators. EU leaders delayed until the year 2015 any major overhaul of their agriculture subsidy program.

The International Conference on Financing for Development ("Poverty Summit") at Monterrey in March 2002, was again a mixture of possibility and problems. More money was pledged, extensive debt relief was committed, and there was a greater sense of donors and recipients working in partnership rather than as supplicants and providers, reflecting an understanding that low levels of poverty in large parts of the world affect the well-being of everyone. The strong message was that the private sector will, through capital investment, be the engine of growth and that efforts must be made to improve the climate for investment by bringing down risk, setting greater certainty in rules and regulations, and combatting corruption. However, the corollary is that the private sector must be subject to clearer standards of accountability and transparency in their international practices. There has been a growing sense among certain corporate leaders themselves that it is good business to be responsible citizens and conduct corporate behaviour in keeping with sound ethical, social and environmental practices. Kofi Annan's Global Compact commits major corporations to responsible international practices. The World Bank is working on a code of conduct for the mining industry. Oil companies such as Shell are now investing in alternative energy sources. The International Gas Association sponsors a competition on sustainable development. At the same time, there continues to be widespread corporate indifference to, and at times deliberate flouting of, any form of corporate responsibility, as we saw in the case of Talisman in the Sudan.

Change will come about as there is an increasing spotlight put on the transgressors and growing realization by the business community that their own interests are best served by working towards acceptable social and environmental goals. Governments can assist with public expenditures to reduce risk. At the same time, they must act to ensure that standards are met. Modern information systems and the increasing whistle-blowing role of NGOs supply the tools for an information-based enforcement system. In the case of massive investment of Canadian capital in major mining projects, for example, the government of Canada has a responsibility to ensure that they are fully sustainable and do not pose risks to the environment.

There will have to be a real effort to introduce into today's myriad business decision making a different way of analyzing the new risk environment, the responsibilities that go with it and the ways in which there must be a much better melding of public and private practices to achieve a responsible and constructive role for the global private sector.

Such a shift could be detected at the 2002 G-8 meeting, held at Kananaskis, Alberta. There we saw a mapping out of a different relationship between rich and poor, between developed and developing countries. As host, Prime Minister Chrétien took the lead in putting aid to Africa on the agenda recognizing it was time to reinvest in Africa, a region with significant, yet unmet, challenges. It wasn't a case of just offering more money, although the prospect for increased funding was indeed an incentive. What was also important was the assumption by the African states under NEPAD—New Partnership for Africa's Development—of the responsibility to pursue genuine development goals, and to monitor and allocate the funds according to very clear guidelines relating to democracy, nation building, capacity building, an anti-corruption agenda, security and growth. The African states have accepted the onus of making NEPAD work, thereby establishing a partnership relationship, not a dependency, with developed donor countries and international financial institutions. The most innovative aspect is an African peer review mechanism, by which members will be reviewed and assessed according to the NEPAD standards—a way of addressing fundamental issues of performance and behaviour at the regional level. If it works, it could break the hold of the international market priesthood. It will now be up to the developing nations themselves to tailor the means to meet the agreed objectives. Channelling assistance through regional bodies overcomes the restrictions of the country-by-country approach, allowing those issues that transcend national political borders, such as AIDS, conflict prevention and water and resource management, to be dealt with in a more comprehensive way.

That at least is the theory. Will the African states in fact develop the cooperative arrangements and be prepared to hold each of their members accountable? Will the developed world come up with the resources in sufficient amounts to make a difference while forswearing the temptation to dictate terms? These are big ifs. But NEPAD does hold out promise, not just for Africans but also for others in the southern part of the globe. When I described the model to a group of senior officials and diplomats in the Dominican Republic, the response was immediate: Did I think it could happen in the Americas as well? It certainly grabbed their attention. And it certainly offers escape from the current development system.

To prove its mettle, this new partnership must meet some severe tests. One is dealing with the AIDS epidemic that is destroying the lives of millions of Africans and crippling their economies. At the People's Summit held in conjunction with the Kananaskis G-8, Stephen Lewis, the UN special envoy for HIV/AIDS, lambasted the NEPAD process for ignoring the pandemic that in 2002 killed 2.4 million people in sub-Saharan Africa alone and led to another 3.5 million infections of HIV. As Lewis and others have pointed out, none of the NEPAD goals can be met unless the disease is brought under control. It saps economic strength, accounting for an annual loss of 0.5 to 1.2 per cent of GDP and undermining any hope of meeting the Millennium goal of 7 per cent growth needed to cut poverty in half. It is impossible to meet the education objectives when the ranks of teachers are being decimated. Even security issues are put in jeopardy because of the large incidence of AIDS among soldiers.

Less prominent in public discussion, but perhaps the most shameful indicator of the contrast between North and South, is the issue of maternal mortality. Half a million women yearly—one every minute of every day—die in pregnancy and childbirth. Ninety-nine per cent of those women are in the South. One out of sixteen women in Africa die from maternal causes, compared to one out of thirty-five hundred in North America. This disparity could be ended if the women of the South had access to skilled health personnel and a functioning public health care system. The problem is that it is health care that gets cut when budget reductions are required. Health care expenditures are decreasing, and public health is not high on the list of donor contributions. Maternal mortality must become a priority under NEPAD.

A further major challenge is to show that the NEPAD process can come to grips with the scourge of conflict and violence. Africa is the site of 40 per cent of present day conflicts, over 70 per cent of casualties. Resolution of conflict is essential to the development of Africa. The early signs are mixed and somewhat disturbing. The failure to deal forthrightly with the repressive situation in Zimbabwe, the wars in Uganda and Burundi, the disruption of west Africa by Charles Taylor and the rape of resources by several African armies in the Congo are just some examples of how difficult exercising real peer review will be. Nonetheless, at their meeting in Abuja, Nigeria, in early November 2002, heads of state of the Africa Union (which has replaced the Organization of African Unity) agreed to establish a NEPAD mechanism to review political governance, not unlike the CMAG process in the Commonwealth. This provides an opening to apply the "responsibility to protect" catechism at the regional level. There will have to be much more education and discussion before it becomes the working mandate of security in Africa, but there is potential for a breakthrough.

By supporting African initiatives encompassing a principle of self-help at the G-8 and following up with serious increases of aid and technical assistance—some $500 million—Canada has gained much credibility with African states and is looked upon as a partner. Now we have to continue to supply ideas, people, resources and advice in a way that is unintrusive yet helpful and which maintains our reputation for integrity. Our stand on changing patent rights for pharmaceutical corporations is seen as a serious commitment to supporting African interests in gaining affordable drugs to treat AIDS. But there is grumbling in some African circles that the aid package is heavily weighted down with too many conditions favouring Canadian industry. The reluctance of officials in DFAIT to advise a proactive stance in trying to resolve the war in Uganda for fear of upsetting the Museveni government is a cop-out. We are in jeopardy of dissipating the goodwill and influence we generated at the G-8 by falling back into shapeless politics and policies. Here is a case where there has to be a broad across-the-departments policy coordinated by the Prime Minister's Office.

More widely, Canada could become a standard-bearer for fundamental reform of the global economic decision-making system by tackling the issue of representation. When he was finance minister, Paul Martin chaired the Group of 20, an association of finance ministers and bank governors that encompassed member states from both the developed and developing nations. He became an advocate of restructuring the debt management system to provide better oversight of looming debt crises and to establish a global form of bankruptcy protection. In a speech outlining his foreign policy position in the leadership race he suggests that a G-20 model be applied to other global issues such as environmental health and poverty reduction.[13] He could expand this agenda to include a democratization of the international economic institutions: greater representation of developing countries through a change in voting structure and a different selection process for choosing the leadership, and much more open decision making and accountability.

The trade investment and development game is far from over. Can the developing countries mount effective leverage to begin changing the terms? The developed world has a strong desire for new rules governing intellectual property, and perhaps developing nations can use this to begin extracting concessions they desperately need.

On the morning of our departure from Ulaanbaatar, the highway led us past the towering chimneys of the coal-generating plant, then, half a mile farther on, to the celebrations of Naadam with the horse races, the wrestling and archery contests and the bright hues of the traditional costumes.

At the airport we were shown the country's latest proud possession, a newly minted Boeing 737, a further step by Mongolia into global trade and commerce, promising more tourists and quicker, cheaper access to world markets for the country's top-quality cashmere sweaters, produced in a massive government plant employing fifteen hundred people. We later learned that the plant was to be privatized in order to raise more capital, and there would likely follow a significant loss of jobs. Mongolians feel they have no choice but to join the international marketplace. The Naadam is great fun to celebrate once a year. The veneration of Genghis Khan and the honouring of things past is a good way to preserve a vestige of history. But nostalgia and custom hold little sway against the power of the marketplace. Can that marketplace be made more people-friendly? That is the hope of many in Mongolia as they strive to keep up in a very tough race on the global track.

In October 2002, the IMF executive board concluded its consultation with Mongolia. What caught my eye in its announcement was the following: "Directors cautioned that the authorities should ensure that the further large increases in civil service wages and pensions do not jeopardize the attainment of a sound fiscal position. They therefore welcomed the authorities' decision to suspend the increase proposed in the 2003 draft budget, while taking early steps to adopt an effective civil service and pension reform strategy, with technical assistance from the World Bank."[14]

Life just got a little tougher and a little less friendly for retired civil servants and their families in Mongolia. But the priesthood has kept the faith.

CHAPTER 14

KYOTO AND BEYOND

THINK OF A PLACE WHERE THE INCESSANT SIGHTS AND SOUNDS OF conflict that so drench our senses are never heard. Imagine a group of people whose vocabulary has three hundred words for reindeer, and only one word for war—and that only to describe what other people do. Dream for a moment of a haven where peace and quiet is undisturbed by the rattle of video games, or reality television, where the air is void of fumes and toxins and the food is caught or harvested in its natural state, with no genome or chemical modifications.

Such a sanctuary can be found in the northern reaches of Sweden amongst the Sami, an indigenous people who have lived in the Arctic perimeter of Scandinavia and Russia for centuries and today follow a nomadic existence as reindeer herders. My family and I spent several days with the Sami in August 2002 as they followed the reindeer to their summer grazing grounds far above the Arctic Circle. We found ourselves welcomed into their tiny homes, treated with unfailing courtesy, given a crash course in their history and culture and entertained with their songs and stories. Most of all we listened to their deeply felt desire to be given the right to continue a way of life founded on a belief in peaceful resolution of disputes and a partnership with the rugged land they occupy. In this respect they differ from the people of Mongolia, who have embraced the pull of globalization.

The summer scenery of this land is a rare combination of mist and mountain, green lichen and dark lake waters, sprays of fuchsia-coloured wildflowers interspersed with low-lying blueberry bush. As we walked the craggy terrain in search of the reindeer, it evoked the seemingly contradictory feelings of solitude and expansiveness found in the Canadian North. But it wasn't the spectacular scenery that made the impression so much as the way in which the Sami have fused with their environment and are engaged in a determined struggle to maintain that way of life against the encroachment of those who want to cut the forests, build power dams on their flowing rivers and spread the detritus of an industrial, carbon-based economy.

These feelings they share with other indigenous people around the globe, who number more than 300 million. Everywhere there is a strong awakening to the protection and advancement of indigenous rights, to pushing back against the history of exploitation and misuse of their land and resources. It was encouraging to hear how the Sami look to the establishment of Nunavut as a self-governing territory, the Nisga'a agreement in British Columbia and Canada's efforts to establish an orderly system to settle land claims as models. They admire the work of Canada's indigenous people in providing leadership both in Canada and in the international arena. The names Phil Fontaine, Mary Simon and Georges Erasmus are well known to the Sami.

Their ambition is to gain from the Swedish state recognition of basic hunting and fishing rights and in the end to gain some degree of control over parts of the northern territory now fully owned by the central government. There is a Sami Parliament, primarily an advisory body but used skilfully and without confrontation or antagonism as a platform for advocacy. Frontal force is not the Sami way.

Another part of the unique, non-combative strategy of the Sami is to use the tools of culture, history, science and education to pursue their aims. At Jokkmokk, the population centre of the Sami, there is a museum and culture centre of extraordinary design blending the ancient with the modern into a tableau of the life and challenges of surviving and flourishing in the demanding climate of the North. It incorporates a research department of taxidermy that preserves and presents the wildlife of the region. The Sami see this as an important way of establishing their legitimate claims to be the stewards of the delicate local ecology as a means of offsetting plans for large-scale developments, such as hydro construction that floods large areas of land.

The Sami and other indigenous people have traditionally faced such serious, disruptive and exploitive threats. But at least these threats are understood and can be countered with lobbying, persuasion and advocacy within their own jurisdictions. Far more menacing are the dangers arising from a global system that is spreading poison, toxics and a warming climate to the northern lands from afar. The remedies need the large-scale cooperation of many governments and the private sector—all far beyond the influence of a small northern population without much political clout.

The Sami have already had a horrifying experience. In 1986 they began to discover that radiation from the Chernobyl nuclear explosion had spread to their region through the atmosphere and had entered the plant life, especially the lichen, a staple diet for the reindeer. The result was that reindeer meat was deemed inedible and thirty thousand animals had to be destroyed. This almost destroyed the Sami themselves, as it deprived them of their main source of livelihood.

Now, like most people of the North, they are experiencing the severe effects of climate change. Rainstorms happen in mid-winter, freezing the ground and hindering the reindeer from breaking through to the underlying grass and lichen. Drought affects them in summer, leaving the reindeer malnourished. Whether there is other damage, as documented in studies in our own North, hasn't yet been determined.

Other northerners share concern over these unsettling developments. The International Institute for Sustainable Development, in Winnipeg, has produced a powerful documentary on the people of Sachs Harbour, on Banks Island in Canada's High Arctic, who are wrestling with disturbing changes to their environment. Autumn freeze-up occurs a month later, the permafrost is melting and unusually large influxes of flies and mosquitoes are becoming a severe hazard for humans and animals. The way of life of the Inuit and the delicate ecology of the circumpolar region are both being transformed.

It isn't just the North. No part of the globe is immune from the effects of carbon dioxide emissions that turn the earth's atmosphere into a virtual greenhouse, disrupting weather patterns, causing dry areas to become more arid and wet areas to have heavier, more concentrated deluges of rain. Polar ice is melting faster. Sea levels are rising. Forests everywhere are receding. Many agricultural areas, from Egypt to Texas, will become dust bowls. The Intergovernmental Panel on Climate Change, a worldwide network of thousands of scientists, has predicted that without some form of mitigation to reduce emissions, the temperature increase over the next hundred years will range from 1.4 to 5.8 degrees Celsius. To put that into perspective, a one-degree increase would surpass any change that has occurred in any one century over the past ten thousand years. The panel also concludes that most of this change is the result of human activity. We are the authors of our own fate— and nature is biting back.

The consequences will be severe, especially for the poorest in the world. Food supplies and the availability of fresh water will be threatened; infectious disease such as malaria will spread; grazing grounds and forests will disappear; and low-lying regions will suffer massive flooding. The World Health Organization acknowledges that "we must assign a much higher priority to population health in the policy debates on climate change,"[1] but admits that so far we have done little to assess the risks. The same lack of serious work applies to assessing the economic and social costs of adapting to and of mitigating the impact. There is a wealth of analysis on costs to industry, but very little on the costs in human terms. But it is important to heed the words of Dr. R. K. Pachauri, chairman of the intergovernmental panel: "The impacts of climate change are expected to fall disproportionately upon developing countries and the poorest communities within those countries."[2] This stark assessment was echoed by the World Health Organization, which estimates that every year five million children, again mainly in the South, die as a result of environmental causes—poor drinking water, pollution, hazardous sites.[3]

The growing numbers of environmental refugees—people forced to leave their homes and livelihoods because of environmental degradation—are perhaps the most tragic evidence of what will befall the globe if we continue to pay only partial attention. It is now estimated that some twenty-five million people have been dislodged or forced to move for environmental reasons. Klaus Toepfer, the executive director of the UN Environment Programme, estimates that the number will double in eight years, a figure representing a staggering mass of human misery. Yet no international program has put the issue on its agenda. The UN High Commission for Refugees sticks to the definition of refugees forged immediately after World War II: a person escaping political persecution. Most environmental refugees are in poor countries that lack adequate resources for resettlement. The best they can hope for is humanitarian aid that keeps them alive, barely. Climate change is a significant cause of their plight, and its source can be found in metaphorical terms in a mom driving her children to a hockey practice in her SUV.

This is the essence of the environmental dimension of the human security argument: that various forms of environmental degradation, caused by human decisions or lack of decisions, harm, injure, kill or dispossess as many people or more as do war or conflict. It is an invisible, quiet, scattered violation, not recognized as a fundamental infringement of the basic right to live in freedom from fear. I remember an ASEAN meeting in Kuala Lumpur in 1997, at the height of the Asian financial crisis, where attention was focused on how to arrange a global rescue of tumbling financial structures. At the same time, Indonesia was lighting fires to clear land for resettlement of urban dwellers, causing deadly waves of smoke to settle over the region; thousands were being hospitalized for respiratory ailments. Regional governments of course complained, but there was no thought of any kind of international action, even though this was a clear infringement of the right of Malaysians, Filipinos and Singaporeans to breathe non-toxic air. If the Indonesian army had wafted poison gas across the region, there would have been a major outcry; the Security Council would have been summoned into session. But because it was an environmental incursion, nothing of the kind took place, demonstrating the major gap that exists between the problems raised by environmental issues and the capacity to deal with them.

Climate change is the mega-headache of environmental security. It is where the most serious fault lines appear between the market and sustainable development; between the need for transcendent global standards and mechanisms and the interests of individual nation-states; between North and South. It is where the principle of the "responsibility to protect" is put to one of its most demanding tests.

It is, as well, one of the toughest tests for Canada. As we saw in the run-up to the parliamentary ratification of the Kyoto Protocol at the end of 2002, there are serious domestic divisions. Deep concern was registered about potential costs to the energy industry and to oil-producing regions, about our competitive position in relation to the U.S. There are undoubtedly significant costs to our economy, and we are striking out on what appears to be a very different course from the U.S., with the pathway to solutions uncertain. Unfortunately, the debate took place in a domestic, continental warp. Rarely was the issue looked at in its global dimensions, with costs and benefits assessed in terms of our being part of a global environmental system. Yet it is an issue of overwhelming importance for our own well-being and for all humankind. It is a defining moment. For that reason it is important that we understand how decisions are made on this crucial issue and where we can make a difference.

HANGING OUT IN THE HAGUE

A few weeks after leaving Parliament in the fall of 2000, I was asked to lead the Canadian delegation to the Sixth Conference of the Parties on Climate Change, meeting at The Hague (COPS). It was a critical meeting: the goals set out in the Kyoto agreement negotiated two years earlier in Japan were to be made concrete, and decisions would be taken on implementation.

I remembered from cabinet meetings in the spring and summer how excruciatingly difficult it had been to draft a government position setting out our negotiating strategy. Domestic considerations had weighed heavily, and the economic costs were constantly introduced as a limit on how far we could go. The appraisal of industry groups, buttressed by arguments from the key economic ministries, was that we simply couldn't afford to meet the Kyoto target of a 5 per cent reduction in carbon emissions from 1990 levels; it would severely impair our growth. Mind you, the calculations never included the costs of the damage caused by climate change or the costs of dealing with that damage. The economists weren't able to, or wouldn't, include a broader assessment of what benefits might accrue from developing technology in alternative fuels that could then be sold around the world.

There was also the orthodox Ottawa mandarins' refrain that we should never take a decision that would separate us too greatly from the Americans, especially in the economic sphere: our competitive position would suffer and our energy sector, highly integrated in a continental basket, would be at a disadvantage with U.S. counterparts. We were members, along with the U.S., Japan, Australia and Russia, of what was called "the umbrella group." Since its job was to coordinate a position in contradistinction to the Europeans and to the Group of 77 that represented Southern countries, we were conscious of keeping well aligned with the Americans on most issues. However, the business community and many Ottawa officials demanded that we should simply be in full lockstep with American positions.

Any negotiating stance would also have to incorporate provincial views, and in Alberta the rumblings already were that this was going to be a re-enactment of the much reviled National Energy Program. In our Western caucus meetings the warnings were dire that if we went too far it would have disastrous electoral effects. Moreover, the Conservative government in Ontario wasn't known for its environmental sensitivity. This was a predicament designed for stalemate.

The compromise that kept this Byzantine arrangement of contending factions together is what can loosely be called the "sinks and credit" formula. Sinks are agricultural lands and forests, which absorb carbon, and because we have an abundance of both we wanted the subtraction of carbon from the atmosphere via sinks to be acknowledged. At the same time, heavy emitters such as the U.S. and Canada can offset their carbon production by paying money—or credits—to net contributors to reduction, such as poorer, non-developed countries, which have limited emissions because they have—so far—few industries or vehicles. In simple terms, a developing country can earn capital for reforestation by selling some of its credits to a jurisdiction that is over its quota.

The environmental movement, however, saw sinks and credits as a way for governments to avoid tough measures to reduce carbon emissions, and felt it was imperative that Canada set out its bona fides as a nation committed to sustainable development. They believed that the Canadian position, one that was followed by all the umbrella group members was a dodge. The NGOs, working with UN environmental agencies, mobilized pressure on various governments, especially in Europe, where a number of coalitions involved Green Party members. The drumbeat was on internationally for action.

It was the task of Foreign Affairs to represent this international aspect of the issue, especially as climate change consistently emerged at summit meetings the prime minister had to attend. Indeed, the prime minister was always on the side of living up to our international obligations, and it had been his intervention that had led to our signing Kyoto in the first place.

Our role at DFAIT was not very public; we weren't involved in the domestic debate. Along with CIDA, however, we drafted a cabinet submission that proposed that over five years $355 million be set aside for international climate change initiatives. This became part of our climate-change strategy and allowed us to put forward proposals for attracting the interest of Southern countries to cooperate on Kyoto.

Going to The Hague offered Canada the chance to be a serious negotiator on a matter that was increasingly becoming a human security concern of the first magnitude. But I was not a free agent—far from it. I had a strict mandate to follow the "sinks and credit" formula, with a sidebar of trying to gain some recognition for nuclear energy as a carbon alternative. I was reasonably comfortable with the idea of sinks and credits, feeling that with the proper safeguards they could be one avenue for meeting our commitments. Just to make sure that there wouldn't be too much freelancing, however, I was to have a nightly conference call with the ministers of foreign affairs, natural resources and environment. Our conference delegation was made up of senior civil servants from all these departments, and each morning I met with the full delegation composed of representatives from provincial governments, business and NGOs. I felt as if I was being heavily chaperoned.

How does one negotiate a set of agreements in the hothouse atmosphere of ten thousand people in a high state of agitation? The answer: not very easily, and not very well. On the controversial subject of how much individual countries could rely on credits and sinks rather than actual reductions, we in the umbrella group found ourselves arraigned against a highly charged European contingent dominated by ministers from the Green Party who held positions in several governments, especially Germany, and who were dead set against any concession. The head of the American delegation, Frank Loy Jr., an experienced and courtly diplomat with close ties to President Clinton, had one very pertinent message— the U.S. administration wanted to sign Kyoto before the presidential election in November, as a Bush victory would stack the odds against U.S. participation. He made it known that he would substantially moderate U.S. demands in return for agreement in principle with the notion of using sinks. The rest of us agreed. There wasn't much give on the European side.

The Group of 77, strangely enough, had as chief negotiators a Saudi ambassador and an aristocratic Philippine woman who had served primarily as an international bureaucrat. Both took a hard line over a major program of aid to developing countries either to moderate the worst effects of climate change or to introduce control mechanisms. I believed Canada could play a distinct role here and I volunteered to take the lead negotiating role for the umbrella group. We were talking about substantial sums of money—in the billions—to be administered through the Global Environmental Facility. But the position taken by the Saudi representative—who for obvious reasons wasn't strongly committed to limiting carbon emissions—was that any funds had to be given unconditionally, with no strings attaching the money to environmental objectives. Many other Group of 77 delegates were a little uneasy with such an uncompromising position, but bloc loyalty held and no agreement was reached. Remembering the anguish of a Mongolian environmental official about the absence of any funding from the international community, I think forlornly of what a billion dollars might now be accomplishing.

An equally frustrating result was the impasse reached over the sinks and credit issue between the Europeans and us. As the meeting wore on, the discussions became intense and at times acrimonious. In discussions with Ottawa, I suggested that we would have to start making concessions, notably to offer the Europeans the position that any claim on using sinks would have to be scientifically verifiable, and to quietly drop our insistence that nuclear energy be considered an alternative to fossil fuel. The Americans and Japanese were also altering their positions. I was particularly impressed by Frank Loy Jr. who genuinely wanted to get a deal and succeeded in gaining approval for major reductions in the American stance on how much leeway would be given to sinks as part of the calculation of Kyoto obligations.

In the early-morning hours of the last day of the conference, we came close. Setting a limit on how much sinks and credits could be used, and agreeing that they would have to be scientifically verifiable, became the basis of a formula generally acceptable to the European delegation with one or two exceptions, in particular the very green minister from Germany. Around five a.m., in the cramped offices of the European delegation, the issue came down not to technical issues but to politics. The Europeans were worried that any appearance of too great a concession would ignite a strong reaction from environmental groups. But the stark reality was that if this deal wasn't accepted, then the U.S. election could bring to power a president and vice-president with close connections to the oil industry and openly hostile to Kyoto. John Prescott, the British deputy prime minister, bluntly told his European counterparts of the risk they were running and left the meeting in disgust at their unwillingness to see that this was the last best chance of having the Americans as signatories. Unfortunately, that meeting ended without an agreement. The Belgian chairman, Jan Pronk, vowed not to give up, and the agenda on implementation was set over to the next meeting, a year hence in Morocco. He told me later in a private discussion that the Europeans recognized they had made a mistake, which made for more productive negotiations at the next COPS meeting.

The seventh COPS conference in Marrakesh did arrive at a deal. Canada was exceptionally well represented by Deputy Prime Minister Herb Gray and we won our case for sinks and credits. The Europeans finally agreed to a formula that gave more concessions in the amount of credit given for sinks. But by that time the damage was done. The newly elected Bush administration rejected Kyoto. The largest emitter had taken itself out of any international process. They might have done so in any event, considering their penchant for breaking treaties, but it was easier for them to disavow an unsigned document. If Al Gore had been elected there would still have been a tough fight for ratification in Congress but at least there would have been a chance.

This U.S. rejection of Kyoto does put us in a unique position. Because we now have targets to meet, there will be a high premium on developing technology and practices to move us towards less carbon dependency. Ratification erased the uncertainty of our position, and drafting an action plan can proceed in a different political atmosphere from one dominated by the question of whether we should join or not. Now the issue is how to design a framework that will enhance innovation and enterprise. That should give us an advantage in developing arrangements with Southern countries to use our technology and to trade credits. We are the only country in the Western Hemisphere in the Kyoto agreement. That gives us a chance to build bridges. Signing Kyoto can be seen as a platform on which to build a more extensive strategy of environmental initiatives with concrete solutions that can be shared with countries from the South.

I received a primer on how to approach climate change at a regional level when the premier of Manitoba, Gary Doer, asked me to chair the province's Climate Change Task Force. It was an eye-opening experience. I saw first-hand the major changes happening in the Northern region—the melting of the ice in Hudson Bay, starving polar bears, the softening of the permafrost, a shrinking boreal forest, the appearance of insects and vegetation never before seen north of the fifty-fifth parallel. I listened to respected scientists such as David Schindler of the University of Alberta describe the severe effect climate change was having on the patterns of water use in the Prairies. Other scientific evidence pointed to the variability and extremes of weather—drought and floods—as a product of the changing temperature.

But the task force also showed me how we can help developing nations build the capacity and resources to do something about climate change. We met businesspeople who are working on alternative technologies and looking for capital to bring them to market; urban officials who have begun to implement conservation strategies and are confident that with the right support they could make a major contribution in reducing Canada's production of greenhouse gases; farmers who have adopted methods of zero tillage in order to restore the carbon absorption in the soil and are engaged in local township plans of conservation and tree planting; and a large assembly of high-school students who demanded new climate change policies to protect their future. There is an impressive array of Canadian talent combined with genuine commitment that could be unleashed on the climate-change challenge for the benefit of both domestic and overseas endeavours.

The problem, once again, is that there aren't yet coherent, cooperative, coordinated policies that can mobilize this force in a broad national undertaking. Overcoming this disconnect between the will and ability of the nation and the incapacity of the political system is a high priority.

In fact, we should be out there proselytizing for Kyoto. We should propose an emissions trading scheme for North America. We should mobilize in Southern regions where we have a political cachet, such as the Americas and Africa, a partnership around climate change similar to that for land mines. As one example, the Dominican Republic is anxious to start a reforestation project on their border with Haiti. Over the years the thousands of refugees who have settled in the region have denuded the forests. One way to finance the project is to develop the forest as a sink and then sell the credit to Canada as a way of meeting our Kyoto requirements. They get a needed forest project; we get help in meeting our obligations.

But Southern countries are naturally suspicious of the climate-change imperative. At The Hague they often suggested that Kyoto was just another way to deprive developing countries of opportunities for growth. That attitude is beginning to change as more and more Southern people realize the huge price paid in environmental degradation. Bridges must be built between North and South, a role we as a participating Kyoto country can play.

Unfortunately, the global system doesn't put much pressure on domestic political systems to meet the bar. International governance on environmental issues is notoriously weak. There are some treaties that have high levels of compliance, such as one dealing with ozone depletion and certain maritime protections, but in general the system is toothless, with minimal standards and limited powers of enforcement. The UN Environment Programme, or UNEP, is confined to analysis, information sharing and conferencing; as yet there is no concerted effort or much political support to enhance its powers. Tinkering is the order of the day, voluntary compliance the commanding ethic. There is enormous reluctance on the part of national governments to relinquish any sovereignty to multilateral environmental organizations that might force compliance with decisions that could reduce economic growth.

Elizabeth May, the executive director of the Sierra Club of Canada, draws a glaring contrast between the willingness of all governments to respond to decisions and accept penalties handed down by the World Trade Organization and their aversion to anything but the most minimal compliance with international environmental bodies. Even avowed unilateralists like the U.S. and dedicated sovereigntists like China are prepared to submit to trade rulings, but they scorn the idea of any enforcement power being given to UNEP.

This takes us back to the basic pattern of economics taking precedence over environment that we saw in Mongolia. Yet if the world continues down this path it will lose the ecological battle or wallow in a sea of inequities that will also eventually swamp the system. Perhaps we can begin on a new course by changing the nature of the debate from one based primarily on sustainable development to one based on economic and environmental security. The concept of sustainable development came about as a way of marrying competing claims between economic development and environmental protection. The idea that growth should take place only when it is environmentally sound and responsible has been an enormously effective way of focusing on those dual objectives. But it hasn't generated the kind of buy-in from national decision makers that results in a readiness to tackle transcendent global issues that threaten the security and well-being of people. Whenever there is a conflict between growth and environmental protection, powerful economic interests usually win. Risks faced by people are not addressed directly by the sustainable-development model; it therefore doesn't provide the necessary imperative for protection. By looking at the landscape with people in it, there is a better chance of creating wider political support.

In 1999 at DFAIT we emphasized the transnational nature of both economic and environmental threats: "A growing number of hazards to people's health—from long-range transmission of pollutants to infectious diseases—are a global phenomenon in both their origins and their effects. Economic shocks in one part of the world can lead rapidly to crises in another, with devastating implications for the security of the most vulnerable."[4]

But we never managed to comprehensively rethink strategy in these fields, and our initiatives, while valuable, ended up playing on the margins. There were just too many other ministries to involve, too many domestic interests to consult, too few resources available. In this respect we were paying a price for the fragmented machinery of government, especially the division between CIDA and DFAIT. If the two had been in the same policy box, it might have been possible to tie development policy more closely into our human security framework. For a while we had a certain synergy and common approach on the peace-building initiative, but not on the other emerging foreign aid and environmental priorities. Thus, it was difficult to ever go beyond the conventional. The height of this folly was demonstrated in our relationship to the regional banks (African, Asian and Inter-American). As the minister of foreign affairs I was the nominal shareholder, and our director reported to me. But the Department of Finance would set the contribution levels and CIDA would set the policy. I can't recall the three ministers ever getting together to talk about a common approach.

The same institutional deficit and division is magnified in managing these issues internationally. The Bretton Woods institutions keep their distance from the international environmental organizations. This is part of the orthodoxy. Whenever I tried to raise issues of child labour, I was told that trade and labour matters had to be kept separate; otherwise the purity of the market would be distorted. As we have seen, the environmental organizations, in particular UNEP, play a useful educational function but have no powers of compliance or enforcement. Even the massive UN meetings that set standards and raise consciousness are not very effective in gaining concrete decisions or implementation.

At the Johannesburg World Summit on Sustainable Development, held in September 2002, little was accomplished to advance environmental standards or enforcement. What *was* valuable was the number of partnerships created between the private sector, NGOs and affected communities to deal with water problems and renewable energy development. Perhaps such networks of international players cooperating over specific problems could be one workable way to respond to environmental issues.

But that still doesn't answer the need for serious international problem solving, for an institution with authority to hold states and individuals accountable for environmental damage that affects the well-being of other communities. Peter Singer, a Princeton University political philosopher, has argued in his book *One World: The Ethics of Globalization* that it should be possible under a strengthened international law for countries suffering serious pollution or degradation as a result of the actions of others to seek damages. He cites Norway, which is pushing for a polluter-pay scheme in Europe after it suffered harmful radiation effects on its coastline from waste material being dumped into the North Sea by a reactor in Great Britain. The next question is whether sanctions or penalties against those whose actions are damaging to others might ultimately be applied. This is the point raised by Elizabeth May. If trade transgressors can be disciplined, should there not be a similar regime for the environment? As Peter Singer asks, "Is it inconceivable that one day a reformed and strengthened United Nations will invoke sanctions against countries that do not play their part in global measures for the protection of the environment?"[5]

A Council for the North

Regional stewardship—integrating the standard-setting, political-bargaining and resource-sharing tasks that should take place at a broad transnational level with implementation by regional organizations and networks—seems to me increasingly plausible. It could be the model for addressing cross-border concerns.

There are already examples of this kind of regional stewardship that balances economic, social and environmental interests. As well as the trilateral environmental and labour commissions under NAFTA and the International Joint Commission for managing shared water resources, the European Union has set environmental policy, brought a transnational perspective to the individual member states, established regional bodies to deal with river and air pollution and advanced common EU positions.

Canada has examples of its own. One of the most successful cases of effective environmental foreign policy, combining the efforts of DFAIT, the Department of the Environment and the advocacy and persuasion of indigenous peoples, was the POPs Convention, an agreement to limit the spread of toxins—specifically, persistent organic pollutants, or POPs—that concentrated in northern waters and affected the health of northern inhabitants. But where we invested the most diplomatic capital and tried the most innovative multilateral approach was in launching the Arctic Council.

The council held its inaugural ministerial meeting in Iqaluit, the capital of Canada's new northern territory of Nunavut, in September 1998, bringing together delegations from eight countries and three international indigenous organizations representing the whole circumpolar region. This high-level forum for promoting cooperation and coordination among the Arctic states and Arctic people, particularly on environmental protection and sustainable development, was the product of several years of painstaking work by a small band of Canadians with allies around the circumpolar region who saw the need to address serious Arctic issues in a collegial way. The single most crucial driving force behind the creation of the council was a remarkable Canadian woman named Mary Simon.

The Arctic comprises about 40 per cent of our land mass, it has critically shaped our identity and it contains some of the most delicate and essential global ecosystems, yet most Canadians don't know much about our North. We think of polar bears, pipelines and the cold Arctic air masses that bring a chill to our bones as most of us huddle along the forty-ninth parallel with the U.S. We give short shrift to thinking about the North as a major frontier, a serious security concern or the site of devastating pollution and the far-reaching effects of climate change. Our foreign policy for the most part focuses on Canada's relations with the U.S., Europe and Asia Pacific rather than on our role as a prime circumpolar player. Yet in the global scheme of things, the North is an area where our freedom to manoeuvre is necessary both for the protection of our own people and for the preservation of our integrity as a country.

The U.S. has never recognized Canadian jurisdiction over much of our northern waters. During the Cold War the Americans and the Soviets used the Arctic as a prime strategic area for nuclear subs. Canadians would be surprised to know just how hot the cat-and-mouse games in our northern waters have been between our southern and northern neighbours. Even after the Cold War, the U.S. is still very active in undersea patrolling. In 1978 the Trudeau government passed the Arctic Waters Pollution Protection Act, which helped to assert our rights in the region, but the U.S. has never acknowledged its application, and we have never made an issue of it because we literally don't have the capacity to enforce its provisions. We have further wounded ourselves by not ratifying the International Law of the Sea, which would give us the right to extend our jurisdiction over Arctic waters. Since the turbot dispute and under pressure from Newfoundland politicians, we have delayed ratification until another UN convention dealing with control of fishing stocks in international waters comes into force. At times there is great illogic in the realm of politics.

Our best strategy under these circumstances is to work to establish agreements and practices that will allow effective, cooperative government of the circumpolar region with due recognition of the rights of its people. This requires a multilateral regime between the appropriate governments and the residents—ergo, the Arctic Council.

I first met Mary Simon in 1991, at a meeting to discuss a northern foreign policy for Canada. At the time I was the opposition critic for Foreign Affairs. The dominating presence in the room was a diminutive and soft-spoken woman representing the Inuit Circumpolar Conference who I quickly learned had determined and well-developed views as well as long experience working on Arctic matters. Born in northern Quebec, Simon had been a CBC reporter and producer before becoming involved in indigenous organizations. Her basic message was that northern people were being ignored internationally; they needed a new forum, and Canada should take the lead in organizing it.

It was several years until I saw Mary again. In the meantime she was appointed Canada's circumpolar ambassador by my predecessor, André Ouellet. In my tenth-floor office she explained her idea for an organization of the eight nations surrounding the Arctic Ocean, but with the special twist of having representatives of the major indigenous peoples as members of equal standing, though minus a right of final vote. But the group would govern by consensus, so the vote really didn't matter anyway. This Arctic Council would address circumpolar issues, coordinate actions and bring the priorities of the North into other international arenas.

There was a problem, Ambassador Simon explained: the Americans didn't want a new forum, and the Nordic countries wouldn't join without the Americans. Negotiations had broken down in late 1995. She asked me to intervene. I negotiated with Warren Christopher, then U.S. secretary of state, to bring the Americans back to the table, agreeing to their condition that security matters not be part of the mandate. We secured a founding meeting in Ottawa in September 1996, and Canada offered to be the chair for the first two years. That was when the tough slogging really began for Ambassador Simon and her small team. The founding document left most of the difficult issues to be worked out in negotiation.

The most contentious matter was defining the rights of full participation for northern people. Most major international meetings invite short presentations by civil groups, followed by polite questions—then dismissal so the real talk can go on behind closed doors. Mary and her team wanted indigenous groups at the table. That gave several governments, especially the U.S. and the Russians, trouble—it's not the way big powers like to operate. But we held firm and used many diplomatic occasions to argue the point.

Eventually we saw a change of heart among many delegations. One key reason was Canada's decision to establish a new territory in the eastern Arctic. Creating Nunavut was seen as an innovative move in granting a form of self-government to indigenous people and showed what could be achieved with a little imagination and boldness. It attracted a lot of international interest and served as the catalyst for shifting attitudes. Still, the main thrust during those first two years was the familiar pattern of dogged, persistent, at times grinding negotiation, leavened by adroit wordsmithing and skilful compromising. Finally, most of the disagreements were settled, and we invited ministers to Iqaluit for September 1998.

Meanwhile, there was the corollary matter of getting our own northern act together. I wanted an explicit northern foreign policy that would get us away from an ad hoc approach. I had a strong personal interest. Throughout my political life in Manitoba I had been fascinated with the Port of Churchill, in addition to dealing with it constantly as a regional concern. Not only was it steeped in the lore of my province as the landing site for settlers and as the home of the polar bear and the blue whale but it was an inland seaport, deep within the mid-continent, and therefore represented an incredible opportunity for the prairie region to overcome the disadvantage of distance. That the railway companies and the grain companies, who had a vested interest in a coastal infrastructure, tried to deep-six Churchill just made me more of a supporter. As I became involved in a proposal to privatize the port, the concept of a transportation link to Russia was raised. The idea of an Arctic bridge whetted my interest, and I began a campaign to give special attention to the Russian North.

Yevgeny Primakov, the Russian foreign minister, proved to be an ally. He was a tough veteran of the old Soviet system, but had a warm personal touch with just a touch of zaniness. His duet with Madeleine Albright in a takeoff from *West Side Story* at an official ASEAN dinner meeting was the boffo performance of the diplomatic borscht circuit. (Every year foreign ministers were expected to humiliate themselves onstage, alas. I usually asked that our presentation be a full chorus so that I could just blend into the crowd.) He was also deeply interested in realigning Russia's relations with countries in the post–Cold War era. One night at the Pearson Building, we and our wives got into a discussion on how little our two countries had developed our polar connections. We reflected on how history might have been different if the mapmakers of the sixteenth century had used a north–south axis instead of an east–west bias. Perhaps it was time to redraw the maps. With Primakov's support, followed by that of his successor, Igor Ivanov, I began a series of visits to Russia and other northern locales to explore some new political terrain.

In meetings in Moscow and later in Lulea, a beautiful little Swedish city inside the Arctic Circle and the place where I returned with my family to visit the Sami people, I met first with representatives of the Russian states, then with members of the Barents Council, making presentations on the Arctic Council idea and talking about the need for stronger circumpolar links. Also present at Lulea was Strobe Talbott, the U.S. undersecretary of state and point man on Russian affairs. He was there to explore with the Nordic countries the vexatious problem of radiation leaks, from Russian subs mothballed in ports on the Kola peninsula, that threatened to contaminate all northern waters. It was fortuitous timing, as I had the chance to sit with this courteous and thoughtful man and gain his commitment to help break the log-jam on the issue of indigenous representation and whether security issues would be included in Arctic Council discussions. He indicated that the U.S. might want to succeed us as chair of the new body: nothing like high-level diplomacy in the High Arctic.

At the Barents Council gathering it became clear that the northern dimension could also engage the Nordic EU members, the key being our common interest in Russia. For Europe, the transition of Russia into a reasonably stable society was a top-of-mind issue. If Canada, through a northern policy, could help, then there was reason to forge a partnership. We had a good case to take back to cabinet.

We were now set for a successful launch of the council. We had ensured full rights of membership for indigenous people. We had the agreement of the Nordic states, Russia and the United States. We had developed a program focusing on northern pollutants, sustainable development, improved scientific research and coordination of efforts on northern youth. We were also in a position to issue a discussion paper for widespread public consultation.

Hosting the inaugural meeting of a brand-new international institution in the far northern capital of Canada's newest territory was a special moment, especially seeing present representatives of all the indigenous northern people, including the Sami. It drew attention to a unique community, one that gives Canada a special character. And it was a dramatic demonstration of how the well-being of our northern people is increasingly interlaced with a global system. It showed why we need a new generation of international bodies to give everybody a voice, regardless of where they live. Mary Simon later told me that the importance of the council was that it made a place where the long-term vision of the Arctic could develop.

It also offers a model for dealing with desert dust-storm problems afflicting East Asian residents; the water shortages in southern Africa; deforestation in Central America; the threat to biodiversity in the Pacific islands—to name just a few areas. All these regions need some form of intergovernmental collaboration. The Arctic

Council model can be grafted on to ensure the participation of all those directly affected.

Canada should have a vision for the Arctic. The North always has a mystical, romantic quality for Canadians, even while we ply our trade to the south. What struck me was that this region could define a strategic place for Canada. It is the canary in the mineshaft of climate change: the melting of the ice pack—affecting sea levels, weather patterns, wildlife migration and vegetation growth—has worldwide consequences. Transportation routes will be substantially altered if there is an open-water route in the Arctic region; every seaport in the world will have to adjust its plans and forecasts if the long-sought northwest passage becomes a reality. Such dramatic changes will emphasize the need to protect the delicate ecology of Arctic waters and thereby set up real issues of jurisdiction and sovereignty.

A northern strategy creates as well the option of much closer economic, political and cultural ties between Canadians and people of the north in Europe, Russia and Alaska, particularly among indigenous communities. In 1999 I travelled to Greenland, Iceland, Finland and Latvia. One of my most enduring memories from the trip was being wakened early on a Sunday morning in a beautiful old guesthouse in Nuuk, Greenland, by the sounds of religious music, mixed with cooking aromas wafting from below. I wasn't sure whether overnight I had been transported heavenward or had sleepwalked into a church service. On coming downstairs, I found the premier of Greenland, Jonathan Motzfeldt, who was also a lay preacher in the Lutheran church, pounding out stirring hymns on an ancient pump organ. Over breakfast he shared his perspectives on both the problems and the opportunities of life in the North. At the root of his beliefs was the need to bind together northern people in order for the rest of the world to pay attention to the uniqueness of their conditions and culture. He argued that if we were so inclined Canada could and should play a leadership role. It could have been Mary Simon speaking.

I heard the same sentiment from the Finnish foreign minister, from my hosts in Riga, who were worried about the Russian presence, and certainly from Icelanders, who saw in the historic ties with the Icelandic population in Canada the chance to strengthen relations. There was a clear invitation for Canada to play an architectural role.

These discussions, and Mary Simon's meetings with indigenous organizations and territorial and provincial governments, set the stage for "The Northern Dimension to Canada's Foreign Policy," announced in June 2000. It is an action plan designed to concentrate northern issues as a priority for Canada. A modest budget of $2 million a year was set aside to assist the Arctic Council, help establish the University of the Arctic and a circumpolar research network, develop economic and trade opportunities and begin implementing a Canada–EU joint plan for northern cooperation. CIDA contributed $5 million for assistance projects in northern Russia, mainly for the support of indigenous people. It was a first if not giant step towards fulfilling the potential that the North can add to Canada's international role.

Markets, Mothers, Migrants and Modified Foods

If you head about six thousand miles southwest from the cool, open tundra of the Sami people in northern Sweden, you will find the sun-drenched, arid highlands and intensely cultivated valleys of the state of Oaxaca, Mexico. It is rich in the diversity of its indigenous people and its agriculture. Throughout the years it has spawned the first known appearance of maize, along with an abundance of herbs and chilies. The rich red dye from the cochineal parasite that grew only on cacti endemic to the region was a source of great wealth for the Spanish during their occupation and gave the Indian people of the area a strong base of independent agricultural development.

Behind the newly restored Santo Domingo monastery in the centre of the city of Oaxaca is a remarkable garden that captures this legacy, presided over by the soft-spoken, intensely committed director of ethnobotany, Alejandro de Avila, who is a pioneer in the study of relationships of plant life to the evolution of human society. One blistering-hot morning in March 2003, my wife and I accompanied him throughout this garden that contains the immense variety of the plant life unique to Oaxaca. At one point he stopped beside a growth of natural maize that can be traced back ten thousand years, and in a calm but worried way told us of recurring evidence that a strain of genetically modified—or GM—corn transported under the NAFTA agriculture system is showing up in the maize species of Oaxaca. Because of the strength of its DNA, this modified maize threatens to subsume and perhaps extinguish local strains. He is not an eco-warrior who condemns outright the application of the new biotechnology, but he is deeply concerned about the implications of GM invasion into Oaxaca and what it means for indigenous people if their staple crop loses the ability to adapt and flourish as it has over several millennia.

Like the Sami museum in Jokkmokk, this botanical garden highlighting the distinctiveness of Oaxaca plant life and its intimate connection to the people of the region is an effort to preserve and promote a distinctive ecology. But de Avila also sees it as a way of meeting the future. Better understanding the evolution and transformations that result from the interplay of human and plant life, and utilizing the rich biodiversity of the area to grow products that are sustainable and usable, such as plant-based energy and lubricants or higher-protein foods, may open new opportunities to recast traditional agriculture. Such new ventures could offer ways of escaping from the debilitating impact of low prices for export commodities such as coffee and from the competition of highly subsidized imports.

It is through such small but creative initiatives sprouting around the globe that we can plot a course of environmental, economic and cultural sanity.

If you arrive in the city of Oaxaca on a Saturday market day, you can see just how important the agricultural base is to the indigenous people. They are spread among five hundred communities, speak more than 150 dialects and are proud of their traditions and long history. For centuries, the market has been their meeting place. Here they gather not only to buy and sell produce and goods but to share each other's company. In *Mornings in Mexico*, D. H. Lawrence wrote about the market in Oaxaca, "To buy, to sell, to barter and exchange. To exchange, above all things, human contact."

Arrayed over a vast area are stalls selling all manner of fruits and vegetables, pottery, building materials, tools, clothing and the basic necessities, displayed with an artistry similar to that exhibited in the ancient ruins of the nearby pyramids of Monte Alban. Into the market, as the morning proceeds, come families from towns and villages far and near. Arriving by bus or on foot, they stream into the maze of the market, multiple shopping bags in hand, ready to bargain. It is yet another spot on the globe where people have shaped a place where a sense of community prevails.

But as we have seen with the nomads of Mongolia, the tribes of Acholiland and the Sami of the North, these distinctive ways of life are threatened. The market at one time occupied a third of the centre of Oaxaca, imparting a vitality and purpose to the core. Along came the rising tide of automobile traffic that strangled the central hub. The market was moved to the city outskirts, leaving the core to sightseers. Today the market faces another challenge. Sam's Club, an offshoot of the ubiquitous Wal-Mart empire, was set up as the nucleus of a large shopping centre. It offers low-cost volume goods, mainly imported, and attracts the patronage of those who can afford a car, leaving the market to the rural campesinos and poorer town folk. What this means for the market as a place of social communication, as a forum for the exchange of goods and ideas out of which a sense of community is fostered, can be foretold by the forlorn experience of countless North American towns and cities where the pull of mass merchandising has led to the hollowing out of downtowns and main streets and a fragmented assortment of freeways, malls, compounds and gated communities— well-known symptoms of the homogenizing effect of the global economy.

For the indigenous people of Oaxaca, the real market they increasingly face is of a global dimension, and like many other marginal groups they find it formidable. As their population increases, their land erodes, unemployment rises, social service funding falls behind demand and they face competition from imported agricultural products, their recourse is to move. Migration to the attractions of the free trade zones of northern Mexico (the maquiladoras) or to the beacon of the U.S. (three hundred thousand Oaxacans reside in Los Angeles alone) is a fact of life. Pulling up stakes from an ancestral home is always personally traumatic; when it involves thousands of people a month, it is a form of social upheaval that strains the ties of family, rends the community and changes the economics. The third-largest source of revenue for the state of Oaxaca is remittances from those who are working elsewhere.

Many of the migrants are young women who go to work in domestic service or the factories of the North, leading to increasing cases of sexual crime and harassment. Children are left behind in the care of grandparents, and family relations suffer. As well, many of the migrants who cross the U.S. border have no legal status, a situation that lends itself to extreme workplace exploitation and the deprivation of basic services of health care and education. It is a sore point that causes great distress in both countries.

This is an intensely human problem, and in a very real way *our* problem. It is happening to people who are our NAFTA partners. It can certainly be argued that the NAFTA requirements for open trade are a contributing factor, as it is clear that the small-scale farmers of Oaxaca have not been integrated into the new export-oriented economy. Yet the present NAFTA framework and certainly our present policy approaches are not designed to help solve such problems. We're back to serious consideration on how to make North America work as a community.

Herein, Oaxaca can also be a guide. In the preceding chapter the problem of maternal mortality was presented as perhaps the most egregious example of the North–South disparity. This I saw first-hand in Oaxaca, as part of a visit of the board of the MacArthur Foundation that was focused on population issues. One morning we gathered in a high-domed, ornate room in the museum of Santo Domingo to listen to the stories of women of the region. They described the high rates of death women experienced because of a lack of health services. Three women a day die in Mexico because of pregnancy-related diseases and complications. Trained health care personnel often aren't in the rural indigenous areas. Where they do exist, husbands often won't let a medical person touch their wife's body. A culture of male dominance still pervades. Sebastiana Vazquez, an Indian woman from the Mixtec tribe who has led a grassroots movement for women's rights in the area, braving condemnation from her family and abuse from officials, summed up this attitude when she said, "Where I come from, women don't have husbands, they have owners."

But it wasn't just the description of the problem that was so striking. What stood out was the impressive alliance of women, working in concert from office towers in Chicago to the Mexican Parliament to the streets of Oaxaca to reform the system. In the case of the Sami, the Arctic Council provides hope. In Oaxaca it was a different kind of organization, less institutional but equally responsive and increasingly effective. My wife commented after this visit to Oaxaca that in a world where so many men were planning for war, it was heartening to see that goodness could still be found.

A CASE FOR GLOBAL REFORM

A healthy global system needs a constant evolution of associations, networks, gatherings and institutions. Climate change, scarce water, burgeoning cities, information divides, mass migrations, energy sources, disappearing fish stocks, disaster relief, income inequity, women's rights—all demand ever higher levels of attention. Existing institutions are overstretched or ineffective. Some are so big they have become immobile. Others are restricted by rigid nation-state procedures or bypassed by big players still operating in a Wild West mode of self-interest. Innovation to solve this sclerosis is in high demand.

All this change is predicated on a serious effort by the wealthy developed states to work in partnership with the South and with the underdeveloped Far North. The promises proclaimed at various summits over the past few years to reform trade practices, increase aid, share technology, set beneficial standards for private investment and assist in combatting environmental degradation must be fulfilled.

So far, the signs haven't been encouraging. The preoccupation with military adventures in the name of fighting terrorism creates a growing sense of grievance in many parts of the world over what they see as indifference and dominance by the most powerful of states—an agenda that undermines efforts to restructure global economic and environmental security. Since September 11 the anti-globalist coalition of Southern countries, environmentalists and development agencies seems to have lost its way. No definable group of governments has enlisted in the cause of economic and environmental structural reform. The movement has not been able to attract popular media interest at a global level. It is a political mission waiting to happen.

Which is why defining the issue in terms of the impact upon people is crucial. Concerns about globalization are as much about culture as they are about economics. Once the connection is made between the rash of natural disasters, extremes in climate, shortage of resources, poisonous air and the dangers to health and livelihoods of people in all regions; once the interdependence between economic inequality and environmental destruction is recognized; once it is understood that the present global system cannot cope with the pressures generated by climate change, then there might just be a springboard for action.

But reform in the arena of economic and environmental security mustn't take too long. Each day of delay, the street children of Ulaanbaatar pay a price, as do the Inuit and Sami of the North, the migrants in sub-Saharan Africa, the slum dwellers of Calcutta, the indigenous people of Oaxaca, indeed our own farmers in the Prairies—all victims, along with many others, of a global governing system that does not work in their interests, does not provide the security and well-being that is their right to enjoy.

PART VII

Searching for Survival in a World of Weapons

CHAPTER 15

DISARMAMENT ON EARTH, DISARMAMENT IN SPACE

THE POTENTIAL FOR WORLDWIDE DESTRUCTION PRECIPITATED BY present stocks of weapons of mass destruction, compounded by the advent of sophisticated systems that can attack information networks or operate from space, is daunting and real. And the carnage of civilian casualties brought on by the excessive availability and use of small arms is staggering. The world's primary response to the new terrorist threat is military engagement. The Bush administration, believing that a show of force and the use of force can ward off all threats and in the bargain advance their hegemonic interests, has built an overpowering military machine. They are campaigning to have all friends and potential allies join in this expanding military complex, controlled out of Washington. In the meantime, other powers are arming themselves to win regional conflicts, and many private organizations of criminals and terrorists are working to acquire weapons of a biological, chemical or nuclear kind.

One of the monumental tasks of our time is to counter this return to a might-makes-right society and to control the supply and use of weapons. In a world brimming with massive destructive power, we all have a responsibility to protect humankind and must put in place the means to do so in a collaborative, peaceful way.

SMALL ARMS

When the Ottawa land-mines conference came to an end, several participants asked whether this kind of process could secure a treaty for the control of small arms. It seemed a natural fit, so I asked my officials to develop a strategy. Certainly, the scope of the problem warranted such an attempt. It has been estimated that three hundred thousand people are killed annually worldwide by small arms in violent conflicts—and another two hundred thousand die from small-arms-inflicted homicide. Millions of civilians every year are wounded or disabled by small arms.

War is now very much a civilian affair. In the First World War, 90 per cent of the casualties were military personnel. In the wars of the last decade of the last century, it was the non-combatants, usually the most vulnerable, the women and children, who accounted, on average, for more than 80 per cent of victims. As we have seen, war today is not primarily a matter of cross-border aggression but is fought internally, amongst warlords, ragtag rebel armies or paramilitaries whose primary aim is to control drugs, diamonds or other resource riches. Or it is a form of official violence, with governments waging war against their own citizens for reasons of ethnic revenge, as in Rwanda or the Balkans.

The automatic rifle is today's most prolific weapon of mass destruction. The AK-47, the M1, the Galils and the AR15s have become the scourge of Africa and parts of Asia and Latin America. Very much a legacy of the Cold War, when thousands were distributed to prop up satellite regimes or supplied to surrogate rebel armies, these weapons have become the prime tool of destruction and disorder in parts of the world where order and legitimate governments are in short supply. They increase the time, lethality and scale of armed conflicts. The arms trade has given rise to the arms trader, a breed of predator who draws down the vast stockpiles of surplus arms left in the warehouses of Northern countries and trades them for diamonds and other portable riches.

These weapons become a source of low-intensity wars involving children in Uganda, Sierra Leone, Liberia, Congo, Colombia, Sudan and elsewhere. In *The Shadow of the Sun,* Ryszard

Kapuściński writes that the modern wars of Africa are mainly children's wars. The orphans of past conflicts become today's recruits, or are kidnapped into service, as with Emma and so many like her. As Kapuściński comments, "The wars of children have been made possible by technological developments. Today, handheld automatic weapons are short and light, increasingly resembling children's toys. The dimensions of weapons are now perfectly suited to a boy's physique. Because the child is capable only of using handheld, short-range weapons, clashes in these children's wars take the form of savagely unmediated collisions. . . . The toll typically is frightful."[1]

The suffering continues long after the initial conflict is over. The inventory of automatic weapons and handguns supplies the tools of criminal action that destabilizes countless societies trying to rebuild after wars. The availability of these weapons is a serious impediment to development and nation building after conflict. The 2002 *Small Arms Survey* reports that "virtually every department of the UN system is exposed to the consequences of armed conflicts, crime, social dislocation, displacement and human suffering that are directly or indirectly related to the unregulated availability of small arms."[2]

These weapons create a culture of violence; in one decade, two hundred thousand Colombians have been killed in violent conflict. People are forced to flee the violence, resulting in vast numbers of internally displaced persons, who when they find their way to a camp discover it is controlled by young thugs with weapons who abuse, rape and otherwise violate. Humanitarian assistance is disrupted as aid workers become targets for the brigands and roving bands of toughs. The litany of despair found in places where guns prevail is long and lamentable.

At the outset, however, it was clear that control of small arms would be a much more difficult undertaking than controlling land mines. The problem was far more diffuse and didn't have the same clear-cut focus. The use of conventional small arms is a legitimate exercise by various agencies of the state, and the intricate small-arms trade links private purveyors with resource companies and unscrupulous governments. Trade in these weapons is huge, and is compounded by the strongly held belief that transfers of weapons to various insurgents and rebel groups is a preferred way of helping bring about desired changes in political regimes—for example in Angola, Afghanistan, South Africa and Bosnia. And how to actually control and verify uses was difficult to fathom. Nevertheless, no situation lent itself more appropriately to a human security policy, so we decided to make it a priority for Canada.

Our action plan had three tracks. First was to support efforts, primarily at the regional level, to address illicit weapons trafficking through improved transparency and weapons registries. Second was to use our peace-building fund to finance various post-conflict small-arms disarmament measures. Third, and most controversial, was to launch a campaign for a convention banning the transfer of military small arms and light weapons to non-governmental entities. This was an attempt to open up for international discussion the reality that much of the proliferation in small weapons occurs as a result of what could be considered legitimate arms sales, either through direct transfer, leakage or pilfering. One way to expose the problem would be a universal system of marking weapons and ammunition. As expected, this initiative evoked an immediate response from the big powers, who saw it as a restriction of their right to support friendly political movements. It had nothing to do, of course, with the fact that these same countries were the biggest sellers of arms. More surprising was the reaction from certain NGOs who cavilled at the idea of restraining the supply of weapons to groups fighting for self-determination or against oppression. We simply couldn't garner enough support, so we switched our tactics.

There was another reason to change tack. In 1998 the UN called for a major international conference on the illicit arms trade. Perhaps we could better achieve our goals by working to shape the agenda, and ultimately the outcome, of that conference by more conventional diplomatic means. At the same time, we reached agreement with the EU on a joint-action plan on small arms, and this Canadian-European common approach would provide a base for close collaboration at the UN conference.

NATO was another place where we attempted to use the inside diplomatic approach. Enlargement into Eastern Europe was the order of the day for NATO. Eastern Europe also sold massive numbers of arms to developing countries. We therefore insisted that one of the conditions of membership in NATO be that any weapons that became redundant as a result of integration with NATO inventory could not be sold on the open market but should be destroyed. In one meeting with representatives from the three countries most eligible for accession—Poland, Hungary and the Czech Republic—I said that unless we were to receive their commitment to this condition, Canada would object to their joining. This tough-love approach had resonance.

As preparations for the UN conference progressed, it became obvious that there was a concerted effort by the UN bureaucracy and the diplomatic disarmament establishment to avoid adopting any of the methodology or lessons of the land-mine experience. This was apparently to be a traditional meeting of nation-states. NGOs would be on the margin.

The conference, held in the summer of 2001, got mixed reviews and results. It did succeed in agreeing on a plan for nation-state action. And it did set in motion long-term UN treatment of the issue, which will culminate in a review conference in 2006. But substantively, there were thin pickings. The NGO community was basically kept on the outside, and the American gun lobby put strong pressure on the U.S. delegation, which led to their forestalling any significant achievement. Despite efforts by Canada, the EU and several other like-minded states, there was failure to agree on marking, regulating civilian possession, increasing transparency and controlling transfers to non-state actors. No universal criteria for export controls or control of arms brokering was agreed to. In short, anything that might have made an appreciable difference was given short shrift.

Why do I think that small arms should continue to be a Canadian priority? One obvious answer is the effect the small arms trade has on development. As the South African deputy defence minister, Nozizwe Madlala-Routledge, said starkly at a disarmament meeting in Beijing, you can't have development when there is a plethora of small arms corrupting the society. The leaders of rich nations frequently sound sincere about the need to address poverty and to adopt enlightened trade and investment policies advocated by the poorer countries. But when it comes to the provision of weapons, the sincerity quickly wears off. At about the same time as Madlala-Routledge was making her plea, British papers were full of news of the Blair government's attempts to sell a multi-million-dollar weapon system to Tanzania in order to shore up defence industry sales, and the U.S. was rearming the warlords of Afghanistan.

All this has special significance for Canada in light of the 2002 G-8 meeting we hosted. One of the important objectives of the African-inspired NEPAD plan is to deal with small arms. Canada has the experience and know-how to provide a great deal of advice and assistance. Working with the Africans, we should seek a comprehensive approach to disarmament and arms-trade restraint on a continent where the scourge of small weapons has been most deeply felt. A major diplomatic effort, for example, to limit the sale of arms from Europe to Africa could be undertaken without running into the interference of the Bush administration. It might not surface on their screen, yet it would add in a very practical way to restraining the transfer of arms.

Regional efforts or agreements between regions are more likely to succeed than an inclusive, global covenant. A global treaty incorporating all the competing interests, working through the consensus-based UN system where big states have a virtual veto, is bound to be limited. Regional agreements are easier to arrive at and address more exactly the needs of that region, even though they are often hampered by a lack of resources for implementation, or by outside interference in conflicts. Now is the time for Canada to assist in rectifying those weaknesses. In their planning and delivery, our development aid programs must take into account the dimension of conflict and security in a particular region and promote efforts to both snuff out the supply of small arms and reduce the demand. As with land mines, the consideration of small arms must shift from a disarmament focus to the impact on people. This may be the most effective way to build towards an international review in 2006 that carries some substance.

THE NUCLEAR THREAT

If controlling small arms is so challenging, imagine how difficult it is to persuade nations to rethink their nuclear strategies. In early June of 2002, a senior DFAIT official called me in response to an article I had written urging the government to once again try to have NATO review its nuclear policy.[3] After the grand declaration by the leaders of Russia and the U.S. that the Cold War was finally over, and in light of the agreement to establish a NATO–Russia Council to cooperate on a range of security matters, I said it didn't make much sense to continue an outmoded nuclear strategy predicated on deterring Russian aggression into Western Europe. We had made an effort to have such a review in 1998, but the nuclear states within NATO had been able to deep-six the initiative.

Conceding my logic, the official lamented that a review was unlikely to happen. Canada was not in a position to resume its efforts for review because the whole foundation of disarmament and arms-control policy was too much in flux, and no one in DFAIT was sure where things were heading. In effect he was saying that the basic architecture of multilateral agreements and treaties carefully built up over the past forty years was being called into question, primarily by the U.S., and no one was sure how to respond.

This came as no surprise. It is clear that the Bush administration does not believe in international negotiation on universal arms treaties. Not that the U.S. had previously been a great booster. The failure of the U.S. senate to ratify the Comprehensive Test Ban Treaty highlighted the withering American commitment to disarmament issues. However, not since the coldest days of the Cold War has there been such outright disavowal of the validity of multilateral engagement, such willingness to break agreements and the adoption of such aggressive pro-nuclear policies as there is under George W. Bush.

After September 11 and the declaration of total war against terrorists and the "axis of evil," this disdain for international, collective action based on commonly accepted rules became even more obvious. Military might is the vogue, and raising questions about restraint is portrayed as disloyal. Pre-emptive action against anyone or any state suspected of harbouring terrorists or building weapons of mass destruction has become an established doctrine, contrary to the precepts of the UN Charter. The new mantra of hard-power thinking includes the buildup of "smart arms" hardware and serious proposals about using a new generation of smaller nuclear weapons to deal with rogue states, along with a commitment to the anti-missile defence program and the affirmation that the U.S. should not be bound by any restraints imposed by international agreements. Anthony Lewis of the *New York Times* puts it this way: "The dislike of treaties reflects an attitude that the United States must be free to do what it wants in the world. . . . It is a sharp break from our postwar premise that, if wisely negotiated, treaties enhance our security."[4]

Further signs of disarray and incoherence in approaches surfaced in 2003. While waging war against Iraq was justified because of the deep suspicion that they were harbouring weapons of mass destruction, North Korea boldly fessed up to having an active program and we were told by President Bush that diplomacy was in order. The message is clear: if you want to avoid being attacked by the superpower, get nuclear weapons before they can make the first move. But what does that do to encourage non-proliferation? At the same time, rapprochement with Russia was heralded as a positive step, even though the accord on reducing nuclear arsenals is really a parking arrangement, not a dismantling formula. There are only minimal efforts being made to restrain India and Pakistan's nuclear sabre-rattling.

This mixed bag of competing postures is confusing for all those concerned about reducing the risks that large arsenals of both nuclear and conventional weapons bring.

MEETING IN BEIJING

A microcosm of these swirling cross-currents played out during an international disarmament meeting I attended in Beijing in April 2002. Largely inspired by then UN Under-Secretary-General for Disarmament Affairs Jayantha Dhanapala, "A Disarmament Agenda for the Twenty-First Century" was co-hosted by the UN and the government of the People's Republic of China. A mix of experts and advocates, ambassadors and officials, politicians and professors assembled in the ballroom of one of the massive hotels that now dominate the Chinese capital for three days of brainstorming on controlling, perhaps reducing, the mountain of weaponry that weighs down the world.

Discussion and debate were certainly energetic, but it was impossible to forge any consensus on a new agenda. Instead, the conference revealed the fault lines that divide the various arms-control and disarmament constituencies and the frustrating inability of multilateral efforts to gain any traction. The prospect of an enhanced arms race, looming weaponization of space, the continuing acquisition of conventional weaponry and fuelling of internal conflicts, the danger of terrorists or criminals gaining access to sophisticated arsenals of biological, chemical or nuclear stocks, and the advent of smart weapons—all this heightened the sense of urgency and foreboding. There was a multitude of risks without any solution. In his opening remarks, Dhanapala drew attention to the doctrine of pre-emptive use of nuclear weapons as needing special attention, a pointed reference to U.S. military thinking.

His overall plea was for an alternative road map, one that reflected the basic principles of the UN Charter with an emphasis on the peaceful resolution of disputes, the role of social and economic development in securing a path to peace and the commitments by nuclear states in the Non-Proliferation Treaty of 2000 to move progressively towards disarmament. He cited a Brookings Institution study that shows the historical cost to the U.S. in the field of nuclear weapons to have been around $5.8 trillion.[5]

Picking up on this theme, Chinese Foreign Minister Tang Jiaxuan reiterated the need for multilateral efforts, especially by the UN, to limit proliferation of weapons and materials. Outer-space weaponization was clearly his preoccupation, and he called for a new treaty limiting further expansion of military development in what he called "the common property of mankind." The Chinese are understandably nervous about the overwhelming dominance of U.S. military power. They see a growing U.S. presence in Central Asia, North Korea named as a charter member of the axis of evil, the promotion of missile-defence agreements with Japan—to say nothing of hints by senior Japanese officials of an interest in acquiring nuclear weapons and the ratcheting upwards of U.S. security guarantees for Taiwan. All this comes at a time when China faces immense domestic pressure to invest in economic development, the environment and energy and to privatize state industries. They don't need the burden of increased arms expenditures, but without some arms-limitation agreements, particularly on space and missile defence, their own hawks will campaign for an accelerated military buildup.

If the Chinese were looking for some comfort, they certainly didn't receive it from the head of the U.S. delegation, Mark Groombridge. A former staff member at the Cato Institute in Washington, a think-tank strongly opposed to international arms-control regimes, and now special assistant to the under-secretary for arms control in the State Department, Groombridge confirmed most of the fears about the uncompromising U.S. attitude towards multilateral dialogue. That the Americans would send such a junior person to represent them was signal enough. His message was equally discouraging. He said the battle against terrorism should be the overriding concern of all nations and justified any and all actions. He made it plain that the U.S. was interested in using outer space as a weapons platform if they thought it necessary and was proceeding with missile defence regardless of the consequence for arms control. It was a chilling display of the "our way is the only way" stance of the Bush administration.

As the session proceeded, I found myself forced to share the skeptics' misgivings about the present state of effectiveness of multilateral disarmament proceedings. There wasn't a lot of new thinking about the proliferation of weapons of mass destruction or how to stem the flow of small arms. Most disquieting was that many participants insisted on preserving the sanctity of the UN Conference on Disarmament, in Geneva, as the place of prime negotiation—even though it has been stalemated for years, not even able to agree on an agenda since 1998. As one observer at the meeting said to me, "The only agreement the Geneva conference has been able to forge in the last few years is where the ambassadors' parking places should be located."

Most of the energy in the room came from the civil activists who argued strenuously for a broad-based coalition of NGOs and like-minded states to campaign for a new disarmament agenda. Rebecca Johnson, director of the British-based advocacy group the Acronym Institute, presented the idea of an Ottawa Process model to tackle weapons in space, which quickly brought a retort from an Egyptian diplomat that bypassing the UN Conference on Disarmament would be a serious breach of international proto-col—which of course was the point. Nobel laureate Jody Williams made an impassioned plea to work outside the traditional diplo-matic forums and open up the disarmament agenda to ordinary cit-izens, out of which could arise strong public pressure to offset the resurgence of strategies to fight a nuclear war and to control the spread of an arms race in outer space. Dr. Ronald McCoy, a kindly-looking obstetrician from Malaysia, said that his bringing twenty thousand babies into the world propelled him into activism on behalf of total nuclear disarmament, and he took great exception to the belligerence of the American delegate. He suggested that the Bush administration had drawn the wrong lesson from September 11. In his view it proved that even the most powerful state on earth was vulnerable, and that such an attack with a nuclear device would have cost far more casualties. Rapid nuclear disarmament and safeguards against nuclear theft should be the priority, not increasing militarism.

One distinct threat identified at the forum was the spread of weapons of mass destruction into the hands of warlords, terrorists, extremists and fanatics. It is now possible for an individual to obtain the materials, the technology and the know-how to manu-facture and deliver lethal weapons. Once again, this is the dark side to the global village. Little progress had been made to adapt the multilateral treaty and enforcement system to address this threat. Attempts in Geneva to negotiate a prohibition against the sale and use of fissionable material have been stalled for years. The American answer as averred by President Bush is frightening in many respects, most simply in the crazy logic of the pre-emptive use of weapons of mass destruction to take out presumed weapons of mass destruction, but it has seemed to be the only option on the

table. The need to forge a strong multilateral response to this problem is self-evident; the capacity, will and intellectual commitment
to do so are suspect.

If there is to be a reassertion of multilateral efforts on disarmament, it will have to come from a coalition representing a broad
range of civil and public interests, along with like-minded states.
This kind of partnership runs counter to the conventional approach
to disarmament negotiations, which have always had a mystique
about them suggesting they are beyond the ken of ordinary folk. It
also presents a challenge to those who see solutions, in particular
to the problem of terrorism, through a hard-power lens: if you let
the NGOs in, then you can't control the agenda, and public opinion might actually divert the chosen course. For civil-society advocates, the experience of the land-mine treaty remains a model of
how to achieve democratic decision making. For the professional
diplomats, it is an incursion into their private preserve. For governments such as those of the U.S., China and Russia who follow a
hard-power agenda, it is anathema to their view of how the world
should be run.

WHO GOVERNS THE BOMB?

Beijing revealed the fracturing of consensus on security concerns,
the fundamental divide between those who believe that one single
power should be the shaping force in determining global relations
and those who believe in an international regime rooted in shared
responsibility and obligations; between those who want to maintain
an elite structure of decision making and those who see the emergence of some form of global democracy. It was the same kind of
dynamic seen on the streets outside any large global conference,
where a barricade divides the protestors and the policy-makers.

Robert Dahl, an eminent American political scientist who spent
his career examining the elusive, time-worn question of who governs,
wrote a book in the mid-eighties called *Controlling Nuclear Weapons*.
In it he poses the question of whether in an age and time where
issues are complex and seemingly remote from the experience of
ordinary citizens it is possible to have democracy. On the manage-

ment of nuclear weapons, his assessment is that decisions have been turned over to a modern version of Plato's Guardians, a class of self-appointed, self-styled experts and insiders who jealously protect their prerogatives to determine the use of these weapons and articulate elaborate theories and threats to justify their control. He writes: "Nothing can have more important consequences for so many people, Americans and others alike, as decisions that may prevent or cause the use of nuclear weapons. If it is also true that these decisions have so far been arrived at pretty much outside the reach of democratic controls, then we must count this as a profound failure in the capacity of contemporary democratic institutions to achieve their purpose."[6]

Dahl's concern takes on added significance today. Global problems are far beyond the scope of governments to handle under the present machinery, and there is a growing disconnect between what people want from their governments and what is in fact being delivered. Nowhere is this more urgent than in the containment of the tools of war. Letting people have more say on governing our policy on nuclear issues would be the most effective way of ensuring that democracy works.

A public-opinion survey conducted in eleven countries in 2002 by the Centre for Public Opinion and Democracy, in conjunction with the Japanese newspaper *Asahi Shimbun*, reinforces this sense of growing alienation on the nuclear issue.[7] The response contradicts the prevailing wisdoms of the decision makers (the Guardians). A "no first use policy" gets strong support even from citizens of nuclear powers, especially Russia (75 per cent), France (68 per cent), the U.K. (64 per cent) and the U.S. (62 per cent). The "no first use policy" gets even stronger endorsement when the question was asked about using the weapons against non-nuclear countries. As you would expect, the numbers in non-nuclear states run ahead of those in nuclear countries: Brazil (76 per cent), Germany (74 per cent), South Korea (73 per cent) and Canada (70 per cent). But the feeling runs against pre-emptive attacks even in the nuclear powers—the U.K. (69 per cent), Russia (68 per cent) and the U.S. (58 per cent).

Most dramatic was the support for a treaty banning nuclear weapons outright. Although this is the stated aim of the Non-

Proliferation Treaty, such a notion is usually ridiculed as being unrealistic and unachievable. The position of the U.S. is that nuclear weapons should once again be considered reasonable options, especially for getting rid of threats from "rogue states," a clear indication of nuclear mission creep. Yet the majority opinion of all those surveyed supports an outright ban: Brazil (89 per cent), Germany (88 per cent), Canada (83 per cent), Japan (77 per cent), the U.K. (72 per cent), Russia (78 per cent) and the U.S. (61 per cent). The sobering side of the results is that most people don't think a ban will happen. Only 41 per cent of Canadians, 35 per cent of South Africans, 26 per cent of Americans and 20 per cent of Japanese believe that someday nuclear weapons will be eliminated. The exceptions to this are Russians, 68 per cent of whom think a ban will eventually take place, followed by the French at 53 per cent.

I can already hear the objections. These survey results are only a one-time snapshot; the questions don't present all the options or complexities; people don't understand the problems associated with policing agreements, non-compliance, verification—all the time-tested arguments. Let's concede all the problems. It doesn't change the fact that a majority of people around the world want to reduce the dangers of nuclear weapons.

The disarmament agenda doesn't reflect public concerns because there is little debate or open examination. Disarmament discussions are still very much a closed shop, with limited opportunity for citizens to have input. There is a failure not only by governments but also by our media, our universities and our think-tanks to address the issue. The Department of National Defence, which doesn't exactly encourage the study of arms reduction, funds twelve security studies programs in universities that have a strong defence bias. With the exception of a few major U.S. foundations and in Canada the Simons Foundation, private funding has withdrawn from the study of disarmament and arms control. There is little critical examination in academic journals or in our media. A profound collective neglect prevails. As Albert Einstein once said, "The unleashed power of the atom changed everything save our modes of thinking."

So how do you energize public engagement? Who will take the leadership? What kind of campaign can be mounted to offset the powerful forces and interests arrayed on behalf of a warrior world? What are we in Canada capable of doing, and are there the political will, public interest and overall competence to tackle the job?

THE FIRST NON-NUCLEAR STATE

In its own quirky way Canada was the first country to decide not to develop nuclear weapons, despite having the capacity to do so. That does set us apart and gives us, in my opinion, a special vocation.

It is history not generally known to Canadians, nor to anyone else for that matter, even though in the scheme of things it was a momentous choice. During the Second World War we became part of the Allied effort to develop an atomic weapon, first as a supplier of uranium, then as part of a research effort in a secret lab in Montreal. C. D. Howe, the powerful czar in Mackenzie King's wartime cabinet, sat as a representative on a Combined Policy Committee set up as a result of an agreement between Roosevelt and Churchill to oversee the development of the bomb. As work proceeded towards the design phase, Canadian scientists became more integrated into the overall Manhattan project. Carson Mark, a mathematician from Manitoba, eventually became head of the bomb design group at Los Alamos. In 1944, the Combined Policy Committee made a top-secret decision to construct the heavy-water plant at Chalk River, Ontario—the precursor to the CANDU reactor and the supplier of the plutonium that was used in the first British atomic bomb, to say nothing of the large amounts we supplied to the Americans.

When the devastating explosion took place over Hiroshima, it came as no surprise to a small handful of top Canadian policymakers. The only comment came from C. D. Howe, who issued the statement: "It is a distinct pleasure for me to announce that Canadian scientists have played an intimate part, and have been associated in an effective way with this great scientific development." Later, Mackenzie King wrote in his diary: "How strange it is that I should find myself at the very centre of the problem, through Canada possessing uranium, having contributed to the production of the bomb, being recognized as one of the three countries to hold most of the secrets."[8]

In those fateful dawning days of the nuclear age, we were an integral part of the small, exclusive club of nuclear-wise states. If we had wanted to pursue weapons production, we were in a prime position to proceed. But we didn't. There appears to have been no inclination to do anything more with the knowledge than develop its peaceful application.

There is no evidence that this was ever the subject of major debate. Aside from a few isolated questions in the House of Commons, Parliament didn't consider the matter. Likewise, there is no record of any cabinet consideration or of any media interest. It just seemed to be an assumption that developing nuclear weapons wasn't something we in Canada would do.

From today's perspective that looks like an odd state of affairs. The possession of nuclear weapons is the prime currency of hard power, a supposed sign of greatness and stature. The French and British hold on to their nuclear status as a way of anchoring their veto-wielding status in the Security Council. The nationalists of India and Pakistan laud their new, if primitive, nuclear capacity as a badge of their coming of age. The security specialists who pore over the military inventories of countries to determine who counts in the power equation see the nuclear arsenal as the *sine qua non* of being a heavyweight, separating the men from the boys. What to make, then, of a country that had the chance to be a founding member of the nuclear club and just wasn't interested?

Furthermore, we were one of the earliest proponents of putting the nuclear genie in an isolation ward with the keys to be held by the UN. We began our multilateral commitment early, and at the time actually shared that faith with our World War II partners, the U.S. and the U.K.—their hardline stance was to come later. In his memoir *Danger and Survival*, McGeorge Bundy, the long-time American diplomat, described a meeting between President Harry S. Truman and Prime Ministers Clement Attlee of the U.K. and Mackenzie King of Canada to discuss the future of atomic energy. In particular he remarks on the role played by Lester Pearson, then the Canadian ambassador to Washington, who in the meetings presented a strong case for international control of atomic energy, under the auspices of the UN, reinforcing the position taken by certain diplomatic and scientific cadres in the American and British establishments against the wishes of the military, which wanted to keep it under full national control. The final communiqué issued by the three leaders signalled a desire for peaceful uses of nuclear energy, the need for international control, the importance of sharing scientific information and *the eventual elimination of atomic weapons.*

Bundy comments, "The role of Canada in the history of nuclear weapons is unique and it seems appropriate here to remark that Canadians' good sense and moderation are visible at many points in the nuclear age. . . . Canada was the first country to decide clearly that it would not itself become a nuclear weapons state, reaching that conclusion openly and with no voice on the other side, in 1945. The Canadians had everything at hand—the uranium, the science, and the technical head start—everything but the desire."[9]

It is somewhat ironic that a tough-minded American diplomat at the outset of the nuclear age is able to capture the essence of the distinctive role that Canada can play amidst the current nuclear threat. He was able to see that there is value from an American point of view in having Canada take a different stance on security issues and work to persuade the Americans of the need to support international cooperation and control. It is a prescription we would do well to remember next time some editorialist, academic or Alliance spokesperson or defence minister bleats out that we have no choice but to fall in lockstep with American policies.

THE NUCLEAR REVIEW: WINDOW OF OPPORTUNITY

I found out just how tricky an exercise nuclear disarmament can be soon after becoming foreign affairs minister. In October 1996, I sent a letter to Bill Graham, then chairman of the House of Commons Standing Committee on Foreign Affairs and International Trade, requesting a review of our nuclear policy. This launched an extensive public process that lasted more than two years and led to difficult discussions in NATO and serious differences with the nuclear-weapon states within the organization.

It was the right thing to do and the timing was opportune, even with the controversy that went with it. The Cold War was over and many of its rigid positions were in flux, including those on nuclear disarmament. There had been the remarkable discussions between Presidents Reagan and Gorbachev in Iceland on total nuclear disarmament, followed by the START II agreements and the indefinite extension of the Non-Proliferation Treaty in 1995. There was some expectation that the Clinton administration would breathe further life into the process.

At the same time, international pressures were building for a reassessment of the nuclear issue. The International Court of Justice had rendered a far-reaching decision challenging the legitimacy of nuclear weapons, and the Canberra Commission on the Elimination of Nuclear Weapons, a group of seventeen leading international figures, initiated by the Australian government, had issued a call for nuclear states to commit "immediately and unequivocally" to eliminating all nuclear weapons. A worldwide coalition of more than six hundred NGOs had launched a campaign to build support for a disarmament agenda; the Canadian component spearheaded a cross-country consultation in eighteen communities, involving a wide variety of participants.

I had my own feelings on the issue. Even with all the post–Cold War efforts, nuclear arsenals still amounted to more than seventy thousand weapons, 98 per cent of them held by the U.S. and Russia. Frustration with the slow progress towards eliminating arsenals was propelling other nuclear wannabes into developing weapons. Indeed, the nuclear powers' continued assertion of the "political value" of nuclear weapons was an open invitation to proliferation. Yet there was a growing climate of public complacency, a belief that the end of the Cold War had taken care of the nuclear problem, and official acceptance, certainly in NATO circles, that the weapons themselves were essential to maintaining a deterrent capacity.

I thought it possible for Canada to challenge the status quo. It wasn't easy. There was no consensus in the government on the issue, so I opted for parliamentary committee.

Once there is a committee report, the government is required to table a response within ninety days; it has to provide its own policy position, as do the opposition parties. It is one way that individual ministers working in cooperation with MPs can engage in creative policy-making. It is one of the most useful pathways for generating discussion, involving the public and legitimizing Parliament as an incubator of initiatives. Unfortunately, it is seldom used.

The standing committee did its work well, travelling extensively and commissioning good research. Of particular interest was the testimony of experts from the U.S. and Great Britain, some of them military people and former security officials. People like Robert McNamara, former U.S. defence secretary, and U.S. Generals Lee Butler, Andrew Goodpaster and Charles Horne had become strong advocates of disarmament. Their testimony about the unreliability of the deterrent system was very powerful considering they had been part of the nuclear priesthood.

With the exception of the Reform Party, a consensus formed around an active Canadian role in altering the nuclear status quo. This generated intense interest and strong lobbying by the American Embassy and the British High Commission, who were in a perpetual state of agitation over the work of the committee. What had them exercised was the possibility that we would issue a "no first use policy." Mavens in our own defence department warned their counterparts in Washington and London that this was part of the grand design of DFAIT, or certainly of the DFAIT minister. The fear was that such a policy would be contagious and would be taken up by other NATO countries. To offset this possibility, American and British diplomats engaged in a variety of persuasive techniques, especially with Liberal members of the committee, including private briefings, dinners and not so veiled warnings of consequences, not unlike those issued by Ambassador Cellucci that our non-participation in the Iraq war could affect border issues. The message of alarm was conveyed directly to me in a number of encounters with NATO foreign ministers, some of them quite curious about what we were doing, others expressing their concern. If I had ever believed that policy-making in Canada is a simple exercise, or that solely domestic forces dictate the result, this experience dispelled such notions. The scrutiny and pressure from outside and the full court press being executed by the nuclear states, especially the Americans, had an effect. You could call it an advancing case of cold feet; several of my colleagues, to say nothing of certain officials in DFAIT and DND, were discovering serious reservations to the nuclear review strategy.

But then we got lucky. Halfway through the committee hearings, in the spring of 1997, an election was called. The work on nuclear policy was delayed until the spring of 1998 at which time the world was shocked out of its complacency by India's and then Pakistan's nuclear tests. Sanctions were applied to the miscreant states. But the world could see that the nuclear states' strategy of using weapons as a political tool and stalling on disarmament had resulted in these two implacable foes—who had waged war twice over the disputed area of Kashmir—arguing that they needed nuclear weapons for their security as well. The need for review became urgent.

In May 1998 a group of middle-sized states (Ireland, Sweden, Egypt, New Zealand, South Africa, Mexico, Brazil and Slovenia) made a concerted effort for a resolution at the UN First Committee calling for a new disarmament agenda, including tough language on the need for NATO to get rid of its nuclear weapons policy, especially its first-use strategy. Once again the nuclear states went into damage control, using blunt language in their opposition. But the vote went against them. Ninety-seven countries voted for, nineteen against and thirty-three abstained, including a majority of NATO members, Canada among them.

In Canada, the standing committee tabled its report in December 1998. It contained fifteen far-ranging recommendations, calling on Canada to reaffirm and demonstrate its commitment to total nuclear disarmament. Most important, it strongly endorsed the notion of a review of nuclear policy in NATO, but didn't get into specifics and didn't address a "no first use policy." That was some relief to our nuclear allies in NATO.

Armed with the committee report and bolstered by the willingness of the defence minister to go along, we were able to get cabinet's support for the principle that a review should be held. We now set about gaining support in NATO. I opened the matter with the other foreign ministers, tying the need for review to the American effort to turn NATO's attention towards weapons of mass destruction. I argued that as long as NATO retained the "political" value of nuclear weapons, it was hard to make the case for restraint. For example, in 1998 the NATO Web site still referred to the utility of nuclear weapons in deterring the massed Soviet armies on the other side of the Oder–Neisse line. With the exceptions of the Germans and the Dutch, it was a tough sell. What I found particularly surprising was the reluctance of the new members of NATO—Poland, Czechoslovakia and Hungary—to consider any change. Perhaps having just acquired the nuclear guarantee, they weren't too anxious to give it up.

Nevertheless, we continued to push. The best we could manage at NATO's fiftieth-anniversary summit, in 1999, was a commitment "to consider options for confidence and security building measures, verification, non-proliferation and arms control and disarmament." It was a thin plank, but strong enough for us to continue our campaign. The crucial decision on such a review would be taken at the NATO Foreign Ministers Meeting in December 1999. We played on recent nuclear testing in South Asia and the rumblings from non-nuclear states about the lack of any demonstrable movement to disarm by nuclear states in fulfillment of the Non-Proliferation Treaty. A review conference on that treaty was scheduled for early 2000, and we suggested that without some signs of progress there could be trouble; a serious review of nuclear policies in NATO could show some momentum. We won the argument, and a committee was authorized to begin work on reviewing options.

Our aim was to see NATO limit the "political" role of its nuclear strategy to one where nuclear weapons would be used only in clear response to a nuclear attack, not in response to conventional or biological or chemical attacks—a far cry from today's pre-emptive proposals. Our other objective was to engage the Russians in a discussion on reducing tactical nuclear weapons. But these ideas were not met with much enthusiasm. One big problem was the inertia, if not opposition, within the bureaucracy of NATO and the permanent representatives to the council. They are basically averse to rocking the boat, and there is still a dominant military culture amongst NATO decision makers.

We might have made some headway if we had not slammed into two brick walls. Once the Bush administration took their seat at the NATO table and September 11 took place, the idea of a serious review was shelved. But this is all the more reason for Canada to again take up the cause. With the new NATO–Russia Council being launched, our goals have even more pertinence today. The blueprint is there, and it would test just how real is this new relationship with Russia.

We painstakingly put together the elements of a distinctive nuclear policy for Canada in the 1990s. It is time to do it again, now that new weapons, the war on terrorism, the "maximum spectrum control" strategy of the U.S., volatility in South Asia, the emerging power of China, and the potential for proliferation of weapons to non-state actors make the risks more complex.

North Korea: Opportunity Lost

Nowhere has the need for new direction been more evident than in the case of North Korea. Its recent bellicosity, manifest in its claims that it is resuming efforts to acquire a nuclear capacity, accompanied by its withdrawal from the Non-Proliferation Treaty, is a serious threat to stability and security. The tragedy is that it comes so soon after what looked like signs of progress on mending fences on the Korean Peninsula. South Korean President Kim Dae-jung's "Sunshine Policy" seeking dialogue with the North Koreans on eventual unification was an enlightened initiative. In 2000, I initiated diplomatic relations with North Korea in the hope that we could add support for this potential rapprochement.

Then things took a turn for the worse. The U.S. named North Korea one of the charter members of the "axis of evil," and their own disdain for the provisions of the Non-Proliferation Treaty and their talk of pre-emptive war set alarm bells ringing in the isolated chambers of the exalted leader of North Korea, Kim Jong Il. There is now a crisis in credibility for the nuclear non-proliferation regime and serious risk of confrontation. The U.S. won't negotiate until

North Korea reverses their decisions, and the North Koreans won't talk until there is some form of non-aggression guarantee from the U.S. The war of words and threats goes on.

Maurice Strong, UN Special Envoy to North Korea, sums the situation up well: "The lesson we can draw from the current Korean crisis is surely that if the underlying conditions which have given rise to it had been addressed at an earlier stage and trust and cooperation amongst the principal parties established we would not be facing a conflict today."[10]

Unfortunately, Canada did not use its initial diplomatic presence in North Korea to provide any grounds for developing trust or cooperation. After September 11, the leadership at DFAIT lost interest in North Korea, as was the case in many other areas of Canadian initiative, and we were somnolent in engaging the Americans on North Korea and suggesting what might be done to build some bridges. Canada can be and should be one of the mapmakers in today's highly charged international environment. We might have made a difference by trying to navigate in a difficult, stormy situation. Instead, we stayed on shore. The result has been a major setback for the non-proliferation regime, created by the contradictory approaches of the U.S. towards Iraq and North Korea—one attacked for having had intentions to develop weapons of mass destruction, the other, at least as I write, being given the diplomatic treatment, even though they clearly admit their intention to proceed with development.

This was only one of several challenges that are undermining the non-proliferation regime. At the annual preparatory committee meeting of state parties of the Non-Proliferation of Nuclear Weapons Treaty (NPT) held between April 28 and May 9, 2003, the stress was evident—nuclear nations were not living up to their disarmament obligations; several states, notably Iran, were limiting inspections; the anomalous position of Israel, India and Pakistan, who possess weapons but are not given standing; and the growing fear that the U.S., and perhaps the United Kingdom, is about to start development of a new generation of small nuclear weapons to tackle "rogue states". With the next review session on the NPT scheduled for 2005 there will have to be a very concerted expenditure of diplomatic capital to alter and upgrade the NPT regime to counteract this erosion of the treaty's validity. If this is not done, then the security that the treaty provides will be diminished, and the threat of a nuclear jamboree will become a twenty-first-century reality.

SPACE

Of equal urgency is the need to finalize a treaty on weapons in outer space.

At a time when there is a wholesale challenge to the legal framework governing not only arms control and disarmament issues but matters of human rights, environment and security, a global campaign to prevent an arms race in space could be a counterpoint around which broad-based agreement could be achieved. It could offer a brake to the unravelling of the global rule of law. Present American actions to move towards a military presence in space—once dismissed as the fantasy of a marginal few who, to use the phrase of one commentator, "had consumed too much Star Trek"—threaten to spark a new arms race. U.S. Secretary of Defense Donald Rumsfeld seems intent on implementing the recommendations of a commission he himself chaired that said it was in the U.S.'s national interest "to deploy the means to deter and defend against hostile acts directed at U.S. space assets and against the uses of space hostile to U.S. interests"—in other words a "space Pearl Harbor." The U.S. Space Command has been given substantially heightened responsibilities and funding; advanced proposals for the missile-defence system outline the possibility of space-based interceptors; and the U.S. says it does not want any limitations placed on its actions in space.

Implicit in this strongly held view is the assumption that the U.S. is so far ahead of all other competitors and has such dedication of fiscal resources that it can establish overwhelming superiority. This may be true. But unless there are controls, other nations will have to try to catch up or at least provide some countermeasures, such as aiming missiles at U.S. space installations. This is certainly the reading one gets from recent Chinese and Russian strategic analysis. Ergo, we have an arms race.

The dangers of an arms race in outer space are infinite. Security, environmental, energy and economic costs would be immense. The peaceful uses of outer space would be severely disrupted, and the highly developed, multi-billion-dollar satellite-communications industry would be put at risk. Space-based sensoring for sustainable-development management through improved environmental monitoring, disaster mitigation and resource management has immense potential, but that and more would be lost. Plans to deploy weapons in space will push aside all other uses and create an atmosphere of conflict, not cooperation.

The international community has long recognized the threats that would arise from an arms race in space. The Outer Space Treaty of 1967 provided a basic framework of international law, incorporating principles of free exploration and no stationing of nuclear weapons or other weapons of mass destruction. Four other treaties and a series of declarations have added up to a hefty body of law, but they don't explicitly limit the kind of weaponry the U.S. is contemplating. At the UN, countless General Assembly resolutions have warned of an arms race in space, but the matter is continually referred to the moribund Conference on Disarmament. The result is that no consolidated treaty has emerged, and given the acceleration of space activity by the Americans, the multilateral system is about to be caught flat-footed.

At the Beijing disarmament conference there was a call for an Ottawa-style process. In this case such a partnership could and should include the private sector. The satellite business has revenue of over U.S.$80 billion and climbing. That constitutes a real stake in keeping an arms race out of space. There is also substantial opposition within the U.S. to a space weapons strategy, including influential members of Congress. Senator Tom Daschle, the minority leader in the senate, has called the notion of putting weapons in space "the single dumbest thing I've heard so far from this administration. It would be a disaster for us to put weapons in space of any kind under any circumstances. . . . It only invites other countries to do the same thing."

There are also questions being asked in the U.S. military. Various military thinkers such as Lt. Col. Bruce DeBlois and Maj.

David Ziegler of the United States Air Force have advanced the idea of space as a sanctuary where there would be a combination of diplomatic efforts to build collective security through shared reconnaissance and surveillance. They both argue that there is no threat to U.S. space dominance as put forward by the Rumsfeld Commission and there are less provocative means than pre-emptive weaponization to deal with the concerns that do exist.

Canada is well placed to champion a coalition movement for a legal regime for space. This is an area in which we have invested time and effort. Unfortunately in trying rationalize Canadian participation in a missile defence program, government ministers have downplayed the risk of space weaponry.

A number of worthy groups and people are promoting a space treaty, they as yet don't match the range of experts, advocates and nations that were behind the land-mine campaign. There is not, for example, a definitive analysis of the effects that a weaponized space would create similar to the exhaustive study carried out by the International Red Cross on the humanitarian toll of land mines. Similarly, the link between outer space and sustainable development could be—but has not yet become—a catalyst for motivating developing nations.

At the same time, the outer space issue has some different ingredients. The degree of skepticism in the U.S. Congress, the potential involvement of the private sector and the work going on in the American scientific community are all elements that need cultivating and that might perhaps pressure the Bush administration to the table. At least there are the makings of a good debate in the U.S. on the issue. Also, key powers such as China and Russia have, for reasons of self-preservation, become proponents of a space treaty. So far, they have insisted on the UN Conference on Disarmament as the vehicle for negotiation. That shouldn't be disabused, but we should also be cultivating their participation in a process outside the conference.

At home we need to address the scarcity of intellectual resources. There simply aren't many Canadian scholars or researchers active in the disarmament field. There is little in the way of research support or opportunity to enlist good graduates. A particular lack is in encouraging good young scientists capable of bringing their knowledge of contemporary technologies to bear on arms-control issues—especially important when we are dealing with new weaponry such as space-based lasers and new information systems. If we are to be a player in arms-control discussions, we must invest in the capacity to marry scientists to good policy work. In the founding days of the nuclear age Canada was listened to when it offered an opinion because our scientists had won respect, knew what they were talking about and could put it into practice. That scientific credibility remains equally important today. Recruiting a cadre of scientists into DFAIT to generate imaginative proposals to counter the space warriors and other opponents of arms control could be a salutary move.

There is a marked difference between active and passive policy-making. It is certainly proper and responsible to go to the right international meetings, make the right noises, offer helpful suggestions and be seen as one of the good guys. But another choice that Canadians should be given is to take on leadership, become the active agent for change, forge alliances and dedicate time, effort and resources to generating support. It is not always easy, and will certainly bring howls of protest from other quarters. But with the future of international disarmament agreements at stake, the issue of weapons in space may just be the Rubicon.

OUR CHOICE

Pressure is building for us to align ourselves with the U.S. military as part of a continental defence strategy. A concentrated campaign is under way by senior elements in the business community on the argument that we need to integrate our security system with the Americans' in order to protect our access to markets and protect against border controls. The pro-military advocates in our universities and think-tanks are demanding that we sign on to further defence and security arrangements with the Americans. Entry discussions on the missile defence program are a sign that these pressures are succeeding. What none of these proponents ever mention, probably because it is not too important to them, is that further military integration would result in the disappearance of a distinctive Canadian voice in the disarmament debate. We would lose our ability to offer good advice and help influence American thinking. Being an appendage just doesn't carry much weight with Washington.

Nor does being a cog in a vast military machine necessarily help our own security. The U.S. military network is immense, far-reaching and extraordinarily powerful. It should be, considering the money that is spent—well over U.S.$379 billion in fiscal year 2003, which is 40 to 45 per cent of all defence spending in the world. Such power was graphically on display during the invasion of Iraq, where the twenty-first-century virtuosity of U.S. military power, information and mobility rolled over the Iraqi armed forces with their 1970s weaponry. It wasn't even a "cakewalk."

This massive concentration of armed might shapes the outlook of U.S. policy. President Dwight Eisenhower originally raised concerns about the corrupting effect of a military-industrial complex that by permeating the political system can set priorities and create demand for ever-increasing defence expenditures. While the budget for the U.S. military goes unchallenged by Congress, social, health and education spending take the cuts. This network has global sway. The leverage of military presence, assistance, training and supply of weapons becomes an important tool in establishing American influence worldwide, affecting the outlook and priorities of other countries.

Dana Priest, the defence reporter for the *Washington Post*, describes in her book *The Mission* a worldwide system of regional commands called CinCs (Commanders in Chief) that have resources at their disposal far outweighing those of their diplomatic counterparts. As a result they have increasingly usurped the role of delivering U.S. foreign policy. As she writes: "In a decade when Congress significantly slashed money for diplomacy, the CinCs' headquarters had grown to more than twice their Cold War sizes. With a combined budget of $380 million a year, their resources were lavish compared to civilian agencies that by law and tradition were supposed to manage U.S. foreign relations."[11]

This is not a benign influence since it sets its own self-fulfilling prophecy—if you have the tools you want to use them. The neo-conservative thinkers who have had such an influence on present-day U.S. strategic thinking have the simple axiom that military dominance assures U.S. security, but it must be applied to send the proper signal to all who might dare challenge that supremacy. Thus military enterprise is the arbiter of affairs and should not be restrained by treaties of control or, heaven forbid, actual disarmament. The prevalent fashion in Washington is to shower disdain on the "wimps" of Europe, and I daresay Canada, because their (our) choice is to restrict military budgets and prompt restraint on military action.

The consequence is serial war and all the instability and global insecurity that goes with it. Those who are in shock and awe at U.S. military might should remember that others can react to this military axiom by following suit and building their own machines as a way of protection—North Korea is just one copycat in its own small but deadly way.

The late W. G. Sebald in his book *On the Natural History of Destruction* describing the firebombing of German cities during World War II captures the essence of what a massive military machine means: "so much intelligence, capital and labour went into the planning of destruction that, under pressure of all the accumulated potential, it had to happen in the end."[12]

At various times in our history we have attempted to counter that inevitable rush to destruction, perceiving our best interest to lie within a system where the tools of war are kept in the chest, to be used only when one is threatened or in recent years to aid those who need protection. This requires military expenditures, but ones designed so as to keep the peace, not to promote war.

It is important to get these considerations out into the open. If we don't have a democratic debate about this, then the insiders will win the day, using their access and money to influence a Canadian decision towards military integration with the U.S. If we don't exercise our distinctive voice, one morning we will wake up to find that our freedom of choice has been given away and we simply aren't credible in the eyes of the rest of the world as a disarmament-friendly people.

PART VIII

The Two Emmas

CHAPTER 16

PUTTING OUR SHIP IN ORDER

I BEGAN THIS BOOK WITH THE STORY OF EMMA: HER KIDNAP BY A rebel group in northern Uganda, her life as a child soldier, her stubborn belief that speaking to international diplomats might better the condition of other war-affected children, and the efforts of various NGOs to alleviate her suffering and help her on the road to a better life. Her story epitomizes all that is wrong with today's world and also what is right. Woven into her story are both the woe of countless innocent victims around the globe and the emergence of universal standards of justice—international treaties and institutions to protect the Emmas of the world and give them a chance to be heard.

When I returned to Uganda in the fall of 2002, the northern region was once again engulfed in war. The LRA had been named a terrorist organization, and the government of Sudan, seeing an opportunity to redeem its tattered reputation, let the Ugandan army chase the rebel group into its territory. Operation Iron Fist involved a massive search-and-destroy mission and the compulsory movement of all civilians in rural areas back into the camps as a way of denying the rebels any form of local support or camouflage. The Museveni government saw a chance to finally rid themselves of Joseph Kony and his followers. The LRA retaliated by attacking convoys of food relief, killing anyone they thought was a government sympathizer and threatening the humanitarian organizations working in the area. Serious starvation and deprivation were once again the plight of the Acholi. And once again the international community paid little attention. The world was preoccupied with the pending American attack against Iraq.

It is not all bad news for Emma. She and her fellow Africans are beginning to ride on a wave of growing awareness that poverty, the AIDS crisis, the environmental despoliation and the resource wars of the African continent affect the entire global community. There are signs of a growing will to take on the challenge. NEPAD has support, and there seems to be a genuine effort by many African leaders to begin cooperating on a variety of economic, environmental and security concerns. An editor of a major newspaper in Kampala told me that he expects to see Africa become a dynamic area of development over the next thirty years. If he is even close to being right, Emma may yet have a promising life.

Emma is very much a child of the last half of the twentieth century. She has inherited the whirlwind of decisions made, opportunities ignored, policies adopted, obligations unmet, noble efforts, failed attempts and acts of generosity and perfidy of the past fifty years.

I want to now tell the story of another Emma, indeed one whose story is just beginning. She is my granddaughter, born into the safety and security of a Toronto neighbourhood just as this book was begun, in the summer of 2001. She is a charter member of the millennium generation. Yet within days of her birth the universe shifted moorings.

Terrorism came to North America with a terrible crash just a few hundred miles from Emma's home. As the World Trade Center crumbled, there was a similar shock to the very meaning of security. Global politics received a jolt and the world's agenda was suddenly dominated by the crusade of anti-terrorism. A Manichean struggle pitting the mighty hegemonic power of the United States against the covert, hidden, deadly network of al-Qaeda has created a seismic shift in the nature of world order. Caught in the undertow, Canada faces renewed pressures from both within and without to sign on to an anti-terrorist doctrine that will fundamentally re-orient our own foreign policy. As Emma grows up, it's conceivable she may never know that at one time we had an independent for-eign policy and played a defining role in the world.

The political space we occupy that gives us some freedom to choose our own course is being squeezed. How to protect that space against further erosion is very much in the hands of this gen-eration of Canadians. In fact, we should be striving to expand our political space and extend our capacity and range; we should be seeking to enhance our role as a global player "with attitude."

This is a story that is not yet written. For the children born in this new century it is a work in progress, a chance for today's polit-ical playwrights to create a new plot and prescribe directions for which they might be thankful, or at least not hold us to blame. Emma from Uganda must live with what the past fifty years has handed her. For Emma in Toronto it is the present that is the cra-dle of her future. Where she will be in fifty years, the kind of world she will occupy, her identity as a Canadian is what's at stake.

This is hard to grasp as we dance to the daily drumbeat. The rush and volume of events are overwhelming, their meaning and significance often drowned in a flood of information and opinion. But we should not be driven by the headlines or the talking heads on CNN. There needs to be a longer view.

NAVIGATING THE FUTURE

I have been struck by how much in this book that seems contem-porary actually had its origins five or six decades ago—the UN sys-tem of international cooperation and the enunciation of universal standards of human rights; the rise of the U.S. as the pre-eminent big power; the Cold War and its legacy of conflict; the period of decolonization; the advent of nuclear weapons and the decision by Canada to eschew their use; the Holocaust and the subsequent war crimes trials, ushering in a new concept of international law; the early debates over economic nationalism. So too the generation born today will be wrestling with the consequences of *our* deci-sions, or lack thereof, fifty years hence.

Richard Falk, who taught me international law at Princeton, has written about how the rapidly accelerating rate of change in our world has heightened our sense of time as it relates to perceived justice and injustice. He says: "Notions of both future and past become more active in our political consciousnesses."[1] Thus, it is increasingly imperative to deal with historic crimes and grievances if there is to be any prospect of reconciliation. Equally, he cites the increasing application of the precautionary principle and the need for an ethos of responsibility in international environmental law to ensure there is stewardship of our scarce resources for the next generation.

This is a message of generational responsibility. The broad notion of human security must be seen through the dimension of time. Any draft prospectus for the next fifty years must accept the responsibility to protect individuals from threat not just here and now but for the future.

So for Emma's sake, and all those like her, I wish to pose questions and raise possibilities, even offer some prescriptions for what should be done to help create a livable future fifty years from now.

This is an exercise in exploration: seeking a far-distant destination, then carefully steering a course guided by the best navigational tools of detection, assessment and forecasting. We should undertake it in a spirit of some adventure, prepared to challenge the unknown, drawing on the will and commitment of those ready to leave the safety of well-known coastal waters and seek out a new horizon. The Oxford historian Felipe Fernández-Armesto, in his massive historical study of the past millennium, makes this observation: "If there was some special spirit abroad in the late fourteenth- and fifteenth-century Latin Christendom . . . it should not be sought in the words of scholars or artists, but in the mentalities of navigators, explorers and settlers. These were the modest heroes who conquered the only new frontier to be added in this otherwise inert or contracting cultural area: a zone of navigation and new exploration."[2]

Exploration is not for the entrenched, the comfortable, the defenders of the status quo, but for sailors, farmers and adventurers who take to the high seas in search of new lands or riches, or maybe a plot of land to call their own. Fernández-Armesto draws a contrast between the outward-looking aggressive approach of the Portuguese,

Castilians and Genoese, who enjoyed the patronage of their rulers and the financing of their bankers, and what happened in China. In the early part of the fifteenth century the Chinese mounted major expeditions that reached the shores of India and Africa. Their ship-building technology and navigational aids were as good as if not bet-ter than the Europeans'. Then came a change of dynasty. The Confucian scholarly class, with their disdain for trade, gained promi-nence and all exploration was shut down. China retreated within its borders. Governments and their "mentalities" do make a difference.

What was true in the fifteenth century holds equally true today. Culture, technology, attitude and governance endow certain groups or communities with the talent to be navigators in the age of glob-alization, just as they did in the age of wind and sail. My argument, often stated in this book, is that Canadians possess qualities suit-ed to this role. We have the right stuff to be explorers, agents of change. Not because of any military muscle or economic might, though appropriate strength in these areas is desirable, but because of the distinctive characteristics of our political, social and eco-nomic system. The parliamentary-federal system of democracy, the Charter of Rights, a pluralistic, bilingual, multicultural society, the appreciation of public goods, a highly professional civil service, progressive education, a skilled high-technology industry, a free media, an active civil non-profit sector—all these give us a base for action. The sense of confidence about our international abilities, the dedication of a coterie of international NGOs and the bur-geoning confidence of our young people add verve to the mix.

These are not immutable attributes. Change is the constant fea-ture of contemporary life. Already the counterterrorism crusade is altering the dynamics of international relations with considerable effect on Canada. Emma could be just on the edge of losing her distinct Canadian patrimony. Equally, though, this uncertain land-scape may open up all kinds of opportunities for Canadians to explore new vistas.

What will tip the balance is how we shape our own society to maximize our strengths and hone our talents. To be good naviga-tors we need our own ship in order, and our voyage begins from home. We need to make the right choices to maintain our distinctive definition of human rights, manage major demographic shifts, strengthen our democracy, enhance our social capital and broaden our capacity to innovate and be a fount of good ideas. This is our starting point if we wish to exercise leadership, set examples and add value to the global community.

New Continental Divides

Canada is undergoing sweeping changes in its social and economic makeup. Professor Larry Bourne of the University of Toronto sent me his paper on Canadian demographic trends based on the 2001 census. It is a fascinating snapshot of a country in the throes of a sea change and a stunning population transformation. Three trends stand out, leading to what Bourne calls the "new divides." One is the concentration of population and economic growth in a few major urban areas, leaving vast parts of Canada in a state of decline. The second is the shift of trade patterns away from east–west towards north–south, leading to further fragmentation between regions and weaker social and political ties. And third is the increasing importance of immigration as the primary source of growth of population, but concentrated in only a few key cities, resulting in even greater diversity and dynamism in some areas while others become more homogenous and stagnant.[3] These divides will have a major influence on the social contract of Canada—the glue that sticks us together—on our outdated structures for federal-provincial relations, and on the degree of political cohesion as we become ever more part of a continental marketplace.

Recognition of these shifts is beginning to occur. Cities are making a comeback and receiving attention on the national agenda. Money for infrastructure is being promised, and urban issues are the subject of intense debate. But the responses are primarily program focused, and do not address the longer-term need to change our governance to encompass the demographic, social and economic punch of our cities.

Our place in the world will be very much determined by what happens in our major urban centres. As Allen Scott, a geographer at UCLA, says, they are the spark plugs of global development and the "platforms from which concentrated groups or networks of firms contest global markets." At the base of the evolving global economic system, he says, "lies a mosaic or archipelago of large city-regions."[4] It is in this emerging network that we must excel through innovation, design, information, finance and governance—the ability of people to work together to define and implement solutions to common problems.

Can the emerging urban reality of Canada help define our course over the next fifty years? The redistribution of people and activity into a few urban concentrations calls for serious structural change, maybe even a form of constitution renewal. The system of government inherited from the nineteenth century can't cope with these changes. Cities must be given a more specific definition than merely being creatures of the provinces. Since the Meech Lake and Charlottetown failures at constitution making, Canadian politicians have had an aversion to such public negotiations. The still delicate problem of Quebec adds to the neuralgia. In the past the adaptation of our federal system has been a crucial instrument to help us govern the diversity of Canada. We have been creative in dealing with the need to recognize aboriginal claims to self-government, as with the establishment of Nunavut. Our federal framework now needs to accept the comparable self-governing requirements of our cities.

Impressive innovation is taking place in Canada on urban issues. Cities are being touted as the appropriate platform to begin addressing global sustainability issues as well as engines for growth. This is the "smart cities" agenda. It is in the cities that tough issues of equity, social tension and democratic rights are being fought out, both in Canada and around the world. It is in the cities, with their complicated systems of services and transportation, where we must work out how to guard against terrorist attacks, providing security without becoming a garrison state. The urban landscape is where future pathways will be decided.

The increasing diversity of our urban cultural mix can be a big plus for Canada. It adds a dynamic quality to those centres that are the gateways for new arrivals. It not only gives greater texture to our cultural mosaic but further strengthens the pattern of group rights that is so much a Canadian trademark. It increases our contact with and understanding of so many other places on the globe.

If we get the right fit for addressing urban issues, and manage well the relations between diverse groups in tight urban settings, then we only enhance our position as a navigator and bolster our ability to provide a model for other parts of the globe. We help to develop the notion of global citizenship, in which people can have several layers of attachment and identity that traverse from the local to the global, and thus build a global democracy that is not tied down to one's membership in a nation-state.

Enlarging the role of our cities, showcasing them as areas of international excellence, developing their capacity to operate in a global economy and highlighting their initiatives to sustain growth, encourage participation and be places of social peace is one sure way to differentiate us from our American neighbour, where cities are suffering from an impoverishment of financial resources and neglect of growing social divisions.

What about the rest of Canada? One of the abiding Canadian traits expressed through various public policies going back to the Trudeau years has been a sensitivity to maintaining some degree of regional equity. Bourne's analysis points to a real risk of a hollowing out of large parts of Canada where there are not the mega-city conurbations such as exist in Toronto, Montreal and Vancouver. As a vast country, nourished by the distinctiveness of our various regions, we cannot afford to let large parts of our community fall behind. There must be renewed effort to invigorate these regions and ensure they are participants in the larger globalizing trends.

In recent years we have allowed this dimension of public policy to be eclipsed by bean-counter economics that have undernourished our regional development agencies, not providing the money to invest in infrastructure and services, and by decisions in education financing, research, transportation and communication that have discriminated against the regions. The reorganization of the airline system after the fall of Canadian Airlines has left smaller centres underserviced. Funding for higher education tied to research chairs and innovation has severely penalized smaller universities and the provincially supported systems in the Prairies and the

Atlantic. The decision not to proceed with broadband, high-speed Internet access to rural northern areas was an unnecessary denial, especially when there were ways of paying for it without draining the public purse. The failure to invest in northern scientific research has left us behind in responding to environmental change.

It's time for redemption. Somewhat paradoxically, many of the trends relating to the challenge of becoming good global citizens open opportunities to redress these domestic omissions. Post-Kyoto plans for emission reductions will put a premium on finding replacements for fossil fuels and testing out new ways of saving energy. Instituting new technologies and developing renewable fuels are activities that can be shared across the country and are particularly adaptable to smaller urban centres and regional hinterlands. One good example is the possibility of biotechnology that creates energy from trees and plants. The move towards a North American community, as described in chapter 5, opens up the possibility for north–south transportation corridors that will connect and bring commerce to all regions of Canada. The changes going on in the North will compel development of transportation, environmental monitoring facilities and support for coastline surveillance. Burgeoning information systems can link everywhere to everywhere; all Canadians should be plugged into the international network. Even in the field of security there are opportunities. Decentralizing strategic military and intelligence services and activities begins to make real sense, as does lessening our reliance on highly centralized energy and water distribution systems. Spreading out the scientific work to deal with the new military challenges offers special opportunities. For example, what about the possibility of investigating antidotes to biological weapons through the Laboratory Centre for Disease Control, in Winnipeg.

Immigration is the crucial, central nub of our meeting the issue of the "new divides." It is a prime determinant of creating a vibrant Canadian community. Since September 11, we've been tinkering, trying to adapt to the paranoia south of us, getting tied in knots over identity cards and refugee security checks. What we must now accept as fundamental to our future is that we need an expanding, open immigration policy to survive and prosper. What is not so obvious is where the new Canadians will come from. Do we continue down the path of trying to skim off the best and the brightest from the developing world, or can we foresee how to relieve some pressures on those areas of the world with large numbers of displaced and uprooted people, whether for reasons of conflict or environment, as we did in the massive movement from Indochina in the early eighties? That's one question.

Another question is where prospective Canadians should settle. Right now the choice is, for the most part, in three major urban areas of Canada, for reasons of cultural affinity and opportunity. This will no doubt continue to be the case, but shouldn't be the exclusive option. Other regions of Canada desire population growth, and it's time to look at incentives. One of the defining moments of Canadian history was the Sifton–Laurier plan to open the West through immigration. Then, the incentives were a plot of land and a free ship and rail ticket. We need a contemporary equivalent.

In my view the answer to these questions is education. The opportunity to come to Canada should include a voucher for higher education, training, certification upgrading, apprenticeship or on-the-job skill development anywhere in the country. An education program should be worked out in conjunction with local and provincial authorities, educational bodies and the business sector, using established Human Resource Councils. It is a way of spreading out the choices for immigrant location through an incentive system.

The weakest part of our immigration policy has been reception and preparation once immigrants have arrived. Cultural communities have been wonderful in assisting new arrivals; families are supportive; there is access to basic services; and there is aid for English- and French-language training. But there is not much more. There is not really a comprehensive approach consistent with our strong definition as a multicultural society. Funding has been drastically cut for multicultural programs and should be restored. This could enable cultural communities to establish long-term settlement programs that set a model for the rest of the world. All these ideas on immigration could be addressed by an action-oriented commission in the mode of the Romanow initiative on health care. It should be open, participatory, and lead to fast government action.

In devoting energy and resources to immigrants, however, we must not forget that we still face the daunting task of closing a historical, still-gaping divide—giving indigenous people in our country the fair, just deal they require to have an equal place with the rest of the community. On the reserve, in the inner cities, in remote communities the struggle for dignity and recognition goes on. One of the great transformations of our time is the active participation of aboriginal people in the life of Canada. Progress has been made with countless projects and shelfloads of studies, but resources are in short supply. Other indigenous people in the world look to Canada for innovative solutions. At the same time, we are properly criticized in many forums, including the UN Human Rights Commission, for discriminatory treatment. It is a serious deficiency in the makeup of the Canadian community when a significant people are denied their full rights. This is the kind of condition that compromises our standing in the global community. Dr. Patricia Spittal, an associate of mine at the Liu Institute, makes the point that on Vancouver's east side, aboriginal women who become addicted to injection drugs suffer the same rate of HIV infection as women in the IDP camps in Northern Uganda.

Our passage into global citizenship should open new avenues for our indigenous people. They possess special talents and knowledge to bring to bear on the need to invigorate our cities and regions, the need to find answers to climate change, the need to establish an active presence in the North for environmental and security reasons. They have a special role to play in creating more extensive global networks of indigenous people to solve common problems of development and security.

Bridging all these "divides" brings opportunities; it also gives us a primer on global citizenship. We have been leaders in using our federal system to define sovereignty in other than traditional nation-state terms—authority can be shared by different levels of government, loyalties and attachments diffused to different commitments. Our Charter of Human Rights has challenged the primacy of the state and put individual and group rights at the forefront, leading to an adherence to and acceptance of international standards of law, a willingness to assume the obligations of international treaties that may override national sovereignty interests. This in turn gives Canadians a sense of belonging to a broader community. Our civil groups in particular see themselves as belonging to a worldwide network of activists and advocates. Now our ability to make a living and preserve our well-being will depend increasingly on our participation in global constellations or networks.

The concept of global citizenship stretches far beyond our own continent. If there is one truth that will dominate the lives of the millennium generation, it is that they will be affected by people, events and actions around the globe. Wherever one resides, a sense of calamity will prevail unless there is a radical change in the way we do business globally. The World Bank forecasts a world population of nine billion and a global GDP of U.S.$140 trillion by 2022—staggering numbers, and ones that will lead to environmental disaster and social breakdown unless policies are dramatically changed to manage this growth in a responsible, sustainable way. Not normally a purveyor of doom, the World Bank warns that unattended these pressures will lead to a dysfunctional global society with enormous demand on basic resources.

It points to existing subsidy policies in food production, discriminatory trade and patent practices, limited sharing of wealth by rich countries and the wave of migration that will sweep the world as a result of increased population growth in poor areas and the continuation of poverty. Similar forebodings of global breakdown are becoming commonplace from a wide variety of sources. The AIDS virus, for example, will not only continue its deadly devastation in sub-Saharan Africa and many other parts of the developing world but is now on a rampage in China, Russia and Central Asia. At the bottom of the rung are over a billion people entrapped in a web of failed states, either embroiled in conflict or recovering from its ravages, and who simply don't have the capacity to be part of the global economy; trade and investment are not their solutions. They can only be rescued by massive assistance from richer countries to build basic health, education and public works—public goods their present governments simply can't or won't provide. This gives further meaning to the "responsibility to protect"—the need for a form of economic governance and intervention.

It does not have to be a doomsday scenario. If we're aware of the shoals, we can alter our course. International collaboration is the route to sharing wealth and changing consumption by industry and consumers in the rich, developed world. That will be the acid test of global citizenship: are we ready to limit or change our present consumerism and levels of economic growth for the sake of cleaner air and water, security against violent climate change and a more equitable distribution of wealth? This is not just a matter for summit meetings and UN conferences. It is a matter of personal responsibility, of individuals making choices from a global perspective that affect their own behaviour and send the right messages politically. I was encouraged to see the response of Canadians during the debate on Kyoto ratification. Soon after Prime Minister Chrétien committed to ratifying the Kyoto Protocol, there was a highly organized effort to scuttle the deal. Certain provincial premiers and business-based lobby organizations immediately denounced the move, claiming that we couldn't afford such commitments, and spent large amounts on advertising their opposition. But public opinion polls showed consistently high levels of support. People understood that this was an issue that went beyond the parochial provincial appeals. We were showing signs of our emerging global citizenship.

In this respect our experience is not unlike that of the Europeans as they wrestle with the multiple tasks of citizenship in the EU. We are both involved in an important transition from conventional notions of national allegiance towards a form of identity with universal standards and institutions. The proposed new European Union constitution will create even stronger transnational bonds and a greater sense of European unity. The European Human Rights Commission is establishing protection for individuals and groups at the local level, just as our own Charter has done.

What is of extreme importance in both Europe and Canada is to ensure that these expanding realms of activity retain a democratic character. In Europe, people grouse about the faceless bureaucrats in Brussels. In Canada, young protestors decry behind-closed-doors decisions under NAFTA. The task we face is not only in changing the nature of citizenship; we must also ensure that as the role of global citizenship grows, it is a democratic one.

DEMOCRATIC REFORM

The nation-state is still important in guiding that democratic trans-formation; how we decide to respond within our own system will be critical to how we respond globally. For that reason it is a prior-ity that we seriously reform the way our national decisions are made. Critics focus on the power of the prime minister. I want to make the case that having a strong executive branch embedded in a parliamentary process, open to a daily test of accountability, is in fact a plus in getting decisions made. In no other system is the gov-ernment leader subject to the same kind of public scrutiny. Can you imagine an American president having to face question period every day? But executive power must be counterbalanced, properly channelled, made relevant to people's needs. Other parts of the system are dysfunctional and what results is a wide gulf between people's interests and the way decisions are made.

First, let me deal with what is called the democratic deficit, the sense of frustration that representation of views and public partic-ipation are limited.

One major problem is our electoral system—the first-past-the-post, single-constituency arrangement. I always enjoyed the privi-lege of being a constituency-based representative. Over time one can build an intimate knowledge of people and their concerns. But I also recognize that this system can lead to gross misrepresenta-tion—a small plurality of votes results in a huge majority of seats—witness the Tory landslide of 1984 or the devastation of the same party in the 1993 election. These huge swings are particularly prevalent at the provincial level.

The other inequity of the system is the under-representation of urban areas, where the disproportion can go as high as three votes in suburban Vancouver equalling one vote in the Interior. The most dynamic regions don't have the voice and clout they deserve, espe-cially in setting an agenda geared to global realities. At the same time, outlying regions must have a clear stake in the parliaments, and not be ignored.

A hybrid electoral system that combines the constituency-based model with modified proportional representation reflecting the popular vote would be one means of further democratizing, and thereby energizing, our politics.

It would also be a way of improving access and opportunity for more women to get elected and exercise their rightful role in the governing of the country. Although many women have held and continue to hold important public positions in Canada, the sad reality is that women are grossly under-represented in our legislatures and cabinets. Women account for around 25 per cent of the Canadian Parliament—that's hardly going to give my granddaughter confidence that she lives in a fully functioning democracy.

I also believe that this inequity affects what we do—or more accurately, what we don't do—globally. It was my experience in Foreign Affairs that women tended to be more supportive of human security than men were, especially when it came to issues such as protecting civilians and peace-building. My sense of this is supported by opinion polls that show a gender gap on such matters as arms control, land mines, Third World development, human rights and the peaceful resolution of conflict. This is not to say that there aren't female hawks—Margaret Thatcher and Condoleezza Rice come quickly to mind; the range of women's views is wide and varied—but overall there seems to be a qualitative difference in the perspective of women on many public policies, and particularly on protecting people.

Because our present electoral-political system prevents this perspective from having full representation, it distorts our decision making. Of course structural reform is not the only barrier. There is a much more complex trap of attitudes on family, money and job requirements and of outright discrimination that works against the political equality of Canadian women. A revised election system, however, would start to ensure that Emma and her sisters eventually have a greater say in what Canada does in the world.

Another way to improve our democracy is to reform the senate. It is anachronistic to have an appointed body making decisions in this day and age. Granted, many highly competent people serve in the senate. But the same people would have even greater influence if they were elected and accountable. Coming from the West, the favourite scheme for me has always been an elected senate based on an equal number of seats per province, where the issues between the different regions could be hammered out, perhaps with an urban criterion to accompany the regional dimension.

An elected senate could assume a special role in debating and reviewing Canada's global commitments and responsibilities. Developing a more democratic global system requires a much higher degree of involvement by parliamentarians. This is a potential that has only barely begun to be tapped. The time and resources of individual members of the Commons are severely restricted by dint of their various constituency, caucus and assembly duties. Yet we need a degree of specialization, where global and international matters would receive more than a passing glance. If the senate were elected, it could bring real credibility to that task.

To think out of the box for a moment, what if Canadians chose through senate election the representatives we send to global organizations? Parliament has timidly started along this path, making certain ambassadorial appointments subject to review by parliamentary committee. But perhaps we should think of more direct election of key posts such as ambassador to the UN, directors on the World Bank and IMF, and our environment ambassador. Candidates could be part of a slate for senate election, allowing each party leader to choose distinguished Canadians as their nominees. They would have to explain and defend their views during election. Once elected, they would have to explain their actions periodically to the other elected members of the senate. Our representation in international organizations would then have a direct connection to our own electoral system, with clear lines of accountability. Think what it might do to engender a serious look at international issues if each party had to nominate people with clear views on a global role for Canada, discussed in a fully transparent electoral campaign, and have those choices ratified by Parliament.

Pending such fundamental changes to the senate, the prime minister should use the power of appointment to install in the upper chamber senior Canadian representatives from international bodies in order to provide some degree of parliamentary link to these organizations. The ambassador to the WTO, the Canadian director on the World Bank and the UN permanent representative should report to Parliament on a regular basis. Its role in holding special debates and as a source of special envoys should be strengthened. Budget allocations must be increased for parliamentary visits, exchanges, membership in international associations, research and public consultation. Parliament is a crucial cog connecting people to the increasingly complex world of decision making on global matters. Until it is made substantially more democratic, its potential to link Canadians to global decisions will be limited.

A third area of democratic reform is to further restrict the distorting influence of money in our national political system, both in the electoral process and in the parties' selection of candidates and leaders. While we are not nearly at the stage of plutocracy experienced in the U.S.—where the political system is dominated by the finances of special-interest groups or by wealthy people with no experience in the political arena but who simply purchase nominations and elections as if they were some luxury bauble—big-money resources nonetheless sway crucial decisions affecting Canada's international role. This power was used with telling effect during the free trade election of 1988. Today money is being channelled through a number of business-oriented think-tanks to promote Canadian support of the right-wing policies of the Bush administration, including opposition to Kyoto, increased defence spending and further military integration. Big money also provides substantial support in leadership contests to maintain a conservative economic agenda opposed to spending on social public goods or investing in added resources for international development and diplomacy. There simply isn't equivalent financial heft behind differing points of view.

Fortunately, reform is on the way. Among the many initiatives Prime Minister Chrétien initiated in his final year, legislation limiting political donations to individuals, and excluding corporations and unions, may have the most profound and long-lasting value. These steps are a good beginning in limiting the power of organizations with big financial resources.

Another way to curb misuse of power and concentrated wealth is to increase the influence and involvement of the public through a broad sharing of information. The water scandal in Walkerton, the revelations on corporate malfeasance washing over North America, the admission of neglect by intelligence agencies in the wake of September 11 are stark reminders of how disclosure and transparency are powerful and necessary tools in a modern democracy. The Internet manages to shatter the control of the expert or the insider. The ability of ordinary people to influence decisions through the glare of information is a substantial, perhaps quantum change in the nature of democratic practice. The potential to short-circuit the gatekeeping of the mass media is at hand.

The populist campaigns for the land-mine treaty and the International Criminal Court were made possible to a significant degree by the power of information technology. The naming and shaming that took place over Angola helped bring about major reform in the international use of blood diamonds. Our establishment of a diplomatic posting in Khartoum opened a window onto the oil revenues received by the Sudanese government in part through the activity of a Canadian corporation, Talisman. Such instances just scratch the surface of the power of disclosure and the use of information technology to mobilize public pressure for reform and accountability. In the future, global networks that keep tabs on governments engaged in human rights abuses, act as verification systems for disarmament purposes and report on environmental and pollution transgressions will substantially broaden the scope of accountability.

GLOBAL LEARNING

The future use of information technology should be one of the most serious of Canadian undertakings. Perhaps its most potent use is in developing a global civic culture that binds people into a global community. The very nature of education is changing fundamentally as we employ multimedia as an interactive learning tool, engaging students in the creation of their own information.

My greatest wish for Emma and her friends would be to see them receive the proper grounding to exercise their full democratic rights

as Canadians and as global citizens. Without a substantial investment in their global education, even the structural reform of our
political institutions will not produce the level of involvement that
is needed. Emma and her cohorts start with a huge advantage.
They are members of the Internet generation, for whom the idea of
borders and boundaries has little meaning. Their cyber universe
encompasses the world; they communicate in an instant with
counterparts to play games, extract information, chat about music
and, alas, peek at pornographic portals. I've seen some remarkable
examples of how information technology opens up incalculable
educational opportunities: grade-seven children in Winnipeg connecting with fellow students in Mexico to plan a campaign to save
the monarch butterfly; young people at a war children's conference
in Accra explaining their circumstances to a group of high-school
students in Canada; the Youth Links project that hooks up young
people in Great Britain and Canada in mutual education about
each other's countries; the virtual University of the Arctic that will
link students in eighteen educational institutions in eight circumpolar countries to share a course on Arctic studies; the on-line literacy programs of the Commonwealth of Learning. All these and
many more equally compelling demonstrations show the potential
to break down barriers, overcome differences and provide a shared
multicultural perspective on global issues. Yet, despite all the
pilot projects and individual initiatives, the effort to construct a
comprehensive network for global-based education is spotty and
underfunded.

The Internet generation has access to sophisticated, technically
awesome computer games, costing hundreds of millions to develop
and promote, that are available from Mongolia to Sweden to
Vancouver Island; Hollywood films extolling action, adventure, war
and violence; reality television, sports extravaganzas and talk-show
diatribes churned out by a mass media controlled by gargantuan
conglomerates. By comparison, the investment put into using the
best graphics and interactive techniques as tools for education is paltry—an illustration of John Kenneth Galbraith's comments about
private affluence and public poverty. One of the more useful and
innovative initiatives of the federal government in the nineties was

to undertake the Internet connection of schools and libraries across Canada, ensuring a degree of equal access. However, limited funds were made available to develop accompanying software or programs to enable the system to be put to innovative public or educational use. Similarly, when I took a proposal to cabinet to extend our connectivity to other countries as part of an international information strategy, it didn't even come close to receiving funding. At the Summit of the Americas in Quebec City, Canada sponsored a program of connectivity in the Americas based on the work done in our human security drug strategy, but resources for program and educational content are still missing.

In a time when we decry the great divides between cultures of the East and West, hear the plaintive wail of commentators in the U.S. about why Americans are not liked, and watch the propagation of historic grievances, fanaticisms and hatreds, bypassing potential tools for an open educational exercise is irresponsible and foolhardy. We need to see that a globally based system of educational programming is a fundamental public good.

There are some issues to examine, and first among them is control. In a world of convergence and consolidation, many of the current mergers and acquisitions in the telecommunications industry are directed at managing the new broadband, high-speed Internet services with a view to limiting use and access. There are attempts to restrict the availability of information in the public domain. Network owners highlight their own and affiliated content, excluding more publicly minded, non-commercial fare, despite widespread public indifference to the multiple offerings on the new digital channels. Even when access for public material is offered, the cost is prohibitive for most non-profit organizations. The effort by former industry minister Brian Tobin to secure a billion-dollar budget to provide high-speed access to as many Canadians as possible was rejected. The cable companies and the telcos are reluctant players in defining a proper public use. Clearly there is a lot at stake, but there is virtually no public debate or input on who will control the information infrastructure of the future. Debate has focused on capacity and speed, not on equity of use and access.

As chair of the Manitoba Climate Change Task Force I saw the potential for a network on climate change tied into community resources such as libraries, schools and community centres. As we enter into post-Kyoto action there should be the means to enhance public understanding of individual responsibility to limit emissions, share innovative, individual and community initiatives, inform on new technologies, plan joint actions with others around the world. An alternative, Web-based forum of information is vital. But who will pay and who has the resources to organize? I don't think we can expect this from the brand-name corporate giants. It will have to be a public use.

This has special meaning when we look at bridging the digital divide, the gap that separates rich from poor, urban from rural and North from South. Here everyone, including the communication giants, expresses their concern. There are major exercises under way, but the missing link is the public use of the space. Lost among all the talk of e-commerce and e-government is the possibility of e-community—a Web-based, borderless, global public network of information connecting researchers around the world to look at common problems of disease, literacy and security, and providing training and education in conflict or crisis management or environmental security.

Here is an exciting role for Canada to play with our information know-how and the skill of our software companies. We have a reservoir of goodwill, good people and good public institutions to span the cyber world and jump over traditional stages of development. By putting a public face on the Internet, we can fulfill McLuhan's prophecy and become the foremost inhabitants of the global village.

But if our aim is a global civic culture, we also have to get our own public space in order—set our own e-community, e-democracy agenda and show the world how it can be done.

Two things should happen. First, there must be a clear policy of access, an open architecture for the Internet. This will require a balanced approach to intellectual property law and new definitions of the public domain.

Second, there must be a way of financing pilot projects and the application and implementation of public uses of the Internet both within and outside Canada. One idea is a public trust fund, as advanced by the Digital Promise project in the U.S. Monies obtained from auctioning the broadband spectrum or granting wireless licences would be dedicated to a special foundation or trust that would, as the authors of the report say, "encourage partnerships and alliances among the nation's and the world's existing institutions and organizations in education, science, the humanities, the arts, civic affairs and government."[5]

Another idea being looked at by tax experts in Ottawa is a levy on e-commerce transactions, a form of cyber GST. Though our Department of Finance has neuralgia over the notion of attached taxation, an argument can be made that a portion of the proceeds from commercial uses of the Internet should be ploughed back into expanding its public uses. This could transform the architecture and function of the information world, and make it a revolution shared by all.

These proposals are prerequisites both for making Canada more democratic and for enabling Canadians to participate fully in shaping our international role. If citizens are not able to be involved in making decisions on complicated contemporary matters affecting humankind, we are in danger of forfeiting democracy. If we do not adapt democracy to a drastically different world, if Canada becomes less fully democratic than it could be, we diminish our chance of showing others the way.

THE GAME PLAN

Democratic governance has to be smart, efficient, coherent and adaptable. We need to overhaul how we manage our international tasks. The problem is a combination of fragmentation in policy-making; underfunded military, diplomatic and foreign aid programs; and the lack of a well-developed strategy for using information technology and educational outreach to expand the global involvement and influence of Canadians. The dialogue process initiated by Bill Graham is a good beginning. While not the full-blown review that was promised, it is an innovative way of using the Internet to reach out to Canadians and present them with options.

As yet, it hasn't commanded the kind of attention that it deserves. One reason is that it is too open-ended, not giving to the public the benefit of well-crafted decisions put forward by the government on key issues. (The dominance of the Iraq issue at the time of its release also put it on the back page.) I believe it can set the stage, however, for a serious debate in the government and in Parliament.

Here are some further prescriptions for reforming government management and resources for a global role.

A global strategy team. The federal government needs a team concept for managing its global policies and activities. A separate committee of cabinet should be formed with the prime minister as chair, the foreign minister as deputy chair, and an executive secretariat to carry out the work of the group. Other ministers should be defence, trade, CIDA, environment, finance, industry, solicitor-general and justice. The committee would plan common and compatible strategies, coordinate efforts, prepare a combined budget and avoid duplication and interdepartmental rivalry. It would see Canada's global obligations and opportunities in all their dimensions, not through the perspective of isolated departments. The strategy group should be assigned a global budget worked out among respective departments. Funding should no longer be the result of an ad hoc competition driven by individual departmental claims, the special pleading of special-interest groups or imperious demands by a resident ambassador from an adjacent country. To further facilitate this approach, the CIDA minister should join the trade and foreign affairs ministers as part of a triumvirate within DFAIT. Maintaining a separate operational role and identity for CIDA makes sense, but there needs to be much closer cooperation among senior officials and ministers in the execution of joint efforts to avoid the kind of fragmentation that occurred over the peace-building program. Synergy at the top would inevitably lead to better cooperation on the ground.

It may also be time to reorganize the machinery of our foreign policy to focus tasks and functions in a more contemporary way. Three areas to consider would be: (1) a separate operating agency to develop the global communication, public diplomacy and education strategy I've described in this book. It would have a clear mandate, a distinct budget, a specialized staff, and be able to work out a variety of contractual arrangements with private, non-profit educational groups both here and abroad; (2) an independent Global Human Security Policy Centre with the capacity to initiate research, analysis and brainstorming, and create and anchor global problem-solving networks; and (3) a Minister for Peace-Building within the foreign affairs portfolio, responsible for identifying and initiating preventative and post-conflict activities and for overseeing the recruitment and placement of Canadians for civil and security tasks in peace-building missions.

It isn't, however, only a matter of reorganization or strategy or innovation. The federal government has to spend more money on its global tool kit. An independent foreign policy does not come cheap.

Diplomatic presence and public diplomacy. One place to start re-investing is the refurbishing of our diplomatic and trade services. Canadian representation should expand in areas that are vital to us, such as the U.S. (a start was made in the February 2003 budget) and other posts in the Western Hemisphere. To maintain a global presence we must open posts in areas where our presence is virtually non-existent, such as Central Asia, and strengthen our representation in China, an emerging global power, and sub-Saharan Africa, where our human-security approach has many friends. This can be done efficiently. A central embassy can service a network of small satellite operations, and facilities can be shared with other compatible-minded countries. Money also needs to be spent on improving the pay, positions and promotion opportunities of our foreign service officers, including those in CIDA and the Immigration branch. Morale is not good. Too many good young officers leave too soon and the chances for postings are limited. All this reduces our ability to be an effective player.

The government could also make much better use of a broad range of Canadians who are not part of the professional foreign service. At DFAIT we tapped into the incredible enthusiasm of young people in an international intern program and created a roster of Canadians who volunteered for human rights duties and for election work overseas. These could be forerunners of cooperative partnership arrangements with universities and colleges, professional, trade and labour organizations and NGO groups to farm out advocacy, promotional, representational and information-gathering tasks. There is no better way to nurture a growing global consciousness.

One beginning is the human security fund. Unfortunately, this program, which builds up intellectual capital to fuel Canadian initiatives abroad, as well as other parts of the human security initiative seem to be a favourite target of the Department of Finance for cuts. What did I say about certain elements in Ottawa not understanding our responsibility as global citizens?

Comprehensive aid. Development assistance is another funding priority. Our contributions currently hover around 0.4 per cent of GNP, a far cry from the 0.7 per cent promised by Lester Pearson. However, Prime Minister Chrétien has committed to doubling foreign aid by 2010, and the recent focus on Africa and NEPAD is a good demonstration of targeting resources and encouraging regional responsibility. Reducing trade barriers adds further value.

What's missing from the Africa initiative is a complementary plan to increase our diplomatic presence, provide military assistance in the event of breakdowns in security, help police the rules against small-arms trading, provide skilled people in administration, and work with the African states to overcome AIDS and with Canadian business to establish codes of conduct for overseas investment. The decided bias against strengthening Canadian presence in parts of Africa where we are under-represented, building our capacity to participate in peacemaking missions or improving our educational and research base on African matters weakens our ability to be actively engaged. It means we have few answers on what to do about human rights abuses in Sudan, the democratic breakdown in Zimbabwe, the resource conflict in Congo, the behaviour of oil corporations in Angola. Building an African policy around the singular pillar of direct development assistance isn't enough.

International assistance is more than a transfer of funds. I think of Sierra Leone, where the need was for a transfer of skill, of knowledge, of military and police support. I think of Mongolia, where the problems are an inequitable international economic system, the lack of international cooperation on desertification and their need for more skilled advocates in international forums. I think of the shortage of diplomatic representation in many parts of the U.S., the short supply of peacekeepers in the Balkans, the lack of good intelligence in Zaire, the tramp steamer that brought our troops back from East Timor, the embarrassment of the federal government not being able to match the international cultural expenditure of the province of Quebec. These are areas where we need to bolster our commitments.

New thinking on development seeks a coherent, coordinated effort to meld the full range of diplomatic, trade, defence, legal and development tools available to a government. It doesn't approach international assistance in narrow terms of fighting poverty but tries to address conflict prevention, emergency assistance, environmental degradation and governance matters simultaneously, all of which requires a much higher level of partnership between governments and private players. Of special importance is a high level of collaboration with Canadians doing business abroad, going beyond the Team Canada objective of trade promotion. Private investment and trade can be engines of growth and help in tackling global poverty. Government engagement with the private sector can help private players reduce the risks from corruption, criminality and strife; ensure their involvement in a country meets acceptable environmental and social standards; and build public trust on the basis of the good reputation that Canada enjoys internationally and by setting the highest standards for corporate citizenship.

Peacemaking, security and defence. Since September 11, pressure groups, the arms industry, editorialists, the senior military brass and the U.S. ambassador, and policy makers in the new government have all been clamouring for increases in defence expenditure. And I agree it should be a priority—although I daresay for different reasons than the defence lobby would wish.

In government I always supported adding to the defence budget when it was designed to improve our capacity for peacemaking, coastal surveillance, disaster missions and special roles such as demining, military training for emerging democracies and service in international missions. What I objected to was the way in which hundreds of millions are spent in development and research on weapons systems that reflect U.S.-determined military objectives such as space-based technology. Many senior officers become far too absorbed into the American military orbit, mesmerized by the glories of interoperability. This is one of our weakest links in asserting a more independent foreign policy.

Where I would like to see increased expenditure is in the supply of equipment, personnel and logistics to support a human security policy. This means transport capable of carrying troops and supplies on rapid-reaction missions for conflict resolution or internationally approved humanitarian assignments; modern naval capacity for sea-based peacekeeping and coastal surveillance, especially in the Arctic; enhanced early warning intelligence gathering through satellite sensoring that we would share with UN peacekeeping operations; efficient health and disaster relief units; and building up a well-trained mobile reserve as a fully competent supplement to regular forces.

I'm mystified why our military planners have not pursued with vigour and imagination a modern, well-trained reserve available for global duties. The use of reservists as civil affairs officers in Bosnia, using a CIDA grant, is a good example of the essential supplemental tasks they can provide. But we haven't done nearly enough to protect reservists' domestic jobs while they are on duty, give them proper benefits, expand their training into specialized peace-building roles or give them an overriding sense of identity as "citizen soldiers" helping to keep the peace. Increasing defence expenditure to emphasize our global citizenship would be a much easier sell to the Canadian public than buying more toys for the boys.

It is crucial that we have the means to adapt to the changing nature of global conflict and security issues, act in concert with other nations in cooperative missions and untie some of the strings that bind us to U.S. military systems and strategy. To cite one example, when the Bush administration threatened to frustrate UN peacekeeping activities as part of their campaign against the International Criminal Court, we along with the Europeans should have said bluntly that they should take their ball and go home. We couldn't, however, because we didn't have the people, the equipment, the intelligence or the will. Our ability as a nation of peacekeepers is becoming frayed and tattered, resting on the memories of past achievements. Yet effective multilateral prevention and post-conflict security is crucial. An assessment of our peace-keeping needs prepared for the Canadian foreign policy dialogue concludes that: "The future of UN peacekeeping is being jeopardized by the official assumption, here and abroad, that the UN is not a priority Organization and that other organizations can better manage its tasks. This trend is short-sighted, risky and it does not reflect the preference of most Canadians. . . . There is a need for policy that demonstrates unequivocal support of the UN. There is also a need for tangible contributions to UN peace operations. Canada's policy and contributions should reflect its commitment to strengthening the only legitimate, universal Organization dedicated to maintaining peace and security, as well as promoting sustainable development, disarmament and human rights."[6]

As one facet of this, we should discuss with the EU joint plans for a rapid-reaction force as part of our transatlantic partnership, since further developing the range and scope of the SHIRBRIG— or high-readiness brigade—agreement is an opportunity to show leadership in this area.

Another place where we need to substantially upgrade our military capacity is in surveillance, monitoring and patrol of our northern regions. While American and Russian submarines play cat-and-mouse in the undersea security zone, we have stood by in silent acquiescence, with only a minimal presence through the Canadian Rangers program, a coastal surveillance unit of Inuit people. But with navigation routes opening up, increased exploration, resource development and the dangers of pollution, we need an appropriate military presence or we will be frustrated by unilateral actions and assertions, particularly from the Russians and the Americans.

Our military can also make a major contribution to a safer world by contributing to a new agenda of arms control and disarmament. Since the land-mines treaty they have had notable success in de-mining training, assisting in verification and developing alternatives to land mines. They could provide the same support in the pursuit of international collective action to deal with biological weapons and cyber warfare, both of which will become increasing threats.

Continuing research into methods of detection, verification and control, and arms removal are requisites for any future agreements. Once our military accept a policy decision, as with land mines, they have shown skill in working with scientists and industry to develop various forms of prevention. As I said earlier, Winnipeg's disease-control centre could be enlisted as part of a defence department effort to protect us against germ warfare. Similarly, our software industry could apply itself to preventing the disruption or destruction of information systems. We need to provide protection for Canadians against terror, but in a preventative way.

These are just some of the ways we can refine our tools of statecraft and prepare Canadians to fulfill the responsibility of global citizenship. We need a clear sense of what we do best and what we should avoid. We must marshal our resources in a comprehensive way, both to preserve our freedom to manoeuvre and to use that freedom to advance international goals and objectives that serve our interests and reflect our values.

How should we put that strategic fit to best use? By reforming ourselves and modernizing our own governance we prepare properly for what lies ahead.

CHAPTER 17

NAVIGATING A NEW WORLD

―――――

THROUGHOUT THE PREVIOUS CHAPTERS I HAVE SOUGHT TO MAP OUT a distinctive course for Canada. The three most important coordinates are: (1) to retain our right to make choices that reflect our own values and interests; (2) to navigate using human security as a lodestar, seeking an international rules-based system that respects and protects the rights of the individual in contrast to a world dominated by military force and naked self-interest; and (3) to build partnerships between governments, business and civil society to tackle the problems we face in common as global citizens.

FROM THE ISLE OF LIGHT

How to bring about this change? How to move from ideas, principles, blueprints and prescriptions to serious reform of the system? And what can we do as Canadians to help bring it about?

First, Canada must play a role as a convener, coordinator and funder of global political networks dedicated to making our security, economic and environmental system more representative, responsive and transparent. We have initiated several such networks—not only on land mines and the ICC but on the protection of children, a hemispheric drug partnership and the Arctic Council. The most ambitious of these undertakings was the Human Security Network, and it represents the kind of network approach where we can apply Canadian "value added."

It originated in 1998 in a curious house on an isolated island in a Norwegian fjord several miles north of Bergen. It was originally the home of Ole Bull and is now a guest facility of the Norwegian government. Bull, a famous and eccentric Norwegian musician, acquired an eclectic taste in architecture as he travelled the world. As a result his home, called Lysoen—or Isle of Light—has Turkish minarets sitting alongside a Russian Orthodox onion-bulb tower, sitting on what looks like the roof line of a Chinese pagoda. It was perhaps an appropriate setting for the birth of an international association that would cut across geographical, political and cultural divides.

To cap the end of a two-day bilateral meeting, Knut Vollebaek, the Norwegian foreign minister, had invited members of the Canadian and Norwegian delegations for dinner on the island. I had just left a G-8 foreign ministers session in London and was looking forward to a brace of cold sea air and Norwegian hospitality after days in over-warm meeting rooms. It turned out to be one of those rare evenings long remembered because of the good food, the good company, the good music and ultimately the good decisions taken. During the day we had been discussing the two countries' increasing collaboration on initiatives of a humanitarian nature. For example, after our partnership on the land-mines treaty, we had teamed up to support a project in Algeria that treated traumatized child victims of the war against terrorism. We had a mutual interest in stemming the proliferation of small arms and various other disarmament issues. We debated the need for a new approach to international relations, and concluded with an agreement to co-operate on a human security agenda. The Lysoen Declaration established a framework for consultation and concerted action to enhance human security, promote human rights, strengthen humanitarian law, prevent conflict, foster democracy and work on Arctic cooperation.

Officials of the two countries then began to translate the declaration's words into action. It was an energizing relationship, and it also got me thinking. If we received such an enthusiastic response from the Norwegians, might there be other countries that shared our interests? If there could be a G-8 centred originally on economic issues, why not form an H-8, a coalition to pursue the objectives of human security? That late spring and early summer I tested the idea out at various international meetings and met with a positive response. Knut Vollebaek and I decided to jointly host an exploratory session at the UN in September with foreign ministers from mostly smaller and middle-sized countries. There was strong endorsement there, too, especially from David Andrews of Ireland, Surin Pitsuwan of Thailand and Wolfgang Schüssel of Austria. The Norwegians offered to host the founding meeting in Bergen, and thus was born the Human Security Network. Knut and I also went public with the idea in an op-ed piece we wrote for the *International Herald Tribune* entitled "For a New Diplomacy to Fashion a Humane World."[1]

The first meeting of the Human Security Network took place in Bergen on May 20, 1999. In attendance were ministers from Austria, Canada, Chile, Ireland, Jordan, the Netherlands, Slovenia, Switzerland, Thailand and Norway. (South Africa opted for observer status, as it didn't feel it could be a full member while serving as chair of the Group of 77.) We agreed on priorities for cooperation and involved representatives from the Red Cross and Red Crescent societies, Save the Children, Amnesty International, the International Campaign to Ban Landmines, the Coalition to Stop the Use of Child Soldiers and the International Action Network on Small Arms, each of whom was asked to present a paper. In her keynote speech, Sadako Ogata, the UN high commissioner for refugees, excoriated the inadequacy of existing mechanisms to address conflict and presented a "ladder of options" to address conflict situations before crisis escalated.

Since that initial meeting, the network has followed through with annual sessions in Lucerne, Petra, Santiago and Graz, each meeting taking a different emphasis and involving a different mix of NGOs. At Lucerne special attention was paid to small arms. At Petra and Santiago the priority was children and the importance of development. At Graz the focus was on human rights. Membership has expanded to include Greece and Mali. The group meets regularly at the UN, and its members seek to introduce the human security agenda into their other organizational involvements. Indeed, a major part of the network's value is in disseminating the human security notion into the broader international agenda. The network helped me get the G-8 foreign ministers to adopt several of the human security initiatives.

It has developed a number of spin-off activities. Thailand hosted a meeting on human security and AIDS, one of the first efforts to introduce the human security concept in Southeast Asia. Chile, in cooperation with UNESCO, hosted a conference on peace, human security and conflict prevention in Latin America and the Caribbean. Andrew Mack of the Liu Institute for Global Issues at UBC is working on an international human security index that will measure the impact of conflict on individuals and communities. Japan has established a commission on human security. The Austrian foreign minister is talking about having the network address the situation in northern Uganda.

What started at the Isle of Light has only been given added urgency by the events of September 11. In a statement, the network said: "These terrorist attacks are a further, horrifying indication of the pervasiveness of threats to people's safety, rights and lives. . . . Innovative international approaches are needed to address growing sources of global insecurity, remedy its symptoms and prevent the recurrence of threats that affect the daily lives of millions of people."[2]

Unlike many of the outpourings of feelings and official statements that followed September 11, this was not a rousing call to arms rooted in retaliation or revenge. It did not assert the need to strengthen borders or amass overwhelming military power. Instead, it recognized the widespread nature of the problem and called for innovative international answers. Most important, it made the risk to individuals the central issue.

We are witnessing today the transformative clash between two global networks, one of terror, unbound by territory, linked by thin tendrils of finance and communication, single-mindedly dedicated to the destruction of its enemy, and the other centred in the world's most powerful state, but with spokes and connections encompassing a worldwide military system, supplemented by diplomatic, corporate, commercial and cultural nodes.[3] One is the way of the fanatic, striking out from the hidden corners of the global landscape, brooking no compromise, drawing strength from the dispossessed of the world. The other is the way of the warrior, using the immense reach of a military apparatus to seduce, shape and when necessary coerce compliance with its own set of goals, values and interests, increasingly disdainful of any international rules of restraint. In its own small, unobtrusive way the Human Security Network, and many groups like it, represents an alternative way, trying to build institutions and practices that promote a rules-based system of global cooperation and the protection of people. Kofi Annan's Global Compact on corporate responsibility and the Jubilee Movement, which has placed the whole issue of debt relief for poor countries onto the agenda of financial institutions, are other examples. This is the way of a navigator, seeking out a secure, safe course for the passengers on board, mindful of their welfare, skirting the shoals and reefs, working in a team with others making the same voyage.

These policy networks can add issues to the global agenda by way of transnational advocacy that breaks the monopoly of various elites and media gatekeepers. They can provide producer and consumer groups with direct links to finance and information and help close the participation gap by linking people of all kinds from all parts of the globe. They can set standards, apply tests of accountability, initiate actions and mobilize support.[4] As such networks start to overlap and intertwine, they can challenge the established one-directional and self-serving power relationships and empower individuals in a form of global democracy. In her address to the Ottawa land-mines conference, Jody Williams said of the network that brought the treaty to fruition, "We are the new superpower." Perhaps a little premature, but a portent of possibilities.

PLOTTING A NEW COURSE

What might those possibilities be over the next fifty years in which the two Emmas will be helping to remake the world?

First would be to continue building a rules-based, cooperative, democratic global system and not give in to those intent on wrecking such a system whether by terror, conflict, greed or imperialism. Submerged in the daily media reports of calamity and violence is the reality of a world that is striving to become more democratic, seeking to resolve conflicts through peaceful means, fostering cooperation on common problems and nurturing the establishment of norms that advance the rights of people. A 2003 survey documents a 50 per cent decrease in the number of armed conflicts since the mid-eighties; a dramatic increase in the number of democracies (nearly double the number compared with 1985) and a comparable decrease in the same time span of dictatorships or autocracies; and a long-term improvement in respect for human rights. The primary tools used to achieve these goals: patient applications of diplomatic conflict resolution, and political efforts at democratic development, institution building, and the negotiation and promotion of human rights.[5]

At the same time there has been a growing consensus on the need to confront injustice, inequity, poverty, environmental threats and disease, and a record of agreement on the Millennium Goals for Development, the Monterrey Consensus on poverty reduction, the Doha trade round, with its focus on development, the establishment of the Global Fund for Infectious Diseases, the land-mine treaty and the protocol on child soldiers, the Kyoto Protocol and the International Criminal Court.

A new system of institutions, practices and norms exists that is slowly but surely advancing human security, freedom and well-being. One of the most important tasks is follow-up, ensuring that the necessary resources, commitment and political will are mobilized to carry through on the promises. This progress, however, shouldn't mask the fact that expectations still far outstrip the performance—conflicts erupt and persist, pandemic diseases threaten, inequalities cause great suffering, children are treated appallingly, there are too many people dispossessed, environmental damage is on the rise. All these conditions if not properly and collaboratively managed can cause major disruption and turmoil affecting everyone. At particular peril are the billion or so people who live where government has failed, where exploitation of resources is rampant and where social and health services are threadbare (sub-Saharan Africa or Central Asia, parts of the Andean area of Latin America and certain islands in the Caribbean). They are "les misérables" of today's global community, calling for an enormous collective remedial effort.

The international consensus required to mount such an effort is presently under duress. The continuing destruction due to civil wars, the risk that government in transition will fail in providing good governance, the sweep of disease and environmental disruption and the growing power of the global underworld all threaten the capacity for global agreement. The looming threat that the most powerful country in the world denies the need for cooperative international action is a particular worry. Indeed the present U.S. administration is applying its immense power and influence towards displacement of the carefully and painfully built, but still incomplete and fragile, rules-based system focused on constructive efforts at conflict management. Clearly there is a need to contend with this challenge.

If Canadians decide that we are prepared to do our part then we mustn't stray off course from a foreign policy based on the belief that the predictable rule of law, and not the arbitrary rule of men, is the best way to ensure security and prosperity for all.

First, we must continue the campaign, along with the Human Security Network, to have the principle of "responsibility to protect" enshrined in the basic mandate of the UN. We must convince enough people of the importance of altering the meaning of sovereignty so that it can't be used to hide oppression and violation of people's rights. We must help the UN redefine the way in which it responds to different kinds of security risks. The Security Council was originally designed to meet head-on the threat of major cross-border aggressions. That task should remain with the council, albeit a council more representative of today's realities. But it is made more difficult by the assertion by the U.S. administration of the right to pre-empt through unilateral intervention where there might be a perceived threat, particularly in response to terrorists with the potential to use weapons of mass destruction. Such an assertion if unchallenged will destroy the carefully constructed international restraints against forceful actions, and set a precedent for anyone to make the same claim.

Let's accept that there may be circumstances when a pre-emptive intervention is necessary. But it should be a multilateral action subject to tests determining whether a real threat exists and whether all other means of recourse have been tried. Here the criteria set out in the *Responsibility to Protect* report can have very direct application. Redefining how international peace and security challenges should be met, in particular delimiting the role of the Security Council to its original mandate of meeting threats to global peace, is the first step towards UN reform and relevance. Once taken, it is possible to shift other situations, such as civil strife, violation of UN conventions, serious abuse of human rights, not threatening any vital interests of any of the P-5) to the General Assembly, where a UN possessed of proper resources can be mandated to act without the presence of a veto.

That could lead to a gradual enhancement of the General Assembly as a place to decide on "responsibility to protect" measures in situations where human security is at stake—humanitarian threats, perhaps severe environmental impacts. There is no reason why the General Assembly working through a mechanism similar to the CMAG group in the Commonwealth, a rotating committee of countries, could not take on a far more active role in the protection of individuals using the criteria set out in the commission report. Changes to the structure and operation of the UN could follow, including a rapid-reaction constabulary and a logistics and early-warning intelligence-gathering capability that can be shared with regional security organizations as they too take on mandates of people-protection. If needed, the General Assembly can request the Security Council to use its Chapter Seven mandate authorizing contributions from members to back up an intervention.

In asserting its right to decision making on human security situations the General Assembly could develop a greater sense of legitimacy. Medium-size and smaller member states could exercise their statecraft there, especially in areas not of interest to the permanent members of the Security Council. For their part the P-5 will have their hands full contending with the initiatives of the U.S. to bypass the council. Even here a strengthened General Assembly could help deflect such initiatives through preventive measures of diplomacy, negotiation, disarmament, monitoring and soft interventions—a way of pre-empting the pre-emptor.

To further strengthen its legitimacy, the General Assembly also needs to become more democratic in its decision making. The time is at hand to begin thinking of a People's Assembly—a second UN chamber directly elected and with a mandate to oversee the protection of people. Using global information networks, it could enable and encourage worldwide participatory political debate and even encompass forms of electronic voting.

Another area in need of attention in a hurry is the field of global disarmament. As we've seen, the volume and sophistication of weaponry is on the rise, with a real threat of proliferation, and at the same time control measures are being weakened. The multilateral system is being bypassed and the prevailing doctrine in the U.S. and increasingly among other states is to reject any restraint on their means of self-protection. The constituency of global arms control and disarmament desperately needs a win. I've argued that one area in which this may be feasible is weapons in space, but that is a future proposition, one that suffers from not being central to the contemporary agenda focused on the potential spread of weapons of mass destruction, especially into the hands of terrorists. That was the mantra driving, at least for public consumption, the war against Iraq. Interestingly, the whole debate surrounding the role of UN inspections in Iraq has raised a precedent about the responsibility of the international community to enforce disarmament when the possession of weapons of mass destruction is considered an imminent threat. At least in the first instance, even the Bush administration conceded a role to the UN to carry out intrusive inspections.

A major debating point in the Security Council was the degree to which the already well established UN presence could be enhanced to ensure compliance. Iraq had already accepted significant limitations on its sovereignty, and the position of many in the international community was that war was unnecessary, just an appropriate, heightened level of UN intervention. For example the Carnegie Endowment for International Peace suggested that inspections teams could be "accompanied by a military arm strong enough to force immediate entry into any site at any time with complete security for the inspections team."[6]

A fundamental principle of the "responsibility to protect" is that when a country is unwilling to accept responsibility for protection then the international community has a right to intervene. This right can apply not only to humanitarian issues but to protect against accumulation of weapons of mass destruction along with the prospect of their being used or transferred. The UN can and should intervene to secure compliance, but in practice that works only if there is support from the U.S., since only they have the clout to make it work. But, given a choice between constantly sending out carrier task forces and using blue berets to defang a potential threat, then it might just have some appeal. This principle could be equally applied to small arms. It would be another way to formulate a role for the UN as disarmer.

Perhaps the most immediate, pressing need for Canadian-sponsored human security networking is in building an international justice system centred on the International Criminal Court. I have already made the case that the ICC can become one of the most effective tools for combatting dictatorship, violations of individual rights, and terrorism. It is the cornerstone for uniform international sanctions against genocide, war crimes and crimes against humanity—the worst crimes known to humanity. It is there to back up domestic legal systems, should they falter. It promises a world where individuals accountable for humanitarian crimes have no place to run, no place to hide from the rule of law. It can have a major role in deterring terrorist activity and its mere existence can, in certain circumstances, supplement, perhaps supersede, the role of the UN in dealing with human security violations. The highly respected UN ambassador from Jordan, Prince Zaid, who played a critical role in guiding the establishment of the court through the UN process, makes the point that the ICC is the best embodiment of a smart sanction—targeting the perpetrators and not punishing the people.

That's the potential. The key issue is to make it happen. The ICC will need substantial resources to get off the ground and prove its worth. One expert estimate is that the budget to undertake proper inquiry, investigation, preparation and prosecution of three to six cases, could be as high as U.S.$150 million, about the cost of ten cruise missiles. The willingness of the state parties to the treaty to authorize that kind of support will take leadership. And that is just one example. On the other side the court will need friends to defend it against those who want to destroy it, primarily the Bush administration, and those (for example the Russians, Chinese and Indians) who view it with suspicion since they want to be free to pursue with impunity acts of force against their own people or immediate neighbours. Offsetting such pressure will also require leadership.

No country is better placed to take on the ongoing stewardship of the ICC and the building of an international judicial system than Canada. We begin with the knowledge and practice of both common and civil law. We have a well-trained legal profession, a respected police force in the RCMP with extensive international experience and a cadre of dedicated officials in DFAIT and the justice department who know the intricacies of international law. We were in the forefront of the campaign to create the court, and one of our distinguished diplomats, Phillipe Kirsch, has been elected its president. We have the confidence of the broad coalition of NGOs involved. We have passed our own ratification legislation that is a model for other countries to emulate. We have the opportunity to mobilize the Human Security Network on behalf of the court. We should take the lead.

The only problem is that this will put us in competition with our powerful southern neighbour. If ever there was a clear-cut choice to make between the compelling, competing pulls on Canadian foreign policy, it is on this issue. The choice made will tell us a lot about where we are going as a country.

Next up for reform should be the global refugee system. Refugees and displaced persons number somewhere in the vicinity of forty to fifty million, and their enormous demand for simple sustenance draws down billions of dollars of aid that might otherwise be spent on development. There is a growing reaction against the acceptance of conventional refugees and a serious shortfall in funding, with the burden of support falling mainly on poor states in the Third World. There is also a tragic inability to find an acceptable rules regime for taking responsibility for internally displaced persons—people uprooted because of internal war, resource scarcity, environmental disaster or degradation—a group that surpasses in numbers the homeless who pass across borders. They are the true lost souls, wandering from camp to camp, never finding a place to call home.

One person who cares is Francis Deng, a scholar from Sudan who serves as the UN's special representative for internally displaced persons, or IDPs. The first time I heard the notion of "responsibility to protect" was when Deng visited me in Ottawa and argued for a clear commitment by the international community to deal with the IDP issue. The UN High Commission for Refugees is hamstrung by an outmoded mandate going back to World War II that limits its task to those who cross borders to escape from political persecution. It's time to insist that if national governments can't or won't protect internally displaced persons and grant them basic rights, then the responsibility should reside with the international community.

Work should begin on a new treaty outlining the rights of refugees and internally displaced persons, relevant to contemporary conditions of displacement and based on the "responsibility to protect." Canada, in association with the Human Security Network, could convene the best minds available to help set standards and propose acceptable measures. This would involve expanding the mandate of UNHCR to cover IDPs and refugees who are escaping starvation and conflict. It clearly would require a different financial formula. And countries would have to agree not only to help with resettlement in the region but where necessary to accept a certain level of migration into their countries.

In the previous chapter I suggested a domestic program of educational vouchers as an incentive to immigration, along with an open system of recruitment and adjustment. That would give Canada the means of accepting more displaced persons and refugees and ensure they would have the wherewithal to settle in. Such an exercise could precipitate a broader global debate and perhaps lead to a network of countries prepared to manage the migration and movement of people beyond the present limited mandates and the restrictions imposed by national immigration laws. Rather than reacting with repressive enforcement measures when poor unfortunates arrive on our shores, we in privileged countries would do much better to seek solutions that enable refugees to either reach a stable existence in their own countries or have controlled access through proper, generous, managed immigration procedures.

The international treatment of human rights should also be on the A-list for reform. Granted, we have come a long way since the early days of the UN Charter and the Helsinki accords. Human rights has a global constituency, with six conventions on universal standards. Strong civil groups such as Amnesty International and Human Rights Watch wield much influence worldwide, and the spread of human rights groups at the local and regional level is impressive. There are, however, two major problems to be overcome.

First, after September 11 the reaction to terrorism has been to suppress human rights, both domestically and abroad. Various governments have passed legislation and tightened enforcement measures that deny fundamental legal rights. Governments that would and should be condemned for abuses against their own people are hailed as loyal allies and their transgressions overlooked. All one has to do is join the anti-terrorist parade and all sins are forgiven.

This retreat on human rights is compounded by the increasing irrelevance and over-politicization of the UN Commission on Human Rights. The annual ritual of resolution making in Geneva has become stale and predictable. Countries use their political influence to water down resolutions, big powers use the session to carry out political vendettas. And who can take the role of the commission seriously when the latest African member is a representative of Robert Mugabe's government in Zimbabwe and the current chair of the commission is a Libyan? Perhaps the nadir of the Human Rights Commission's performance was the 2001 Durban conference on human rights that turned into a slugfest over Zionism. Louise Arbour, the new high commissioner, has an opportunity to initiate reform proposals, and potentially inaugerate a new regime of activism for the commission.

What is needed is a shift in tasks and approach. The UN Human Rights Commission should become the centre of an information-based network of investigation, disclosure and transparency, able to expose abuses and unafraid to point the finger. It should become the 911 of global human rights, able to respond quickly to assist those who experience what they feel to be a violation, or to blow an early whistle on signs of major rights violations. It should be an information network, tying the various centres of human rights activity together, an electronic source bank that can assist local rights groups fighting cases or trying to protect individuals and minorities. Canadian technology and know-how can help design and implement such a system, provided the resources are made available.

A global human rights information centre could also revive the commission itself, which could become seized with matters brought directly to it by those oppressed and in danger. The hearings and debates could even go worldwide, with evidence and testimony given on-line by victims and witnesses.

This should be seen as a long-term proposition. Existing commission members will not easily surrender their prerogatives and stranglehold, especially when it means they themselves become more vulnerable to critique and condemnation. Addressing the conditions of membership would be a start. Human Rights Watch has set out standards that might be the minimum basis for election to the commission. Willingness to accept human rights inspectors unconditionally is one, not being the subject of a condemning resolution is another, and being a signatory to the major human rights conventions is yet another—hardly onerous obligations. Changes of this kind would begin to revive the body, make it more credible and set the stage for a more elaborate human rights mandate.

A recent visit I made to the beautifully designed open-air Nairobi headquarters of the UN Environment Programme (UNEP), the UN's flagship organization on environmental matters, was a source of some sadness and a little irritation. I was in East Africa on a fact-finding tour, meeting with skilled and dedicated groups and individuals involved in conservation efforts on the African continent. At UNEP, however, though greeted politely and given full attention, I could sense the contrast—its lack of ideas, relevance and direction. UNEP does provide information, holds conferences, undertakes different research projects and has a prestigious ministerial forum—all useful undertakings. But as the spark plug for environmental renewal and action commensurate with the seriousness of the issues, it sputters. I saw no chance of it evolving into a worthy competitor with the World Trade Organization in pursuing environmental interests in balance with commercial considerations. To imagine it having any serious influence over nation-states or corporations that pollute with impunity and degrade with disregard is just wishful thinking.

This failing seems to be recognized by officials of UNEP and they would be the first to argue for strengthening the organization. There are increasing calls for a World Environment Agency that would corral all the different treaties and conventions, funding sources and programs under one roof. President Jacques Chirac of France has made a strong case for such an institution, and ultimately I believe it is a goal to strive for. But many experts are nervous about too great a focus on the idea of a new institution as they're afraid it will divert attention from other more immediate efforts. David Runnals of the Winnipeg-based International Institute for Sustainable Development has made some very practical suggestions that could become the building blocks towards the eventual creation of a World Environment Agency. UNEP should be strengthened by giving it a respectable budget (it is presently just over U.S.$100 million). Various agreements and programs in comparable areas, each with their small little secretariats, should be bunched for common administration. Sustainable development clauses should be written into trade agreements, ensuring that in determining disputes environmental considerations are not given short shrift. And there should be much greater assistance to Third World countries to increase their capacity to act on environmental matters. These make good sense as immediate measures.

At the same time I believe work should begin on the creation of a world environment network that goes beyond the classic multi-lateral structure that represents only nation-states. It should be a multi-stakeholder partnership, bringing together government, civil groups and business with equal standing and responsibility. Canada could start the ball rolling by inviting different think-tanks, universities, NGOs and business organizations to submit proposals, hold a competition, get the creative juices bubbling.

One key to gaining traction with the public, with governments and with the environmental movement would be to link this new global network to our fundamental need for environmental security—for protecting the environment to limit risks. That means giving some environment agency sufficient power, authority and resources to make a difference, to hold environmental transgressors to account, to resolve disputes and to be the central pulse of global environmental action. In a world where trying to get buy-in on Kyoto is difficult, such an organization looks a long way from fulfillment. But that doesn't mean we shouldn't begin to build support for it.

There are some encouraging signs, especially in the increasing engagement of the private sector and their willingness to form partnerships with environmental groups, the involvement of international financial institutions and the emergence of collaborative regional bodies like the Arctic Council. A combination of major U.S.-based foundations and the World Bank have funded a U.S.$250-million worldwide conservation fund. Shell Oil is working with locally based NGOs to introduce solar power for homes with solar energy in developing countries. Public-private partnerships have been set up to supply clean water and to begin addressing cross-border water-management issues.

The onus is on government to define its role within these new constellations. Governments must set standards, erect regulatory frameworks, supply resources, work out collaborative cross-border arrangements, transfer authority to private actors. One model worth considering is beginning to take hold in the Albertine rift region of east-central Africa, one of the most critical preserves of biodiversity in the world, and best known as the home of the

mountain gorilla. A network of parks has been established, strad-
dling the borders of five countries. A dedicated alliance of local
and international scientists and conservation groups, supported
by funding from international donors, works to help protect the
parks and preserve their various species. The private sector is being
recruited to help develop viable economic products such as natural, herbal health remedies that are conservation-friendly both
within the parks and on the buffer regions. Governments of the
region are beginning to work together to promote ecotourism. All
this in an area racked by war and poverty. Cooperation amid chaos.

Despite such innovative structures, some issues must be resolved
if there is to be a serious environmental security regime. One is the
huge economic disparity in the world that leads to environmental
conflict. The plundering of natural resources and the environmental
exploitation of poor countries cry out for broad, pre-emptive, cooperative action. NGOs have led the way in blowing the whistle on
extractive resource companies that abuse the environment and contribute to conditions of conflict. (The work of Global Witness and its
campaign to have corporations publish what they pay to governments
for resource concessions is one good example.) The Security Council
initiative on Angola that led to the Kimberly process for marking
where diamonds come from is another model. One of the most
important tasks for a World Environmental Network would be the
establishment of a regime of transparency to track resource extraction activities, combined with the ability to go to court and prosecute
renegade companies. That's one reason to eventually establish a
World Environment Agency. We need an organization that can draw
on substantial resources and perhaps one day operate under some
form of international taxing power, perhaps levied against polluters or
those who break treaty commitments. We need organizations that
can meld together the various international agencies and operations
that oversee conventions on the law of the sea, desertification and
the ozone layer, to name a few. And we need an organization with sufficient weight and authority to be an equal partner with the WTO
and the international financial institutions, to make sure that environmental security has equal standing in determining global policy. If
the trade purists are going to argue that the WTO shouldn't confuse

its mandate by introducing environmental issues, then they should agree to a worthy global organization with the power to assure that commerce doesn't always trump environment.

How would a World Environment Agency acquire that kind of clout? One way is to have the kind of multi-partner membership already suggested. But the essential element is to endow such a body with the authority to hold both public and private players accountable for good environmental security practice. That means having the power to require disclosure, verify compliance and ultimately impose penalties or prescribe international enforcement. It doesn't mean having a group of green berets march ashore to intervene when some perpetrator is destroying a rain forest or producing exorbitant volumes of toxic gases. It does mean borrowing from the WTO the idea of penalties based on impartial adjudication. Perhaps a judicial procedure where individuals are held to account should be considered—more naming and shaming. And, who knows, maybe there *should* be a corps of green berets who can go in to clean up a waste site, help protect biodiversity "hot spots" and inspect alleged transgressions. I could think of no better way of enlisting the energies of today's young people than to invite them to become part of a global environmental youth corps.

Again we can make a difference by kick-starting the debate and offering alternatives to the present ideological and conceptual straitjackets.

Finally, in this scheme of global reform, I come back to the centrality of building an international information network dedicated to public purpose. Already the impact of the Internet is profound and far-reaching. But so much more can be done. Canada should take the lead in expanding the options and choices on how to use global networks and fit them into our priorities.

One imperative would be to set up a major global learning network to give students a chance to focus on matters of human and environmental security and peace—a different way of looking at the world. Already the UN has training and educational institutions, such as UPEACE, UN University and UNITAR. UNESCO has a broad mandate to promote peace studies and support widespread education. These could form the backbone of a system of global learning that could help transform the culture of our world from one based on war and conflict to one based on cooperation and collaboration. I believe there is the public appetite. At a large public gathering organized by the University of British Columbia to examine the concept of global citizenship, one of the constant refrains from the audience was a demand that universities establish a learning network around global issues so people can find out and understand what is going on. If centres in different parts of the world could create an interactive learning experience, would we not begin to escape today's overheated nationalisms and create a true global culture? This is a goal worthy of Canadian talent.

A second goal is the search for e-democracy at the global level. We cannot build stronger transnational institutions without finding better answers to how people can participate in their decisions. The vast growth of NGOs has been one important expression of this emerging form of citizenship. But dominated as they usually are by professional staff and small, somewhat exclusive boards of directors, they are often not very democratic in the way they make decisions or are held accountable. Protests on the street are another effective way to give people a voice, but they are unreliable as a source of serious debate and deliberation. And massive international conferences are never democratic. The inclusive access and extensive participation offered by new information systems needs to be explored. In the future, one of the most challenging tasks will be to give people a real sense that their voice will be heard. We need to connect parliamentarians worldwide and plug individual citizens into a form of direct digital democracy.

Tennyson's poetic vision of "a parliament of man, the federation of the world/ There the common sense of most shall hold a fretful realm in awe/ And the kindly earth shall slumber, lapped in universal law" may just be a possibility in the lifespan of the two Emmas. The new information age offers us the chance.

THE ROAD AHEAD

This agenda of international collaborative action within a framework of rules and laws may seem strangely at odds with the temper of our times. Most talk of the future paints a dismal picture of unrestrained American dominance, mixed with anarchy let loose by the forces of criminal fanaticism.

What I have presented here is an alternative road map. It is not unrelated to the dominance-doomsday scenario, but it takes into account that under different leadership the U.S. is capable of using its immense power to create strong international institutions and uphold the rule of law. Those Americans who argue for a return to a constructive role for the U.S. can be greatly helped by close friends setting out a blueprint. Similarly, effective global institutions grounded in democratic practices and following human security principles are the best means of countermanding and controlling the global underworld.

Working on an agenda of this kind is not only a good fit for Canadians, it is also the right thing to do. Canadians can help set the right navigational coordinates, but to do so we must enhance, not reduce, our freedom of action and guard against forces in our country that want us to travel only in the company of our powerful neighbour.

There is no sure way to navigate this world. No yellow brick road leads to a guarantee of salvation at its end. Each and every one of us will be called upon to broaden our global perspective, explore new options, honour different ideas and voices—above all the voices of youth—and show resiliency in the face of the unknown. It is a journey we Canadians take together by deciding together, not because other nations choose for us. Though we welcome their company and their perspectives along the way.

Canada is only one community amongst many. We have no pretensions about wielding a big military stick, nor do we have any whiff of manifest destiny. But we can offer ideas, skills, resources, a political commitment to working with others to find practical, peaceful solutions, and a sense of quiet optimism about the future. We can hold out hope for many around the world. We can mark the road towards a horizon where justice, security and fairness beckon. We can set a beacon to guide both Emmas as they define their own pathway into this new century.

Traveller, there is no path. Paths are made by walking.
—Antonio Machado

NOTES

PREFACE TO THE PAPERBACK EDITION
1. Winston Churchill, "An Age of Great Events And Little Men" November 21,1901, Philanthropic Society Dinner, Liverpool, as reprinted in *Never Give In—The Best of Winston Churchill's Speeches* ed. by Winston S. Churchill, Hyperion Press, New York, N.Y. 2003 p.13.

PROLOGUE: CANADA AND THE WORLD
1. See Pew Research Centre "What the World Thinks 2002" December 4, 2002.

PART I: EMMA AND US
CHAPTER 1: THE ROAD TO GULU
1. In spring 2003, there were increased efforts at peace negotiations, and both the EU and Human Security Network took up the issue. The Liu Institute partnered with Human Rights Watch and the Center of Human Rights at Makerl University in Uganda to prepare a report on child violations that was presented to the UN Human Rights Commission's annual meeting in Geneva.
2. Cynthia Ozick, "Of Christian Heroism," *Partisan Review* 59, no. 1 (1992): 47.
3. Giorgio Agamben, *Homo Sacer: Sovereign Power and Bare Life*, trans. Daniel Heller-Roazen (Stanford: Stanford University Press, 1998).
4. Navid Kermani, "The Flower Children of Banda Aceh," *Times Literary Supplement*, November 1, 2002, p. 16.

PART III: BORDER CHOICES
Chapter 4: How to Make Love to a Porcupine
1. Stephen Chase, "Canadians Divided on NAFTA," *The Globe and Mail*, December 9, 2002.
2. Wendy Dobson, "Shaping the Future of the North American Economic Space," *C. D. Howe Institute Commentary* 162 (April 2002).
3. "Dispute Management and Dispute Settlement Considerations in Bilateral Treaty Arrangements between Canada and the United States." Report of special legal counsel to the minister of foreign affairs, 1998.
4. Michael Byers, "Canadian Armed Forces Under U.S. Command." Report of the Simons Centre for Peace and Disarmament Studies, Liu Institute for Global Issues, University of British Columbia, May 2002.

Chapter 5: The North American Condo
1. Abram Chayes and Antonia Handler Chayes, *The New Sovereignty: Compliance with International Regulatory Agreements* (Cambridge, Mass.: Harvard University Press, 1995), p. 1.
2. Stephen Flynn "Transforming border mangement in the post-September 11 world," p. 38. <www.maxwell.syr.edu/campbell/governance_symposium/security.htm>.

PART IV: HUMAN SECURITY
Chapter 6: The Ottawa Process
1. Alex Vines, "The Crisis of Anti-personnel Mines," in *To Walk Without Fear*, ed. M. Cameron, R. Lawson and B. Tomlin (Toronto: Oxford University Press, 1998), p.120.
2. Human Rights Watch and Physicians for Human Rights: A Deadly Legacy (New York Human Rights Watch 1993).
3. Vines p.125.
4. *Landmine Monitor Report 2001* "Major Findings," <www.icbl.org/lm/2001/findings/>.
5. William J. Clinton, "Address to UN General Assembly," September 26, 1994.
6. Lloyd Axworthy, "Address at the Closing Session of the International Strategy Conference Towards a Global Ban on Anti-personnel Land Mines," Ottawa, October 5, 1996.
7. *Landmine Monitor Report 2002* "Major Findings," <www.icbl.org/lm/2002/findings.html>.
8. Ibid.
9. *The Economist* (November 10–16, 2001), 16.

Chapter 7: Chronicle of a Death Foretold
1. *The Responsibility to Protect: Report of the International Commission on Intervention and State Sovereignty.* <www.dfait-maeci.gc.ca/iciss-ciise/report-en.asp>
2. *The International Response to Conflict and Genocide: Lessons from the Rwanda*

Experience, Steering Committee of the Joint Evaluation of Emergency
Assistance to Rwanda, March 1996. <www.reliefweb.int/library/nordic.>
3. Joe Jockel and Joel Sokolsky, "Lloyd Axworthy's Legacy: Human Security and
the Rescue of Canadian Defence Policy," *International Journal* 56, no. 1 (Winter
2000–2001): 1.

CHAPTER 8: RESPONSIBILITY TO PROTECT
1. Michael Ignatieff, *Virtual War: Kosovo and Beyond* (Toronto: Viking, 2000),
p. *xxx*.
2. World Report on Violence and Health (WHO), p. 217.
3. Martha Crenshaw, "The Global Phenomenon of Terrorism" in *Responding to
Terrorism: What Role for the United Nations?*, a report of the International Peace
Academy, October 2002.
4. Lloyd Axworthy, Notes for an Address at G-8 foreign minister meeting,
Cologne, June 9, 1999, Department of Foreign Affairs and International Trade.
5. Virtually every day Heidi Hulan, from my staff, and Jill Sinclair, probably
the individuals most responsible for getting the commission organized, would
submit another list of names and people to call. It was the closest thing to
what a prime minister must do in assembling a regionally balanced but pre-
sentable cabinet. We were very fortunate in those who agreed to serve, especially in the co-chairs, Gareth Evans and Mohamed Sahnoun, both ex-foreign
ministers. We also recruited the likes of Michael Ignatieff, Cornelia
Samarunga, Ramesh Thakur, Edwardo Stein, Carlos Ramos, General Klaus
Naumann, Lee Hamilton, Gisele Cote-Harper, Cyril Ramaphosa and Vladamir
Lukin. A new wrinkle added to the commission was the setting up of an advisory board made up of present or former ministers designed to give further
leverage in establishing political support and credibility. I chaired the advisory
board after resigning from Foreign Affairs in the fall of 2000. I was joined on
the board by Robin Cook from Great Britain, Rosario Green from Mexico,
Maria Soledad from Chile, Amre Moussa from Egypt, Senator Patrick Leahy
of the United States, George Papandreou of Greece and Surin Pitsuwan of
Thailand, among others.
6. *The Responsibility to Protect: Report of the International Commission on
Intervention and State Sovereignty: Synopsis.*
<www.dfait-maeci.gc.ca/iciss-ciise/pdf/Commission-Report.pdf>.
7. Ibid., p. *xi*.
8. International Committee of the Red Cross, *The People on War Report*, prepared by Greenberg Research. <www.icrc.org/eng>.
9. Wesley Clark, "An Army of One?" *Prospect* 81 (December 2002): 12.
10. *Human Rights Watch Report: Afghanistan*, vol. 14, no. 7 (C) (November
2002), p. 4. <hrw.org/reports/2002/afghan3/herat1002.pdf>.

11. Marina Ottoway et al., "Democratic Mirage in the Middle East," *Carnegie Endowment for International Peace Policy Brief* 20 (October 2002). <www.ceip.org/files/pdf/Policybrief20.pdf>.

12. John Lloyd, *Financial Times* (London), December 27, 2002.

CHAPTER 9: A NEW COURT FOR A NEW CENTURY

1. Philippe Kirsch was subsequently elected a judge of the ICC, in February 2003, and made president of the court, a well-deserved recognition of his talent and commitment—another Canadian "global citizen."

2. For the complete text of the Rome Statute, see <www.un.org/law/icc/statute/romefra.htm>.

3. The Liu Institute through its International Justice Strategies Forum and Vancouver dialogue process is trying to promote these exchanges and global policy networks for international justice.

4. Michael Howard, "What's in a Name? How to Fight Terrorism," *Foreign Affairs* (January/February 2002).

5. Human Rights Watch, "United States Efforts to Undermine the International Criminal Court," briefing note, September 2002.

CHAPTER 10: THE CROWDED GLOBAL VILLAGE

1. Robert Cooper, "The Post Modern State," in *Re-ordering the World: The Long-Term Implications of 11 September*, ed. Mark Leonard (London: Foreign Policy Centre, 2002).

2. Andrew Cooper, "More Than a Star Turn: Canadian Hybrid Diplomacy and the OAS Mission to Peru," *International Journal* 56, no. 2 (2001): p. 290.

PART V: THE UNITED NATIONS
CHAPTER 11: REWIRING THE UN

1. Centre for Public Opinion and Democracy, Liu Institute for Global Issues, "Global Poll Shows World Perceived as a More Dangerous Place" (May 16, 2002) <www.ligi.ubc.ca/_media/_releases/020516release.pdf>.

2. "Views of a Changing World," The Pew Global Attitudes Project, Pew Research Center, Washington D.C., June 2003.

3. See *Responding to Terrorism: What Role for the United Nations?*, a report of the International Peace Academy, October 2002.

4. Don Hubert, "Resources, Greed, and the Persistence of Violent Conflict," chap. 7 in *Human Security and the New Diplomacy: Protecting People, Promoting Peace*, ed. Rob McRae and Don Hubert (Montreal: McGill-Queen's University Press, 2001).

5. United Nations Development Programme, *Deepening Democracy in a Fragmented World: Report 2002*. <www.undp.org/hdr2002/complete.pdf>.

CHAPTER 12: REBIRTH OF A COUNTRY

1. Lansana Gberie, *War and Peace in Sierra Leone: Diamonds, Corruption and the Lebanese Connection*, Partnership Africa Canada, Ottawa 2002, p. 14. <www.partnershipafricacanada.org/hsop/>.

2. *The Responsibility to Protect: Report of the International Commission on Intervention and State Sovereignty: Synopsis.* <www.dfait-maeci.gc.ca/iciss-ciise/pdf/Commission-Report.pdf>.

3. "Breaking the Conflict Trap: Civil War and Development Policy," World Bank, 2003. <econ.worldbank.org/prr/civil war/prr>.

PART VI: ENVIRONMENTAL SECURITY

CHAPTER 13: THE MACHINE IN THE GARDEN

1. For a full discussion see Wayne Nelles "Reconciling Human and National Security in Mongolia: A Canadian Perspective," Program on Asian-Canadian Policy Studies, Institute for Asian Studies, University of British Columbia.

2. Erla Swingle, "The Cities: Challenge for Humanity," *National Geographic*, November 2002. <magma.nationalgeographic.com/ngm/0211/feature3/assignment1.html>.

3. David Lamb, "Awash in Trash: Crisis in Asia's Cities," *International Herald Tribune*, September 7, 1991.

4. UN Centre for Human Settlements, *Cities in a Globalizing World: Global Report on Human Settlements 2001* (London: Earthscan, 2001).

5. *UN Declaration on Cities and Other Human Settlements in the New Millennium*, S–25/2, August 16, 2001.

6. Larry Rohter, "Brazilians Find a Political Cost for IMF Help," *New York Times*, August 11, 2002.

7. Kenneth Rogoff, "The IMF Strikes Back," *Foreign Policy* (January/February 2003).

8. Oxfam International, "Rigged Rules and Double Standards," April 2002.

9. Ha-Joon Chang, *Kicking Away the Ladder: Development Strategy in Historical Perspective* (London: Anthem, 2002).

10. "Deepening Democracy in a Fragmented World," United Nations Development Programme Report 2002. <www.undp.org/hdr2002/complete.pdf>.

11. *Miami Herald*, July 27, 2002.

12. J. F. Rischard, *High Noon: 20 Global Problems, 20 Years to Solve Them* (New York: Basic Books, 2002), p. 92.

13. Paul Martin, "Canada's Role in a Complex World," Canadian Newspaper Association Conferencec, April 30, 2003.

14. For the full text of the public information notice, see <www.imf.org/external/np/sec/pn/2002/pn02130.htm>.

CHAPTER 14: KYOTO AND BEYOND
1. World Health Organization, "Climate Change and Human Health" (May 2002), p. 6.
2. World Health Organization, "WHO calls for urgent action to prevent 5 million children's deaths," press release, April 7, 2003.
3. WHO, "Climate Change."
4. Canada, Department of Foreign Affairs and International Trade, *Human Security: Safety for People in a Changing World* (Ottawa, April 1999), p. 2.
5. Peter Singer, *One World: The Ethics of Globalization* (New Haven: Yale University Press, 2002), p. 50.

PART VII: SEARCHING FOR SURVIVAL IN A WORLD OF WEAPONS
CHAPTER 15: DISARMAMENT ON EARTH, DISARMAMENT IN SPACE
1. Ryszard Kapuściński, *The Shadow of the Sun* (Toronto: Alfred A. Knopf Canada, 2001), p. 149.
2. Graduate Institute of International Studies, *Small Arms Survey: Counting the Human Cost* (Oxford: University of Oxford Press, 2002), p. 157.
3. Lloyd Axworthy, "It's Time to Ban the Bomb," *The Globe and Mail*, June 3, 2002.
4. Anthony Lewis, "Abroad at Home: Bush the Radical," *The New York Times*, July 23, 2001.
5. Stephen Schwarz et al., *Atomic Audit: The Costs and Consequences of U.S. Nuclear Weapons Since 1940* (Washington, D.C.: Brookings Institution, 1998).
6. Robert Dahl, *Controlling Nuclear Weapons: Democracy versus Guardianship* (Syracuse, N.Y.: Syracuse University Press, 1985), p. 5.
7. Centre for Public Opinion and Democracy, Liu Institute for Global Issues, "Global Poll of Security in Eleven Countries," May 16, 2002.
8. Both noted in Gordon Edwards, "Canada and the Bomb," *The Gazette* (Montreal), August 9, 1998.
9. McGeorge Bundy, *Danger and Survival: Choices About the Bomb in the First Fifty Years* (New York: Random House, 1988), p. 149.
10. Maurice Strong, "Peace, Security and Sustainability" (speech delivered at Simon Fraser University, B.C.), January 16, 2003.
11. Dana Priest, *The Mission: Waging War and Keeping Peace with America's Military* (New York: W. W. Norton and Company, 2003), p. 71.
12. W. G. Sebald, *On the Natural History of Destruction* (Toronto: Alfred A. Knopf Canada, 2003), p. 65.

PART VIII: THE TWO EMMAS
CHAPTER 16: PUTTING OUR SHIP IN ORDER
1. Richard Falk, *Human Rights Horizons: The Pursuit of Justice in a Globalizing World* (New York: Routledge, 2000), p. 178.

2. Felipe Fernández-Armesto, *Millennium* (London, Toronto: Bantam Books, 1995), p. 161.

3. Larry Bourne, "New Continental Divides," 2002.

4. Allen Scott, *Global City-Regions: Trends, Theory, Policy* (Oxford: Oxford University Press, 2001), p. 14.

5. *The Digital Promise Report*, Executive Summary. <www.digitalpromise.org/report/1ExecutiveSummary.pdf>.

6. Peter Langille and Tania Keefe, "The Future of Peacekeeping." <www.ligi.ubc.ca/_media/_reports/030602/future_of_peacekeeping.pdf>.

CHAPTER 17: NAVIGATING A NEW WORLD

1. Lloyd Axworthy and Knut Vollebaek, "Now for a New Diplomacy to Fashion a Humane World," *International Herald Tribune*, October 21, 1998.

2. "Statement by the Human Security Network Concerning the Terrorist Attacks in the United States of America, 11 September 2001," New York, November 12, 2001.

3. This idea of competing networks is from Richard Falk, *The Great Terror War* (Northampton, Mass.: Olive Branch Press, 2003).

4. For a comprehensive exploration of global policy networks see Wolfgang Reinicke and Francis Deng, "Critical Choices: The United Nations, Networks and the Future of Global Governance," Ottawa: International Development Research Centre, 2000.

5. "Peace and Conflict 2003: A Global Survey of Armed Conflicts, Self-Determination Movements and Democracy," Monty G. Marshall, Ted Robert Gurr, CIDCM. <www.cidcm.umd.edu/peace_and_conflict_2003.asp>.

6. Carnegie Endowment for International Peace, "Iraq: A New Approach" (August 2002). <www.ceip.org/files/pdf/Iraq.Report.pdf>.

Index

LLOYD AXWORTHY has been a Member of Parliament and a cabinet minister in several portfolios including employment and immigration, transport and foreign affairs. He served as Director and CEO of the Liu Institute for Global Issues at the University of British Columbia. Currently he is the President and Vice-Chancellor of the University of Winnipeg and has been appointed a Special Envoy of the UN Secretary-General to facilitate a peaceful resolution to the dispute between Ethiopia and Eritrea. Among other awards, he has won the CARE International Humanitarian Award and was nominated for the Nobel Peace Prize. In 2003 Lloyd Axworthy became an Officer of the Order of Canada.